Lawrence Durrell's Poetry

Lawrence Durrell's Poetry

A Rift in the Fabric of the World

Isabelle Keller-Privat

FAIRLEIGH DICKINSON UNIVERSITY PRESS
Madison • Teaneck

Published by Fairleigh Dickinson University Press
Copublished by The Rowman & Littlefield Publishing Group, Inc.
4501 Forbes Boulevard, Suite 200, Lanham, Maryland 20706
www.rowman.com

Unit A, Whitacre Mews, 26-34 Stannary Street, London SE11 4AB

Copyright © 2019 by Isabelle Keller-Privat

Extracts from *The Collected Poems 1931–1974* by Lawrence Durrell, London: Faber, 1980, quoted by permission of Faber and Faber Ltd. United States rights by Curtis Brown on behalf of the Beneficiaries of the Literary Estate of Lawrence.

All rights reserved. No part of this book may be reproduced in any form or by any electronic or mechanical means, including information storage and retrieval systems, without written permission from the publisher, except by a reviewer who may quote passages in a review.

British Library Cataloguing in Publication Information Available

Library of Congress Cataloging-in-Publication Data

Names: Keller, Isabelle, author.
Title: Lawrence Durrell's poetry : a rift in the fabric of the world / Isabelle Keller-Privat.
Description: Madison [N.J.] : Fairleigh Dickinson University Press ; Lanham, Maryland : Copublished by Rowman & Littlefield Publishing Group, Inc. [2019] | Includes bibliographical references and index.
Identifiers: LCCN 2019004751 (print) | LCCN 2019009131 (ebook) | ISBN 9781683930631 (Electronic) | ISBN 9781683930624 (cloth) | ISBN 9781683930648 (pbk)
Subjects: LCSH: Durrell, Lawrence—Criticism and interpretation. | Durrell, Lawrence—Poetic works.
Classification: LCC PR6007.U76 (ebook) | LCC PR6007.U76 Z7256 2019 (print) | DDC 821/.912—dc23
LC record available at https://lccn.loc.gov/2019004751

Contents

	Introduction	1
Chapter 1	A *Private Country*: The Poet's Secret Cartography	9
Chapter 2	*Cities, Plains and People*: Lands of Exile and Introspection	43
Chapter 3	*On Seeming to Presume*: The Dream of a Secret Belonging	77
Chapter 4	"Dreams bursting at the seams to die": *The Tree of Idleness*, The Mauled Dream	129
Chapter 5	*The Ikons*: Greece in the Mind's Eye	175
Chapter 6	*The Red Limbo Lingo*: "Thus words in music drown"	225
Chapter 7	*Vega*: The Star of Poetry	267
	Conclusion	305
	Bibliography	315
	Index	327
	About the Author	331

Introduction

> *A great Poet must be, implicitè if not explicitè, a profound Metaphysician.*
> *He may not have it in logical coherence, in his Brain & Tongue;*
> *but he may have it by Tact: for all sounds, & forms of human nature*
> *he must have the ear of a wild Arab listening in the silent Desert,*
> *the eye of a North American Indian tracing*
> *the footsteps of an Enemy upon the leaves that strew the forest;*
> *the touch of a Blind Man feeling the face of a darling Child.*[1]

Lawrence Durrell's poetry does not stem from a self-evident choice but is rather the fruit of a lifelong questioning. As early as April 1945, his publisher and mentor T. S. Eliot asked him in one of his letters: "Are you primarily a poet or a prose writer?"[2] A subsequent letter, dated from September 1945, leads us to surmise that Lawrence Durrell has failed to answer the question convincingly and warns the young writer of the inevitable choice that lies ahead:

> I didn't ask you whether you were a poet. I wanted to know whether you were a poet or a novelist, which is not the same question. I am satisfied that you could be either: I don't believe that in twenty years you will find that you are both. That is incompatible with the laziness necessary for poetry.[3]

By then Lawrence Durrell has already published at Faber's, under T. S. Eliot's supervision, his first poetry collections, which precede his first novels: *Quaint Fragments* appeared in 1931, *Ten Poems* in 1932, and *Transition: Poems* in 1934. Yet it is in his drama pieces that T. S. Eliot deciphers the poet's hand. Shortly after having read *Sappho*[4] he writes to Durrell in July 1938, "It is refreshing to find a poet who does understand that prose comes first and that poetry is merely prose developed by a knowledge of aeronautics."[5] Such a definition is particularly enlightening, for it welds humor and insight and underlines both the necessary distance that underpins poetry and the fundamental, ungraspable essence of an art that displaces language toward a new horizon. A timeless, hazardous man-made science, it enables man to challenge spatiotemporal boundaries. One may then remember French contemporary poet Jacques Ancet raising the eternal question of the definition of poetry:

> There is the world, my language and something else. It is this something else I call poetry.
>
> Poetry's language does not state, does not describe, does not narrate, does not convey any message: it disseminates.
>
> The rise of a new dawn in today's language, such might be the very essence of poetry.[6]

Only much later and indirectly, through a letter addressed to Diana Menuhin in 1960, does Lawrence Durrell assert his ambition as a poet: "In other words I hope that finally I will be judged as a poet and not as a novelist, and the job will 'float' like a poem."[7] And it is the violinist's wife who confirms Durrell's poetic gift:

> As with writing, so with music—the total is never there, only the minuscule, only the need—nay, the sacred duty—to correct like some self-appointed helmsman adjusting the wheel, the sextant—all to his own personal compass of course with the polarities of his own idiosyncratic reactions, emotions and tastes [. . .].
>
> Yes, you are basically a poet and your mind not only can delve into the place where words dissolve into symbols which then dissolve into elusive ideas and have, with the alchemist's hand of the poet, to be recaptured, made into solid metal if not gold, reshaped and re-assembled [. . .].[8]

A musician and a steersman, the poet is also the alchemist who molds a new language, a language that does not stand against prose but is born out of the prose. Durrell appears to follow in the wake of Mallarmé, who invited poets to apply the principles of hermeticism to poetry. As the critic Hugo Friedrich explains:

> In an article entitled *Magie*[9] [. . .] he [Mallarmé] writes: "I assert that there exists between the old practices and the spell poetry will always cast a secret

equivalence." Thus, poetry is the art of "conjuring on purpose a shadow, an unnamed object, through allusive, always indirect, words" and the poet is "the wizard of words."[10]

Hence Durrell's poetry is to be thought of as this new language that comes to life where it is least expected, this rift tearing apart the prose lining and summoning the reader to be sensitive to the music of words, to listen to the secret spell that gives every line its vibrant, pulsing strength. "I think really I'm a poet," Lawrence Durrell finally asserted during an interview on the BBC in 1960, before concluding, "in poetry perhaps I'm not of sufficient size myself; but it leaks into my prose. [. . .] It's certainly slightly poetic prose."[11]

Thus, although his poetry collections are not numerous, Durrell confirms the prevailing role played by poetry throughout his opus, suggesting that his entire work should be read from a poetic perspective, at a slant away from the prose, not unlike Baudelaire's prose poems, which were born from the "miracle of a poetic prose, a music devoid of rhythm and rhyme, both lithe and jolty enough to marry the lyrical cadences of the soul, the fluctuations of dreams, the tremors of conscience."[12] Indeed, shortly after its publication in 1960, Durrell defined *The Alexandria Quartet* as "a sort of relativity poem," adding, "I knew I was going to write a sort of Big City Poem in a special form."[13]

Modern poetry, unlike the novel and the epic poem, is characterized by the constant rivalry between narrative coherence and discontinuity, thus determining two antithetical yet simultaneous reading patterns that, according to critic Christian Doumet, "generate tension and contradict one another: narrative coherence is undermined by brevity and fragmentation; discontinuity, by the tightness of a submerged story line."[14] This is the reason why, according to Hugo Friedrich, poetry gives rise to "a tension that creates disquiet rather than quietude in the reader's mind."[15] Such a tension is redoubled for Durrell's reader who confronts a twofold loss: that of the poetic form when he approaches the prose, and that of the narrative pattern when he tackles the poem. Lawrence Durrell's poetry is then not only "the place of the other,"[16] as Bernard Sesé contends, it is also the other place that finds its way beyond the boundaries of poetry collections and haunts the prose, thus opening up a new space, the space of linguistic and symbolic otherness. It is the space of a promise never quite fulfilled, the space of renewed hope, of a dream-born freedom.

The poetry collections published between 1943 and 1973 are coeval with the prose works. *A Private Country* (1943) and *Cities, Plains and People* (1946) were written at the same time as *The Black Book* (1938) and *Prospero's Cell*

(1945). *On Seeming to Presume* (1948) and *The Tree of Idleness* (1953) coincided with the publication of *A Marine Venus* (1953). *The Ikons* (1966) and *The Red Limbo Lingo* (1971) were issued shortly before *Tunc* (1968) and *Nunquam* (1973) while *Vega* (1974) came out concurrently with the first volume of *The Avignon Quintet*, *Monsieur* (1974). Hence all seven poetry volumes appear to map out a new poetic experience that develops in symbiosis with the prose, sketching out an art form that branches out and expands regardless of "rhythm and rhyme," attuned to "the lyrical cadences of the soul, the fluctuations of dreams."[17] Through a disjunctive writing Durrell unveils a new vista that unfolds edgewise, at an angle to the text and to the world. As Bo Carpelan said, "the poem creates an experience, it gives us new eyes, new senses."[18]

The various poems initially published in these seven collections over thirty years were reissued in *Collected Poems* in 1980, but the original organization that gave each collection its coherence and singularity was lost. Thus, although James A. Brigham's conscientious edition does retrace the chronological development of Durrell's poetic output, it does not enable the reader to get a clear idea of the workmanship that characterizes each collection. This is why I have chosen to return to the material reality of these original publications, to their historical and literary context, to the details of their composition, which does not necessarily respect temporal or spatial unity. Ultimately, I will show how, through a thorough study of the architecture and pace of Durrell's original poetry books, our interpretation of his entire poetic production may be redefined. Each collection functions both as a unique piece that stands out as a complete whole by itself and as one of the many links making up the lifelong chain through which the poet elaborates his secret vision of the world and carves out his personal poetic universe. While retracing the chain of Durrell's poetic experience, the reader is simultaneously brought to embrace the chain of writers summoned between the lines: Shakespeare, Blake, Keats, Coleridge, Wordsworth, T. S. Eliot, W. H. Auden, Dylan Thomas, as well as Nerval, Rimbaud, Valéry, Propertius, Virgil, Cavafy, Seferis, to cite but a few. Therefore, any merely chronological or thematic reading of Durrell's poetry quickly appears inadequate: each poem demands to be read "A Rebours," to quote Durrell's reference to Hyusmans in *The Alexandria Quartet*.[19] It unfolds as the nexus of a protean, heterogeneous intertwining that shapes out its destiny and hints at the mysterious process of creation. As each poem orients the reader backward, it also bears the impetus of the ongoing form it belongs to, revealing what Rilke called a "wonderful, wide open pattern"[20] that imposes its own rhythm to the reader and leads him to and fro amid the manifold temporal, spatial, textual, symbolic, and literary strata.

Thus, although Lawrence Durrell's poetic production seems to be overshadowed by his prose work, poetry is of paramount significance to the understanding of his writing. Indeed, he started his artistic career as a poet, despite becoming famous for the first time as late as 1957 thanks to *Justine*, the first volume of *The Alexandria Quartet*. A close reading of the echoes that keep reverberating between the poetic and narrative pieces leads the reader to realize that Durrell builds up his oeuvre in the subtle interweaving of poetry and prose, calling for a "watchful, a true reader between the lines—where all the writing is done,"[21] where the reading act is transformed, where the world is reshaped.

This is how we are led to follow Durrell on Corfu through the poems "Carol on Corfu" and "Summer in Corfu," both published in *A Private Country* in 1943 and, simultaneously, through the residence book *Prospero's Cell*, published in 1945, before we eventually return to the selfsame island in "Cities, Plains and People," the eponymous poem of his subsequent collection issued in 1946. Geographic, formal, textual, and temporal boundaries are thus progressively blurred, a technique that is highly reminiscent of the "Notes for landscape tones. . ."[22] opening the first description of Alexandria in *The Quartet*. It is as if the prose and the poems harbored inner crevices, unchartered leeways making room for the other text, for this estranged presence that lies beyond the reach of the chosen genre, reminding the reader of the porous essence of semiotic frontiers, of the brittle nature of stylistic conventions, of the quintessential uncertainty of any art form. Such a practice extends far beyond Durrell's early work; while writing *Tunc* and *Nunquam*, which were eventually republished as a single volume under the title *The Revolt of Aphrodite* in 1974, he was composing *The Red Limbo Lingo, A Poetry Notebook*, which he introduced on the dust jacket as:

> [. . .] strange thoughts, in prose or verse, in English or French, around the notion of blood—from its sacrificial aspect, one might have said, to its association with vampires, but he [Durrell] doesn't seem to set them apart. [. . .] But a notebook of this sort is like a constellation, a star cluster of thoughts which may set off poems on quite other preoccupations. And the train of ideas is, in fact, followed by twenty-one new poems [. . .].[23]

Playing with limits is, as I shall argue later, an integral part of Durrell's aesthetic and philosophic conception of the essence of poetry understood both as an artistic practice culminating in the materiality of the poem and as the patient ripening of a personal poetics. The reader thus faces the difficult task of genre classification: for instance, how is the second chapter of *Clea* to be construed? The narrative momentum is frozen in this prose poem that captures the reader's eye and ear as early as the first words. The introductory sentence is fraught with a musical rhythm that makes the entire chapter float between fiction and poetry, detached from the narrative context where it belongs, like another of those visual mirages haunting the Alexandrian desert:

```
  /   x   /    x / x     / x / x   x  /  x
Ancient lands / in all their / prehistoric / intactness:
  /  / x /    / x    /     x  x  / x    / x  x  / x
lake so/litudes / hardly / brushed by / the hur/rying feet of / the centuries
  /    x    / x x  / x    / x  /    x / x /    x / x   x   / x
where the / unin/terrupted / pedigrees / of pelican / and ibis / and heron
x  /    x    /    / x x   x x   /    x / x
evolve / their slow / destinies / in complete / seclusion.²⁴
```

The writing mimics the inner breath of the landscape through a ternary rhythm. The alternating anapests (xx/) and dactyls (/xx), giving way to the binary tempo of the iamb in the end, echo the crescendo movement that expands from the tetrameter to the pentameter and hexameter before reverting to the pentameter one more time. The numerous alliterations in /l/ and /s/ combine with the assonances in /ɪ/ and /iː/ to produce a soothing, flowing lilt. The landscape expands, contracts, and reverberates. Confused perspectives betray a writing that conjures up characters and landscapes only to wipe them out instantly, while casting an entire chapter into the margins of the novel, transforming it into a poetic oddity, not unlike "those exquisitely beautiful and mysterious objects,"²⁵ fruit of the Austrian Baron's alchemical experiments in Da Capo's letter. Durrell's poetics thus fascinates and traps the reader's eye, inviting him both to track the missing generic coherence and to enjoy the bewitching power of a prose that momentarily sheds its story line to develop into a hypotyposis marrying writing, music, and painting.

Such an example clearly evinces the impossible classification of Durrell's output and the necessary to-and-fro movement that brings the reader to embrace poetry and prose in a single glance. What is to be learned, then, from these all too scarcely studied poetry collections about Durrell's poetry and the nature of its relationship to the prose? Are they merely the harbingers of the novelist's accomplished art or do they point to a further, private achievement? What do they tell us about the specificity of Durrell's oeuvre? I contend that the chronological development of his poetic works points to the deepening of a complex poetic space that serves the elaboration of a secret symbolism wrought between the lines. This twofold interconnection between prose and poetry, and between poetry and drama, testifies to the creation of a unique poetics. One may remember the few lines by Angelos Sikelianos that Durrell penciled into the first edition of A *Private Country* he presented to Eve Cohen: "Eyes closed I look at you and am never sated, I am never sated of seeing you"[26]—the contrast between the verbs "to look at" and "to see" suggests the enduring presence of an inner vision that haunts the poet's eye forever. Lawrence Durrell's poetry remains faithful to the vision of the inner eye, following the steps of the Greek poet as much as those of Wordsworth and the Romantics.[27] The poet is thus to be conceived as this artist who keeps looking back, but this retrospective and introspective gaze has freed itself from the subject's will: it takes possession both of the work and of its author, it challenges temporal linearity as much as logic. The experience of poetic vision is then intimately linked to the experience of an ontological dispossession. Beyond the sudden bereavement of forced exiles, or the various losses Lawrence Durrell underwent, his writing hints at a deeper, deliberate surrender that is the very essence of poetry, as Gérard Pfister points out: "Orpheus simultaneously sings the beauty and the loss of the loved one: because he saw her, he lost her; because he lost her, he sings her. The poem is both vision and dispossession."[28] Reading Lawrence Durrell's poetry amounts to groping slowly back toward this intense loss that gives the poet his voice, a voice delivered from material, autobiographic, or temporal contingencies, a voice that reaches out to the reader and opens up the possibility of a new being-in-the-world that Phaon's words in *Sappho* adumbrate:

> There is no real meeting or parting
> In this world, once you have learned the truth,
> Nor yet in any other.[29]

Notes

1. Samuel Taylor Coleridge, "Letters," July 13, 1802, *Selected Poetry*, Harmondsworth: Penguin, 1996, p. xiii.

2. SIU archives, The Lawrence Durrell papers, Collection 42/1/4 [Correspondence 1942–1946].

3. SIU archives, The Lawrence Durrell papers, Collection 42/1/4 [Correspondence 1942–1946].

4. T. S. Eliot agreed to the publication of *Sappho, A Play in Verse*, which was published by Faber in 1950. Its postscript makes Durrell's literary and aesthetic aims fairly clear: "This verse play [was] written with the object of marrying up pace, plot and poetry [. . .]," p. 187.

5. SIU archives, The Lawrence Durrell papers, Collection 42/1/4 [Correspondence 1942–1946].

6. Jacques Ancet, quoted by Pfister Gérard, *'La poésie, c'est autre chose,'* 1001 *définitions de la poésie*, Paris-Orbey: Arfuyen, 2008, p. 30.
7. Letters to Diana Menuhin 1957–1984, SIU archives, VFM material, manuscript shelf list catalog: letters from Lawrence Durrell, VFM 1672.
8. Undated letter probably written during the year 1977. SIU archives, The Lawrence Durrell papers 2nd accession, 1990, collection 163/14/2.
9. Stéphane Mallarmé, *Magie, Œuvres complètes II*, Paris: Gallimard, 1967.
10. Hugo Friedrich, *Structure de la poésie moderne*, Paris: Librairie Générale Française, 1999, p. 188.
11. Lawrence Durrell, "Coming in slightly at a slant," interview with Huw Wheldon. *Lawrence Durrell: Conversations*, ed. Earl G. Ingersoll, London: Associated University Presses, 1998, p. 54.
12. Charles Baudelaire, "A Arsène Houssaye," *Le Spleen de Paris: Petits poèmes en prose*, Paris: Gallimard, 2006, p. 104.
13. Lawrence Durrell, "Letting the book breathe by itself," interview with William G. Smith. *Lawrence Durrell: Conversations*, pp. 60, 62.
14. Christian Doumet, *Faut-il comprendre la poésie?* Paris: Klincksieck, 2004, p. 89.
15. Hugo Friedrich, *Structure de la poésie moderne*, p. 14.
16. Bernard Sesé, quoted by Pfister Gérard, *'La poésie, c'est autre chose,'* p. 197.
17. Charles Baudelaire, "A Arsène Houssaye," *Le Spleen de Paris: Petits poèmes en prose*, p. 104.
18. Bo Carpelan, quoted by Pfister Gérard, *'La poésie, c'est autre chose,'* p. 54.
19. "A copy of *A Rebours* lay face down on the floor" of Clea's apartment on the night of Justine's disappearance. (Lawrence Durrell, *The Alexandria Quartet*, London: Faber, 1974, p. 180).
20. Rainer Maria Rilke, *Lettres à un jeune poète*, Paris: Librairie Générale Française, 1989, p. 47.
21. *The Alexandria Quartet*, pp. 379–80.
22. *The Alexandria Quartet*, p. 18.
23. Lawrence Durrell, *The Red Limbo Lingo*, London: Faber, 1971 [n.p.].
24. *The Alexandria Quartet*, p. 686.
25. *The Alexandria Quartet*, p. 809.
26. The original dedication to Eve reads as follows: "και εας κυττάω μέ σφαλισμένα μάτια / και δέ χορταίνω, δέ χορταίνω να εας βλεπω. ΑΓΓΕΛΟΥ ΣΙΚΑΛΙΑΝΟΥ."
27. We may remember here Lawrence Durrell's profound admiration for the great poet of English Romanticism, which he not only edited and prefaced (*Wordsworth: Selected by Lawrence Durrell*, Harmondsworth: Penguin Books, 1973, pp. 9–21) but also repeatedly commented upon in his critical essay *Key to Modern Poetry* published in 1952.
28. Gérard Pfister, *'La poésie, c'est autre chose,'* p. 50.
29. Lawrence Durrell, *Sappho*, London: Faber, 1969, p. 113.

CHAPTER ONE

A Private Country
The Poet's Secret Cartography

At the time when *A Private Country* was first published, in 1943, Lawrence Durrell was already "exiled from exile":[1] sent away from Greece, he discovered an Egypt that beat to the rhythm of military defeats and progress, where refugees from everywhere, soldiers and deserters, poets and diplomats converged and met. The first poem in this collection was written from Mykonos, shortly before Durrell left Kalamata, and clearly signals Greece as this intimate anchorage that he will never cease to fathom although he has already lost it. Throughout this first collection published by Faber and the various poems that appeared simultaneously in the *Personal Landscape* review under the direction of Robin Fedden and Bernard Spencer in Cairo, Greece stands out as this absent presence that is the true spring of the poetic imagination, the deeper root of the uprooted suffering subject, the original rift where all writing is born.[2]

The Dragoman-Prophet: The Poet's Mask

A Private Country opens upon a poem that seems to promise the narrative of an entire life, that of Stefan Syriotis:

> Fangbrand
> A biography
> *To Stephan Syriotis in his island of oblivion, Mykonos*[3]

Stefan Syriotis, the friend who introduced Lawrence Durrell to the islands of Mykonos and Delos and, more importantly, to a thriving network of Greek friendships, acts as the tutelary figure keeping watch over the early beginnings of Durrell's poetry, the careful guardian of the very first lines of the collection. It is indeed thanks to such varied and close friendships that Durrell learned to discover and love Greece, as he himself wrote several years later:

> I had begun to understand Greece through the friendships I had made with the young people of Athens, a remarkable body of spirits—some of fortune, some poor—but all endowed with the riches of the buoyant Greek nature. [. . .] Of exceptional beauty and style, the type to which they belonged was always recognizable on Greek coins or sculptures in the museum. [. . .] These young men were an education in themselves. It is a pleasure to put down their names—each had something personal to teach me through his attitude to life and his intrinsic Greekness. I think of Andre Nomikos, painter; Stefan Syriotis, high functionary; Matsas, diplomat; Seferis, poet; Elytis, poet [. . .] Stefan Syriotis spent his summer hidden in Mykonos with his small boat, living in seclusion almost, and coming back to the little hamlet of Mykonos only for provisions of lentils and rice and wine. For the rest, he led the life of a seabird, swimming on faraway beaches, reading and sleeping away the days until he needs must return to Athens and his job. [. . .] It was to Stefan that I owe my first visit to Mykonos and, by the same token, to Delos [. . .]
>
> Mykonos at that time was little frequented because of faulty and haphazard communications with Athens; but it was a choice and secret place which Athenians loved, and which they kept very much to themselves. It was a compliment to be made free of this little club of Mykoniots *d'élection* [. . .].[4]

Stefan Syriotis is the initiator and dragoman who sketches out a new path for the poet, unveiling a sheltered and secretive land.[5] This particular island interestingly became the object of an ethnographic study that, taking up Durrell's phrase the "Mykoniots *d'élection*," describes the island of the 1940s as a secluded space, a mythical haven peopled only by the intellectual and artistic elites in want of a temporary abode:

> Thus the sense of exclusivity attached to the island was established early on; it was taken over by charismatic and privileged groups who in turn initiated, in the first instance, the 'elite' of their day and age. The cosmopolitan Greeks, ship owners, artists, intellectuals and their keepers arrived and thus begins the whole snowballing scenario of acquaintanceship. For quite a few decades [. . .] the island remained a paradise for the few.[6]

This heavenly realm where exceptional personalities can meet and mix, this intellectual crucible of nomadic sensibilities is brought back to life in Durrell's poem through the creation of a mythical figure. Syriotis is then no longer the "high functionary"[7] Durrell recalls in *The Greek Islands*. He disappears and gives way to a mythical hero, metamorphosing into Fangbrand—an outlandish name that subsumes the scorching burn of the firebrand and the venomous fangs of the snake, suggesting the everlasting imprint of the land on the poet's flesh and soul. From the very first lines, Fangbrand is a hybrid figure crossing geographic, temporal, historical, and fictional borders:

> Fangbrand was here once,
> A missionary man,
> Borne down by the Oxus,
> Pursued by the lilies,
> Inhabited by the old voice of sorrows,
> In a black hat and sanitary boots. (l.1–6, A *Private Country*, p. 7)

The presence of the Oxus suggests Alexander the Great, who crossed the unruly river on his way to Central Asia, while the lilies evoke both the myth of Persephone taken away by Hades into the world of Shades as she was picking a lily, and that of the metamorphosis of Hyacinthos, Apollo's lover, into a lily. This first stanza projects the spectral shadow of Fangbrand born from the flux of a time beyond memory and foreshadowing a world of hidden grief. The ominous figure in "a black hat and sanitary boots" forces the reader to face the present chasm of darkness out of which Fangbrand radiates hope and light. Throughout the poem Fangbrand impersonates the "missionary man," whose surprising isolation and silence make the inner voice of the land even more vibrant. When man's voice is no longer heard, one may listen to the sea and the earth:

> The blue circlets of stone,
> On a sea blotted with fictions [. . .] (l.11–12)

> The Ocean's peculiar spelling
> Haunts here, cuddled by syllables
> In caves perpendicular, a blue recitation
> Of water washing the dead [. . .] (l.13–16)

Space itself metamorphoses as the frontiers between the human and the mineral, the earthly and the watery realms merge and blur:

> His brows that bent like forests
> Over the crystal-gazing eyes;
> His brows that bent like forests,
> A silver hair played on his neck. (l.25–28)

The syntactic structure, with its two relative clauses devoid of any head clause, comes apart at the seams, just as the human body breaks apart to merge with the land. The boundaries between the inner and the outer world, between the subject and the surrounding space, fade out. It is as if space opened up from within to hint at what lies beyond the visible:

> Pulpits whitened by the sea-birds,
> Mean more than just a house, rock,
> A tree, a table and a chair. (l.40–42)

These lines already pave the way for the poetry that is yet to come: they usher in the living word of a prophetic landscape that will develop a few years later in *Cities, Plains and People*, where the poem "Two Poems in Basic English" opens upon:

> Ships. Islands. Trees
> These ships, these islands, these simple trees
> Are our rewards in substance, being poor.
> The earth a dictionary is
> To the root and growth and seeing,
> And to the servant heart a door. (l.1–6, *Cities, Plains and People*, p. 53)

This prophetic language strikes the reader as both metaphorical and deeply imbued with a keen sensual awareness of the land's "substance" to which Fangbrand bears witness as this paradoxical missionary who is first and foremost characterized by his gifts as a silent listener:

> [. . .] the one voice
> Saying 'Renounce', the other
> Answering 'Be'; the division
> Of the darkness into faces
> Crying 'Too late' 'Too late'. (l.50–54)

Fangbrand's art rests in his expectant, heedful attitude, which makes him the receptacle of a word he is the only one to hear and serve as its oracle, not unlike the Delphic Pithia. The penultimate stanza concludes "Fangbrand / Died with his art like a vase" (l.134–5), thus confirming the unique intimate relationship between landscape and character, a relationship that cannot be conveyed in words and that is to be approached as a mystery.

This mystery is none other than that of human nature, divided between the voice of the ego and that of the spirit, torn between possession and renunciation:

> And always the awareness
> Of self like a point, the quiver
> As of a foetal heart asleep in him. (l.58–60)

The critic Ray Morrison reads this inner rift as the sign of the deep influence that the symbolist tradition has played in Durrell's poetry and as the harbinger of his "heraldic universe":

> Durrell, in "Fangbrand" [. . .] seems to sum up and put on display all he has absorbed about symbolism. Through an enigmatic, quick-changing flow of symbols, the poet suggests Fangbrand's dilemma and the spiritual changes occurring in him [. . .] he dies with "his art like a vase", his life a symbolist work of art, the poem Durrell has written. [. . .] During this time, Durrell brings together materials from Taoism, Georg Groddeck (1886–1934) and his psychology, the Greek world, and his deepening sense of love, experienced at moments through his marriage and the birth of his daughter. Most of these influences coalesce around and help to define what Durrell calls his Heraldic Universe.[8]

Therefore, the poetic space conjured up in Durrell's early collections sketches out a new universe that heralds a singular, intimate birth—that of the acute perception of the self and of the surrounding world that can only be understood within the silent exile of a memory that keeps retracing its own steps:

> Continuous memory, continual evocations.
> An old man in a colony of stones,
> Frowning, exilic, upon a thorn,
> Learning nothing of time [. . .] (l.61–64)

There can be no traditional learning process, no linear progression, but only a constant resifting of the past that echoes the relentless undertow of the sea at the end of the poem: "[. . .] nothing grows, / But the ocean expunges" (l.131–32). Fangbrand, a true antiprophet, makes no revelation, no prophecy, and this paradox is the very object of the poet's writing, the source of his constant brooding upon the frailty of man's spirit and flesh that, instead of ruling the world, blends with the sea:

> It seemed to him here at last
> His age, his time, his sex even
> Were struck and past; life
> In a flood carrying all idols into the darkness [. . .] (l.73–76)
> His body he left in pools
> Now dazed by fortune, like an old
> White cloth discarded where
> Only the fish were visitors. (l.91–94)

Fangbrand's dispossession of his own self brings about a feeling of freedom and relief as he comes closer to his own essence:

> Truth's metaphor is the needle,
> The magnetic north of purpose
> Striving against the true north
> Of self: Fangbrand found it out,
> The final dualism in very self,
> An old man holding an asphodel. (l.103–8)

This inner split is the price to pay for the one who is in search of freedom, not material but spiritual freedom that grows out of man's awareness of his dualism and of his encounter with his mortal nature. In that respect, Fangbrand is reminiscent of Jonah, the antiprophet in the Old Testament who not only refuses to obey God's command because he fears prophesying but welcomes the waters of chaos that entrap him and, instead of pleading for salvation, is thankful for being reunited with God.[9] The figure of the "old man holding an asphodel" thus marries the Christian and the Greek traditions.

Abandoning himself to "a flood carrying all idols into the darkness" and stepping into the underworld, he is finally endowed with the sight of the spirit. He metamorphoses into a *vanitas* comprising the traditional symbols of decay and of the ephemeral nature of life:

> He regarded himself in water,
> The torrid brow's beetle,
> The grammarian's cranium-bone. (l.115–17)

Leaving nothing behind him, neither book nor paper (l.125–26), taking away every sign of material presence, Fangbrand erases all traces; the "white island" (l.124) only bears the insubstantial imprint of his spiritual quest:

> [. . .] the luminous island
> Of the self trembles and waits,
> Waits for us all, my friends,

> Where the sea's big brush recolours
> The dying lives, and the unborn smiles. (l.146–50)

"The luminous island" radiating life is that of art that always outreaches its own object, but it also stands for the underlying hope that precedes and outlives any work of art. Fangbrand consequently appears as one of the poet's many masks, the projection of an ideal alter ego that deepens and expands man's connection with the universe, echoing Durrell's letter to Miller written from Kalamata in 1941: "I walk about like a free man and sniff the wind and relive my past incarnations as a goat, a tree, and a centaur."[10]

Therefore, the poet's secret cartography sketches out an ontological quest: it does not merely chart the poet's sensibility and past emotions, the private contours of a modern mind. It stands out as a philosophical endeavor to define both the artist and the man, for, like Pursewarden, his alter ego in *The Alexandria Quartet*, Durrell drew no line between life and art: "You see, Brother Ass, there is life and then the life of my life. They must belong as fruit and rind. [. . .] It is not really art which is at issue, it is ourselves. [. . .] (Art occurs at the point where a form is sincerely honored by an awakened spirit.)"[11]

However, one should not confuse the author's life and the work of art itself, far less try to interpret the man from his texts. Thus, we may remember how Darley, the narrating character in *The Alexandria Quartet*, tries to rebuild Pursewarden's character after his death with the naïve enthusiasm of a young writer who turns into a sleuth, ends up befuddled, and finally admits: "He was only to be seen now through the distorting mirror of anecdote or the dusty spectrum of memory."[12] Significantly, this scene is followed by the discovery of Nessim's telescope aimed at the very spot on the beach where, just a few moments ago, Darley and Justine were conspiring to recapture Pursewarden's portrait. The textual irony showing the "secret agent"[13] watched by his lover's husband is redoubled in the following volume where Balthazar points at Darley's inability to grasp Pursewarden's true nature: "[. . .] he does not seem to resurrect on paper into a recognizable image of the man I knew. He seems to be a sort of enigma to you."[14] The author thus remains this pervading, tantalizing presence that cannot be circumscribed. Similarly, although *A Private Country* does enable the reader to follow Durrell's peregrinations, the collection is not primarily concerned with retracing the poet's steps. The various geographic beacons suggest a symbolic space where

> As long-drawn echoes mingle and transfuse
> Till in a deep, dark unison they swoon,
> Vast as the night or as the vault of noon—
> So are commingled perfumes, sounds, and hues.[15]

Greece: The Chosen Land, The Point of Cleavage

While retracing the poet's footsteps across the various cities and countries that acted as so many milestones in Durrell's life and career, the reader soon realizes that this very private country cannot be mapped out but keeps dissolving and reforming like the shaky fragments of an ever-moving kaleidoscope. The tutelary figure of Fangbrand standing on the threshold of *A Private Country* clearly signals Greece as the chosen land explored throughout the following poems: "Carol on Corfu," "Summer in Corfu," "In Arcadia," "To Argos," "At Corinth," "On Ithaca Standing," "Father Nicholas His Death in the Ionian," "A Noctuary in Athens," "Nemea," or "Exile in Athens." The various titles evince the ambiguous status of the Greek islands and cities that work both as spatial references giving a realistic anchorage to the text and as the object of discourse that progressively metamorphoses into a living, organic subject that the poem celebrates and to which it gives voice.

That "Carol on Corfu" and "Summer in Corfu" face each other on a double page leads the reader to question the role of the island both as object and place of discourse. The first poem, which clearly follows the symbolist tradition, gives tongue to the lyrical "I" who delivers the mysterious music of the land:

> This is my medicine: trees speak and doves
> Talk, woods walk: in the pith of the planet
> Is undertone, overtone, status of music: God
> Opens each fent, scent, memory, aftermath
> In the sky and the sod.[16] (l.11–15)

The run-on lines, anadiploses, anaphoras, or paranomases characterizing this poem reverberate the inner music of the text, which seems to well up from the land itself, from every single geological, phonetic, and prosodic cleft. The poet's "I" seems to merge with the island, and the writing is the very "salt of the poem,"[17] just as man is "the salt of the earth."[18] Thus the poet, communing with the world, is at one with the I/land he celebrates.

The second poem, "Summer in Corfu," is also an ode to the island of Corfu, more specifically an ode to summer aimed at mysterious addressees that the poet considers as his brothers. Despite the changed perspective suggested in the title by the preposition "in," the poem is to be read as the second movement of the first ode. "Summer in Corfu" significantly detaches itself from its geographic bearings and explores the mystic allegory of fertility as the island metamorphoses into a woman's body:

> [. . .] The season
> Like a woman lies open, is folding,
> Secret, growth upon growth. The black fig
> Desire is torn again from the belly of reason.
> Our summer is gravid at last, is big.[19] (l.7–11)

The two poems retrace the slow symbolic fulfillment of the land: "Carol on Corfu" enacts the poet's (re)birth carved in the clay of words—"With the madman's verve I quicken, / Leaven, liven body's prime carbon, / I, per se I, alone" (l.8–10)—while "Summer in Corfu" stages the incarnation of the life-giving soil.

Time is the land's accomplice: summer, the time of fruition, offers a euphoric counterpoint to the last lines of "Carol on Corfu," ending on the drab note, "Now feather and beak have gone" (l.20), and brings about the blooming powers of the island: "New beaks for the flesh,[20] / From the black mint / Steel for new flint" (l.4–6). Space and time are happily attuned on the mythical land of writing.

The last stanza metamorphoses all human beings into island children, sacred fruit, just as the real island is metamorphosed into a mythical locus, an object of eternal desire and a symbol of immortality:

> All you, who know desire in these seas,
> Have souls or equipment for loneliness, loneliness,
> Lean now like fruitage. The Hesperides
> Open. This the limbo, the doldrum.
> Seal down the eye of your Cyclops,
> Silence Time's drum. (l.12–17)

The garden of the Hesperides opens up its doors to all those akin to the poet who have been sorely tried by desire and loneliness and are ready to bear fruit. By alluding to the golden apples that granted the immortality much coveted by ancient heroes, the poet suggests that writing is to be seen as the crossing point toward a mythical elsewhere and as the object of a never-fulfilled desire. The entire poem is indeed this fruit about to be born and the clue to an unmapped space-time, a "limbo" where the boundaries between the geographic and the mythical dissolve, not unlike those of the ancient Greek garden hovering somewhere on the edge of the encircling Ocean world. Significantly the promise of the opening garden leads to "Silence": the stanza ends on the mysterious "limbo." The peaceful decrescendo of the final trimeter and the shift from trochee to spondee as well as the masculine rhyme (drum/drum) forcefully marks the end of the poet's discourse and ushers in the realm of the ineffable. Having given up the necessarily imperfect physical perception of the one-eyed "Cyclops," the poet's disciple can travel from the recorded time of the classical metrical beat to the unrecorded time that the entire poem aims for. The blank space that stretches at the end of this last, shortened line opens up the text to the silence of unspoken echoes. For that matter, Corinne Alexandre-Garner's analysis of *Prospero's Cell* can be applied to Durrell's poetry: "[. . .] the tales of ancient times and those of the present day coalesce. [. . .] We have entered the world of Baudelaire's 'Correspondences.'"[21]

Yet Greece is not only the land where the poet experiences the harmony of the world. It is also the space of differentiation where the cleavage between the ancient world and the modern European one symbolized by England is made most poignant. This is why the collection confronts "In Arcadia" and "To Argos," conjuring up two spaces that call for diametrically opposed perspectives whether one chooses to favor a sensual or a rational connection with the land.

"In Arcadia" offers the reader a world where man can be at one with nature:

They invented this valley, they taught
The rock to flow with odourless water.

Fire and a brute art came among them.

Rain fell, tasting of the sky.
Trees grew, composing a grammar.[22] (l.3–7)

Unrefined though they may be, the Dorians knew how to invent a landscape where elements commingle, where man and nature partake of the same essence. Their disappearance, as mysterious as their arrival, still permeates and affects the most ephemeral organisms and the most minute aspects of natural life: "the brown bee," the "world of bushes," "the awkward patience of the ant" (ibid.). Arcadia is therefore not so much equated with an unspoiled area as with a harmonious era when unity prevailed over dualism. This era can only be revived through the poetic vision that sees through the past mysteries brought down by the river where the layman sees naught: "All travellers recorded an empty zone." Yet the poet remains sensitive to the resounding breath of the past—"Something died out by this river: but it seems / Less than a nightingale ago"—and seems to share Keats's haunting question: "Was it a vision, or a waking dream? / Fled is that music:—Do I wake or dream?"[23]

Facing "In Arcadia" on the opposite page, the poem "To Argos" contrasts "the dead ones / Who are lying under these mountains" and "our own fastidious / Heroes" to conclude upon the rift separating the Greek land from the English language:

> Truly, we the endowed who pass here
> With the assurance of visitors in rugs
> Can raise from the menhir no ghost
> By the cold sound of English idioms (l.37–40)

Unlike the Greek land, where contraries are happily married—"The roads lead southward, blue / Along a circumference of snow" (l.1–2)—England is synonymous with a colorless cold, with a language Durrell deems impervious to the eternal and the sensual, with the crude indifference of "the modern girls [who] pose on a tomb smiling," with a society that has become symbol-blind: "The hyssop and the vinegar have lost their meaning" (l.47). The hyssop, which is linked to the purification and redemption rituals in the Book of Psalms and the vinegar, in which Booz invites Ruth to dip her slice of bread, fleetingly evoke a primeval society in which man was surrounded daily by "forest-groves of symbols."[24] This is how Greece paradoxically turns out to be the very space where the poet experiences dispossession and loss. The repeated line "This is what breaks the heart" (l.24 and l.48) evinces the poet's painful wrench and his hopeless desire to recreate a harmonious cycle through this prosodic and musical mirror to the peaceful image of the "circumference of snow."

The reader may then realize the subtlety of the constant opposition between here and elsewhere that underlies the entire collection. Greece and England, the mythical past and the present times coexist as the two poles of a constant and essential tension that reverberates throughout Durrell's poems. And it is the same principle of a vibrant, painful dualism that is, according to Durrell, the true source of the poet's birth:

> There is a pleasant fancy which is a far eastern one, namely, that you have two birth-places. You have the place where you were really born and then you have a place of predilection where you really wake up to reality. One day you wake up and it's there, and in your inner life, in your dreams and so on and so forth, it's the place of predilection that comes forward and which nourishes you.[25]

Poetry is the privileged mode of expression of this fundamental polarity that shapes out Durrell's entire opus. It is all the more meaningful in Durrell's case, the Anglo-Indian boy who always entertained a peculiar and uncomfortable relationship with the word "home." "Home" naturally referred to a strange and foreign land, away from and at odds with the motherland, inevitably leading to a confusing idealization. Thus, we may remember the tender and nostalgic words uttered by the young Walsh Clifton, Durrell's heavily autobiographical alter ego, shortly before his departure for England:

> He knew, of course, that England was where everyone should go; that was the dream that induced the colonial to save his pay. He remembered the Abbis family: they had left for England last summer. He remembered their exultation and happiness. Mr. Abbis was huge and broad-shouldered and as brown as wood-smoke; he had chattered for weeks on end of going home; of getting his daughters educated at home; of settling down at home; always "home." The two girls had boasted openly, proudly of it. They, too, used the word "home." Walsh found it a peculiarly inspiring word, but applied to England it meant less than nothing.[26]

The very titles at the heart of the collection enable the reader to understand that poetry is the secret place where Durrell recreates the original uprooting and relives the rift that lies at the core of his artistic sensibility.

"At Corinth," the poem following "To Argos," dwells upon the opposition between the world inhabited by Greek myths and that of the scientific discourse upon mythology. Two realities are pitted against each other: that observed by visitors and tourists who have been influenced by their bookish memories and that of the man who pays attention to the land and comes to meet the spirit of the place. Between "a place in a book" (l.5) and "the quotation of visitors" (l.24) the two stanzas in free verse develop a vision unspoiled by any scientific knowledge, as if the land were slowly breaking free from the learned frame of reference in which it had been confined. The antithesis between the two visions of Greece is the cornerstone of a renewed vision of the relationships between man and the universe. For Durrell is not merely concerned with revisiting the classics and following in the wake of Seferis or Sikelianos, whom he was the first to translate into English. Indeed, he contributed to the fame of modern Greek poetry at a time when it was mostly unknown abroad.[27] He also distinguishes himself by elaborating a Greek landscape that outlives its literary heritage. Far from rejecting the poetic tradition ("[. . .] we whose blood was sweetened once / By Byron or his elders in the magic" l.27–28), he summons his reader to take up the road to Corinth once more in order not so much to experience what the language of myths tells us about the place but to become aware of what our senses tell us about the place, to become sensitive to the language of place. "The touch of flesh, / Our fingers pressed upon eyelids of stone" (l.8–9) introduce a silent, sensorial, instinctive, ephemeral, and intimate relationship with the place that is no longer the passive object but the active source of the poetic utterance.

This reversed perspective affects the stylistic, syntactic, and prosodic patterns: the parentheses at the end of the first stanza reveal what lies precisely beyond the visible world—"[. . .] the touch of flesh / [. . .] (Our fingers pressed upon eyelids of stone)" (l.8–9)—the subject of the infinitive concluding the first stanza disappears in the wake of the "dissolving moon" (l.12), while the beginning of the second stanza plays on the comma to introduce "The scent of the exhausted lamps" (l.16) as a deceptive apposition to the figure of the lovers. By joining the earth and the sky in "stars come soft to pasture" (l.18), or subverting the geographic journey in "this land of doors" (l.3) into a dream-born wandering ("all doors lead to sleep" l.19), the poem, although following the classical iambic rhythm, upsets our relationship to space and naturally leads to the progressive detachment from a faulty reading ("What lies beneath the turf forbids / [. . .] / The intrusion of a style less pure / Seen through the camera's lens, / Or the quotations of visitors" l.20–24). The intuitive foreknowledge of what "lies beneath the turf" and can neither be seen nor rationally apprehended suggests the powerful presence of the underworld, which, since the dawn of time, has ruled man's fate and continues to do so by forbidding any unfaithful, secondhand approach that could be subsumed in simple "quotations." The poet, like Hermes, is entrusted with a firsthand message that he conveys in this unexpected letter. "Writing [. . .] home," the poet addresses the world and discloses a new, unheard-of reality that cannot be summed up in a quote but that breaks free from the words to inhabit the silence of the smile:

> My skill is in words only:
> To tell you, writing this letter home,
> That we, whose blood was sweetened once
> By Byron or his elders in the magic,
> Entered the circle safely, found
> No messenger for us except the smiles. (l.25–30)

The symbolism of this poetic letter revisits and revives classical mythology: the old messengers are replaced by the modern poet who shakes off his masters' authority and directly approaches "the magic" of place. Bridging geographic and historic gaps as well as literary and philosophical traditions, the poem suggests the ambiguous presence of a writer haunted by past writings of place acting as a go-between who has successfully "entered the circle" of poetic initiation. While paying homage to his "elders," the poet turns his gaze toward disembodied "smiles" heralding the smile of Tao he will later come to identify with the essence of poetry: "[. . .] the poem (the ideogram of a perfected apprehension)."[28]

Thus, Durrell invites his reader to ponder both upon the discourse on space and the language of space, to rethink our deciphering of the outer world and of its reverberating echoes in the mind's eye. He steers him toward an acute receptiveness to the familiar beneath the symbolic and to the ephemeral beneath the eternal through a deliberate subversion of classical values:

> Owls sip the wind here. Well,
> This place also was somebody's home,
> Whipped by the gulf to thorns,
> A house for proverbs by the broken well.
> Winter was never native here: nor is.
> Men, women, and the nightingales
> Are forms of Spring. (l.31–37)

The poem concludes on a narrative that conveys the voice of the poet who has elected the auspices of the owl, Athena's bird, the symbol of intuitive knowledge, of the keen penetration that can read signs in the dark. This is how the owl comes to epitomize the poet himself who through the sheer evocative power of words can summon the invisible and the inconspicuous: the statues that "dissolve" (l.11), "the scent of the exhausted lamps" (l.17), the owls that "sip the wind" (l.31). The poem "At Corinth" thus questions our reading of place and of the various discourses it has engendered, and it suggests that every place should be read as a mysterious code that cannot be broken by reason but is meant to bring back to life all our senses.

Sensorial perception precisely reaches its climax in the wan light of "a dissolving moon" (l.12), in a land where "all doors lead to sleep" (l.86), where ratiocination no longer rules. Only there and then can sensorial notations capture the ephemeral and the unremarkable ("less penetrating than the touch of flesh" l.7) through a prosody that marries visual and auditory rhymes. The echoes between "Hunting" and "Haunting" in stanza 1 or the play on sibilant sounds in stanza 2 ("Here stars come soft to pasture") testify to the preciseness and complexity of a text that, like the land itself, calls for the reader's absolute alertness. The space of the poem, like that of the Greek land, can only be descried by those who can notice the changing rhythms, the unexpected associations of abstract and concrete notations, of the animate and the inanimate realms, of the earthly and the magical. The ultimate twist lies in the unique rhyme of the entire poem, the word "home" that appears twice in the last stanza. In the first occurrence, "home" refers to the land once inhabited by Byron[29] and where Durrell was introduced to the world of British and French poetry, while the second is a wide-open abode defined in the following line: "A house for proverbs by a broken well" (l.34). This is where writing springs from, the place of wisdom where water hides to surge again out of the rubble of the past, where men, women, and nightingales join in unison. The poem conjures up the place of creation previously mentioned: "a place of predilection where you really wake up to reality [...] the place of predilection that comes forward and which nourishes you."[30]

Therefore, far from being a mere symbol, place becomes the proper matter and subject of the text: it welcomes the poet and guides his voice. The poetics of place is the crucible of Durrell's poetry, as shown in the issues of *Personal Landscape*, which Durrell launched with his friends Robin Fedden and Bernard Spencer in 1941 in Cairo. They comprised British and Greek contemporary poems as well as some of Durrell's poems and meditations on poetry. Issue no. 2, published in March 1942, highlights Durrell's artistic project and sketches out the very specific reading mode that his poems seek to elicit:

> Logic, syntax, is a causal instrument, inadequate for the tax of describing the whole of reality. Poems don't describe, but they are sounding boards which enable the alert consciousness to pick up the reverberations of the extra-causal reality for itself.
>
> Poems are negatives; hold them up to a clean surface of daylight and you get an apprehension of grace. The words carry in them complete submerged poems; as you read your memory goes down like the loud pedal of a piano, and all tribal, personal associations begin to reverberate. Poems are blueprints. They are not buildings but they enable you to build for yourself.[31]

The first part of this quotation delineates the role poetry plays in Durrell's writing: it is the least imperfect mode of expression because it enables the writer's voice to shake off the constraints of syntactic and causal logic. Paratax, floating syntagmas, displaced punctuation marks, incomplete sentences, imperfect rhymes are part and parcel of Durrell's poetic writing.

Unlike his novels, plays, or residence books, his poems are not "buildings" but "sounding boards" that bring back to consciousness the echo of an underlying world that transcends causal reality. In that respect the poet's intention does not differ significantly from the novelist's as defined by Pursewarden in *The Alexandria Quartet*: "Or is art simply the little white stick which is given to the blind man and by the help of which he tap tap taps along a road he cannot see but which he is certain is there?"[32] Just as the narrator Darley, who questions his ability to rebuild through memory the lost Alexandria, the poet is very much aware of his limited powers. He knows the poem can only unveil an indirect and incomplete vision of the world. If fiction may be considered as necessarily partial, distorted, and imperfect—"refracting truth by the disorders inherent in my own vision"[33]—poetry is fundamentally more indirect, more distant from its object. But these characteristics are not considered as flaws: they are the signature of this singular genre and they warrant its authenticity. The constant oscillation between these two genres singles out Durrell's work where the novel is conceived of as a perpetually broken, recaptured, and tenuous narrative line, sending the reader back to the poem that welcomes all forms of discontinuity—logical, chronological, syntactic, causal—and where words, freed from any narrative purpose, reverberate as so many unwritten poems offered to the reader's imagination. Poetry is then not the place for "building" but for diffracting sounds and meanings. Each word bears the print of the past wor(l)ds and of their infinite connections with a future poetic birth. Poetry's fate is then not dissimilar from that of Man as described by Sabine in Durrell's *The Avignon Quintet*: "We each have as many destinies stacked up inside us as a melon has seeds. They live on in potentia so to speak. [. . .] All of you, all of us have as many destinies as the sands of the seashore."[34] Just as Sabine tentatively reads her friends' palms, the reader gropes through the many "negatives" of Durrell's poetic world. This is how the poem creates a new, out-of-reach place: that of the "apprehension of grace," the promise of an ungraspable infinite that haunts the reader's imagination, poetry's unalienable home.

Therefore, Durrell's reader is assigned a specific place and role: standing at the crossroads between genres, he is expected to "build for [him]self,"[35] or in other words to follow the path toward the awakening of all senses where true knowledge lies. His Odyssey takes him to Ithaca where the poet, following Caliban,[36] requires the greatest heedfulness: "Tread softly, for here you stand / On miracle ground, boy" (l.1–2). The submerged intertextual reference spurs the reader to decipher the verb "read" hidden within the imperative "Tread" and to realize that any form of intellectual approach runs the risk of deflowering its object. "A breath would cloud this water of glass, / Honey, bush, berry and swallow" (l.3–4) may also be understood literally and metaphorically: the breath of poetry may both spoil the perfection of the place and instill a new life. The poem is thus conceived of as this paradoxical, fragile place of collaboration and rebirth where the poet, like Prospero, comes face to face with his quintessential vulnerability, his humanity.[37]

The reader is therefore summoned to tread the mythical Greece of the "saint"[38] (l.11), that of self-knowledge and renunciation, to "stand" (l.1) on a shifting ground that takes him from one I/land to another before floundering under the steps of the poet whose "dark anvil" (l.15) awaits the "complete submerged poems" yet to be born.

The Submerged Landscape

A Private Country is divided into three main movements. After the overture that introduces the reader to the Greek land and shapes out the writing of place that underlies his poetic and novelistic production, the second part of the collection paves the way for the oncoming rift. The death of Father Nicholas ("Father Nicholas His Death in the Ionian"), the relentless "quantum of misfortune" that weighs on the poet's mind ("A Noctuary in Athens"), or Agamemnon's tomb in Nemea ("Nemea") stage various forms of loss that are magnified by "Exile in Athens" and "In Crisis," both set in the context of the Second World War. "Exile in Athens" significantly revisits the tragedy of war by extolling the potency of the poet's dream:

> To be a king of islands,
> Share a bed with a star,
> Be a subject of sails. ("Exile in Athens" l.21–23)[39]

The ballad form, marked by shorter lines, a narrative pattern, and the inclusion of a burden, such as in "Fourteen Carols And" or "Five Soliloquies Upon the Tomb of Uncebunke," is characteristic of this second movement. Resorting to Christian, Roman, and Shakespearian references that remind one of the black humor that underpins *The Black Book* ("This, my black humour," "Five Soliloquies, I" l.20, *A Private Country*, p. 43), such pastiches signal the poet's return into "the European waters" mentioned at the end of "Daphnis and Chloe." The following prosodic forms, such as the lullaby to Ping-Kû,[40] which recalls William Blake's "A Cradle Song," the homage to Rimbaud in "'Je Est Un Autre,'" or "'The Sonnet of Hamlet'" (the latter two being introduced between quotation marks the better to resurrect long-gone voices), evince a striking displacement within the geographic bearings of the collection. The modalities, themes, and musicality of these poems reveal the poet's return toward the European sphere where Greek myths are the objects of a rationalized scientific discourse, where the darkness of war prevails, as exemplified in "Journal in Paris to David Gascoyne," which Durrell wrote shortly after his friend, the surrealist poet David Gascoyne, entrusted him with the typescript of his *Paris Journal*.

However, the collection ends on a last journey back to Greece. The two concluding poems, "Matapan" and "At Epidaurus," alternately unveil a pain-stricken land ("An end of everything known"[41]), and a victorious country that has always healed distressed souls and is about to open up its mysteries: "Unlocking this world which is not our world."[42] Likewise Cape Matapan, although caught in the midst of World War II, looms up undefeated ("Guarded by the green wicks of cypresses" 1.89). Despite its suffering it will never cease to sing, just as the poet who, while despairing to hear its music, simultaneously asserts its indomitable strength. The last line, "It is too far to hear the singing," captures both the loss and the eternal resilience of the lost object. As Roger Bowen aptly remarks:

> Cape Matapan was the last landfall on mainland Greece as Durrell sailed in the caique from Kalamata to Crete. [. . .] This was a world that might not be seen again, but the poem, as it evolves, moves outward from that possibility. [. . .] He [Durrell] is *not there*, but if he is too far away to hear the singing, he knows it is going on. The harmony, the completeness of it all, is there, even if his witnessing of it must remain on trust.[43]

Although the presence of the Greek land may be interpreted as the clue triggering a backward reading of each poem and hinting at the inner architecture of the whole, the exact boundaries between each part of the collection cannot be delineated. *A Private Country* cannot be read as a series of well-ordained sequences but rather as a broad and expansive movement that keeps blurring frontiers between the Greek, the Parisian, and the English eras that have nurtured the poet's inspiration. Furthermore, the poems that had partly been published prior to the collected edition in poetry reviews (quoted at the end of the table of contents[44]) do not follow one another in chronological order. Therefore the progress offered to the reader is neither historical nor autobiographical. Durrell is not so much concerned with remembering the past as with experimenting, unfolding the world of sensorial perception, giving the reader access to the secret ripening of poetry through a composition that has been minutely organized. His introductory notes to his *Selected Poems* in 1956 and 1964 as well as the meticulously annotated 1964 edition are explicit enough. Durrell took up again his own 1956 edition and amended the table of contents to show where the new poems should be inserted, adding on the first page the following note: "Alan here are the new poems. I have indicated their place in the index."[45]

Likewise, Alan Ross's quotation in his introduction to the 1977 edition clearly suggests Durrell's profound desire to build up a unified whole though the arrangement of each poem: "Of the order within the volumes themselves Lawrence Durrell has said: '. . . I have always tried to arrange my poems for balanced readability—like one does a vase of flowers. How silly it would be to arrange the flowers in the order of their picking . . ."[46]

At the same period, the French poet André Frénaud was drawing the reader's attention to the subtle organization of seemingly disjointed units, claiming that "[. . .] the composition of the book [enables one] to understand something of the secret geographies of a personal labyrinth."[47] This hypothesis has been further developed by the critic Christian Doumet:

> [. . .] the notion of composition sends us back, from a readerly as well as a writerly perspective, to the experience of a *submerged form*, recognizable by the reader (although this is not necessary), acknowledged by the writer himself (although this is not always the case), as the inner narrative of the book of poems.[48]

The reader cannot fail to notice the clever strategies of displacement that characterize this *"submerged form"* and partake of the "inner narrative" underlying Durrell's poetry books: linear logic is systematically shattered while the poet's secret peregrination replaces the expected geography. This is why "Egyptian Poem" does not mention Egypt, where Durrell was then exiled, but the lost Greek world, the Ionian land of the central stanza that harbors life and wisdom:

> In the Ionian villa among the marble
> The fountain plays and the sea's piano,
> And by the clock the geometric philosopher
> Walks in white linen while death
> Squats in the swallow's eye.[49] (l.8–12)

Challenging the death drift that holds sway over the world and the text "the geometric philosopher," whose perfection seems to seclude him from historical contingencies, looms up like a surrealist vision on the outskirts of the underworld. The postponed subject at the end of line 9 upsets the syntactic order and interrupts the reading, imposing a slower progress that makes the music of the fountain and the sea even more poignant. The elements composing the scene (the Ionian villa and the marble, the fountain, the sea, the clock, the philosopher's white figure) are strongly reminiscent of Chirico's paintings. Juxtaposing conflicting planes and temporalities that arouse feelings of unsettling familiarity, this poem draws upon the painter's technique to which Durrell will explicitly resort again in his *Avignon Quintet*.[50]

The presence of the muzzled dogs and the entrapment of the lyrical voice "between the born and the unborn" suggest the Asphodel Meadows where the dead lead an ethereal life. Yet, as "Carol on Corfu" asserted earlier, the poet's voice is not made of such perishable substance ("Let flesh falter, or let bone break / Break, yet the salt of a poem holds on," "Carol on Corfu," 1.2–3): "Egyptian Poem" conveys the poet's refusal to abandon the land that has fostered his art ("Exempt me") as well as his trust in the powers of the spirit ("I have friends in the underworld").

Significantly, the poet's voice is brought back to life at the heart of the collection through the reincarnation of "the geometric philosopher" into Conon in the eponymous poem "Conon in Exile." The philosopher implicitly recalls the historical figure of Conon of Athens, who led the Athenian fleet in 407 BC during the Peloponnese war and who, having been defeated, fled for Cyprus in 405. Having obtained a new fleet from the Persians, he conquered Cythera and the Aegean Sea and went back victorious to Athens in 393. Thus Conon embodies the figure of the defeated yet triumphant general whose exile paves the way for glory. The character summoned in the poem takes after Homeric figures: he befriends the ancient heroes and goddesses (Penelope, Ariadne, Io) whose stories are artfully rewritten, and his love-stricken fate turns him into another alter ego of the poet himself, who emerges at the end of the poem as the archetypal figure of exile and dispossession, placing his hope, like the ancient general, in the "blue Aegean."

Interestingly, the "imaginary Greek philosopher" is explicitly introduced as another of the poet's masks in the prefatory note to the final version of the poem published in *Collected Poems 1931–1974*:

Author's Note
    Conon is an imaginary Greek philosopher who visited me twice in my dreams, and with whom I occasionally identify myself; he is one of my masks, Melissa is another; I want my total poetic work to add up as a kind of tapestry of people, some real, some imaginary. Conon is real.[51]

The five irregular stanzas of "Conon in Exile" suggest a narrative pattern that mimics epic poems while the last two lines enact the peaceful return of the hero:

By our blue Aegean which forever
Washes and pardons and brings us home. (V, l.16–17)

Conon, the poet-soldier and the philosopher-lover (combining the Janus-like figures of Pittakos and Phaon in *Sappho*), at once "imaginary" and "real," and who was only loved for his words, comes to grasp his own insufficiencies at last:

> Even in these notes upon myself I see
> I have put down women's names like some
> Philosophical proposition. At last I understand
> They were only forms for my own ideas,
> With names and mouths and different voices.
> In them I lay with myself [. . .] (V, l.9–14)

Exile becomes synonymous both with solitude and with a certain form of blindness: it is the dark mirror in which the poet beholds the harrowing pain of estrangement, his inability to relate intimately to others and the dissociation of self whence a new vision may arise. This is why the philosophic treatises are pastiches of ancient texts: *The Art of Marriage, Peace in the Self, Of Love, Of Love and Death* bring no happiness to the lover, and cut him further off from any living soul. Finally the philosopher undergoes Ariadne's fate and metamorphoses into "a spider in a bottle" where he becomes the object and the subject of his own scrutiny and discovers the gaping void he has wrought for himself, "Knowing only coitus with the shadows." However, the last two lines strike a hopeful note: just as "the blue" that promises the eternity of an unheard yet breathing land at the end of "Matapan," "our blue Aegean" at the end of "Conon in Exile" suggests an oncoming redemption. Only by nurturing a new awareness of himself and of others may the poet hope to free himself from the abyss of a self-centered and nostalgic outlook and reach out to the "huge tear about to drop from the eye of the world."

When Space Challenges Time

The implicit yet persisting connections that arise between the various poems that compose the three movements of the collection lead us to consider the long series of couplets entitled "'The Sonnet of Hamlet'" as the unexpected development of the obsessing feeling of estrangement that seeps through "Conon in Exile" and "Matapan."

"'The Sonnet of Hamlet'" is undeniably the longest and most complex poem in the collection, and it is also the most unsettling one. Its fourteen stanzas composed of seven unrhymed couplets devoid of the classical iambic rhythm create a hiatus between the easily recognizable pattern and its subverted form, just as the quotation marks in the title suggest a distanced perspective, as if to mirror the inner split between the poet's and the poem's "I." Indeed, the first sonnet stages Hamlet's voice while the following ones rebuild the fragmented narrative of the character's story. However, Durrell's personal imagery keeps interfering with Shakespearian images:

the second sonnet juxtaposes the poisoning of the King of Denmark and the image of the phoenix that appears repeatedly in Durrell's fiction.[52] The third sonnet heralds a rebirth that takes place in the fourth sonnet where Hamlet's voice vanishes. The ongoing flow of time is momentarily frozen in the fifth sonnet, which builds up a surprising prayer to the Virgin. The new voice and tone is all the more perplexing as submerged Durrellian visions are brought back to the surface, suggesting a Mediterranean elsewhere at odds with Hamlet's world: "the hollow curvature of the world" (IV, l.1), "the owls" (IV, l.12), "the Cretan eikon" (V, l.6). The following sonnet is a love and death song. Hamlet's voice seems to have expired, and the "candles smoking on a coffin" shed light on the body's decay and on the eternity of love. The seventh sonnet enacts the central upheaval of the poem: Hamlet is no longer the subject but the object of discourse and merges with the figure of Christ: "nailed between the thieves of love" (VII, l.2). Yet this Christ-like figure has not shed the ancient rites: it crosses into the world of Shades with "the obol in the lips," having entrusted the poet with Ophelia's skull and passed on the pain of an ill-fated love that permeates the writing: "I take the round skull of the nunnery girl / [. . .] I hang my heart, being choked upon a noun. / I hang her name upon this frantic pothook." (VII, l.9; l.13–14). The noun "pothook," which refers both to the curved iron rod for hanging a pot over the fire and to the S-shaped stroke in writing, signals the metatextual mirror whereby Hamlet's paroxystic madness contaminates the entire poem: "the mirages of dazed ladies" (VI, l.10), the "Barbarian ladies with their fingernails, / [who] Strip off her simple reason like a wedding-dress" (XVIII, l.12–13), and "The widow walking in a rubber mask" (IX, l.6) evince a distraught conscience haunted by Hamlet's madness and looking in vain for a teleological order. The poet's anguished mind sketches out a labyrinthine world whose "[. . .] maps were stifled with him in the maze" (XIV, l.13), trapping him like the Minotaur in the same darkness that Lawrence Lucifer built around himself in *The Black Book*: "The darkness which I myself am beginning to inhabit, to construct incongruously for myself on the rocky northern cliffs of this Ionian island (perhaps, who can tell, even interpret by the tapping of these metal *pothooks*[53] on the paper you hold before your eyes)."[54] The twelfth sonnet brings back Hamlet's voice, whose anaphoric address to the reader ("You have Ophelia / You have my mother") draws attention to the slow metamorphosis of the tragic chess game into a portentous nightmare. "The suit of love gored by the courtier's fang," the "mother folded like a rag," the "pawn [played] against the prince," and the descriptions of the "marble statues [that] bleed," as in *Julius Caesar*, foreshadow the end of time, the last stage of "the Babylonian fable" (VII, l.11) announced in the central sonnet, the point when the "piercing harps" (VII, l.12) are no longer heard. Babylon emerges as the antithesis to the heavenly Jerusalem: "the magi [are led] to the child's foul crib" (XII, l.13) while the poet takes Christ's place, "nailed up between two thieves" (XII, l.14).

The last two sonnets function as a sarcastic yet tender conclusion inviting the reader to walk toward those lands where he may "wake up to reality":[55]

> Then walk where roses like disciples can
> Aim at the heart their innocent attention.
> [. . .]
> Then suckle the weather if the winter will not,
> Seal down a message in a dream of spring (XIII, l.1–2; l.9–10)

The figure of the poet embodied by "the frigid autist pacing out his rope" (XIII, l.12) foreshadows the poignant end of the carefree buffoon, magician, and beggar of the last lines, already turned to "ash" and dressed "to dance upon the void" (XIV, l.9), who retraces his slow progress toward death:

> And when hemp sings of murder bless your boy,
> The double fellow in the labyrinth,
>
> Whose maps were stifled with him in the maze,
> Whose mother dropped him like the seedless pod. (XIV, l.11–14)

The artist is this Janus-like figure who stands at the crossroads of life and death, of laughter and tears, of hope and darkness. Lost in the labyrinth of signs, abandoned by his mother like an empty shell, he nevertheless yields the fruit of hope: "My mercy in a wallet like berry bright" (XIV, l.10). The postponed adjective paradoxically enhances the only source of light that rescues the text from the abyss of madness and despair. The choice of the word "berry" suggests its homophone "bury" and invites the reader to wonder whether the poet's gift does not precisely arise from such a symbolic death.

"'The Sonnet of Hamlet'" goes far beyond a mere homage to Shakespeare or an exercise in style: it is the place where the poet delves into his relationship to life, to death, and to the other, developing the meditation that was born in *The Black Book* where Lawrence Lucifer signed "Affectionately Yours, Hamlet's little godchild"[56] and that Durrell further expatiated upon in his letters to Henry Miller.[57] "'The Sonnet of Hamlet'" also explores the notion of self-sacrifice that is to play a major role in the entire opus, the realization of the poet's exile from his own self, of this death to oneself as the hearth of creation. Durrell is in fact investigating the question of the relationship between death and creation that had been analyzed by Otto Rank in *Art and Artist,* where the psychoanalyst examines the necessary sacrifice that underlies creation, as is the case in *Hamlet:*

> He needs, as it were, for each work that he builds, a sacrifice which is buried alive to ensure a permanent existence to the structure, but also to save the artist from having to give himself.[58]

This paragraph is followed by a footnote:

> Shakspere's [sic] *Hamlet* and Mozart's *Don Juan* are familiar examples of the reaction after a father's death, [. . .] These works are supreme examples of artists negotiating with the problem of the Beyond. [. . .][59]

Durrell's predilection for Hamlet, just as the juxtaposition of obsessive images; the dissociation of the subject; the intertwined literary, ancient, and Christian references; the ethereal nature of the female body that keeps vanishing and reappearing as a lover, a nun, or a skeleton, are to be read as the various modalities of the original sacrifice that shapes out the complexity of Durrell's work. The poet seeks to make us experience the living, palpable, and suffering matter that is the true texture of writing so as to make us grasp the stakes of this perplexing relationship to a beyond that is both terrifying and omnipresent, and that pervades the war poem anthology to which Durrell contributed. We may remember Sidney Keyes's evocative lines in which the poet's persona embodies a soldier looking for peace and finding himself with an arrow in his hand, unable to avoid war.[60] Reading this poem, one immediately recalls Keats leaving for the war front at the end of *The Alexandria Quartet* as well as Death Gregory's prophetic words in *The Black Book*: "Books should be built of one's tissue or not at all."[61]

This is why the poems published in *A Private Country* cannot be read independently from *The Black Book*, which was written at the same time as most of the poems in this collection. The novel, like the poems, is anchored in the Greek island of Corfu, and the entire narrative arises from the loss of the beloved land:

> While the sea pushed up its shafts and coils under the house, we lay there in bed, dark as any dungeon, and mourned the loss of the Mediterranean. Lost, all lost; the fruiting of green figs, apricots. Lost the grapes, black, yellow, and dusky. Even the ones like pale nipples, delicately freckled and melodious, are forgotten in this morning, where our one reality is the Levantine wind, musty

> with the smell of Arabia, stirring the bay into a muddy broth. This is the winter of our discontent. [. . .]
>
> Do not ask me how. Do not ask me why, at this time, on a remote Greek headland in a storm, I should choose, for my first real book, a theatre which is not Mediterranean.[62]

The first paragraph evinces the melodious flow of a poem with its anaphoras, alliterative sequences, and the visual strength of its nominal structures. The "muddy broth" is reminiscent of the witches' cauldron in *Macbeth*. The wrench from the magic island, which is to be reborn as Prospero's island in the residence book, is first and foremost a temporal and cyclic wrench, coinciding with the arrival of winter and throwing the writer into a hostile elsewhere. Thus, *The Black Book* paradoxically unveils, from the shores of the Ionian Sea, the reversed image of the Greek world. It is the figuration of exile within and through writing that precedes the actual exile from Greece in 1940. Naturally it is a symbolic exile, quite distinct from the autobiographical one depicted in *Pied Piper of Lovers*, and which ceaselessly calls into question the notion of frontiers: "Our world is a world of strict boundaries, outside which we dare not wander, not even in our imagination; whose seasons come and go without any sense of change"[63] asserts the narrator at the onset of the novel. The reader soon realizes that this winter season is just as symbolic as the character's exile: it is the temporal nucleus where Lawrence Lucifer's inner exile will be developed and relentlessly probed—

> January brings the first raw cleavages of weathers—a blind hint of the merchandise which begins to fructify under the snow. Foxes' ears underground, odorous, odorous. From the chalk breasts of Ion an Ionian asphodel. As always, the weather I am continually referring back to is spiritual. Winter is more than an almanac: it is dug in invisibly under the fingernails, in the teeth—into everything that is deciduous, calcine. [. . .] That is why I am marking down these items in the log of that universal death, which I have escaped.[64]

The writer deals with a very specific form of exile: it is an ontological condition that initiates a wandering that shatters our representations of the world and of the text. Through parataxis, nominal sentences, and a careful handling of rhythm, Durrell invites us to listen to the text as a poetic construct. Hamlet reappears in *The Black Book*, and the reader understands that the freedom the narrator hankers after rests upon this contest with the death anguish: by welcoming his symbolic death, the narrator, just as Darley diving into the waters to rescue Clea at the end of *The Alexandria Quartet*, can hope to attain the ultimate fulfillment that the last lines of the novel adumbrate—"From between your legs leaking, the breathing yolk, the durable, the forever, the enormous Now. This is how it ends."[65] The investigation of the artistic conscience that is conveyed through the exploration of Hamlet's figure in Durrell, is shared by an entire generation of writers. It is at the root of *The Michael Fraenkel–Henry Miller Correspondence Called Hamlet*, which was published in 1939 and that Durrell commented on and analyzed in depth in his early letters to Miller.[66] Miller's opening letter to Fraenkel interrogates the symbolic network attached to Hamlet within contemporary philosophical, literary, and aesthetic criticism:

> If there is any success in our endeavor it will be in laying the ghost. For Hamlet still stalks the streets. [. . .] None of us have become naturally modern enough to waylay this ghost and strangle it. For the ghost is not the father which was murdered, nor the conscience which was uneasy, but the time-spirit which has been creaking like a rusty pendulum. In this book it should be our high purpose to set the pendulum swinging smoothly again, so that we synchronize with past and future. Are the times out of joint? Then look to the clock! Not the clock on the mantelpiece, but the chronometer inside which tells you when you are living and when you are not.[67]

This reflection, which was shared by all members of the Villa Seurat,[68] seeps through Durrell's entire work, which never ceased to question man's relationship to time. Michael Fraenkel's short essay published in 1939 and entitled "A Late Note on Hamlet" concludes upon these resounding lines that are symptomatic of the questioning that haunted an entire generation:

> Hamlet has died. Time! [. . .] We are aware of death. The sense of life is beginning to stir within us. We proceed, always bearing in mind the fact of Hamlet's death, our *death*. [. . .] Thus, by an *art morphology of the creative memory* we save ourselves from the stagnant flux, the timelessness in which we were mired; art saves us to ourselves; delivers us from the blind, aimless movements of biology. Thus, whereas we stood before with Hamlet in a present that was death, in a permanent winter of the spirit, we now move in life, toward a first spring.
>
> In this artistic redemption we develop a new art of reading. We learn to read in a new direction. We do not begin with the beginning, with the Watch on the platform; we begin with the end—with *the rest is silence*. [. . .]
>
> We stand naked in wonder and expectation: the light of a new world has fallen upon us.—Here is a new way of telling time, reading the heavens.
>
> True, it's not real time, real life, but only reminiscent time. But what other time is there?[69]

It is from the perspective of "reminiscent time" that belongs to silence that "Journal in Paris" is written. Like "'The Sonnet of Hamlet,'" this poem is not a mere homage to David Gascoyne but unveils a shared vision of the world, a similar refusal to submit to the arbitrary division of time and reality. It asserts the hope in the "redemption" brought about by art. The incomplete list of the days of the week (Monday, Tuesday, Friday, Saturday, Sunday) partly reproduces the architecture of the journal, in particular, the sequence of October 1936. Gascoyne's fragmented day list ("Last Sunday," "Next morning," "On Tuesday," "Saturday," "On Friday," "On Saturday") culminates in a dark premonitory cry that paves the way for Durrell's poem: "*Mais ne pensez-vous pas que c'est un grand moment de drâme, maintenant que le monde va éclater en flames rouges et que tous les individus se désintègrent?*"[70] The French, italicized sentence signals the point where the text and the world cave in, heralding the frozen dead end of Durrell's "pit":

> But today Sunday. The pit.
> The axe and the knot. Cannot write.
> The monster in its booth.
> At a quarter to one the mask repeating:
> 'Truth is what is
> Truth is what is Truth?' (l.18–23, A Private Country, p. 29)

The nominal sentences, the fragmented lines, the disjointed time, and the disfigured face combine with the disrupted syntax and prosody to suggest the dislocation of form and meaning. The anguished investigation of temporality within a divided world where, as in Shakespeare's play, "time is out of joint,"[71] is intimately linked to the questioning of the artist's role. Durrell's quest meets Gascoyne's, whose poem "Apologia," published the same year as *A Private Country* and adopting the Macbeth-like perspective of "a most furious fool," attempts to confront the chaos of the world through a creation bent on discovering a truth that eventually evades him since only the unwritten poem can be held to be true.[72] Durrell's conception of truth differs from Gascoyne's absolute truth, which leads to an aporia. It is a substantial truth incarnated in the poetic act. One may recall his refusal to give any inkling of a formal, theoretical definition in "The Kneller Tape": "Truth? What do we know about truth? I hunt among facts and only seem to recognize what I would call truth by one quality—its *poignance*."[73] This conception saves Durrell's writing from the aporia Gascoyne seems to have fallen into, for truth is not conceived of as an unreachable absolute, like Gascoyne's never-to-be-written poem, but rather as a synaesthetic experience that affects the inner self. Poetry is a weapon that touches, hurts, and awakens man's conscience, initiating a timeless collaboration between poet and reader involved in the same process of spiritual rebirth, which David Gascoyne artfully described in his journal: "The power of Poetry alone redeems the world, and reunites the blind, confused and fragmentary elements of universal experience within the circle of significance. The supreme task: that of synthesis. How to invoke the welding flame?"[74] Symbolically, *A Private Country* ends on the poem "At Epidaurus" and on the hieratic gesture the thaumaturgic poet teaches to his reader:

> Then smile, my dear, above the holy wands,
> Make the indefinite gesture of the hands,
> Unlocking this world which is not our world.[75] (l.52–54)

The opening doors of Epidaurus where man's spirit and flesh used to be healed suggest the primordial function of poetry inherited from the Greek tradition: the healing and the redemption of man that is accomplished, in Durrell's writing, through the harmonious encounter of the poet and his reader. "At Epidaurus" builds up such a world delivered from "the penetration of clocks striking in London," which is best symbolized by the stillness of Greek temples:

> A formula for marble when the clouds
> Troubled the architect, and the hill spoke
> Volumes of thunder, the sibyllic god wept. (l.26–28)

The perfect harmony between the human and the divine, the terrestrial and the celestial, conjures up a world that is evocative of Otto Rank's conception of ancient Greece:

> The Greeks were the first, and perhaps the only, people to live really on earth and in the light of the sun—hence their sharp dividing-line between the upper world and the under, in which the dead led a bloodless, soulless existence. [. . .] While the Egyptian lived below the earth, and the Christian above it, the Greek, with all its spiritual requirements, stood firmly planted upon it [. . .][76]

Durrell's private cartography is deeply rooted in a Greek world attuned to man's material and spiritual needs: it is a shelter ("Here we are safe from everything but ourselves"), a place open to exploration ("Here the lover made his calculation by ferns"), a crossing point ("We, like the winter, are only visitors"), and a place of revelation ("All causes end within the great Because"). The Greek land functions as the sanctuary of a creative and healing imaginary. Thus Durrell regenerates the antique conception of the imagination as described by Giorgio Agamben:

> [. . .] the imagination which, by virtue of its 'unreality', is nowadays excluded from knowledge, was on the contrary considered by the ancients as the ideal medium. As the mediator between the senses and the intellect accomplishing through fantasy the marriage of the sensible shape and of the intellect, it fulfils in ancient and medieval cultures the same role as experience does in our society. Far from belonging to the realm of the unreal, the *mundus imaginabilis* has its own real plenitude just as the *mundus sensibilis* and the *mundus intelligibilis*; it influences their connection, that is to say knowledge. [. . .] one easily understands why dreams in the ancient world entertained a specific relationship to truth (as was the case of the divination *per somnia*), as well as with effective knowledge (as is the case of medical therapy by incubation).[77]

Having reached the last pages of *A Private Country*, the reader cannot but be struck by the complexity of the entire collection. While alluding to the literary magazine *Personal Landscape* to which Durrell contributed from Cairo, the collection mostly comprises poems written in Greece, including "Egyptian Poem," and the mythological network it summons (Agamemnon, Penelope, Ariadne), just as its topography (Corfu, Argos, Corinth, Ithaca, Athens, Epidaurus) suggests a private Greece that is the true spring of the poetic imagination. This is why the Greek land of the collection of poems functions as an elsewhere that enables Durrell to escape both Europe at war with its frightening visions of Hamlet and the stifling atmosphere of Egypt, where the war is a haunting presence. Greece is both a unique and a fragmented territory on the edge of present space and time and a purely imaginary and personal land, explicitly located in a symbolic place. As "the ideal medium" of our understanding of the world it is at once an imaginary and a very real place. It partakes of the same harsh reality as the crevices, pools, and rocks of its shores, it shares the precise contours of its luminous snow lines and winding bays, it reverberates the echoes of the oracles, it is the only living reality that haunts the reader when he closes the book. It is the living spring of the Durrellian space-time that will be made explicit in the introductory note to *The Alexandria Quartet*: "Only the city is real." Likewise, one might say about *A Private Country*: "Only the island is real." This early collection confirms the poet's awareness of an eternal, inviolable I/land, a graspable yet intimate reality—that of the Greek land that is the quintessence of life because it is in the image of Man, it is an extension of the microcosm. By sending the reader back to the tholos of Epidaurus through a poetic architecture that plays on circular effects (whether syntactic, conceptual, or lexical), the end of the book opens onto the omphalos announcing "this world which is not our world" (l.53), that of magic and creation, the poet's true home. Durrell's poetry responds to the geocentric Greek architecture described by Otto Rank:

> The great architectural buildings [. . .] were no longer, as in the East, macrocosmic reflections of heavenly designs, but extended microcosms: that is, not only enlarged, but elevated, beings. [. . .]
>
> Symbolically interpreted [. . .], the navel stands for the visible sign of the animal origin of man, but at the same time of his selfness and independence [. . .], it is at this point that man begins to construct his world-system so as to reunite himself with, not to say to magnify himself into, the cosmos.[78]

The collection ends on the poet's rebirth in a land that is both a symbolic and a material anchorage, the crucible where the poet molds his artistic identity and foresees his slow progress toward a transcended ego, the prerequisite step to the construction of his heraldic universe.

One may then surmise that the following collection *Cities, Plains and People* (1946) opening on the Levant ("Levant") will keep exploring the same intimate yet real cartography in order to sketch out new possible worlds, thus echoing Otto Rank's definition of artistic creation:

> [. . .] the creation, namely, of material and spiritual values—the values of culture, art, and religion—not as an imitation of nature, but as a macrocosmization of man, pointing him towards a new spiritual reality that is created out of himself and exists only through him. [. . .] To this end, however, he must sacrifice part of his actual life, his possibilities of earthly happiness, creating a spiritual cosmos analogous to the heavenly one; and thus he becomes himself a maker of worlds, but, at the same time, his own world-stuff out of which and by which he creates.[79]

To build from this, the next chapter uncovers how the concept of a geocentric art enlightens Durrell's writing and enables the reader to grasp the painful necessity of the original loss at the heart of creation. This loss, which can take many diverse forms (exile, separation, physical and psychological estrangement, bereavement), is the hallmark of *Cities, Plains and People*.

Notes

1. Corinne Alexandre-Garner, "Regard d'exil—Naître de l'Inde: Lawrence Durrell," in *Cahiers du SAHIB* no. 4, Université de Rennes II, 2ème trimestre 1996, p. 24.

2. See I. Keller-Privat, "De l'autre côté des frontières: l'écriture poétique chez Lawrence Durrell," *Migrations/Translations*, Paris: Presses Universitaires de Paris Ouest, 2016, pp. 397–416.

3. The biographical anchorage of the poem is similarly underlined in its later publication in Lawrence Durrell, *Collected Poems*, London: Faber, 1960, p. 92, where the inscription only differs slightly: "*For Stephan Syriotis* (Mykonos, 1940)."

4. Lawrence Durrell, *The Greek Islands*, London: Faber, 1978, pp. 235–36.

5. We may remember Lawrence Durrell's fondness for this particular poem, "the only piece of my personal mythology which comes off 100 percent," as he said to T. S. Eliot in 1942 (Ian S. MacNiven, *Lawrence Durrell, A Biography*, London: Faber, 1998, p. 226).

6. Pola Bousiou, *The Nomads of Mykonos: Performing Liminalities in a 'Queer' Space*, New York, Oxford: Berghahn Books, 2008, p. 41.

7. *The Greek Islands*, pp. 235–36.

8. Ray Morrison, *A Smile in His Mind's Eye: A Study of the Early Works of Lawrence Durrell*, Toronto: University of Toronto Press, 2005, pp. 62–63.

9. "When my soul fainted within me I remembered the Lord: and my prayer came in unto thee, into thine holy temple. They that observe lying vanities forsake their own mercy. But I will sacrifice unto thee with the voice of thanksgiving," Jonah 2: 7–9.

10. Lawrence Durrell and Henry Miller, *The Durrell-Miller Letters, 1935–80*, Ian S. MacNiven, ed., London: Faber, 1988, p. 148.

11. Lawrence Durrell, *The Alexandria Quartet*, London: Faber, 1974, p. 751.

12. *The Alexandria Quartet*, p. 137.

13. "[. . .] we talked of him, confirming and denying and comparing, like secret agents rehearsing a cover story, for after all the fallible human being had belonged to us, the myth belonged to the world," *The Alexandria Quartet*, p. 137.

14. *The Alexandria Quartet*, p. 281.

15. Charles Baudelaire, "Correspondences," translated by Roy Campbell, *Poems of Baudelaire*, New York: Pantheon Books, 1952, http://fleursdumal.org/poem/103.

16. Lawrence Durrell, *A Private Country*, London: Faber, 1944 (first published in 1943), p. 12.

17. "[. . .] yet the salt of the poem holds on," "[. . .] The salt of the poem lives on," (l.3; l.18, *A Private Country*, p. 12).

18. "Ye are the salt of the earth [. . .]," Matthew 5:13, The Holy Bible, Authorized Version.

19. *A Private Country*, p. 13.

20. I have retained the original punctuation of the stanza, i.e., the comma instead of the full stop that has been inserted at the end of line 4 in the final edition of the *Collected Poems*.

21. C. Alexandre-Garner, *Lawrence Durrell: Dans l'ombre du soleil grec*, Paris: La Quinzaine Littéraire, Louis Vuitton, 2012, p. 56.

22. *A Private Country*, p. 14.

23. "Ode to a Nightingale," *Lamia, Isabella, and Other Poems* [published in 1820], in *The Works of John Keats*, Hertfordshire: Wordsworth Editions Ltd., 1994, p. 233.

24. Charles Baudelaire, "Correspondences," translated by Roy Campbell, *Poems of Baudelaire*, New York: Pantheon Books, 1952, http://fleursdumal.org/poem/103.

25. Lawrence Durrell, *Blue Thirst*, Santa Barbara: Capra Press, 1975, p. 22.

26. Lawrence Durrell, *Pied Piper of Lovers*, Victoria, Canada: ELS editions, 1935, p. 55.

27. Lawrence Durrell translated *Six Poems from the Greek of Sikelianos and Seferis*, (Rhodes, 1946) and *The King of Asine and Other Poems* (translated from the Greek by Bernard Spencer, Nanos Valaoritis, Lawrence Durrell, with an introduction by Rex Warner, London, 1948). The latter translation is mentioned by G. Seferis in his journal (*A Poet's Journal: Days of 1945–1951*, Cambridge, MA: Harvard University Press, 1974, January 12, 1945, p. 73).

28. Lawrence Durrell, *A Smile in the Mind's Eye*, London: Faber, 1982, p. 20.

29. See Roger Bowen's analysis: "[. . .] Durrell finds an affirmation for himself in the examples of other artists. [. . .] His identity as an artist is validated by their examples and by *his* example as an interpreter, critic, recreator, and in the case of 'Byron,' as a mime." Roger Bowen, *Many Histories Deep: The Personal Landscape Poets in Egypt, 1940–45*, Madison: Fairleigh Dickinson University Press, 1995, p. 158.

30. *Blue Thirst*, p. 22.

31. "Ideas about Poems II," in Lawrence Durrell and Robin Fedden, eds., *Personal Landscape* no. 2, Cairo, March 1942, p. 2. [SIU]

32. *Clea*, *The Alexandria Quartet*, London: Faber, 1974, p. 756.

33. *The Alexandria Quartet*, p. 734.

34. Lawrence Durrell, *Quinx, The Avignon Quintet*, London: Faber, 1992, p. 1335.

35. "Ideas about Poems II," *Personal Landscape* no. 2, Cairo, March 1942, p. 2. [SIU]

36. We refer the reader here to Caliban's words in the end of act 4, scene 1 (l.194) in Shakespeare's *Tempest*: "Pray you, tread softly," *The Complete Works of William Shakespeare*, London: Henry Pordes, 1993, p. 19.

37. Such is indeed Durrell's interpretation of *The Tempest*, which he develops in a letter dated from July 1940 to Henry Miller: "Here is the outcast holy man in his cell on Corcyra; his retreat is really voluntary, because he is dealing with reality, his many inner selves. [. . .] in the epilogue you have the clue to the whole artistic stance. The gesture of renunciation is pure wizardry; artist laying down his medicine, releasing his spirits, and putting himself AS A HUMAN BEING at their mercy." *The Durrell-Miller Letters 1935–80*, p. 140.

38. "On Ithaca Standing," *A Private Country*, p. 19.

39. *A Private Country*, p. 26.

40. Ping-Kû was the nickname given to Durrell's elder daughter, Penelope.

41. "Matapan," l.27, *A Private Country*, p. 75.

42. "At Epidaurus," l.57, *A Private Country*, p. 79.

43. Roger Bowen, *Many Histories Deep: The Personal Landscape Poets in Egypt 1940–45*, pp. 147–48.

44. These are *The New English Weekly, Purpose, Diogenes, Poetry (London), Delta, Seven, The Fortuna Anthology, Personal Landscape* (Cairo), *Experimental Review,* and *Proems.*

45. Lawrence Durrell, *Selected Poems 1935–1963*, London: Faber, 1964, [n.p.].

46. Lawrence Durrell, *Selected Poems*, edited with an introduction by Alan Ross, London: Faber, 1977, p. 11.

47. André Frénaud, "Réflexion sur la construction d'un livre de poèmes," *La Sainte Face*, Paris: Gallimard, 1968, p. 252.

48. Christian Doumet, *Faut-il comprendre la poésie?*, Paris: Klincksieck, 2004, p. 91.

49. *A Private Country*, p. 73.

50. See Corinne Alexandre-Garner and Isabelle Keller-Privat, "'Manufacturing Dreams' or Lawrence Durrell's Fiction Revisited through the Prism of De Chirico's Metaphysical Painting," *Deus Loci* NS 13 (2012–2013), pp. 85–109.

51. Lawrence Durrell, *Collected Poems 1931–1974*, London: Faber, 1985, p. 107.

52. See Lawrence Durrell, *The Black Book*, London: Faber, 1977 (first published in 1938), as well as the later set of novels, *The Revolt of Aphrodite* (first published in 1974).

53. My emphasis.

54. *The Black Book*, p. 218

55. *Blue Thirst*, p. 22.

56. *Blue Thirst*, p. 136.

57. Durrell considered Hamlet as the epitome of the artist's struggle: see *The Durrell-Miller Letters 1935–80*, p. 45.

58. Otto Rank, *Art and Artist* (1932), New York: Norton, 1989, p. 49. [Bibliothèque Lawrence Durrell]

59. *Art and Artist*, p. 49.

60. *Return to Oasis, War Poems and Recollections from the Middle-East 1940–1946*, introduction by Lawrence Durrell, London: Editions Poetry London, 1980, p. v.

61. *The Black Book*, p. 121.

62. *The Black Book*, pp. 19–21.

63. *The Black Book*, p. 22.

64. *The Black Book*, pp. 101–2.

65. *The Black Book*, p. 244.

66. See in particular letters from December 1936 to January 1937, *The Durrell-Miller Letters 1935–80*, pp. 30–50.

67. Michael Fraenkel and Henry Miller, *The Michael Fraenkel–Henry Miller Correspondance called Hamlet*, éditions du Laurier, London: Carrefour, 1962, p. 13.

68. The Villa Seurat, situated in the 14th arrondissement in Paris, was an artists' residence that hosted writers and painters long before Henry Miller's arrival in 1934. It refers, metonymically, to the network of philosophers, writers, poets, painters, and

photographers that momentarily gathered in Paris around Miller: Michael Fraenkel, Anaïs Nin, Alfred Perlès, Lawrence Durrell, David Gascoyne, Henri Michaux, and George Brassaï were among its faithful figures.

69. Michael Fraenkel, *Death Is Not Enough: Essays in Active Negation* (1939), London: Carrefour Publications, 1962, pp. 159–60.

70. David Gascoyne, *Collected Journals 1936–1942*, London: Skoobs Books Publishing Ltd., 1991, pp. 29–30.

71. *The Tragedy of Hamlet*, act I, scene 5, l.195, Oxford: Oxford University Press, 1994, p. 196.

72. David Gascoyne, "Apologia," *Collected Poems*, Oxford: Oxford University Press, 1984, pp. 65–66.

73. Earl G. Ingersoll, ed., *Lawrence Durrell: Conversations*, London: Associated University Presses, 1998, p. 73.

74. David Gascoyne, *Collected Journals 1936–1942*, 20.V.38, p. 155.

75. *A Private Country*, p. 79.

76. Otto Rank, *Art and Artist*, p. 146.

77. Giorgio Agamben, *Enfance et histoire* (1978), Paris: Éditions Payot & Rivages, 2002, p. 45.

78. *Art and Artist*, pp. 169, 190. These lines have also been underlined by L. Durrell in his personal copy [Bibliothèque Lawrence Durrell].

79. *Art and Artist*, p. 203. These lines have also been underlined by L. Durrell in his personal copy [Bibliothèque Lawrence Durrell].

CHAPTER TWO

Cities, Plains and People
Lands of Exile and Introspection

Unlike A *Private Country*, whose title markedly echoed Robin Fedden's collection *Personal Landscape: An Anthology of Exile*,[1] *Cities, Plains and People* steers away from the autobiographical context that saw the publication of Durrell's first poems, along with those of World War II poets such as Terence Tiller, Bernard Spencer, George Seferis, Keith Douglas, G. S. Fraser, Olivia Manning, or Diana Gould. The eponymous title of the final poem signals an autotelic dynamics that entices the reader to consider it as the key to the metatextual nature of Durrell's poetic space. The poet's private landscape becomes the space of an introspective questioning.

The Poet's Inner Lands

The very first poem in the collection, "Eight Aspects of Melissa," is conceived as a structural echo to the sixteen sections of the last poem, "Cities, Plains and People," thus endowing the textual space with a symbolic depth and a musical resonance that function as code. Those eight fragments composing Melissa's abstract being suggest the four axes structuring a Buddhist mandala: they point to the four corners of the cosmos and to their various reduplications and extensions throughout the poet's work. Thus, the eight themes pave the way for a symbolic and spiritual journey that relies on an infinity of mirror effects. Such is the case with the first one, "By the Lake," which opens on a series of embedded refractions calling forth the frail shadow of Melissa, who will later take shape in *The Alexandria Quartet*. The yet-unborn

Melissa conjures up a second anachronic memory: that of Justine inviting the narrator Darley to look at his characters through several reflections.[2] As a result, the reader feels utterly baffled when trying to circumscribe the very textual space she or he is contemplating: the first lines of the poem—"If seen by many minds at once your image / As in a prism falling breaks itself"[3]—ring like a metatextual comment upon the reading process itself with which this modernist writing keeps toying endlessly, losing the reader "In roundels of diversion like the moon."[4]

The mysterious addressee of these lines, whose shimmering body eventually vanishes, comes to inhabit the poet's eye and acts as the very mirror upon which the figure of the lover is eventually projected. "Rootless" and "Fatherless," her existence is subsumed in "the smallest / Wish or kiss upon the rising darkness," an ephemeral, hypothetical contact that testifies to the unreal and inaccessible essence of the beloved. The many comparisons through which the poet attempts to encompass this fleeting presence are shattered by the interplay of postponed adjectives and broken lines that materialize, at the heart of the poetic inspiration, the violence of an inner rift. "Eight Aspects of Melissa" thus comes to symbolize the various paths of a complex spiritual journey through which Melissa embodies the polyphonic nature of the poetic voice, as Lawrence Durrell clearly stated in a later note to "Conon in Exile"—"Conon is an imaginary Greek philosopher [. . .] he is one of my masks, Melissa is another"[5]—and as the last poem of *On Seeming to Presume* equally suggests: "Melissa, nurse, augur, special self."[6] Therefore, it is no wonder that Melissa should lead us into the steps of the "Three little magi under vast Capella"[7] that illuminates further the deathly pain of our survivors' world. From one fragment to another, the voice takes us deeper into darkness: light is a lure, and the "ocean of shipwrecked mariners"[8] rises like an indomitable "visitation"[9] that pervades the poetry and the prose[10]:

> They dipped in this huge pond and found it
> An ocean of shipwrecked mariners instead,
> Cried out and foundered, losing one another.
>
> But some sailed into this haven
> Laughing, and completely undecided,
> Expecting nothing more . . .[11]

Concluding "*They* wrote those poems," the poet points to those who welcome dispossession and loss, those who have embraced "the mad friendship of bodies"[12] and the "farewells"[13] and made it their new "haven." Such is the poetic space from which they can approach a wholeness that is "completely undecided" because it welds together opposite forces. Poetic creation, rooted in the experience of loss and madness, thus appears as the only means through which man may overcome human pain by the harmonious marriage of the yin and the yang. It operates as a transcending power that has been analyzed by the philosopher Edgar Morin:

> We recognize poetry not only as a means of literary expression but also as an alternative consciousness which arises from participation, fervor, wonder, communion, exhilaration, excitement, and of course, love which embraces every form of expression of altered perception. Poetry is freed from myth and reason and simultaneously welds them together. The poetic state conveys us through madness and wisdom beyond madness and wisdom. . . .
> If poetry transcends madness and wisdom, we must aspire to live in the poetic state and strive to prevent prose from drowning our lives which are necessarily woven from prose and poetry.[14]

This is how the poet's introspective journey calls forth a reassessment both of poetic creation and of the complexity of readerly responses as the reader is equally obsessed by those random "Visitations," "Left like an unknown's breath on mirrors."[15] References to the yet unwritten yet germinating *Alexandria Quartet* abound in *Cities, Plains and People*, hinting at the fascinating gallery of characters that will take flesh later on in the prose but whose presence can already be felt, thus abolishing temporal and textual borders: "the explorer, / The soldier and the secret agent,"[16] "The face. . . turned as sadly as a hare's,"[17] "The cool muslin dress shaken with flowers"[18] or the "Burning, particular, fastidious and lost / . . . figure"[19] build up a dreamlike universe where the reader proceeds in a dazed state, convinced that he has been walking around "forever in the same place / Same town, and country, sorting letters"[20] that only spell his unfathomable loss.

The poet's slow analytic work that relies on imperfect and fragmentary refractions through hazy temporal strata eventually leads him to contemplate his own reflection in the voice of Petron, "the Desert Father"[21]: "'I dare not ask for what I hope, / And yet I may not speak of what I fear.'"[22] The mystic figure is but another alter ego of the poet, who conceives of writing as a leap into the unknown: "artists like antennæ boring into the unknown through music or paint or word suddenly strike this Universe where for every object in the known world there exists an ideogram."[23] More or less at the same time, and in the same publication, his friend, the Greek poet George Seferis, insisted on the sharpness of perception that singles out the poet's skill: "All poems written or unwritten exist. . . . The special ability of the poet is to see them: that's why the poets are sometimes called seers. The faculty of seeing them makes the poet, the faculty of painting (*i.e.*, writing) makes the talent of the poet."[24]

The poet as a seer is a classic topos that Durrell revisits through the shifty contours of an unstable "I." Using various addressees and building up a protean persona that may turn out to be successively a lover, a magician, a mystic, or a prophet, the poetic voice undergoes multiple reincarnations, like so many aspects of Melissa. Each new theme or fragment corresponds to a new enunciative shift that endeavors to circumscribe an ever-elusive subject, what the French symbolist poet Stéphane Mallarmé called "l'absente de tous bouquets,"[25] "the missing flower in every bouquet." This is best felt in the last fragment, "A Prospect of Children," where the poet focuses on the abstract figure of a sleeping child. The closed eyes and lips offer inklings of the unknown and the unformed, of the irrepresentable. The sealed face lost in sleep challenges the seer poet: it stands as the perfect, self-enclosed representation of the unchartered past, present, and future that also sends the poet back to the mystery of his own, defunct, childhood. Just as in Rimbaud's poetry, which made a strong impression on Durrell, "the unknown is the object of vision."[26] As Yves Bonnefoy explains:

> The unknown is the unmasked essence of things per se; it is a momentum in its astounding immediacy, rather than a figure, a dynamics rather than an aspect, a mode of sharing rather than a mode of looking. . . .
> Thus the unknown is simultaneously a source of light, a rhythm, the ultimate act . . . , *bliss*—and, in any case, the negation of language in its everyday use.[27]

The seer poet must be capable of approaching the unknown that lies within him and beyond, the shifting sands of time through which a sleeping child's face reveals to him both his own vanished child face and the mysterious universe he could then behold. The poet becomes this voice inhabited by an inner exile that places him on the edges of the world and of his own self. Through this estrangement the reader comes to grasp the momentum of the unknown that vibrates through the lines. Poetic writing truly becomes the place of a living experience, as the French poet Pierre Jourde explains:

> Poetry turns language not only into a means of expression, but also into a place of experience; it is not just a formal or linguistic experience but an experience in being. Poetic love . . . , as Agamben says, is 'the attempt to experience the event of language itself as a fundamental poetic and love experience'. This does not mean expressing a past experience, a specific love affair, but what, within speech, corresponds to the dynamics of desire attempting to point, at the heart of things, to their presence.[28]

Durrell's "place of experience" is all the more poignant and intense as it points to an ever present and absent object: a childhood that encapsulates "the restless inventories of feeling,"[29] a presence long lost that functions as the irrepresentable heart of poetic speech. This last fragment thus invites the reader to reconsider Durrell's poetic work through a cluster of references pointing toward an unreachable origin that functions as the vanishing point where structural and semantic lines seem to converge.

The Vanishing Point

The poem "For a Nursery Mirror" in *Cities* reminds the reader of another, previous, childhood lyric, "To Ping-Kû Asleep," which was initially published in *A Private Country* and appears on the same page as the former in *Collected Poems* (p. 103). The mirrored poems keep refracting this impalpable and evanescent reality that haunts the eye of memory. This endless *mise en abyme* of the tantalizing "Image of the Dancer in water,"[30] simultaneously conjuring up the abstract and yet real form that shall rise[31] from the vacuum of the blank page, echoes the young poet's meditations on the art of poetry in the Cairo-based World War II poetry journal *Personal Landscape*:

> Since words are inadequate they can only render all this negatively—by an oblique method.
>   'Art' then is only the smoked glass through which we can look at the dangerous sun. . . .
>   Poems are negatives; hold them up to a clean surface of daylight and you get an apprehension of grace.[32]

Durrell's lines suggest a twofold intertextual mirror effect: that of St. Paul's epistle ("For now we see through a glass darkly"[33]) as well as that of Polonius's cue in Hamlet ("By indirections find directions out").[34] The time of childhood thus stands out as this "dangerous sun," this frightful object that art can only mirror at an angle and that reverberates through a multiplicity of imperfect prisms across Durrell's entire opus, both poetry and prose. Poetic writing appears then as the privileged medium through which the author explores the ontological imperfection of his art, thus building up a metatextual contemplation on the inadequacy of language that partakes of the very essence of poetry *per se*. As Benoît Conort has explained: "the poem denounces its very illusion."[35] This can be felt throughout Durrell's poetic output. In his first collection, *Quaint Fragments* (1931), he questions his own material: "Words? They are not large enough. / The sense is never minion to the word."[36]

Similarly, the poem "Pearls," facing "For a Nursery Mirror," concludes on the imperfect essence of poetry:

> Something is incomplete here
> [. . .]
> Like this unbroken coast,
> Like this half-drawn landscape,
> Like this broken torso of a poem.[37]

"Not large enough," words are akin to the devouring folds of the coat of Nessus: they burn the poet's soul without allowing him to shake them off, they travel far in time, imprinted deep into his skin, they escape temporal and spatial boundaries, they resist semantic stability. In a later poem, "Swimmers," published in *The Red Limbo Lingo* in 1971, Durrell ponders again upon their mobile, transgressive nature:

> [. . .] I tried
> To write you only the syntax failed,
> Each noun became a nascent verb
> And all verbs dormant adjectives.[38]

The only avenue left to the poet is that of a moving writing that follows in the wake of the symbolic, semantic, and linguistic shifts. The run-on line in the first two lines quoted above mimics, at the prosodic level, the grammatical fluidity, the wandering essence of a word that shall never be made to capture its own object. Vibrant with the very echo of unfathomed possibilities, freed from the constraints of denotation, the poetic word is envisaged as a self-renewing flux, an unstoppable lifeline that accounts for the supple melodic momentum that defies categorization and approaches the ineffable. As Conort has said, poetry is the art of "formulating what cannot be said," i.e., an utterance that builds upon the polysemic instability of words that cannot be circumscribed by discourse. This process further develops in "At Rhodes," included in the cycle of "The Anecdotes,"[39] a long poem that, like "Cities, Plains and People," is composed of sixteen fragments:

> If space curves how much the more thought,
> Returning after very conjugation
> To the young point of rest it started in?
>
> The fullness of being is not in refinement,
> By the delimitation of the object, but
> In roundness, the embosoming of the Real.[40]

The reality to which Durrell refers is the heraldic reality defined in *Personal Landscape* as "a continuous self-subsisting plane of reality towards which the spiritual self of man is trying to reach out through various media."[41] Such is the reality, as opposed to the factual, mundane one, of which the time of childhood partakes: the "roundness," the fecund embrace of words, the "curves" of a writing that brings together the beginning and the end—in faithful homage to T. S. Eliot's *Four Quartets*[42]—build up a new life cycle.

This is how the fleeting images of childhood can be traced back throughout Durrell's earlier poems. Like T. S. Eliot's time, they "Point to one end, which is always present."[43]

"Inconstancy," which first appeared in 1931 in *Quaint Fragments* before being reissued in *Collected Poems*, opens up on the preceding complement that sets the tone for the remainder of the poem: "Child, in the first few hours I lived with you."[44] Childhood belongs to a previous era, a short-lived past, and refers less to a period in time than to a moment of rupture:

> The fleeting moments laughed in mockery;
> Fled with the light abruptness of a dream . . .
> Time was asleep . . . Night and the stars remained
> The bitter emptiness of nothing gained,
> The queer half-witted stagnancy of Love
> Passed like a covert whisper in the night.[45]

This rupture characterizes both the syntactic and the prosodic structures. The semicolon at the end of the first line cuts the subject from the verb in the second line while the polyptotons and the synonyms (fleeting, fled, passed) highlight the poet's inability to capture time and seize the depth and intensity of its passive nature: "Time was asleep . . . Night and the stars remained." The ellipsis signals the caesura at the center of the line, the rift between two worlds: what vanishes—the sleepy, stagnant folds of time embracing the child—and what remains—the starry night and the bittersweet memory of a long-lost time, the awakening of pain. The end of the stanza symbolically sends us back to the beginning, to the primal object of loss: the "whisper" of Love that eludes the poet's grasp. The poet precisely stands at the crossing point of two time frames, in this painful in-between that harbors the hidden hope for a "whisper" conveying both the breath and the words of love into the present night of writing.

Another poem from *Quaint Fragments*, "Sonnet Astray," asserts the tragic death of youth:

> Life is a loneliness, and heritage
> A whispered mockery; yet, first to go,
> Killed by the fitful ravings of a sage
> Was youth; youth has been dead a painted age ago . . .[46]

The poet is not merely dealing here with his own youth, but with the birth of his own poetic awareness: the heritage he seeks to denounce is the very symbolist tradition he has made his own. The symbolist elements (". . . the whiteness and the godliness / Wings of the twilight") link up with the classical pattern of a rhyming lyric to debunk the expected form of the sonnet and give birth to a voice that goes "astray." The surface dichotomy opposing the "child-like" and the "senile with age" suddenly breaks apart with the oxymoron that conjures up, within the space of a single hemistich, a paradoxical truth, an unexpected opening:

> The wisdom of a fool that seeks and finds
> An emptiness, a gaunt penultimate stage
> Before perfection![47]

The poem steers away from the mimetic rendering of a past experience in order to convey its symbolic reconstruction that transcends the loss of childhood and unveils a new aesthetics and a new ethics:

> Sometimes the gross pendulum of time
> Is swung back an aeon;
>   And I,
> Bewilderingly wonder at my great foolishness
> To leave you forever alone that night by a star swept sea,
> With the laughter of the dark surf in your eyes . . .
> Godless, and yet so very much a God.[48]

This ultimate stanza that hinges on the typographic, syntactic, and prosodic dismantling of the second line mimics the portentous swing of the "gross pendulum of time," opening consciousness to a new time scale that challenges linearity and offers, retrospectively, the image of a vanished yet insistent gaze through which the poet, although "Godless," keeps alive his hope in a godlike presence. Just as in Corinthians, madness paves the way for a new kind of wisdom that defeats reason. Thus "Sonnet Astray" ultimately surpasses the symbolist heritage by questioning the very essence of poetry for, as Jacques Ancet asserts, "the poem listens, through language, to the unknown that keeps coming, endlessly. It is an experience. Not the reproduction of an experience that would precede it but which arouses and creates it in the fabric of the text." The epanadiplosis on the last line of the poem enhances the dualistic nature of the poetic experience that steers away from mimesis to enter the world of tentative correspondences, thus testifying to the strong influence of Otto Rank's study *Art and Artist* on Lawrence Durrell's writing: "To me, however, the whole science of art seems to be permeated . . . with a far-reaching dualism which . . . reflects the dualism inherent in the problem of art itself."[49]

Therefore, the reader is progressively led to realize that childhood is not to be taken as a realistic but as a symbolic motif that answers to Durrell's definition of the ideogram—a fundamental symbol that can refer to various semantic units, a linguistic materialization of the mobility of meaning. The numerous mirror effects that build up through explicit motifs—such as the mirror or the lake—or implicit ones—whether syntactic or prosodic ones—keep reverberating the ideogram of childhood. Indeed, "For a Nursery Mirror" in *Cities, Plains and People* and "To Ping-Kû Asleep" in *A Private Country* (both dedicated to Durrell's daughter Penelope) shift the perspective. The child embodies the other, a mysterious being wrapped in the secrecy of sleep who is singled out as different and differing, as the first lines of "To Ping-Kû Asleep" exemplify: "You sleeping child asleep, away / Between the confusing world of forms." The run-on line marks out the disjunction between the syntactic and the prosodic unit, as if the sentence were unable to reach out to this inaccessible world, "the confusing world of forms." The lexical and rhythmic echo "asleep, away" that is resumed in the dichotomy "you lie / And the pause flows" on the next lines and before the image of the child "Asleep in the body of the nautilus" concludes the stanza, creates a textual mirror effect that belies the both pregnant and unreal nature of refractions. Incidentally, the reader is also led to remember another chiaroscuro scene associating the face of the sleeping child and the light of the night lamp in Durrell's first novel, *Pied Piper of Lovers*: "Above him the night-light kept wicked vigil over a sleeping child and a collection of treasures on a table."[50] The impalpable, confusing refractions are further developed in "For a Nursery Mirror," where the child is subsumed in the thrice-repeated "Image," as if the poet were attempting to conjure up a departed spirit through an incantation that allows us to hear the inner decomposition of the poet's voice: "Image, Image, Image answer" (l.1) / "'Image, Image, Image'" (l.7). The second stanza, placed between quotation marks, does not give access to the child's voice but instead to the broken echo of the poet's initial utterance that keeps reverberating and fragmenting in the repetition of the last two lines of stanzas 1 and 3 ("A bird's beak poking out of the flesh, / A bird's beak singing between the eyes"; "From the hit of the wind of Death, / From the chink of the pin of Day") and in the final fearful symmetry of the very last line ("This is the body, / this is the blood"). From one collection to the next, the reader cannot fail to notice the shift from a euphoric to a dysphoric undertone in the second poem.

"To Ping-Kû Asleep" ends on repeated anaphoras and run-on lines that build up a victorious transition from childhood to womanhood:

> Sleep and rise a lady with a flower
> Between your teeth and a cypress
> Between your thighs[51]: surely you won't ever
> Be puzzled by a poem or disturbed by a poem
> Made like fire by the rubbing of two sticks?[52]

The rubbing of sticks and of words evokes a primitive, unsullied world that comes to fruition at the end of the collection in "Letter to Seferis the Greek" where "The girls with flowers in their teeth"[53] embody the perfection and the seductive powers of the writer's Greece, which stands for the ideal symbol of harmony, completeness, and fruitfulness. The same symbol was already at work in Durrell's early novel *Panic Spring*, published in 1937:

> The long blue Ionian nightfall, splintered by lights among stone columns, had given him the vision of Greek women, ripe as marble, natural as fruit to be plucked, lingering among the shadows of the waters, laughing upon the mouths of the young men . . . , mimosa sweetening the still air across the bays and islands, and the girls with pomegranate flowers in their mouths.[54]

The violent image of the cypress rising between the thighs combines here with the ominous symbolism of the pomegranate flowers that connect the fate of those young Ionian girls to that of Persephone tricked by Hades into eating seeds of the pomegranate that condemned her to spend six months in the year in the underworld. It would then seem that the joyful connotations of "To Ping-Kû Asleep" are subtly undermined through a play on distant similarities that are consubstantial to poetry. As Michel Deguy has explained: "*poetry has to do with apparition despite appearances. It links things—from a distance.*"[55] Thus the poem seems to break textual boundaries and lead us to a new perspective that challenges appearances, and readerly logic, only to make us keenly aware of the bare necessities of poetry:

> One must repeatedly gnaw at generic borders in order to tie up, each time and in a new way, the purpose and the workmanship. . . . Every form is allowed for because the problem with these forms is the space where they are made visible and where they make imagined possibilities visible. . . . "Poetry" is displaced

literature, if ever it is literature. . . . Poetry: what for? To leave behind a trace of something displaced which is still on the move.[56]

This displacement, orienting the reader toward unexpected margins of meaning, is at the core of Durrell's poetics.

This is how we move from the deceptively joyful tone of "To Ping-Kû Asleep" to the darker one of "For a Nursery Mirror," where the ascending dynamics is replaced by a downward move into the lovers' flesh, at the delicate junction where "The wet part is joined to the dry," in the painful crack between light and darkness, life and death, creation and chaos. The obsessive echo of polyptotons ("joined" l.8; "joints" l.9) as well as the sharp focus on "the soft red clay" (l.13, 18) and on "the wound" (l.12, 19) take the reader into the depths of an unfathomable world where birth metamorphoses into death, into a Christian sacrifice: "This is the body, this the blood." This last line brings to a climax the biblical metaphor that haunts the poem ("'The earth is a loaf'" l.6; "the joints of Adam" l.9; "the soft red clay" l.13) while debunking our expectations. Where we expected flesh and life, we are rewarded with blood and pain: that of the flesh torn through by the singing bird, that of a birth that looks like a crucifixion and that sends the reader back again to Durrell's novel *Pied Piper of Lovers* and his alter-ego protagonist:

> The child was born in those first days of monsoon, when the ground was rapidly becoming a living clot of humidity, and the ravines mere waterways for the passage of such debris as the wind had torn from the hillsides: when the clouds moved in menacing night-patrol above a cowed earth.[57]

Birth in the novel amounts to a violent expulsion from the womb of the earth that carries away the wreckage washed down by the wind and the rain and opens up the great wound of India's harrowed body standing for the child's mother we are never shown. The soil becomes this living flesh that the text relentlessly plods, foreboding future displacements (the doctor's face replaces the mother's, the father's that of the child). Durrell's decision to forbid the reprint of this strongly autobiographic novel does not just testify to the author's modesty. It also highlights his desire to provide his reader with something more than the mimetic reproduction of a past experience and to instead present a symbolic network that connects the poetic rhythm with the dramatic power of words that are freed from intimate connotations. The deliberate erasure of autobiographic echoes gives free rein to the logic of association that turns the reader's gaze away from the specific toward the universal and that foregrounds Durrell's philosophic outlook. This is why the two poems summon a simultaneously real and imaginary addressee: the little girl asleep in "To Ping-Kû Asleep" *is and is not* the daughter who shared the poet's life. She is the embodiment of the figure of absence that haunts Durrell's writing, and she comes back as such in the second poem, "For a Nursery Mirror." The poem is indeed addressed to a missing child (the preposition "To" is significantly replaced by "For"), as if he/she had long been gone and were but a hazy memory ("Whether son or whether daughter") that encapsulates the idea of a child. It is no longer a child as such, a living being, but a Platonic idea, that is a place, the place of emergence of childhood, the place where all living possibilities are born, in keeping with Plato's doctrine developed in *Timaeus*:

> [52a] [. . .] a third Kind is ever-existing Place, [52b] which admits not of destruction, and provides room for all things that have birth, itself being apprehensible by a kind of bastard reasoning by the aid of non-sensation, barely an object of belief; for when we regard this we dimly dream and affirm that it is somehow necessary that all that exists should exist in some spot and occupying some place, and that that which is neither on earth nor anywhere in the Heaven is nothing. So because of all these and other kindred notions we are unable also on waking up to distinguish clearly the unsleeping and truly subsisting substance, owing to our dreamy condition, [52c] or to state the truth—how that it belongs to a copy—seeing that it has not for its own even that substance for which it came into being, but fleets ever as a phantom of something else—to come into existence in some other thing, clinging to existence as best it may, on pain of being nothing at all.[58]

This is why childhood is much more than a traumatic experience. It is the trace of a loss that keeps haunting the poet since it can only exist as a defunct object: the consciousness of childhood is irremediably linked to its end.

By offering to the living conscience the prospect of its oncoming death, the image of childhood operates in the same manner as Yorick's skull that brings Hamlet back to the time when the King's jester used to bear him "on his back."[59] Yet this ghostlike survival of the past also reorients the subject's gaze forward: it is "a phantom of something else—to come into existence in some other thing"; it is the source of an endless process of renewal, the breath of the creative spirit, "barely an object of belief"; it occupies a place that cannot be identified, the place of constant displacements, of drifting bonds constantly reborn. It is a place that cannot be put into words and that Phaon seeks to explore in *Sappho*, the play Durrell wrote in Rhodes in 1947:

The three most beautiful forms are
Ships, women, and musical instruments,
Their properties must somewhere intersect:
But this is only seen by mad poets
For whom there are no single images
But a continual marriage of attributes.[60]

Similarly, "there are no single images / But a continual marriage of attributes" whose interplay conjures up Durrell's ideogram of childhood that even defies biographic narratives. As Corinne Alexandre-Garner aptly points out:

Legend holds that Lawrence Durrell was born in the Himalayas on 27th February 1912. Although the date is true, the place is purely fictitious; however, it reveals the spiritual birth place of the artist who enjoyed saying time and again that, according to the Chinese, we have two birth places: the one where we were born, and a place of predilection where we awaken to reality. . . . It is the place of a kind of revelation of the inner world that dwells within each one of us. Durrell, who was born in Jullundur, near the border to Pakistan which he left when he was one year old, has no memory of the town where he was actually born.[61]

As soon as one considers childhood as an image, as the moving image of a receding place that keeps "clinging to existence as best it may," one becomes aware of the shifting forces at work in Durrell's writing, of the fundamental fleeting emptiness upon which our entire world rests and is forever reborn into "some other thing."

Transmuting Loss

Childhood comes powerfully to the fore in the central poem of the collection, "In Europe." Never ceasing to "gnaw at generic borders,"[62] as Jean-Patrice Courtois has said, this poem explicitly toys with the dramatic genre and stages the dialogue of three characters (Man, Woman, Old Woman) lamenting the disappearance of borders, the end of a stable world, a balanced and peaceful universe:

Nothing disturbed such life as I remember
But telephone or telegram,
Such death-bringers to the man among the roses
In the garden of his house, smoking a pipe.[63]

This atmosphere of blissful harmony sends us back to that of "Letter to Seferis the Greek" that concluded the cycle of *A Private Country*:

> ... history with all her compromises
> Cannot disturb the circuit made by this,
> Alone in the house, a single candle burning
> Upon a table in the whole of Greece.[64]

This self-enclosed, Edenic world, sheltered from the turmoil of History, has been irretrievably lost, and the poet's voice has been smashed to pieces. The characters' retorts in this radiophonic piece, which the reader is nonetheless asked to read silently on the page, dramatize the fragmentation of the poetic voice. The systematic breaking up of the generic and of the semantic patterns climaxes in the image of destroyed childhood that pervades the text and testifies to the downfall of civilization per se, which Durrell openly excoriates in his residence book on Rhodes:

> I saw the dying child, no less a symbol—but of what? Our world perhaps. For it is always the child in man who is forced to live through these repeated tragedies of the European conscience. The child is the forfeit we pay for the sum of our worldly errors. Only through him shall we ever salvage these lost cultures of passion and belief.[65]

Throughout the poem, "the children," who are given no voice, are the founding absence that lays bare the tragic impotence of Europe, and yet they also stand, silently, for this ideal place that every character hankers after, a place of redeemed hope smashed to smithereens by History:

> Woman
> The children have become so brown,
> Their skins have become dark with sunlight,
> Man
> They have learned to eat standing.
> ...
> Woman
> If only the children—
> Man
> Were less wild and unkept, belonged
> To the human family, not speechless,
> Old Man
> And shy as the squirrels in the trees:

Woman
If only the children
Old Man
Recognised their father, smiled once more.[66]

The children, burned beyond recognition, are standing, as if to judge the world that has orchestrated their destruction. They come back to haunt man and woman in a speech that conjures up two simultaneous and incompatible codes: that of dramatic cues where the syntactic unity is oddly missing and that of the poem where prosodic unity is challenged by the dialogic structure. Eventually the object of discourse proves the impotence of discourse itself through the tragic chorus in which old man and woman join voices to recapture an image that evades them and comes to symbolize the impossible redemption of a forsaken future: "They have got the refugee habit, / Walking about in the rain for food, / Looking at their faces in the bottom of wells."[67] In the dark mirror of wells the poet contemplates the black whole of History that echoes in the aposiopesis of the woman's incomplete line "If only the children—." The only thing we are left with, in this postapocalyptic world, is the dismantled fragments of a meaningless language:

Woman
Peoples and possessions,
Lands and rights,
Titles, holdings,
Trusts, bonds.
Old Man
Mean nothing any more, nothing.
. . .
Woman
All we have left us, out of context,
Old Man
A jar, a mousetrap, a broken umbrella,
A coin, a pipe, a pressed flower
Woman
To make an alphabet for our children.

Losing what we had, entering into a new contact with disseminated objects "out of context" like ourselves, is the starting point wherefrom a new coherence, a refunded relationship to the world, can be imagined. This new relationship is announced at the end of the poem by the woman's paradoxical renunciation of the world, which frees her "From fear of wanting, fear of hoping, / Fear of everything by dying." However, she also appears to have shed that last fear, and the acceptance of her impending dissolution coincides with the announcement of the vanished frontiers.

> Woman
> . . .
> We can die now.
> Old Man
> Frontiers mean nothing any more. Dear Greece!
> Man
> Yes. We can die now.

The poems ends on the acceptance of death and on the invocation to an eternal Greece that defeats even death, that resists the perishable frontiers, a Greece that belongs neither to geography or to History but to a boundless space-time. Greece thus stands as a counterpart to the image of destroyed childhood: it may well have been ransacked and torn apart by war, yet its ideal essence is the true anchoring of the poet's meditation on life, death, and on man's insanity. Only through the acceptance of death can this symbolic Greece function as a place of rebirth.

This explains why Greece also looms large at the end of the collection concluding on Prospero's "evergreen / Cell by the margin of the sea and land."[68] The last and long poem "Cities, Plains and People" opens upon a symbolic childhood—"Once in idleness was my beginning"[69]—anchored in a mythical Tibet that Durrell never inhabited. Through the deceptive autobiographical reference, the poet reorients our gaze once more toward T. S. Eliot's *Four Quartets*. The repeated occurrences of "In my end is my beginning"[70] invite to us to listen to the circular motif developed by Durrell and to realize that the origins he is exploring are indeed those of art. Similarly the reappearance of the figure of Prospero, at the beginning and at the end of the poem, confirms the structural and metatextual circularity of a text that is built on the principle of "little mirrors in the light,"[71] refracting light, dazzling the eye, and calling us, out of actual space and time, "in space-time void"[72] where the emerging figure of Prospero eventually replaces that of the poet. Poetry flows from this "space-time void"[73] that defeats logic and discourse and opens up the text like "the cave of the silver echoes"[74] that Durrell foresaw in an early poem from 1931. For despite the realistic references that lie in the margins of "Cities," giving the reader the impression of entering the secret folds of the poet's life, the markedly disjunctive prosodic and narrative pattern of the poem materializes "this honeycomb of silence"[75] for which the poem aims and where the past is transmuted. This is how the last line of the first fragment—"Until your pain become a literature"⁷⁶—acquires a prophetic ring that warns the reader of the constant displacement that rules Durrell's writing. As Corinne Alexandre-Garner and I have explained elsewhere in a detailed analysis of this particular poem:

> Words are inadequate, yet the space opened up by the writing of poetry creates a fabric of interwoven flashes of memory mingling rhythms and sounds, replacing the sensual impressions of childhood.
>
> Despite the poet's professed hopelessness, despite the "heap of broken images"⁷⁷ that haunt him—"Bombers bursting like pods" (Part XV, l.1), the dilapidated cities of Athens and Bremen, "A mass of rotten vegetables" (Part XV, l.10)—the poet transfigures this disquieting waste land into Prospero's island, which welcomes us in the last section of the poem with its "lime-green, odourless / And pathless island waters / Crossing and uncrossing [. . .]" (Part XVI l.2–4). Prospero, the idealised poetic persona, the distorted reflection of Eliot's old Tiresias, symbolically lies at the heart of an "evergreen / Cell by the margin of the sea and land" (XVI, l.7–8). Inhabiting the world of creation, he is a borderline spirit, a dual creature, belonging both to the amorphous, protective waters and to "The rocky island" (Part VIII, l.6). In his recumbent, sleepy figure in sunlight holding "the Apple in his hand" (Part XVI, l.12), the reader recognises the beginning of a new world, "once in idleness" (Part I, l.1).⁷⁸

The Greece of writing is born out of these broken forms and bears witness to the poet's victory over the repeated uprooting and loss, the dispossession and renunciation that have punctuated his artistic struggle. This process has been analyzed by Rank in a passage of *Art and Artist* that Durrell annotated in his copy as "pure gold":

> In this sense the general problem of the artist . . . is contained in the two notions of deprivation and renunciation. . . . But the two aspects are complementary, like outer and inner, society and ego, collectivity and individuality. The great artist and great work are only born from the reconciliation of the two— the victory of a philosophy of renunciation over an ideology of deprivation.⁷⁹

At the Heart of the Cleft: The Emergence of Seizure

The Greece that emerges from the collection of poems is necessarily a shimmering, evanescent entity that is refracted through the fragmented prism of the poems. As the poem "Pearls" suggests, there can be no end and no beginning to the voice that celebrates a perpetually unfinished landscape:

> Something is incomplete here
> Something in the story is unfinished,
> A tale with no beginning
> The fragment of a voice that interrupts,
> Like this unbroken coast,
> Like this half-drawn landscape,
> Like this broken torso of a poem.[80]

Durrell's unachieved poem mesmerizes the reader by the very perfection of its incompleteness. The regularity of its anaphoras, the carefully balanced syntax, the narrative coherence all testify to a poem that precisely meets its designated end—a maimed landscape poem. Behind the apparently perfected construction, the missing head, and the broken torso, the emptiness that the writing mimics in the series of disjointed noun phrases is highlighted by the unpredictable prosodic pattern alternately playing on trimeters and pentameters, trochees and iambs. Placed at the beginning of the collection, the poem "Pearls" operates as a programmatic piece that invites the reader to explore the clefts of writing and envisage every poem as so many pearls encircling a headless sculpture. The comparison of writing to a faceless body is an old one that dates back to Montaigne, who established a parallel between Baroque painting and his writing in the *Essais*, which he sees as "crotesques [. . .], rappiecez de divers membres, sans certaine figure."[81] The absence in which the text is rooted can thus also be read, paradoxically, as the sign of a metatextual, veiled presence.

Through the tension between opposed poles ("unfinished" / "no beginning"; "unbroken" / "broken"), the poet suggests unexpected parallels ("story" / "tale" / "coast" / "landscape" / "poem") and leads us to pay heed to the other fragments of voice circulating throughout his poetry. One typical instance is "Conon the Critic," previously encountered in *A Private Country*.[82] His face is never revealed, and his utterances are delivered as poetic fragments in *Cities*, whereas the first publication of the text in *Personal Landscape: An Anthology of Exile* specified "Conon the Critic, on the Six Landscape Painters of Greece, by Lawrence Durrell (Prose)."[83] Therefore, it would seem that the genre is equally "incomplete," "unfinished," and fluctuating between prose and poetry, such that both genres are summoned only to be interrupted.

This method, which is characteristic of Durrell's writing, accounts for another famous poem, "Freedom." It initially appears in the play *Sappho* in 1947 before it is included in various collections,[84] where it is alternately published as an extract from the play and as a poetic piece per se, which is in keeping with its initial function as an epigram composed by Sappho.[85] A poem embedded within a verse play, and then included in several poetry collections, the text never ceases to haunt and baffle the reader's memory. Less a text than a mirror, playing on a variety of echoes (alliterations, anaphoras, polyptotons), the poem calls for a variety of projected images not unlike Plato's cave. This blurring of enunciative sources and textual origins was already foreshadowed some ten years earlier in "Conon the Critic, on the Six Landscape Painters of Greece," whose sections, hovering between prose and poetry, resemble imaginary quotations of fictitious artists that mesmerize the reader and defeat any rational analysis. Partaking simultaneously of prose and poetry, these mysterious statements suggest the structure of the *Ko-an*, those paradoxical parables through which the master leads the disciple to a deeper spiritual vision. According to D. T. Suzuki, whom Durrell read extensively, the *Ko-an* "denotes some anecdote of an ancient master, or a dialogue between a master and monks, or a statement or question put forward by a teacher, all of which are used as the means for opening one's mind to the truth of Zen."[86] Just like the *Ko-an*, Durrell's poem takes various forms and, although seemingly absurd, leads the reader to investigate the relationships between the subject, space, and its perception. "This landscape is not original in its own mode," says the first line, for what makes a landscape original is the gaze that the prose poem explores. Peter of Thebes offers us a synaesthetic approach where smell and taste combine with vision. Manoli of Crete experiences physical and spiritual fusion with the landscape: sensorial sensations blur and lead the subject to a spontaneous union with the outer world that annihilates borders and make man and the universe at one with each other. Such is "the Way" sought by Buddhists, as Chuang Tzu explained in a passage underlined by Durrell:

> The Way has never known boundaries. . . . So [I say,] those who divide fail to divide; those who discriminate fail to discriminate. What does this mean, you ask? The sage embraces things. Ordinary men discriminate among them and parade their discriminations before others. So I say, those who discriminate fail to see.[87]

Durrell's poem can only make sense if we consider it as an exploration into a new mode of vision that embraces the boundless world of writing and disregards generic borders. Thus, it is barely surprising that the poem should echo the residence book on Corfu and, within, the transcription of his poetic correspondence with the Greek writer Kostan Zarian. The poem is therefore embedded twice in the prose: that of Durrell's narrative and that of his letter to his friend. It functions as a spiritual window opening onto the inner world of timeless meditation:

> Zarian sends me a poem about the island in Armenian to which he adds an English translation. Writing of Corcyra he says: 'The gold and moving blue have stained our thoughts so that the darkness is opaque, and we see in our dreams the world as if in some great Aquarium. . . .'
>
> Since I have nothing else I reciprocate with my poem on Manoli, the landscape painter of Greece: 'After a lifetime of writing acrostics he took up a brush and everything became twice as attentive. Trees had simply been trees before. Distinctions had been in ideas. Now the old man went mad, for everything undressed and ran laughing into his arms.'[88]

The perfect echo between *Prospero's Cell* and the poem not only shatters the boundaries between residence writing and poetry, it also testifies to Durrell's unrelenting quest for a renewed vision of the world in which the minute and the impenetrable come to man's encounter, abolishing any need for the superfluous ploys of art, offering an immediate, uncalculated communion through which man's essence is refunded. The island of Corfu, just like the I/land of the poem, abolishes the distance between the inner and the outer world, the human and the nonhuman, and metamorphoses the subject. Manoli embodies the new perception dreamed of by Zarian, whose acute sensitivity shatters ontological boundaries. The landscape is not so much described as experienced. Just as man dwells in the landscape, the landscape dwells in him. This reciprocal relationship annihilates the hierarchy between the thinking subject and nonhuman matter, and poetry stands out as the only truthful medium that reinstates a legitimate order and places the landscape at the heart of human action.

This explains why the third character in the poem, Julian of Arcadia, defines Arcadia neither as a landscape nor as an aesthetic and philosophic concept but as an ideal space for which every artist aims. One immediately recognizes a metatextual allusion to the poem "In Arcadia" in *A Private Country*,[89] where the barely perceptible presence of the persona of the poem creates a unified space-time and erases logical link words so that "There is no feeling of 'Therefore' in it."[90] The "good poem" would then deploy, in the image of "In Arcadia," an ideal, boundless time-space that can detach itself from causality and float freely, to which no "origin, reason meaning"[91] can be ascribed.

Such a poem illuminates the theory developed by Durrell, who held that "pure poetry evokes, prose relates. . . . Prose can be constructed, but poetry comes from nothing. It surprises even the poet."[92] Poetry should then no longer be seen as the artful mastery of a literary set of techniques but as the emergence of a seizure.

This is what accounts for the reversal of the gaze that characterizes the following fragment, "On Spiridon of Epirus," where the landscape turns into a subject imprinting in the painter's eye "the form lying under."[93] The painter's work, a visual displacement of the poet's invisible handling of words, metaphorizes the latter's desire for the vanished picture, for the emergence of the Platonic idea: "Thus one day there remained only a picture-frame, an empty studio, and an idea of Hero the painter."[94] The abstract image that arises in the ensuing section, "On Hero of Corinth," offers a perfect counterpoint to the last one in "On Alexander of Athens," where the painter, using the opposite technique of excessive representation, "exhausted both himself and his subject in his art,"[95] absorbing reality into art, draining out the world of its substance and leaving the reader endlessly "looking for a way back from art into life."[96] Conversely, Durrell's poetry is not exhaustive but suggestive. It is not descriptive or didactic, but initiatory, thus reasserting the essence of the art, which Jean-Luc Nancy has subsumed as follows:

> As a consequence, poetry is also negativity inasmuch as it denies us, in the access to meaning, what would determine this access as a passage, as a way or a path, and posits it as a presence, as an invasion. Rather than an access to meaning it is an access of meaning. Suddenly—and easily—being or truth, heart or reason shed their meaning and the difficulty is there, it seizes you.[97]

This moment of seizure is repeatedly asserted, as if the poem was designed to prevent us from ascribing a fixed meaning to the sequence of words, as if the poet's voice remained a haunting presence, or what Nancy called "the *praxis* of the never-ending return of the same: the very same difficulty, the very difficulty itself."[98] Indeed the poem reappears at the end of the collection under the title "Conon in Alexandria."[99] This second poem attributed to Conon is placed at a turning point within the collection, at the onset of the third movement, which leads us away from the world of the Greek islands and of Europe and into Egypt. Conon's voice is no longer superseded by the polyphony of quotations but dramatizes the lyrical "I" of the exiled persona and reverberates Durrell's own exile. As Roger Bowen has explained, Durrell "creates a fictive speaker from another era who is . . . not hesitant to reiterate his loss of Greece. . . . To create *another* exile is to escape from one's own; the path of invention is the path of transcendence."[100] Therefore, we realize that what looked like a sequel to the first poem orchestrates a radical rift: the enunciative source and the prosodic pattern signal the stark difference between both texts. However, they both raise the same question, a displaced question that never ceases to return.

The structure of the poem relies on repetition and difference. It is divided into two symmetrical parts, the first one being composed of three sections marked out by asterisks and the second of two only, equally separated by asterisks. The first four sections are made of three quatrains followed by a distich composing four sonnets alternating iambic and trochaic rhythms while the last section is made of two quatrains followed by a tercet and a concluding final quatrain. Such a structure reveals the twofold nature of the poem as a whole, and simultaneously, as the combination of independent units. Here lies the true challenge of poetry: capturing unity in a fragment, opening man's consciousness to an extended form of presence that lies beyond.

Significantly, "Conon in Alexandria" opens up on a description of Alexandria that exemplifies the advice we were given in "On Spiridon of Ephesus" ("Look at this landscape for five years. You see little but something attentive watching you"[101]):

> Ash-heap of four cultures,
> Bounded by Mareotis, a salt lake,
> On which the winter rain rings and whitens,
> In the waters, stiffens like eyes.[102]

The echo between the two texts does not merely bridge the gap between prose and prosody: it also rings as an answer to Eliot's *Ash-Wednesday*; to *The Wasteland*, "for you know only / A heap of broken images";[103] as well as to *Four Quartets*, "Old fire to ashes, and ashes to the earth / Which is already flesh, fur and faeces."[104] Alexandria thus stands for the place of a spiritual downfall that is also a place of passage from birth to life, ashes to the waters of renewal, which implicitly echoes the Book of Samuel[105] and the Book of Psalms.[106]

The dead waters of the lake turned into "eyes" metamorphose the landscape and the text into a mirror of the poetic gesture itself, preparing the reader for the following poem, "Mareotis," which concludes: "Now everywhere Spring opens / Like an eyelid still unfocused, / . . .—a landscape like an eye."[107] The persona of the poem is sent back to the endless refractions of his own gaze, as if he was never meant to escape the contemplation of a disaster whose impossible description breaks up the enunciation. The distich ending this first sonnet tears the syntax apart, as if to mimic the loss of a forbidden paradise that vanishes in the blank space of the page, while the enunciator begins to doubt his choice of words:

> A solitary presumed quite happy,
> Writing those interminable whining letters,

> On the long beaches dimpled by the rain,
> Tasting the island wind
>
> Blown against wet lips and shutters out of Rhodes.
> I say 'presumed', but would not have it otherwise.[108]

The second sonnet takes us backward through an inner journey that leads us from the steps to Pharos into Greece: "the familiar papers," "the plate of olives and the glass of wine," "the almond-candles and the statues" operate as ideograms of Durrell's previous poems on Greece. The mirror of the landscape opens up a textual and scriptural mirror to the poet who contemplates the rift tearing him apart from his own former selves. The ultimate mirror is that of self-reference in the third sonnet where the poet's "I" addresses Conon: "Would you say that later, reading / Such simple propositions, the historian / Might be found to say: 'The critic / In him made a humour of this passion.'"[109] The interplay of voices culminates in the distich—"'Two equations of a mind conscious of ideas, / Fictions, not kisses, crossed the water between them'"?[110]—and blurs the enunciative sources, as if the poem was inhabited by two identical voices reverberating in "a universe too large"[111] to be comprehended. The final question mark disturbs once more the cohesiveness of the poem and suggests a dialogue where questions are left unanswered. This dismantling of the poetic voice climaxes in the last two sections abounding in imaginary quotations, whether italicized, when they report past utterances, or not, and when they are purely hypothetical. Such a technique foreshadows the enunciative and scriptural mirrors that Durrell will set up in *The Avignon Quintet*[112] later on and also paves the way for the contemplative space of the desert that he will develop in *The Alexandria Quartet*. The last section concludes indeed on the inner eye of the desert:

> You might have added: 'The desert, yes, for exiles.
> But its immensity only confines one further.
> Its end seems always in oneself.'[113]

The desert stands as the ultimate place of self-renunciation, of the quest for an ineffable absolute in an endless meditation. The characters briefly mentioned in this last section are the objects of an abstract analysis—"a woman's body," "The lovers," "a man"—through which the poet attempts to decipher a form of eternal truth. As imaginary entities, hypothetical beings, or illusory perceptions, they are all the objects of a boundless meditation by the mysterious Conon. The poem becomes the very desert space where questions reverberate endlessly, where words bring no relief, where an unfathomable presence is both veiled and unveiled. As George Didi-Huberman has explained: "the desert—spacious, empty, monochrome—is probably the most appropriate visual place to acknowledge this absence as something infinitely powerful, commanding."[114]

This absence is materialized in the poem by an incomplete page: "A letter unfinished because the ink gave out." This gap in the text, this interrupted exchange, opens up a new perception that is neither pictorial nor poetic nor musical but mediated by the voice of an absent presence:

> I have passed all this day in what I would call patience,
> Not writing, alone in my window, with my flute,
> Having read in a letter that last immortal February
> That 'Music is only love looking for words'.[115]

This final image echoes the minimal picture concluding "On Hero of Corinth"—"a picture-frame, an empty studio"[116]—and exposes the aporetic essence of representation: that of an intradiegetic subject who stops writing, takes the place of the reader, and acts in turn as a mirror to the mysterious, unnamable other.

This is how we are artfully brought back in the end to the beginning, to the "little mirrors in the light," to Durrell's poetry that operates as the mirror of Zen described by Suzuki:

> Zen often compares the mind to a mirror free from stains. To be simple, therefore, according to Zen, will be to keep this mirror always bright and pure and ready to reflect simply and absolutely whatever comes before it. [. . .] Here is no logic, no philosophizing; here is no twisting of facts to suit our artificial measures; here is no murdering of human nature in order to submit it to intellectual dissections; the one spirit stands face to face with the other spirit like two mirrors facing each other, and there is nothing to intervene between their mutual reflections.[117]

Poetry, not unlike Zen, would open the doors to an ineffable perception that illuminates the mundane and places man in a new relationship to himself and to the others. "Not writing, alone in [his] window, with [his] flute,"[118] the poet divests himself of the husks of words to commune with "the island wind"[119] of the initial sonnet, inviting his reader to step beyond the frame and hear what the words cannot say but which the poem may whisper to the attentive ear—the secret music of a quest fraught with echoes: "Le vent se lève! . . . il faut tenter de vivre! / L'air immense ouvre et referme mon livre."[120] In Durrell, as in Paul Valéry's poem, the call for life resonates long after the book has been closed.

Listening to the Voice of the Poem

We are thus led to reread and listen to Durrell's musical poems from a new perspective. Poems such as "Water Music"[121] in *Cities*, "Carol on Corfu" and "Nemea" in *A Private Country*, or the poem "Echo" dedicated to Nancy and Ping-Kû on the first page of the collection, as well as earlier poems such as "Lyric" (1934) or "Lines to music" (1938), highlight the quintessentially musical nature of every poem and arouse the reader's desire to read the text as one would a music score, taking the time to listen not only to the persona's lyric "I" but also to the perfection of the form, what Jean-Luc Nancy calls "the mechanical completion that gives access to infinite meaning."[122] Through the various syntactic, symbolic, prosodic, and rhythmic variations every poem reasserts the continuity of the poetic gesture, its resistance to death, its persisting reverberation in the reader's sensorial consciousness that "Carol on Corfu" extols: "the salt of a poem holds on / . . . The salt of the poem lives on."[123] The reader thus encounters a text that forces him to listen to the silent page. In "Water Music" the play on alliterations and assonances, anaphoras and paranomases, polyptotons, and unexpected compound nouns partake of the cyclic structure of the poem in which the end sends the reader back to the first and to the penultimate stanzas in a self-reflexive gesture that points to the resistance of the poetic voice analyzed by Christian Doumet:

> For the written page would not resemble a shroud, a casket or a screen for someone who could not *read* it. On the contrary, it is essentially a tool that designates; it is the place where the reader also becomes the writer; the hearer becomes the speaker and reciprocally. The undecidability of these postures is the sign of the hospitality of the text about which one should reread some pages in *Of Grammatology* by Jacques Derrida (Derrida insists several times on the idea of "the voice that keeps silent"). He would help us, in words that have now become familiar, to understand better what a written poem is: it is, obviously, the translation of a voice, but of "the voice of being" which remains "silent, mute, insonorous, wordless, originally *a-phonic*".[124] For such is certainly the exact status of the voice of the poem: it is the vocal persistence of the dead [. . .] haunting the ruminations of the living.[125]

Indeed, the "sulky beauty" of "Water Music" unfolds like a minor movement, like the musical signature of the poetic act pointing to the mysterious presence of a subliminal voice that emerges and is drowned again in the crashing of waves, revealed and preserved, and that reaches out to us from the depths of an ever-shifting territory.

Similarly, "Nemea" in *A Private Country* functions as the cave of echoes allowing the reader to hear the "low music" of Sacheverell Sitwell's meditation on death in his long poem *Agamemnon's Tomb* where Agamemnon is endowed with a golden mask.[126] S. Sitwell's poem is organized as a musical composition in three movements—a meditation on death and burial followed by the celebration of Agamemnon's tomb and ending on a tragic chorus announcing the approach of death and inviting the reader to listen to the music of life in the singing fountain. Such a structure clearly paves the way for the musical architecture of Durrell's poem, which conjures up the same elements in a striking celebration of Sitwell's piece:

> Only the drum can celebrate,
> Only the adjective outlive them.
> . . .
> Tone of the frog in the empty well,
> Drone of the bald bee on the cold skull,
>
> Quiet, Quiet, Quiet.[127]

Instrumental music and vocal music answer each other in a similar surge of life, but it is a secretive music played *mezzo voce* "in the empty well," in "the cold skull," a music that arises from the presence of insignificant beings (the frog or the bee) and that softly resists death in the unremarkable, insignificant resilience of the signifier, in the silent displacement of the vowel from "quiet, quite quiet" (l.2) to "Quiet, Quiet, Quiet" (l.14; 17).

This music outlives the poem and the collection and silently resurfaces several years later in the mnemonic journey spurred by Durrell's recollections in *Reflections on a Marine Venus* where the reader recognizes, between the lines, an ancient melody:

> In the silence we could hear the water gurgling somewhere down and there, below the earth. . . . I suddenly remembered other moments of time spent in this landscape, time printed upon silence with all its real colours up: the faint burring of honey-bees in Agamemnon's tomb: one glittering spring day, the noise of snow melting among the meadows at Nemea. . . . all isolated moments existing in a peculiar dense medium of their own which was like time but not of it. Each moment to itself entire, populating a whole continuum of feeling.[128]

Visual and auditory perceptions mirror one another on either side of the series of colons, creating a timeless, shifting painting that abolishes narrative linearity, breaks up syntactic logic, and freezes the last movement of the sentence in a nominal syntagm. The residence book marks its deliberate estrangement from the genre of the travel book. It unravels a static meditation on space, a timeless dwelling in the landscape that allows for the emergence of the invisible: the sensorial perception of an unworldly time-space. The narrative dissolves and reveals its poetic strata, veering away from the initial, implicit, reading contract. Instead of a story, we are given a prose poem that dismantles the prose and becomes the true event at the core of the text. We enter a distinct temporality, the temporality of the poem that Gaston Bachelard has analyzed thus:

> Every true poem includes the elements of still time, a time which does not abide by the beat, a time we shall qualify as vertical to distinguish it from the time that runs horizontally like river water. . . . In the poetic instant, our being goes up or down, rejecting worldly time which would translate ambivalence into antithesis and simultaneity into successiveness.[129]

The very same "vertical time" rules "Two Poems in Basic English," which opens upon the repetition of the three elements composing the title of the first poem—"Ships. Islands. Trees"—and reworks them in an increasingly complex syntax metamorphosing those three simple items into iconic signs that refer the reader not to their denotative meaning but to their semiotic value so that ships, islands, and trees are both far less and far more than the mere objects they stand for. Like "the cold skull" in "Nemea," they echo with the possibility of their past semantic functions of which they have been divested and compose a new "dictionary": "This earth a dictionary is / To the root and growth of seeing, And to the servant heart a door."[130] Their reordering in the second stanza shatters the conventional relationships between objects and annihilates the easy equation between the signified and the signifier as if to prove that poetry is the art of precipitating new encounters:

> . . . these living
> Instruments of space,
> Whose quiet communication is
> With older trees in ships on the grey waves:
> An order and a music
> Like a writing on the skies
> Too private for the reason or the pen;
> Too simple even for the heart's surprise.[131]

The poem ends on the ineffable: this "quiet communication" between shapes and sounds that makes "older" and "order" rhyme, however imperfectly, just as "skies" and "surprise" or "space" and "waves," suggesting an infinite number of possible textual and sensorial webs through which meaning is simultaneously woven and unwoven. The reader is left with a writing that is as difficult to circumscribe as the moving skies, a poetic gesture that escapes the narrow limits of the page and the simplicity of a private bliss that seizes the poet unawares. The discreet mosaic in gray and blue of timeless ships, islands, and trees unveils for a fleeting moment the possibility of a harmonious universe that the second poem will shatter to pieces.

"Near El Alamein," which Durrell refused to include in the larger contemporaneous trend of war poetry,[132] takes up the same iconic elements to explore the death drift of the world. The sinking sand, the empty houses in the first stanza are set in sharp contrast against the same houses and gardens men dream of in the second stanza before they are killed. The sea is paradoxically associated with the army as the only living matter:

> Units of the dead in these living armies,
> Making comparison of this bitter heat,
> And the living sea, giving up its bodies,
> Level and dirty in the mist,
> Heavy with sponges and the common error.[133]

As a shroud concealing and simultaneously revealing the corpses, the sea is the exact counterpart to the desert, which surrenders the soldiers' empty helmets ("Green bulbs in the hollow sand here"); sullied by man, it mirrors the desert and sends the reader back to the first stanza and its initial line: "This rough field of sudden war." The sand and the sea visually, symbolically, and phonetically embrace each other. They are both smooth and empty spaces of wandering and loss, endless blank spaces where humanity faces both its finitude and its insignificance in the greater order of the universe, preparing the reader for the symbolism that pervades *The Avignon Quintet* where the desert becomes an overpowering presence.[134]

Throughout *Cities, Plains and People* Durrell's poetry invites us to listen to the becoming of writing, a writing that transcends the various forms of death—whether personal or historical—and conjures up the possibility of an undreamed future. The reader's eye is caught in the web of a text that keeps playing between the lines, between genres, forms, and temporalities, building up a silent conversation that takes place in the margins. The essence of the poem lies in this constant, disrespectful, and creative displacement.

Notes

1. Lawrence Durrell and Robin Fedden, *Personal Landscape: An Anthology of Exile*, London: Editions Poetry Limited, 1945. See Roger Bowen, *Many Histories Deep: The Personal Landscape Poets in Egypt, 1940–45*, Madison: Fairleigh Dickinson University Press, 1995, and Jonathan Bolton, *Personal Landscapes: British Poets in Egypt during the Second World War*, London: Macmillan Press, 1997.
2. "I remember her sitting before the multiple mirrors at the dressmaker's . . . and saying: 'Look! Five different pictures of the same object. Now if I wrote I would try for a multi-dimensional effect in character, a sort of prism-sightedness," Lawrence Durrell, *The Alexandria Quartet*, London: Faber, 1974 (first published in 1962), p. 28.
3. Lawrence Durrell, *Cities, Plains and People*, London: Faber, 1946, p. 7.
4. *Cities, Plains and People*, p. 7.
5. Lawrence Durrell, *Collected Poems 1931–1974*, London: Faber, 1985 (first published in 1980), p. 107. This only appears in the complete volume of Durrell's poems and was not included in *A Private Country* in 1944.
6. "The Anecdotes," "XIII In Paris," Lawrence Durrell, *On Seeming to Presume*, London: Faber, 1948, p. 55. 1.) Many other invocations to Melissa can be found in the sixteen fragments composing this long poem.
7. *Cities, Plains and People*, p. 8.
8. *Cities, Plains and People*, p. 9.
9. *Cities, Plains and People*, p. 12.
10. See *The Alexandria Quartet*, pp. 833–34.
11. *Cities, Plains and People*, p. 9.
12. *Cities, Plains and People*, p. 9.
13. *Cities, Plains and People*, p. 9.
14. Edgar Morin, *Amour, Poésie, Sagesse*, Paris: Seuil, 1997, pp. 9–10.
15. *Cities, Plains and People*, p. 12.
16. *Cities, Plains and People*, p. 9.
17. *Cities, Plains and People*, p. 10.
18. *Cities, Plains and People*, p. 10.
19. *Cities, Plains and People*, p. 10.
20. *Cities, Plains and People*, p. 10.
21. *Cities, Plains and People*, p. 10.
22. *Cities, Plains and People*, p. 10.
23. "Ideas about Poems," *Personal Landscape: An Anthology of Exile*, p. 72.
24. "Mathaios Pascalis His Ideas about Poems," in *Personal Landscape*, p. 78.
25. "Je dis: une fleur! et, hors de l'oubli où ma voix relègue aucun contour, en tant que quelque chose d'autre que les calices sus, musicalement se lève, idée même et suave, l'absente de tous bouquets," Stéphane Mallarmé, *Avant-dire au* Traité du verbe de René Ghil (1886), *Œuvres complètes*, Paris: Gallimard, 1945, pp. 857–58.
26. Yves Bonnefoy, "La Poésie objective," *Two Cities*, Paris: May 1960, p. 8.
27. "La Poésie objective," pp. 9–10.

28. Pierre Jourde, "Nerval, la voix, l'irreprésentable," *De l'irreprésentable en littérature*, Jean-Marc Houpert, Paule Petitier (dir.), Paris: L'Harmattan, 2001, p. 155.
29. *Cities, Plains and People*, p. 13.
30. *Cities, Plains and People*, p. 16.
31. The verb "rise," placed at strategic points within the prosodic pattern of the two poems, emphasizes the carnal and symbolic essence of begetting.
32. "Ideas about Poems" in *Personal Landscape*, p. 73.
33. Corinthians 13: 12.
34. William Shakespeare, *Hamlet*, act 2, scene 1.
35. "Entretien avec Benoît Conort," in Jean-Michel Maupoix (ed.), *La Poésie pour quoi faire? Une enquête*, Paris: Presses Universitaires de Paris Ouest, 2011, p. 19.
36. "Love Poems," in *Collected Poems*, p. 39.
37. *Cities, Plains and People*, p. 17.
38. Lawrence Durrell, *The Red Limbo Lingo*, London: Faber, 1971, p. 43.
39. *On Seeming to Presume*, p. 50.
40. *Collected Poems*, p. 204.
41. "Ideas about Poems" in *Personal Landscape*, p. 72.
42. See T. S. Eliot's "In my beginning is my end," "East Coker," *Four Quartets, Collected Poems 1909–1962*, London: Faber, 2002, p. 184.
43. "Burnt Norton," *Four Quartets, Collected Poems 1909–1962*, p. 178.
44. *Collected Poems*, p. 18.
45. *Collected Poems*, p. 18.
46. *Collected Poems*, p. 19.
47. *Collected Poems*, p. 19.
48. *Collected Poems*, p. 19.
49. Otto Rank, *Art and Artist*, New York: Norton, 1989 (first published in 1932), p. xxxvii.
50. Lawrence Durrell, *Pied Piper of Lovers*, James Gifford, ed., Victoria, Canada: ELS editions, 2008 (first published in 1935), p. 49.
51. The choice of such a violent image in a poem addressed to a little girl is obviously meant to shock the reader out of his or her comfortable assumptions, thus leading him to question the very title and to sense the darker side of the image of childhood that will be developed in "For a Nursery Mirror."
52. Lawrence Durrell, *A Private Country*, London: Faber, 1944 (first published in 1943), p. 49.
53. *A Private Country*, p. 71.
54. Lawrence Durrell, *Panic Spring, A Romance*, Victoria, Canada: ELS editions, 2008, p. 74.
55. Michel Deguy, *L'énergie du désespoir ou d'une poétique continuée par tous les moyens*, Paris: PUF, 1998, p. 2.
56. *La Poésie pour quoi faire?*, pp. 31–32.
57. *Pied Piper of Lovers*, p. 1.

58. Plato, *Timaeus* [52a–52d], *Plato in Twelve Volumes*, vol. 9, translated by W. R. M. Lamb, Cambridge, MA: Harvard University Press; London: William Heinemann Ltd., 1925.

59. Hamlet, act 5, scene 1, l.177, p. 329.

60. Lawrence Durrell, *Sappho*, London: Faber, 1967 (first published in 1950), scene 3, p. 83.

61. Corinne Alexandre-Garner, *Lawrence Durrell: Dans l'ombre du soleil grec*, Paris: La Quinzaine Littéraire, Louis Vuitton, 2012, p. 25.

62. *La Poésie pour quoi faire?* p. 31.

63. *Cities, Plains and People*, p. 29.

64. *A Private Country*, p. 72.

65. Lawrence Durrell, *Reflections on a Marine Venus*, London: Faber, 1953, p. 183.

66. *Cities, Plains and People*, pp. 27–30.

67. *Cities, Plains and People*, p. 30.

68. *Cities, Plains and People*, p. 72.

69. *Cities, Plains and People*, p. 57.

70. T. S. Eliot's "East Coker," *Four Quartets, Collected Poems 1909–1962*, p. 184.

71. *Cities, Plains and People*, p. 57.

72. *Cities, Plains and People*, p. 70.

73. *Cities, Plains and People*, p. 70.

74. "Echoes I," first published in *Quaint Fragments*, 1931. *Collected Poems*, p. 21.

75. *Cities, Plains and People*, p. 58.

76. *Cities, Plains and People*, p. 58.

77. T. S. Eliot, "The Wasteland," in *Collected Poems 1909–1962*, London: Faber, 2002, p. 63.

78. C. Alexandre-Garner, I. Keller-Privat Isabelle, "When Elsewhere Is Home: Mapping Literature as Home in Lawrence Durrell's 'Cities, Plains and People,'" *Études Britanniques Contemporaines* no. 37, December 2009, pp. 83–84.

79. *Art and Artist*, pp. 416–17.

80. *Cities, Plains and People*, p. 17.

81. Michel de Montaigne, *Essais*, Livre I, Chapitre XXVIII, in *Œuvres complètes*, Paris: Gallimard, 1962, p. 181.

82. "Conon in Exile," in *A Private Country*, pp. 51–52.

83. *Personal Landscape*, p. 6.

84. "Freedom" appears in an edition of *Selected Poems* in 1956 and in 1964 as well as in the *Collected Poems* in 1960 and in 1985. The poem is also taken up in a series of audio recordings issued by Argo Record Co. Ltd. in 1962 with the title *The Love Poems of Lawrence Durrell*, among which Durrell has also recorded his reading of "Water Music," "Episode," "By the Lake," "A Portrait Theodora," "Conon in Exile," "To Ping-kû Asleep," "Cradle Song," "Heloise and Abelard," "John Donne," "La Rochefoucauld," "Poggio," "Levant," "Alexandria," "The Anecdotes," "Song of Zarathustra," "Ballad of the Oedipus Complex," "A Ballad of the Good Lord Nelson," "Ballad of Psychoanalysis," and "Bitter Lemons."

85. *Sappho*, scene 2, p. 69.
86. Suzuki, *Essais sur le Bouddhisme Zen*, Paris: Albin Michel, 2003, p. 296, note (1), 102.
87. *The Complete Works of Chuang Tzu*, New York: Columbia University Press, 1968, pp. 43–44.
88. Lawrence Durrell, *Prospero's Cell: A Guide to the Landscape and Manners of the Island of Corfu*, London: Faber, 1962, p. 20.
89. *A Private Country*, p. 14.
90. *Cities, Plains and People*, p. 33.
91. *Cities, Plains and People*, p. 33.
92. Earl Ingersoll, ed., *Lawrence Durrell: Conversations*, Madison: Fairleigh Dickinson University Press, 1998. p. 63.
93. *Cities, Plains and People*, p. 33.
94. *Cities, Plains and People*, p. 34.
95. *Cities, Plains and People*, p. 34.
96. *Cities, Plains and People*, p. 34.
97. Jean-Luc Nancy, *Résistance de la poésie*, Bordeaux: William Blake & Co., 2004, p. 11.
98. *Résistance de la poésie*, p. 11.
99. *Cities, Plains and People*, pp. 49–51.
100. Roger Bowen, *Many Histories Deep: The Personal Landscape Poets in Egypt, 1940–45*, p. 150.
101. *Many Histories Deep: The Personal Landscape Poets in Egypt, 1940–45*, p. 33.
102. *Cities, Plains and People*, p. 49.
103. "I. The Burial of the Dead," *The Waste Land* in *Collected Poems 1909–1962*, p. 53
104. "East Coker," *Four Quartets* in *Collected Poems 1909–1962*, p. 184.
105. "He raises up the poor out of the dust, and lifts the needy out of the ash heap," 1 Samuel 2: 8.
106. "He raiseth up the poor out of the dust, and lifteth the needy out of the dunghill," Psalms 113: 7.
107. *Cities, Plains and People*, p. 52.
108. *Cities, Plains and People*, p. 49.
109. *Cities, Plains and People*, p. 50.
110. *Cities, Plains and People*, p. 50.
111. *Cities, Plains and People*, p. 50.
112. See the dialogues between Blan and Sut and the mirror of textual columns in *Quinx* (Lawrence Durrell, *The Avignon Quintet*, London: Faber, 1992, pp. 1187–91).
113. *Cities, Plains and People*, p. 51.
114. Georges Didi-Huberman, *L'Homme qui marchait dans la couleur*, Paris: éditions de Minuit, 2001, p. 11.
115. *Cities, Plains and People*, p. 51.
116. *Cities, Plains and People*, p. 34.

117. *Essais sur le Bouddhisme Zen*, 61.
118. *Cities, Plains and People*, p. 51.
119. *Cities, Plains and People*, p. 49.
120. Paul Valéry, *Charmes, Œuvres I*, Paris: Gallimard, 1957, p. 151. This is not the only intertextual encounter with Valéry's "Cimetière Marin," as we shall see later in our study of "Mistral" in chapter 6. Durrell's admiration for the French poet is well known; he even compared him to Seferis: "Basically Valéry is very close to Seferis. It's the gnomic quality, the density." In the same interview he drew a parallel between his own writing strategies and Valéry's: "I was a terrific word-hunter, an avid collector of images before the Eternal. But I was like Valéry when it came to the first line, 'the gift of the gods.' I would often have to wait ages for it"; "Listening for the novel's fetal heartbeat," interview with Marc Alyn 1972, *Conversations*, pp. 142, 147.
121. This poem, whose title is evocative of Haendel's three orchestral suites composed between 1717 and 1736, is part of the series of recordings read by Lawrence Durrell and published by Argo Record Co. Ltd. in 1962 under the title *The Love Poems of Lawrence Durrell*.
122. *Résistance de la poésie*, p. 14.
123. *A Private Country*, p. 12.
124. Jacques Derrida, *Of Grammatology*, Baltimore: Johns Hopkins University Press, 1998, p. 22.
125. Christian Doumet, *Faut-il comprendre la poésie?* Paris: Klincksieck, 2004, p. 40.
126. Sacheverell Sitwell, *Agamemnon's Tomb*, Edinburgh: The Tragara Press, 1972, [n.p.].
127. *A Private Country*, p. 25.
128. *Reflections on a Marine Venus*, pp. 122–23.
129. Gaston Bachelard, *L'Intuition de l'instant*, Paris: Stock, 1931, pp. 104–5.
130. *Cities, Plains and People*, p. 53.
131. *Cities, Plains and People*, p. 53.
132. Jonathan Bolton explained: "As Durrell later wrote: 'We artists are not interested in policies but in values—this is our field of battle.' [*Clea*, 760] And that is the field of battle he enters in 'Near El Alamein,' fully determined to ensure that such values as love, imagination, and the idea of things do not become casualties of war." *Personal Landscape*, p. 40. In his introduction to *Return to Oasis: War Poems and Recollections from the Middle-East 1940–1946*, Lawrence Durrell analyzes "the temper of those times when poetry counted so very much.... It was not a question of morale, it was literally a question of spiritual survival. In this context even the war had its uses" (pp. xxvi–xxvii).
133. *Cities, Plains and People*, p. 54.
134. See *Monsieur*, "The sand of the desert could have been snow" (*The Avignon Quintet*, 112); *Constance*, "[the desert] as much an entity as the Atlantic" (650); and *Sebastian*, "the uncompromising sea of sand curling and flowing away into the empty sky" (1022).

CHAPTER THREE

On Seeming to Presume
The Dream of a Secret Belonging

On Seeming to Presume resorts to the same technique as *Cities, Plains and People*: it bears the title of an eponymous poem that appears this time not at the end but at the center of the collection, which opens up like an Eastern diptych. Although published in 1948, it was written in October 1946 and traveled several times to and back from Faber, where T. S. Eliot made the final corrections on the last manuscript sent from Buenos Aires in January 1948. "On Seeming to Presume is now a good job, likely to promote the Durrell reputation,"[1] he concluded in his last letter to Durrell. "Green Coconuts: Rio" and "Christ in Brazil" were written in Argentina, but the greater part of the poems was composed in Greece.

As opposed to the coming years during which the poet's creative urge was undermined by depression, *On Seeming to Presume* belongs to a remarkably fertile era. Durrell's artistic and personal development expressed itself through various forms: poetry, fiction, residence writing, and drama. And just as he was simultaneously writing his poems, his "labyrinth book,"[2] *Cefalu*, his second island book, *Reflections on a Marine Venus*, and his first play, *Sappho*, he was also exploring diverse artistic media, such as watercolor and pottery, which he practiced when he was not writing, or poring over the archaeological, geological, and political past of the island. Rhodes can thus be considered as the crucible of a personal and artistic fulfillment that will leave a lasting imprint upon Durrell's work where the visual and the tactile blend, turning the artist's language into a place of encounters where even linguistic boundaries are transcended: "I am beginning to write little things in French now, and in Greek. I feel a wonderful fluency,"[3] he gleefully exclaimed to Henry Miller. As a child in India Durrell had already experienced the sense of innate fluency that a polyglot environment fosters as he was simultaneously learning English as well as Hindi and Urdu with the "ayah" who looked after him. He recovers in Rhodes the trilingual dwelling of the world, which he equates with completeness. Moreover, unlike *A Private Country* and *Cities, Plains and People*, both achieved when Durrell was in exile, *On Seeming to Presume* revels from beginning to end in the Greek light that first struck Durrell when he reached the island in January 1946 and gave rise to one of his most poetic letters to Henry Miller where writing vies with painting:

> I've just come back from Patmos where Cohen and I spent Xmas with Father Porphirios. . . . Shattering whiteness and play of light. Like stepping into the silver of a mirror, or into the heart of a crystal. . . . While we were sitting talking to the Abbot . . . the sky slowly darkened, swelled, became bitumen grey and then black with clouds; the sea like a lake of pitch. It was like a chapter from the Apocalypse. Then the rain broke green from rents in the cloud, breaking open pencils of light which played on the darkness like the beam of searchlights in close focus. Strange moving pencils of green rain racing across the sea like fingers.[4]

"The heart of a crystal" inevitably brings us back to the "dark crystal" in the residence book *Prospero's Cell* and in "Letter to Seferis the Greek,"[5] the penultimate poem in *A Private Country*. The poet is thus reborn in the literary and symbolic place of writing, which nurtures a synaesthetic awareness to the world, as expressed in another letter to Miller: "Life at times begins to get its old prismatic hue."[6] Unsurprisingly, this correspondence reads as an ode to the island that will shape Durrell's subsequent writing. This explains the odd familiarity one experiences when reading the hypotyposis of the harbor of Alexandria lit up by the flare of the bombs in *The Alexandria Quartet*. The "pencils of light"[7] turn into "white fingers of powder-white light"[8] and sketch out another Apocalypse: "It had begun to swell up, to expand like some mystical rose [. . .] We were staring at the burning embers of Augustine's Carthage, I thought to myself, we are observing the fall of city man."[9] Not unlike the island, the city inflates and irradiates, shimmering upon our retina like an unearthly vision, before it returns to the world of myths that bore it.

Rhodes: The Land of Epiphany

Just like Alexandria prophetically blooming in the glare of war, the isle of Patmos opens the collection upon a terrifying and dazzling revelation that will never cease to haunt the poet and resurfaces some thirty years later in the prose of *The Greek Islands*:

> The punch-drunk numerologist who gave us this magnificent doom-laden poem is said to have conceived and executed it in a cave, over which stands now a chapel dedicated to St Anne and the Apocalypse. . . . The wind howls outside and, inside the dark-rock chamber, you hear the mountain teeming with invisible springs, the noise of water everywhere macerating pebbles, the drip, drip of rain at the entrance. . . . Pencils of white light moved about the sky like searchlights in the pitch-dark afternoon. . . . It is all painted stark white, and the towers and steeples are patterned in cubist motifs of great beauty . . . [10]

The first page of this Rhodian collection guides the reader toward the eternal beauty of "The Island of the Rose," which Durrell will never cease to praise.[11] However, the poem discloses a temporal shift through which the landscape does not arise out of the stormy light of early evening but at dawn, the better to signal the start of a new writing born from the harmonious welding of space and time:

> Early one morning unremarked
> She walked abroad to see
> Black bitumen and roses
> Upon the island shelf[12]

The "bitumen grey"[13] of the sky in Durrell's letter to Miller has turned black, as if to sharpen contrasts, and pave the way for a sensorial experience through which visual notations progressively give way to auditory and tactile ones. The first and the second stanzas hinge on the echo between the song of thrushes and that of the larks "from the Grecian meadows," as if to materialize the distance between the austere cliffs and the fertile hinterland where the music of life flows "Like semen from the grape." Patmos stands for the oblique angle wherefrom Durrell reenters the "renewed landscape" of Greece and reasserts the necessary slanting perspective through which writing transmutes geography into a creative space. Indeed Patmos, although it is part of the Southern Sporades, stands out as a unique, self-contained island, at odds with the Greek world, as Durrell explains in *The Greek Islands*:

> The most northerly, and in a queer sort of way the most anomalous, of the group is Patmos, which lies like a tortoise in a spatter of atolls . . . What makes it seem strange is that it is wholly a Christian land, with no whiff of ancient Greece about it.[14]

The first stanza stages a world apart through the image of the thrushes locked in their solitary chant, like John of Patmos in a prophecy that is forever coming:

> Thrushes repeat their clauses
> From some corruptible tree
> All copied in herself.

The song of birds conspires with water music to offer to the persona of the poem a new road that stretches across the sea, in the void left by the two stanzas that, although separated by a full stop, are syntactically and semantically linked by the temporal clause:

> When from the Grecian meadows
> Responsive rose the larks,
> Stiffly as if on strings,
> Ebbing, drew thin as tops
> While each in rising squeezed
> His spire of singing drops
> On that renewed landscape
> Like semen from the grape.

The rhythm of the sea ("Ebbing") and of the rain ("singing drops") joins the earth and the sky, suggesting an ascending movement through which the poem turns into a vision. The voice of the poem echoes like a prophecy metamorphosing the mundane into a pure, ethereal line that rises toward a fruitful beyond. Run-on lines, alliterations, and assonances accompany the soaring birds that fade "thin as tops," suggesting both their vertical momentum and their surreal union with that part of a volatile liquid mixture that distills first—the chemical meaning of "top." The melodic line transmutes into a celestial vision that, like St. John's, announces "a new heaven and a new earth."[15]

Therefore, Rhodes belongs to a mystical land that resorts to biblical symbolism to point toward a revelation that is not a religious but a sensual and spiritual one. The anonymous "She," like Melissa in the previous collection, materializes a subject inhabited by a poetic grace that opens up a new Eden in the margins of the world that is the poet's true I/land. The residence book makes the symbolic reality of Rhodes explicit: "Patmos, I thought, was more an idea than a place, more a symbol than an Island. . . . Some day I shall find the right way of dealing with it in words. . . ."[16] Only through poetry can Durrell summon the Platonic idea Rhodes stands for. "Patmos" is thus to be read as a key Durrell gives us at the onset of the collection to unlock the world of poetic creation.

This initial and initiatory poem foreshadows "In the Garden: Villa Cleobolus," which opens up the second half of the diptych, right after the eponymous poem. The poem harbors in its folds the symbolic and prophetic inklings that Durrell will deploy five years later in *Reflections on a Marine Venus* in the chapter "In the Garden of Villa Cleobolus." The title of the poem points to the paring down of language through the substitution of the colon for the preposition, which is evocative of the strength of poetic language dismantling the syntax to produce a visual and rhythmic echo that defeats the logic of belonging. The semantic suspense induced by the mirroring pattern suggests the central place devoted to the Garden. The progressive displacement of the villa, which gives way to an all-encompassing garden dissolving man-made boundaries in the embrace of its luxurious curves, foreshadows the later prose:

> so dense is the packing of oleanders and small pines and so heavy the shadow in which the house is set that sound itself becomes blurred and mingles with the hushing of the sea along the beaches eastward [. . .] Presently the servant comes swaying down the dark path with a rosy branch of candles shielded in the coarse red coral of her hand: to sweep up the ash-tray and discarded books and set out supper-places.[17]

Interestingly, the poem comes before the prose and explores the palpable density of silence, revealing a synaesthetic world in which olfaction, our most spontaneous and uncontrollable sense, comes to the fore and endows inanimate objects with a haptic presence:

> Mixtures of this garden
> Conduct at night the pine and oleander
> Perhaps married to dust's thin edge
> Or lime where the cork-tree rubs
> The quiet house, bruising the wall:

The garden and the house face one another at each end of the first stanza and delicately meet through the run-on line that fleetingly joins dust and lime. The subtle overlapping of disintegrated and solid matter, just as that of the vegetal (cork) and the mineral (wall), of visual, olfactory, auditory, and tactile sensations suggest the symbolic potency of "the quiet house, bruising the wall" materializing the unaccountable pain of dwelling. The colons of the final line ushering in the second, shorter stanza belie the anxiety haunting the poetic voice. The ample breathing of the sentence, unfolding over five irregular stanzas, and concluding on a series of interrogatives, is mimetic of the poet's desire and inability to enfold a world that will perpetually evade his grasp. Adding a temporal dimension to the poem, the second stanza dramatizes the urge to resist the onrush of time that the servant's arrival forebodes:

> And dense the block of thrush's notes
> Press like a bulb and keeping time
> In this exposure to the leaves,
> And as we wait the servant comes,

The conjunction "and," the postponed verb, and the atemporal present participle blow up the sequence that is abruptly ended in the last line where the servant's interruption heralds the passage from dusk to night. The time dimension introduced by the servant coincides with a delicate painting that calls for sharpened sensations: the fragile light of the candle heralds the substitution of auditory perceptions for the more rational visual ones, just as the closed books pave the way for more intimate questionings.

Like a Greek vestal, the servant moves through a garden that is progressively reconfigured as a temple where every object acquires a symbolic meaning and an intense presence that sets it apart from everyday reality. She symbolically stands at the junction between light and darkness, between inside and outside, the known and the unknown, the memory and the dream:

> Brings with her from the uninhabited
> Frontiers of the darkness to the known
> Table and tree and chair
> Some half-remembered passage from a fugue

The run-on lines creating a semantic link and a prosodic gap between "uninhabited" and "Frontiers," just as the symmetrical pairing of "the darkness" and "the known" on the same line, evoke the amphibological essence of frontiers in Durrell's work: they partake of the known and the unknown, they operate as a threshold opening up dark spaces of inquiry, anxiety, and desire that utterly transform the subject. Writing "for the dead and the unborn,"[18] as Pursewarden says in *The Alexandria Quartet*, the poet also writes from this unchartered frontier land where he locates his true bearings. This is why the table, the tree, and the chair exist on an immemorial and symbolic plane: they are objects abstracted from matter through the process of poetic disfiguration analyzed by Christian Doumet—"To disfigure would thus mean to free things from figuration, to restore them to their mobile existence which replaces in them the assertion of being by the questioning of being."[19] Far from the mimetic representation of the lost garden of the past, and hence, from the narrative of *Reflections on a Marine Venus*, the poem steers away from the mere naming of things to question their essence, as fickle and labile as "Some half-remembered passage from a fugue." The isotopy of music introduces the shift from the assertive to the questioning mode in the ensuing stanzas where verbs of action in the present tense and run-on lines transform the Wordsworthian "tranquil restoration"[20] into an untranquil exploration "into the life of things":[21]

> And you think: if given once
> Authority over the word
> Then how to capture, praise or measure
> The full round of this simple garden,
> All its nonchalance at being,
> How to adopt and raise its pleasure?

Just as in the end of the first stanza, the colons herald a new line of thought that shatters the dominant assertive mode. The poetic voice announces its incapacity to circumscribe an almost divine "word," which rejects the fetters of syntactic and semantic logic and summons within the secluded space of the garden the infinite realm of idleness and plenitude that evades the grasp of the world of action. The three infinitives "capture, praise or measure" amount to a negative definition of poetry by naming what it is not: neither capture, nor praise, nor measure of a lost time and space, but rather, the intimate progress out and toward himself of a subject placed under the spell of "The full round of this simple garden." Thus, the poet opts for minimal action that borders on contemplation and enables him to relish time and space like a fruit:

> Press as on a palate this observed
> And simple shape, like wine?
> And from the many undeserved
> Tastes of the mouth select the crude
> Flavour of fruit in pottery
> Coloured among this lovely neighbourhood?

We are reminded here of Durrell's pottery artifact that served then as tableware in the villa Cleobolus but, more importantly, of the fruit of knowledge the poet yearns for, a metaphysical "treasure" that cannot be "Confined within the loving chamber of a form, / Within a poem locked."[22] It belongs to this "Beyond" that symbolically introduces the penultimate stanza and heralds the new horizon toward which the last lines tentatively reach out:

> Perhaps not this: but somehow, yes,
> To outflank the personal neurasthenia
> That lies beyond in each expiring kiss:
> Bring joy, as lustrous on this dish
> The painted dancers motionless in play
> Spin for eternity, describing for us all
> The natural history of the human wish

This last stanza, where the first pair of colons makes way for the hesitating voice of the persona, while the second pair creates a syntactic and semantic rift, reads as an ode to the fragmented and unstable nature of the poetic search. Indeed the ambiguity of the grammatical mode of the verb "bring" leaves room for two possible interpretations: one can either read it as an infinitive following "To outflank" or as an imperative suggesting a new departure. In the first case, the two infinitive clauses are devoid of a main clause; in the second case, the addressee of the imperative form remains eternally absent. Is the injunction meant for the reader, or the poet, or both of them? Unless it were a plea aimed at the landscape? The answer matters less than the question. The dismantled syntax destroys mimetic representations of, and responses to, the world and allows for the rise of a context-free vision. "The painted dancers motionless in play / Spin for eternity" beyond the rim of the dish, beyond the embrace of the lovers: they are the visual materialization of an immaterial dance that escapes the potter's wheel, the symbolic lines that point to an unachieved earthly harmony where the flesh of the world is recast. One recognizes here the hand of John Keats and understands the palimpsestuous and rebellious essence of this second Genesis. Indeed, the poem simultaneously summons the Great Masters and breaks free from them in a prosodic and syntactic form that evinces a fundamental openness to tonal modulations by allowing for infinite interferences and disruptions. The joint presence of music, pottery, and dance—of the auditory, the tangible, and the ethereal—molds a new reality where matter and abstraction meet, converting the surface plane of the vision into the tridimensional plane of experience: that of "the human wish."

The Black Pearl of Writing

In Durrell's poetry "the human wish" is the touchstone of our humanity and belies the omnipresent awareness of a founding loss. Although he is enjoying to the full the poetic fertility Rhodes fosters, "the personal neurasthenia"[23] is lying in wait, secretly preying upon every kiss so that the precious pearl of writing is inseparable from the intense pain that haunts the poet's work, as his letter to Henry Miller evinces:

> Guess I haven't got over the loss of *my* small daughter yet—that's the real *crux*. However we compose ourselves slowly around our pains like the oyster round the grains of sand—and out of it come pearls, black pearls—in the case of the oyster at any rate. So far I have shed only pus and lymph these six years, but the pearl is forming. I feel it.[24]

The diptych pattern that structures the collection throws the reader into a complex Greece that both contrasts and joins opposite images, such as those of "Patmos" at the onset of the first half of the collection and that of "The Lost Cities" in the second half. Through the simultaneous conjunction and disjunction of the two poems that mirror each other like two hinged panels, the poet allows us to touch "this painful contact point between outer reality and human conscience,"[25] which is, according to Pierre Reverdy, the true source of poetry. "The Lost Cities" foreshadows those of the fourth chapter of *Reflections on a Marine Venus*, entitled "The Three Lost Cities,"[26] where the narrator describes the ancient cities Ialysos—whose name has become Phileremo—Cameirus, and Lindos. However, a comparative reading shows that the cities described in the narrative both *do* and do *not* resemble those of the poem. The inscription "(for Paddy and Xan)" seems to refer to the characters of *Reflections on a Marine Venus* where a footnote explains:

> The bat infested underground water-conduits of Cameirus I never had the courage to explore until one memorable day when Paddy and Xan and the Corn Goddess shamed me into following them down its dark tunnels.[27]

The poem might thus be interpreted as the nondiscursive refraction of this travel experience, leading the reader to feel rather than to follow the poet's slow transformation as he progresses through this underground maze. But the labyrinth conjured up in the poem proves to be a radically different one in which the reader loses both his geographic and textual bearings:

> One she floats as Venice might,
> Bloated among her ambiguities:
> What hebetude or carelessness shored up
> Goths were not smart enough to capture.
> The city, yes: the water: not the style.

> Her dispossession now may seem to us
> Idle and ridiculous, quivering
> In the swollen woodwork of these
> Floating carcases of the doges,
> Dissolving into spires and cages of water:
> Venice blown up, and turning green.

Where we expected a Greek town, we are given Venice, a displacement that heralds that of the incipit of *Bitter Lemons* where Venice is both displaced and disfigured:

> Cloud and water mixed into each other, dripping with colours, merging, overlapping, liquefying, with steeples and balconies and roofs floating in space, like the fragments of some stained-glass window seen through a dozen veils of rice-paper. [. . .] The glass palaces of the Doges are being pounded in a crystal mortar, strained through a prism.[28]

This displacement, which is characteristic of Durrell's entire oeuvre, operates in a different way in both cases. Whereas *Bitter Lemons* staged Venice as a threshold paving the way for the narrator's sea voyage and playfully disfigured a recurrent literary and pictorial *topos* in travel literature, the poem turns Venice into a screen. The hypertrophied city in the first stanza paves the way for the metaphor in the second where Venice becomes a piece of rotten flotsam, a pale echo to "the ship's huge shadow"[29] in "The Rime," and utterly dissolves to swallow Cameirus, which becomes invisible. We are left with the distorting prism of a "floating" city that evades the poet's grasp, just as the lost cities have evaded the traveler's, who can only describe the surface city where the yawning chasms suggest unfathomable depths:

> It lies there in the honey-gold afternoon light listening to the melodious ringing of water in its own cisterns [. . .]
> In the silence we could hear the water gurgling somewhere down there, below the earth. An owl whistled once, twice, and we heard its creaking flight from one tree to another, like the rustle of a linen skirt.[30]

The poetic prose of the narrative does not so much reveal the object of the poem as its symbolic echo. Space is indeed materialized through what it cannot contain: the music of water and birds that, although they belong to the place, float free, unattached, and open the doors of anamnesis. The sunken city of the prose is not to be watched but rather to be listened to as the soft lapping of its secret streams bathes the channels of personal memories.

The superimposed cities, far from leading to a new composition, amount to the disintegration of the object of the poem: "swollen woodwork," "floating carcases," "Venice blown up, and turning green" turn the reader's gaze toward the process of decomposition, away from the cities, suggesting the overpowering work of time upon space and matter and the poet's inability to capture reality before its dissolution. Cameirus is not even named, just as the city in the third stanza, although the "red wells" and "the potter's thumb" remind one of the red clay and antique artifacts of Ialysos.[31] Significantly, the following stanza is dedicated to Carthage, the epitome of urban annihilation, as if to remind the reader that the poem is not so much about "cities" as about the experience of their loss. Though these cities are often deprived of a name and of their very existence, the poem explores the process of disappearance and fragmentary emergence, which is at the root of the disfiguration through which the poet tears things and beings away from their realistic anchorage. In so doing, he allows them to float free from autobiographic, geographic, or logical discourse and established unexpected relations between apparently disjointed space-times. This is how "The Lost Cities" progressively metamorphoses into a meditation upon the transient essence of cities and the frailty of man's grasp upon matter, substituting a secret and intimate place for our hackneyed common place:

> That fluent thumb which presses
> On history's vibrating string,
> Pressing here, there, in a wounded place.

The repetition of "press" and the jerky rhythm of the last line mold the very matter of the stanza. The "fluent thumb" is both that of the ancient potter and of the poet who signals in the "vibrating string" of history the shifting focus from the lost cities to the cities of loss until their disappearance illuminates the writing process:

> 'No wonder. A river once turned over
> In its sleep and all the cities fled.'

The unidentified voice musing upon "A few drops of ink or salt" opens the poem to the persona's inner voice, foreshadowing the dried-up rivers of one of the last poems:

> The big rivers are through with me, I guess;
> . . .

> Yes, the big rivers, except the one of sorrows
> Which winds to forts of calm where dust rebukes
> The vagaries of minds in silent poses.[32]

The river veering away from the city and from life is the very same one encountered thirty years later and whose slow parting stretches across time and space, whether that of "Greece which is not yet Greece" in "The Lost Cities," or that of the Thames, the Nile, or "black Brahmaputra" in "Last Heard Of." The unhurried shifting waters draw a disfigured space-time where geographic and temporal landmarks merge and vanish, where memory takes refuge in inanimate objects: "This orchard, painted tables set outside / A whitewashed house, / And on the rusty nail a violin."

Space is thus reconfigured as what Christian Doumet calls "a sound-matter extracted from a psychic geography":

> The word is not a concretion of erudite memory, but a nebula of affects: it returns to what it probably was when it first appeared to us. . . . Language recognizes itself both as a common ground for exchange *and* as an unnamable substratum.[33]

The fifth stanza conjures up this "unnamable substratum" through daily objects that only exist inasmuch as they belong to "a psychic geography," free from any real city, while delineating the poet's only living reality, left unspoiled by "the devastator," "uncherished by its tenants" but that inhabits poetry. As the city vanishes, the poet is left with the ultimate inanimate object: "Rhodes, death-mask of a Greek town." The singled-out last line, expelled from the body of the poem, characterizes poetry as the place where death and survival meet, as a crossroads where the poet faces his own mortal nature and leaves the reader with the immortal shapes of death. Rhodes carved out, seen as a shared funeral object, an object of remembrance that, like any ancient tragic mask, is made to be exchanged, invites us to reflect upon the traces of eternity imprinted upon our mortal civilization. Interestingly, *Reflections on a Marine Venus* points toward the unnamable that the poetic experience throws us into: "It is as if you had been leaning against a door leading to a poem when suddenly it swung open letting you stumble directly into the heart of it."[34] Such is the door that the poem attempts to open: the intensive resurrection of a sensible experience that defies time and marries the finite and the infinite. Rhodes stands out at the heart of the collection as the emblematic "wounded space" of an inner voyage that projects poet and reader into unchartered territory.

Founding a New World

The metamorphosis of Rhodes is further developed in "Rodini," "Phileremo," and "The Parthenon." The central question to "Rodini"—"Is there enough perhaps to found a world?"—sums up the essence of the poet's inquiry and of his problematic relationship to space. This particular poem addresses the founding of a new world where "Rodini" looms up like a still life from the first line—"Windless plane-trees above Rodini"—to the last one—"we lie under the windless planes." The immobile landscape is mirrored by a motionless, passive subject who, once tempted by "the pencil or the eye," opts for inaction. The landscape thus becomes the only active subject:

> Where of late trees have become ears in leaf
> Curved for the cicada's first monotony
>
> Hollow the comb mellow the sweetness
> Amber the honey-spoil, drink, drink.[35]

Inanimate and animate patterns mirror one another in a world devoid of human authority and refract the musical and gustatory harmony of a language that plays on run-on lines, symmetry, alliterations, and onomatopoeias to hint at the inner consonance that springs from silence:

> In these windless unechoing valleys
> The mind slips like a chisel-hand
>
> Touching the surface of this clement blue

Penetrating the world of silence allows the mind to approach the impalpable, the "clement" horizon that is the realm of tapering trees, before plunging into the disorderly one of human solitude: "The same disorder and the loneliness— / The what-we-have-in-common of us all." "Rodini" is the space where Durrell attempts to solve this dichotomy, as he explains later on in *Reflections*:

> In their star-dances savages try to unite their lives to those of the heavenly bodies—to mix their quotidian rhythms into those great currents which keep the wheels of the universe turning. Poetry attempts to provide much the same sort of link between the muddled inner man with his temporal preoccupations and the uniform flow of the universe outside.[36]

In order to do so he conjures up an unruffled landscape ("windless," "unechoing," "odourless") within which the only moving spirit would belong to a human being who has freed himself from the binary opposition between mind and body in order to become the very "chisel-hand / Touching the surface of this clement blue." The conversational tone of the fragmentary dialogue in the second half of the poem creates an enunciative rift, amplifying the world of disorder heralded by the disjunctive dash at the end of stanza 6. However, the twelve unrhymed couplets sketch out a cyclic pattern that transcends its inner breaches: the heteroclite composition of the compound noun in "The what-we-have-in-common of us all" creates a common subject made of heterogeneous, floating entities—the community of potential poets—while the mysterious addressee in "of what you said once" conflates with the enthralling vision of the "dark hair with its sudden theft / Of blue from the darkness of violets" where the human and the vegetal, the earth and the sky are joined. Durrell's poem illustrates what Jean-Christophe Bailly calls "the pronominal scene" by building up an addressee, a "you," and a community, a "we," made of indistinct, "insular and protean"[37] beings that compose an ideal, inclusive community that does not imprison the subject but instead confronts it to the Other. The second-person and first-person plural in the poem evince a fundamental awareness of the instability of the "I" who recollects the others he used to be and conceives of the self as "a provisional sequence within an infinity of possible shapes."[38] Therefore "I" and "you" are no longer opposed, nor are their singularities annihilated in what Bailly calls "a factitiously united mass."[39] This is why the persona of the poem can successively take on the fleeting features of "the solitary Turk," the lover or the "penitents." It becomes as fluid as time itself, akin to the "odourless water-clock of hours" that heralds the poet's pure, disembodied self ("the lustration of penitents"). Thus the poet inhabits this ancestral time, both motionless and fluent, which brings us back to the beginning, "where we lie under the windless planes." Space thus belongs to a recovered temporality and to an eternal, fluid community, uniting the ancient and the contemporary in a redeemed present.

    The disfiguration of space is carried a step further in "Phileremo," where both the text and the title of the poem blur the topographic referent. Indeed "Phileremo" refers both to the "philosopher in search of human values" and to the Greek city whose "stones" and "cistern" are described in *Reflections*. The poem opens upon the improbable gaze which the Renaissance Italian poet Antonio Fregoso,[40] also called Phileremo, lover of solitude, might have cast, had he been still alive, upon the two-faced city: the antique one and the one destroyed by German and Italian mines during the Second World War. The philosopher's perspective contrasts with the darker symbolism—"A philosopher in search of human values / Might have seen something"—

hiding behind the ominous "Black boots with cracked eyes and . . . / . . . rich in historical error." To the philosopher's untold interpretation, the poet substitutes the historian's reading of clues: "Old wall we picked the moss from, reading / Into it invasions by the Dorian or Medes." The position of "reading," acting as a hinge between the two lines, emphasizes the crucial role of the interpreter and paves the way for the following stanza exposing the risks of a blind, erroneous reader who relies upon "education" and annihilates the object of vision: "But the bearded arboreal historian / Saw nothing of it all, was nothing then." Ironically, the earth speaks to those who cannot read—"The stones spoke to him"—and induces a descent into the subject's growing awareness:

> The stones spoke to him. Reflected there
> In a cistern I heard you thinking: Europe
> Also, the whole of our egopetal culture
> Is done for and must vanish soon.
>
> And still we have not undergone the poet's truth.[41]

The third person is not just the object of discourse: he becomes a mirror into which the poet perceives the quintessential disjunction of our European consciousness; he is the estranged other who refracts our intimate self and spurs another, textual refraction, as the reader recognizes another text. The poem "In Europe," in *Cities*, partook indeed of the same dysphoric vision, as if ancient tragedies were mirrored by modern ones in a never-ending deathly momentum, which is further substantiated in the residence book:

> Here we set our backs to the sea and the village, and our faces to the bulk of Phileremo, the flat-topped mountain which was Ialysos once, and which has offered a first-class defensive site to a hundred armies, Greek, Frankish, Roman, Turkish, German. [. . .] Directly beneath we see the slight [s]tump of excavated ground where the city of Ialysos once stood, and can even discern among its furrows traces of ancient wall. Of the minefield, however, there is no discernible trace from this range.[42]

The art of the poem is to unfold what is precisely not "discernible": the refraction of a thought pondering upon the death drift of our world, a world where wars are no longer confined by boundaries, a world threatened by entropy that the Old Man in "In Europe" foretold: "So many bridges to the end of the world. Frontiers mean nothing any more . . ."[43]

The critical position of "Europe" at the end of line 2 disrupts the rhythmic pattern and acts as a metonym for a universal collapse that affects syntax and prosody as much as our conscience. The poem brings to the fore one of Durrell's core preoccupations: the conflicting relationship between man's ego and the outer world, which urged him to try and build bridges between Western and Eastern philosophy throughout his poetry and his fiction, as *The Avignon Quintet* evinces:

> Neurosis is the norm for an egopetal culture—Freud exposed the roots as a dentist's drill exposes the pulp chamber of a tooth—the aching root is guilt over uncommitted sins! Civilisation is a placebo with side-effects.[44]

Abandoning the "egopetal" vision, the last stanza opens up local space to the elements and reverses the perspective of the residence book: "the flat-topped mountain" becomes "that haze of flats" and turns our gaze back toward the sea—

> Could we comfort us in more than this
> Blue sea and air cohering blandly
> Across that haze of flats,
> The smoking middens of our history—
> Aware perhaps only of the two children
> Asleep in the car beside a bear in cotton gloves?

The poem ends on an unanswered and incomplete question that superimposes upon the "smoking middens of our history" the unaccounted-for presence of unconscious children who can explain or solve nothing but whose very existence, in its stark, unrefined reality, undermines the death drift of our adult civilization and rings as a diffracted answer to the Woman's repeated plea in "In Europe," "If only the children."[45] The dash ending the antepenultimate line sketches out a new sort of bridge, a threshold into another vision, which forebodes a new mode of being into the world.

"The Parthenon" stages the ultimate disfiguration by leading the reader away from the Greek temple and toward the cities, "capes and islands"[46] that turn the poem into a living temple to the act of writing. The first stanza shifts the perspective toward the archetypal, unnamed city, "the city," which is slowly dematerialized and looms up as an ethereal, uncanny entity:

> [. . .] say the city
> Swam up here swan-like to the shallows,
> Or whiteness from an overflowing jar
> Settled into this grassy violet space,
> Theorem for three hills,
>
> Went soft with brickdust, clay and whitewash[47]

Not so much a city as a "theorem," it stands as abstract speculation that must be demonstrated in order to exist and that determines its very essence: it glides weightless in the sibilant alliterations of the first lines, and its whiteness creates an unearthly contrast against the "violet space." The names engraved on its walls partake of the same fleeting existence ushering in a space as fragile as human life: "On a plastered porch one morning wrote / Human names, think of it, men became the roads."[48] A new universe is thus born that takes roots in "the investigation of shade an idle boy / Invented"[49] and where the heavy stones seem to ignore gravity ascending into the sky "as a wish grew up."[50] At this precise point the poem veers away from its apparent object and offers the reader an abstract architecture:

> Joining action and reflection in the arch,
> Then adding desire and will: four walls:
> Four walls, a house. 'How simple' people said.
>
> Man entered it and woman was the roof.

The poem reveals a deeper structure: that of human conscience trapped in the logic of causality that leaves no room for freedom as the anadiplosis linking lines 2 and 3 evinces. This arbitrary chain breaks up the former ideal vision as syntax becomes binding—"Now syntax settled round the orderless"—and as the punctuation disrupts the smooth breathing of the lines through the use of colons, full stops, and quotation marks that create an enunciative disjunction. The last line clearly signals man's fall from the world of idle invention embodied by the boy into the realm of temporality that wounds. And although art is unable to save the lost world, its sensual geography retains the ideal weightlessness of the past in its unnamed "cities / made of loaf-sugar, tamed by gardens, / Lying hanging by the hair within the waters." This unsubstantial presence can still be felt despite the heavy ego of "Men of linen [. . .] on marble chairs / In self-indulgence murmuring 'I am, I am.'" To those who can only decipher material clues in the archaeological remains of a dead city and cannot see beyond "a jar of red clay," the poet opposes those who can penetrate the eternal relations of the natural world, which thrives in an everlasting present:

> Though grown from causes we still share
> The natural lovely order, as where water
> Touches earth, a tree grows up,
> A needle touching wax, a human voice.

The bare syntax, and the progressive erasure of time references (from the simple present to the present participle and to the ellipsis of the verbal syntagma), are telling of the simplicity and proximity of this universe that underlies our civilization. The pendulum effect arising from the perfect balance between the hemistiches of the last two lines and underlined by the polyptoton "touches / touching" induces a perfect symmetry between the movement of the water and that of the needle of the gramophone. The tapering tree mirrors the ascent of the human voice and enacts the perfect harmony between man and nature.

The following stanza contrasts this eternal realm against the world fragmented by time where the material artifacts—"the brush, the cone, the candle, / The spinning-wheel and clay"—attempt to make up for the initial loss, this "original joy" that cannot be reiterated. The artist's attempt at regenerating the ideal world is necessarily imperfect:

> Lost even the flawless finishing strokes,
> White bones among the almonds prophesying
> A death itself that seemed a coming-of-age.

Yet from this very imperfection emerges a world where the bones of the dead come in touch with the almonds of life. Thus, man's inevitable progress to his doom marks the advent of a symbolic fruit. Indeed, the almond, protected by two envelopes, symbolizes the three steps leading to God[51]: the first envelope, which is bitter and temporary, is that of the Ten Commandments; the second, protective one is that of God's teaching; finally, the kernel gives access to truth itself: that of a death, which is not an end per se but an achievement. Although Durrell's almond is devoid of any form of religious teaching, it retains its biblical symbolism and acquires a metaphysical meaning by opening, through the run-on line, onto a death that acts as a revelation, granting the artist what his art failed to achieve. The apposition of the last two lines blurs the syntactic structure and gives the image the force of a condensed clause, so that the ultimate vision is not "lost" but is granted withal. Death as a prelude to the true vision, as a sign of the inner awakening that frees the poet from finitude, eventually prevails in the last collection where the ultimate poem concludes:

> You show us all the way the great ones went,
> In silences becalmed, so well they knew
> That even to die is somehow to invent.[52]

However, this much-desired achievement announced in "The Parthenon" and confirmed in "Seferis" perpetually eludes the poet. The ultimate collection, *Vega and Other Poems*, ends on a blank page,[53] where poetic invention really belongs. "The Parthenon" unfolds a landscape that progressively metamorphoses into a suffering female body wherefrom the only hope rises from "the darkness"—the counterpart to the blank page—that is to say from the unfigurable. The subject is trapped in space, unable to escape from the matter of mortality:

> Lastly the capes and islands hold us
> Tame as a handclasp,
> Cause locked within effects, the land—
> This vexed clitoris of the continental body,
> Pumice and clay and whitewash
> Only the darkness ever compromises
>
> Or an eagle softly mowing on the blue . . .

The subject is locked in an anthropomorphic space whose anguished embrace and wounded body stand as metonym for the anxiety of the modern Western subject. "Cause locked within effect" mirrors "Joining action and reflection" and emphasizes the twofold meaning of the term "reflection" (as refraction and meditation). The macrocosm also reflects the microcosm in a land where the geological ("pumice"), the architectural ("whitewash"), and the human ("clay" is understood as the potter's clay in "a jar of red clay" and as human flesh[54]) merge. The poem thus conjures up the materials of a second, imaginary Genesis that endeavors to answer Rodini's question: "Is there enough perhaps to found a world?"[55] "Brickdust, clay and whitewash" (stanza 2), "Chapters of clay and whitewash" (stanza 11), and "Pumice and clay and whitewash" (stanza 15) build up a new, mobile architecture that digs into our mundane matter to refashion our relationship to the world and opens our consciousness to the impalpable: "the darkness," "the blue." This nominalized adjective inevitably sends the reader back to *A Private Country* where Durrell first composed, stroke after stroke, the luminous and unfigurable essence of his Greek landscape: starting from "The blue circlets of stone, / On a sea blotted with fictions"[56] in the very first poem, he proceeds on his way to Argos where "The roads lead southwards, blue / Along a circumference of snow"[57] until "Father Nicholas," where the definite article introducing the nominalized blue turns the color into a referential absolute: "And the blue will keep."[58] Finally, "Letter to Seferis the Greek" operates the ultimate consecration through the demonstrative adjective that adds proximity to this intangible presence: "this blue, this enormous blue."[59] In "The Parthenon" "the blue" is fraught with an unspeakable hope that recalls Paul Valéry's azure:

> Patience, patience,
> Patience dans l'azur !
> Chaque atome de silence
> Est la chance d'un fruit mûr ![60]

The soft gliding of the "eagle mowing on the blue"[61] transforms the azure into a tender soil that holds the promise of a fruit in the indefinite future of the ellipsis concluding the line. And yet uncertainty rules the last stanza, where the poet's anguished question "And yet, Geros, who knows?" sends us back to the earlier meditation on our doomed history ("A vexing history, Geros [. . .] / And nothing has redeemed it"). Eventually, the poem is torn between the peaceful "blue" and the anguished "shriek" that announces the reconciliation of "Lands and Islands,"[62] in Odysseas Elytis's own words that introduce the poem.

> And yet, Geros, who knows? Within the space
> Of our own seed might some day rise,
> Shriek truth, punish the blue with statues.

The last stanza attempts to solve the dichotomy between the whole and the fragment, the macrocosm and the microcosm that the persona's communion with the island achieves. The new "seed" would thus be that of the I/land that Durrell, the "born islomane," defines in *Reflections*:

> . . . there occurred the word *Islomania*, which was described as a rare but by no means unknown affliction of spirit. . . . These born 'islomanes' . . . are the direct descendants of the Atlanteans, and it is towards their lost Atlantis that their subconscious yearns throughout their island life . . .[63]

The ellipsis opens up the narrative space to the lost city, just as the ellipsis concluding the line "Or an eagle softly mowing on the blue . . ." opens up "The Parthenon" to the impenetrable light of the island where the sky and the sea merge into each other. However, this new human seed is inseparable from the experience of pain and anguish, and man's creation—in the shape of "statues"—sends us back to the "Men of linen sat on marble chairs" and to "our egopetal culture"[64] denounced in "Phileremo," while the piercing cry of truth—"Shriek truth"—echoes the cleft of "this vexed clitoris" a few lines earlier.

The ambiguity that characterizes the logical link between the last two lines of the poem evinces how Durrell breaks away from the figuration of the Greek land that shaped the previous collections in order to put to work the question of space in its relation to time, independently from any geographic anchorage. Such is the hidden meaning of the name "Geros," the mysterious addressee of the poem, a Janus-faced being who designates both the old man and the one who can resist time. The Greek land, torn apart between the mainland and its islands, bearing the imprint of man's work and of eternity, operates as the ideal place where the poet can question man's relation to space, and hence, to his own mortality.

Facing Finitude

The disfiguration of the Greek space is part and parcel of the slow excavation process through which the poet interrogates death. This is particularly striking in the poem "Penelope" where Penelope addresses Ulysses in a barely identifiable landscape ("hill," "shoreline," "delta," "sea") as if to suggest, in the minimalist décor of the scene, the universal nature of the separation enacted. This separation is initially materialized by the geography, which enhances the rift at the heart of the textual space where each line functions as a self-contained unit:

> Look, on that hill we met.
> On that shoreline parted.[65]

The symmetrical structure and the antithesis "met / parted" highlight the elision of the subject in line 2, thereby enhancing the paradoxical syntactic link between two distinct sentences that are nevertheless united by a prosodic run-on line that contradicts the punctuation and forces the reader to adopt simultaneously opposed viewpoints. This geographic and textual rift further develops in the second stanza where the syntactic isolation of the final dactyl ("Of oracles to back them. I remained.") reads as a striking counterpoint to the last iamb of the first line in the first stanza ("we met."). Durrell toys with the rules of classical prosody, combining binary and ternary rhythms while avoiding any regularity in order to dramatize the poetic space. Indeed, the fifth stanza breaks free from the easily recognizable scansion of the third and fourth ones through the interplay of run-on lines and parataxis that upset the rhythmic pattern and open up the textual space to what has not been revealed:

> The augurs in the delta have not *once*
> Foreseen this dust upon an ageing eyeball,
> Vitreous as sea-spun glass, this black
> Sperm of winter-sea we walk beside,
> The marble onanism of the nymphs.

The separation of the lovers is negated through the petrifaction of the gaze that retains forever in its "ageing eyeball, / Vitreous as sea-spun glass" the infinitesimal weight of "Tears." The last line can either be understood as the direct object to the verb "Foreseen" or as an apposition to "this black / Sperm" whereby the movement of the sea freezes into an oneiric sculpture. This darkening eye, this stained sea, this lifeless, self-centered pleasure compose the hidden truth of the oracles. In this italicized "*once*" underlined by the print and the intonation, the poem gives voice to a fragmentary, unseemly vision that breaks through an unsteady, faltering stanza. Death acquires the contours of a poetic space where the syntactic, prosodic, and lexical matter implode ("sea-spun," "winter-sea"), where movement is annihilated, where opacity prevails.

The same process of petrifaction is at work in the paradoxical celebration of the advent of life that unfolds in the eponymous poem "On Seeming to Presume," where space is crudely abolished:

Where earth and water plan
No place for him, no home
Outside the confining womb[66]

Coming to life, which is a coming into the world, is conceived of as an expulsion and a banishment into a sort of nowhere land where the subject's only contact with the outer space is mediated by "the rubber forceps," which heralds an unrelenting cycle of deeper ruptures: those of the self caught between "I will," "I must," and "I ought" where the modals evince the progressive affective dissociation of the subject from the duties imposed upon him. The Shakespearian intertext dramatizes this cleavage by staging a dispossessed subject who becomes the receptacle of a particular poison: that of a cultural code transforming him into a dead man alive. From one stanza to the next, the subject embodies a phantasmagoric Hamlet who moves on toward his death. The denial of any spatial anchorage signals the doom of the human figure unable to find any new dwelling beyond "the confining womb" it was torn from. The tragic-comic tone of the poem that blends themes from *Hamlet* and *The Tempest* in a ballad rhymed by italicized burdens evocative of a Greek chorus unsettles the reader, who is torn apart between the insidious light ring of the form and the tragic fate encapsulated in the two words "no home," which point to the very last poem in the collection.[67]

This homeless figure is none other than the poet himself, who can only find a new abode in literature, hence the multiple echoes to Shakespeare and T. S. Eliot—"So how should I presume?"[68]—that end up in the reincarnation

On Seeming to Presume 99

of the persona as the Bard in "The Critics."⁶⁹ Once again, Durrell plays on classical prosody (pentameters, quatrains, end rhymes, and crossed rhymes) without ever allowing for an easy identification of the rhythmical pattern, and deliberately jostles the reader to suggest a new critical space at the heart of the poem that becomes the very tool of a heuristic approach:

> Yet under it perhaps may be discerned
> A something else afoot—a Thing
> Lacking both precedent and name and gender:
> An uncreated weight which left its clue,⁷⁰

Reverting to the Shakespearian lexicon, the poem stages an unexpected apparition whereby Shakespeare becomes one of the poet's many masks. This "Thing / Lacking both precedent and name and gender" suggests the overpowering presence that takes hold of the poet's fate, "Making him run up bills, / Making him violent or distrait or tender." Likewise, it drives him away from the mundane and from himself and into a world of imaginary quotes. "'Words / Added to words multiply the space / Between this feeling and my expressing it . . .'" sends us back again to Hamlet—"Words, words, words"⁷¹—that is, to an ever-expanding palimpsestuous realm where past and present, real and imaginary voices meet, conjuring up a new, poetic dwelling:

> '. . . Time smoulders
> Like a burning rug. I *will* be free.' . . .

The suspension points concluding this penultimate stanza herald a final reversal through which the poet, seemingly reaching his aim, suddenly widens the gap between desire and its achievement in a theatrical somersault:

> And all the time from the donkey's head
> The lover is whispering: 'This is not
> What I imagined as Reality.
> If truth were needles surely eyes would see?

One easily recognizes here the trick played on Titania by Puck, who disguised Bottom with a donkey's head in *A Midsummer Night's Dream*.⁷² However, unlike Shakespeare's comedy, which ended on a joyful revelation that banished all former illusions, the poem offers no remedy but only the hypothesis of a total, yet improbable, perception that inevitably suggests the biblical phrase "It is easier for a camel to go through the eye of a needle than for a rich man to enter into the kingdom of God!"⁷³ Durrell sheds light on the poetic questioning that characterizes the entire collection, which repeatedly attempts to define, in a humorous tone, the poet's impossible task that Shelley had already grappled with: "A poem is the image of life expressed in its eternal truth."[74] Durrell's poetry endeavors to respond to the same challenge, opening up a space of freedom and a new angle of vision through which art points to a wordless form of wisdom that inhabits both his poems and his fiction. Thus, we may remember Balthazar's words on the selfsame quest for the truth:

> Fact is unstable by its very nature. Narouz once said to me that he loved the desert because there "the wind blew out one's footsteps like candle-flames". So it seems to me does reality. How then can we hunt for the truth?[75]

The desert wind in *The Alexandria Quartet* is the emblem of the unstable nature of reality and epitomizes the fluctuating essence of the truth.[76] This train of thought, which is voiced by Balthazar, as well as by Darley, Justine, or Pursewarden,[77] often coincides with poetic fragments that shatter the linearity of the prose, such as the beginning of the third part of *Justine* where the city is reshaped under the khamseen threading its way into every nook and cranny of Alexandria:

> From time to time a cracked wind arrives from directly above and stirs the whole city round and round so that one has the illusion that everything—trees, minarets, monuments and people have been caught in the final eddy of some great whirlpool and will pour softly back at last into the desert from which they rose, reverting once more to the anonymous wave-sculptured floor of dunes. . . .[78]

Alexandria is engulfed by the whirlwind that upsets even the structure of the sentence itself. We may indeed notice the problematic punctuation that introduces between dashes the group "trees, minarets, monuments and people" but forgets to end the enumeration and later substitutes these four subjects for the indefinite pronoun "everything," so that the reader finds a verb in the plural where he expected a singular. The movement of the sentence imitates that of the wind by upsetting the original syntactic structure that is brought to end on three dots, as if to convey the boundless scale of the phenomenon. Yet this rendering of atmospheric upheavals also conveys the permanence of the natural phenomenon: not only is the whirlwind a regular phenomenon but the poetic writing reverberates the unchanging nature of the atmospheric event—the self-reverberating adverbial "From time to time" is echoed by "round and round" as well as by the semantic mirroring of "eddy" and "whirlpool" or of "back" and "reverting." Thus, the wind, although it ravages the landscape, sketches out a perfect cycle, bringing the city back to the desert where it first came from. Thus, the depiction of the all-invading khamseen contains the seeds of a renewed genesis and is consequently perceived less as a destruction than as the reviving of origins, showing behind "the anonymous wave-sculptured floor of dunes" from which Alexandria first loomed out, the deep recesses of the city's birth.

The disfiguration of the Greek space in *On Seeming to Presume* that paves the way for the poet's meditation on human finitude consequently heralds the poetic and symbolic preoccupations that will later on lead to the progressive excavation of the fictional space. Should one then consider the links sketched out between the various poetry collections and Durrell's prose writing as the clues to a wider architecture whose various pieces may point toward an underlying whole? Such a critical desire for an all-embracing logic that would structure the entire opus is partly encouraged by the author's own words and simultaneously defeated by a writing that refuses any form of *telos* and adopts a strong Eastern stance, which led Durrell to confess in the later years: "I have a personal vagueness which corresponds to the Tibetan. . . . Finally I am an old man now, and everything seems to be falling apart . . . I believe there is truly something that remains, that lasts, in places."[79] Rather than the linear and logical development of former works, Durrell's various texts build up a continuum of interlocked images and sensations that echo one another endlessly. The reader is deliberately lost in the intricate Chinese box pattern through which he is expected to plunge deeper into conceptually nested arrangements that are never quite the same and never quite estranged from one another. He shares with him a poetic excavation through which life itself is refunded, as Yves Bonnefoy has beautifully explained:

> He [the poet] excavates, if I may say so, a world which is thus entirely his out of the indistinct mass of his living milieu. This excavation reshapes his life, becomes for him the very matter of his experience, reality itself.[80]

The Greek landscape would then only exist as this place of symbolic and psychic excavation where Durrell repeatedly digs out the fluctuating forms and sensations of "something that remains, that lasts, in places."[81]

The Rose of Poetry

Thus, the links established between the collections are rather to be thought of as an intricate pattern through which the poem both discloses and overlaps a previous echo, allowing the reader to experience through the translucent material of the text how "Words / Added to words multiply the space."[82] This fractal-like structure is best exemplified in "Eternal Contemporaries: Six Portraits"—which reads as an echo to "Conon the Critic on the Six Landscape Painters of Greece" in *Cities*—where the rose epitomizes the visionary intensity that characterizes the Greek land. Quotation marks have disappeared, as if to give us access to the poet's own voice, which is nevertheless filtered through a series of gazes meant to deepen the perspective. The first fragment, entitled "Manoli of Cos," opens up on a description of the rose adorning the rudder of the boat only to end on a symbolic and literary blow-up of the rose, which takes up the entire poetic space and becomes the source of absolute vision:

> This is not the rose of all the world,
> Nor the rose of Nostradamus or of Malory:
> Nor is it Eliot's clear northern rose of the mind,
> But precisely and unequivocally
> The red rose Manoli picked himself
> From the vocabulary of roses on the hill by Cefalû.[83]

This negative definition conjures up an entire gamut of roses that the reader is expected to both decipher and discard in order to search for the poet's own rose, for the personal "matter of his experience, reality itself,"[84] as Bonnefoy expressed it. However, the second half of the stanza qualifies the flower with an adjective and a relative clause that only make the mystery thicker: it is the equivocal rose *par excellence*, the rose that shelters in the secret folds of its dark petals an infinite number of interpretations.

In the long enumeration of roses the reader also recognizes the silent echo of Yeats's roses—"Red Rose, proud Rose, sad Rose of all my days,"[85] "Rose of all Roses, Rose of all the World!"[86]—which shines throughout the stanza and gives coherence to the mosaic of alchemical, poetic, and botanical roses. The rose becomes the flower of language itself—not unlike Gertrude Stein's self-generating tautology "A rose is a rose is a rose is a rose"[87]—which partakes both of the mundane and of the poetic reality and which subsumes Durrell's quest up to the very last notebook:

> First paint the rose in its physical form as a pure flower. Next forget the physical form and paint the perfume. Next forget everything and paint the idea of the rose—any rose. Remember that the rose was not created by nature but by man, a compilation of tensions, like a wine or a watercolour. Once you become a painter you realize that everything about it is imaginary except the thorns.[88]

"The vocabulary of roses on the hill by Cefalû" is none other than that of the poet delving into the soil of writing to create a new language, a lingo that will give birth to the penultimate collection, *The Red Limbo Lingo*, where language becomes the essence of poetry, as foretold by Pursewarden in his notes to Clea: "Language is not an accident of poetry but the essence. The lingo is the nub."[89] Inventing a language that is poetry in essence, transcending the dialectics of language as this "moving and all too impure matter"[90] that Valéry used to denounce, such are the stakes of Durrell's writing, which is deeply rooted in Shelley's poetic vision:

> In the infancy of society every author is necessarily a poet, because language itself is poetry; and to be a poet is to apprehend the true and the beautiful, in a word, the good which exists in the relation, subsisting, first between existence and perception, and secondly between perception and expression.[91]

Such is the relation Manoli embodies: he is the second dragoman after Fangbrand in *A Private Country*, steering his boat between the sacred and the mundane, between life and death, and inviting the reader to undertake the same crossing "between existence and perception, and secondly between perception and expression" that will lead him to comprehend the rose neither as an object of the visible world nor as an intellectual image, but as a flux, as a current linking the word to the object, the subject to the world. At such cost may the truth pierce our eyes like needles, when the object and the sign both vanish to summon, beyond words, beyond the dead scene, a new relation to the world that Pierre Reverdy has described as follows:

> There are no words more poetic than others. For poetry does not lie in words any more than it does in the sunset or in the effulgence of dawn—nor does it lie in sadness more than in joy. It rests in what words become when they reach the human soul once they have transformed sunset or dawn, sadness or joy. It rests in the transmutation that is brought about by the power of words upon things and in the reactions that operate between one another through their combinations reverberating upon the mind and the senses.[92]

Words in poetry are then, as Durrell expresses in his last notebook, "a compilation of tensions," a personal dictionary that consists not in signifiers and signifieds but in relations, in "transmutations." It is "the vocabulary of roses" that captures things in their ineffable substance and turns language into what the contemporary French critic Thierry Maulnier once called "the magical tool of an exchange between reality and its shadow, the unknown, . . . the mirror where the invisible face of the world is refracted."[93]

This "compilation of tensions" is felt most prominently in the five subsequent poems that compose "Eternal Contemporaries." Recapturing the pattern that underlay "Conon the Critic on the Six Landscape Painters of Greece," Durrell builds up timeless mythical characters, some of whom are easily recognizable figures of Greek Orthodox Patristics, such as Basil the Hermit, while others conjure up Durrell's Greek friendships, like Panagiotis of Lindos, until we meet A Rhodian Captain, the archetypal emblem of the seafarer who mirrors Manoli of Cos, in the first poem, and embodies the ageless and motionless crossing into eternity, challenging our notions of space and time. The journey is then no longer a spatial but a temporal one through which the six poems unfold a spiritual progress. "Mark of Patmos" and "Basil the Hermit" accomplish an inner exile that conjures up a new reality:

> Mark has crossed over to Mount Olivet,
> Putting aside the banneret and the drum.
> He inhabits now that part of himself
> Which lay formerly desolate and uncolonised.
> He works that what is to pass may come
> And the birth of the common heart be realised.[94]

Starting like a prophecy from the Mount of Olives, "Mark of Patmos" points to a new departure toward the Promised Land conceived of as an intimate space where passivity and renunciation prepare the subject for a new world. "The birth of the common heart" is anything but common, for it is rooted in the sharp awareness of the common, of the insignificant: "A flower dropped / In the boat by a friend." The flower, which none other may have noticed, is the essential link that ties up this second poem to Manoli's "red rose" in the first poem; it is the fragile, ephemeral yet eternal thread of life that defies death:

> Feeling, not that something momentous
> Had begun, but that their common childhood
> Had foundered in the Syrian seas and ended.

The fundamental point of origin remains hidden: the eye can only grasp the stark divide between past and present, between him and "the island loafers" who see no new beginning but death. Mark of Patmos truly embodies the persona of the poet who has freed himself from death, as Durrell will later explain in his essay *A Smile in the Mind's Eye*: "The poet is one whom death cannot surprise, for he has taken up an imaginative emplacement within it by his poems."[95]

"Basil the Hermit" stages a similar detachment. Basil, an exile, withdraws from the society of pleasure seekers and thus embodies the perfect anchorite[96] whose body becomes the living metaphor of spiritual aloofness:

> His inner prohibitions were a sea
> On which he floated spellbound day by day.
> World and its fevers howled outside: within
> The Omen and the Fret that hemmed him in,
> The sense of his complete unworthiness
> Pressed each year slowly tighter like a tourniquet.[97]

The outer space paradoxically flows into the inner self, abolishing the very notion of self and finally emptying out the subject. Stopping his prayers, he abandons his hold on reality and acquires a material weightlessness that makes him sensitive to an ontological "worthlessness" that foreshadows the Bodhidharma's quest in *The Avignon Quintet*: "With only his eyeballs for probes he exhausted the contents of the blank wall. . . . In this critical wall he saw a mirror reflecting the whole irretrievable inward chaos of man."[98] Just as in the novel where the Bodhidharma's endless meditation abolishes the distance between the subject and the object, between the conscience of the blank wall, and the wall itself, the poem enacts the conflation of space and subject, of the object and the source of contemplation that are no longer separate but partake of the same substance, as D. T. Suzuki has explained:

> When Buddhists declare all things to *be* empty they are not advocating a nihilistic view; on the contrary an ultimate reality is hinted at, which cannot be subsumed under the categories of logic. . . . The Absolute refuses to divide itself into two: that which sees and that which is seen.[99]

The poem conjures up the emptiness of Zen spiritual exercises through which the ego is abolished and which the following poem, "Dmitri of Carpathos," further delves into. The fourth poem surprisingly superimposes the icon of the saint and the image of the card players:

> Four card-players: an ikon of the saint
> On a pitted table among eight hands
> That cough and spit or close like mandibles
> On fortunate court-cards or on the bottle
> Which on the pitted paintwork stands.[100]

Two semiotic icons[101] are symbolically opposed and pitted against each other: a sacred and a secular one meet on the plane surface of the table. They are clearly distinguished in the first line where the colons ending the first hemistich signify both the separation and the reverberation of opposites. However, they are eventually conjoined in the fifth line in the syntagm "the pitted paintwork" where the "ikon" and the "pitted table," simultaneously separated and linked by the run-on line (l.1–2), are strikingly brought together. The superimposition of the two planes sliding upon each other suggests an intersemiotic relationship that relates the poem both to a previous textual icon—"Greek Church: Alexandria" in Cities[102]—and to the pictorial tradition of seventeenth-century Flemish tavern scenes. In the encounter of spaces, art forms, texts, and genres the past participle "pitted" plays a symbolic role: it characterizes the surface pockmarked by the sailors' rough hands, by the passing of time, imprinted by the coming together of opposed worlds. The ultimate icon metamorphoses the very matter of representation: the "four card players" are subsumed in the metonymy of the "eight hands / That cough and spit or close like mandibles"—a simile that lays bare the animal instinct at the heart of man's action—while the "ikon of the saint" turns into a "pitted paintwork." The players' human nature and the saint's presence are erased, paving the way, in the second stanza, for the apparition of a sailor who stands as a counterpart to Basil the Hermit. He is the embodiment of "complete unworthiness":

> Among them one whose soft transpontine nose
> Fuller of dirty pores pricked on a chart
> Has stood akimbo on the turning world
> [. . .]
> In wine or poppy a drunkard with a drunkard's heart
> Who never yet was known to pay his round.

The sailor's worthlessness matches that of "his rotten boat" that "like a gypsy burns and burns." The great fire marks a decisive step: "something climbs the hill / And stands beside him at the tavern table / To pluck his drunken elbow like a child." The poem ends at the point when the drunken sailor is about to recover his awareness, when the annihilation of matter heralds a possible rebirth.

Similarly, "Panagiotis of Lindos" joins the celestial and the marine worlds through the comparison between the birds nibbling at their feathers and the sailors mending their nets. Birds and sailors are both set upon a hypothetical task: capturing an elusive object—"Needles passing in a surf of lights." The needles of truth in "The Critic"[103] as well as those of "Fangbrand"—"Truth's metaphor is the needle"[104]—are here recaptured and expanded to orient the reader's gaze toward Durrell's recurring fishing metaphor whereby poetry is conceived of as the art of the ungraspable. We may remember his interview with Stephen Gray in 1965—"Poetry's much more delightful and exacting [than prose]. It's more like fly-fishing: you can't guarantee that you don't pull up an old boot—I do frequently—instead of a fish"[105]—as well as Blanford's words in *The Avignon Quintet*: "The poetic reality of which I speak, and which Sutcliffe might have deployed in his unwritten books, is rather like the schoolchild's definition of a fishing-net as 'a lot of holes tied together with a string.' Just as impalpable, yet just as true of our work."[106] On the contrary, Panagiotis, who embodies the perfect philosopher, has chosen to relinquish his hold on the material world:

> Panagiotis has resigned it all
> For an enamel can and olive shade
> His concern a tavern prospect,
> Miles of sweet chestnut and borage.[107]

The tavern and wine are no longer synonymous with confusion and destruction but pave the way to spiritual knowledge through a harmonious blending: "Mixing leisure and repose like wine and water, / Tutor and pupil in the crater."

Forsaking his desire for material possessions and achievements, Panagiotis enters "his dark sleep" that paradoxically leads toward a new light that invades and kindles the sky, the sea and the shores:

> His dark sleep is bruised by each
> Sink of the sun below the castle
> Where the Sporades have opened
> Their spokes, and the whole Aegean
> In brilliant soda turns the darkening bays.

Upon the very moment when the sun goes down into the earth the islands are bathed in light, just as the subject is submerged by the inner light that flows into the text as it flows into the unresisting, sleeping conscience that has shed the ego. The white light that dissolves the dark contours of the shoreline is redolent of the magnesium flare of earlier photography and invites the reader to look, behind the distorted shapes conjured up by the poet's artifice, for the essence of forms. The fluent run-on lines, the melodious interplay of alliterations and assonances further enlarge the expanding embrace of the sinking sun that lights up the world from within.

The last poem, "A Rhodian Captain," closes the circle upon the only anonymous figure in the series who, through his love for olives and wines, echoes Panagiotis, and embodies the quintessence of the Greek sailor who, having traveled far and wide, enters the realm of silence and solitude:

> Ten speechless knuckles lie along a knee
> Among their veins, gone crooked over voyages,
> Made by this ancient captain. Life has now
> Contracted like the pupil of an eye
> To a slit in space and time for images—
> All he has seen of sage and arbutus:[108]

Offering a close-up upon the subject after the wide shot upon "the whole Aegean" that concluded the previous fragment, "A Rhodian Captain" opens up another invisible space: the unremarkable, illegible journey of the veins furrowing his skin, as if space, like life, "contracted." The ultimate vision is precisely born from this contraction that foreshadows the advent of a new life. The dash on line 5 is mimetic of the in-between space where the inner vision arises and paves the way, on the other side of the colons, through the interwoven branches of the Mediterranean plants, for a timeless memory that marries the sky, the earth, and the sea: "Touched berries where the golden eagle crashes / From its chariot of air and dumb trap: / Islands as fortunate as Atlantis was . . ." The suspension points suggest the looming vision of a recovered eternity that remains invisible to the eye and where the various spatiotemporal strata are interpolated. Like Ulysses, whose story is that of an eternal return to Ithaca, the Rhodian Captain remains "in truth, outside the doorpost," like the drop shadow of Prospero who stands, at the end of *Cities* "by his open door."[109] He is the presiding prophet who holds the vine and the olive, the eternal emblems of a symbolic Greece that the very first poem of the collection celebrated: "On that renewed landscape / Like semen from the grape."[110] Like its flowers, grapes, plates of olives, Durrell's Greek land is a code one must learn to read.

The Mandala of Writing

The eternity heralded by "A Rhodian Captain" is that of death, of the lost Atlantis that the poem remembers and commemorates as the harbinger of future losses, announcing the cities and islands of the last poem, "The Anecdotes," whose sixteen fragments echo those of "Cities, Plains and People." Beyond the mere structural symmetry, the two poems present striking similarities that set them apart in the entire body of Durrell's poetic output. Indeed, their structures recall the intricate pattern of the Kalachakra mandala, which is also called the vessel of the great journey and which has been analyzed in depth by Sylvie Crossman:

> The Kalachakra mandala serves as an initiation to one of the most complex Tibetan teachings and has been considered for two thousand and a half years as the utmost expression of Emptiness.
> Shakyamuni appeared on a full moon night under the shape of Kalachakra, a four-headed god who looked at the four cardinal points and carried various objects in his twenty-four arms. He was holding a goddess in his embrace.
> The word "kala" in Sanskrit means "time" and "chakra", wheel. Kalachakra is also traditionally referred to as "the Wheel of Time" because time is the cosmic manifestation of omniscience, that is, time understood as space-time, capable of embracing all time—past, present and future, the human world as well as the solar system, a truth with no beginning and no end that cancels causality. Kalachakra was the eternal, bottomless emptiness of the universe, the wheel of the world.[111]

The symbolic power of this quaternary structure that underlies the poetic form is then obvious: the two poems answer each other, uniting the space-time of the two collections, embodying "the Wheel of Time" that coalesces the inner and the outer, the microcosm and the macrocosm. The painstaking colored sand composition, which projects a three-dimensional palace on a plane surface, offers an ephemeral, fragile, and mobile icon that seems to whisper to the initiated: "Come, child, / I will teach you in depth / The rites of the secret way / You are the vessel of the great journey."[112] Likewise, "Cities, Plains and People" and "The Anecdotes" echo each other and orient the reader's gaze toward the same journey.

We may recall that "Cities, Plains and People," which concluded the collection just as "The Anecdotes" did, offered a retrospective journey into the poet's biographical, literary, and spiritual progress. The sixteen poetic fragments—a form with which Durrell is then experimenting for the first time—are completed by marginal notes in italics that appear either on the left or on the right-hand side of the page, thus enhancing the patchy nature of the poem. Like a map legend, they give a geographic, contextual, literary, or spiritual anchorage to the main body of the text while reflecting its prosodic form. The reader is thus able to follow the poet's great journey and retrace the various space-times that contributed to his poetic initiation: "India," "Rimbaud," "Paris H.V.M. Anaïs Nancy Teresa," "Corfu," "Athens. Katsimbalis, Wallace and Anna Southam. Seferiades Stephanides," "Dostoevsky," "Alexandria [. . .] Classical Chinese Philosophy," "E. Graham Howe." However, these marginal notes, far from being merely explanatory, expand the various space-times, broadening the possible connections. Instead of anchoring the poem in the mundane world of causality and chronology, they delicately interweave centuries and spaces, literary and philosophic references—whether explicit or implicit—and build up a complex pattern of echoes to the references scattered in the main body of the poem: "Blake," "Dante and Homer," "St. Augustine," "Jerome," "Prospero," "Wordsworth," "Keats," "Valéry, Gide or Rabelais," "old Moll Flanders," "Buda," "Tao," "Hamlet and Faust," "Rimbaud," "Lawrence," or "T.S. Eliot" with whom the text engages in an ongoing conversation.[113] The poem ends on a last displacement: "Beirut" is indeed the place where the poem was written and that of the writer's most excruciating exile as, having lost his daughter and wife who fled Alexandria during the Second World War, he meets them one more time in Beirut before losing them forever.[114] "My wife's in Syria, and my daughter, and my heart" he writes to T. S. Eliot in August 1942. Just as *On Seeming to Presume*, "Cities, Plains and People" is built "round the grains of sand,"[115] round the pain of loss.

However, although "The Anecdotes" take up the same structure, they are markedly different. The marginal notes have disappeared and the poem resorts to a deceptive linearity. Each fragment bears a title that anchors it in a specific space. Yet these are oddly duplicated either through an exact repetition—"I In Cairo" followed by "II In Cairo," "XII In Rhodes," followed a few intervals later by "XV In Rhodes"—or through slight variations—"III At Rhodes," and "IV At Rhodes" followed by "XII In Rhodes," where the changed preposition opens up an imperfect echo with dissimilar spaces introduced by the same preposition: "XIII In Paris," "XIV In Beirut." The journey expands to include new spaces while many space references are scarcely mentioned within the text, such as in "I In Cairo," where we only see the hand of the torero—"Fingers spread themselves apart, / And then contracted to hand again, / Attached to an arm, leading to heart"—mirroring the hand of "A Rhodian Captain." Yet unlike the hand of the Greek sailor that stands "In the shade of the eternal vine . . . / With the same tin plate of olives," the torero's suddenly disappears:

> And I suddenly saw the cottage scene
> Where the knocking on the door is repeated.
> Nobody answers it: but inside the room
> The fox has its head under the madman's shirt.[116]

The hand knocks in vain at the door of a home devoured from within, the fox has taken the place of the heart that has stopped beating. The poem reveals a "room" inhabited by death, a dark counterpoint to the "world of little mirrors in the light,"[117] which opened up the Himalayas of "Cities."

This ominous materialization of the world of pain was already foreshadowed by the last lines of "Cities":

> To all who turn and start descending
> The long sad river of their growth:
> The tidebound, tepid, causeless
> Continuum of terrors in the spirit,
> I give you here unending
> In idleness an innocent beginning
>
> Until your pain become a literature.[118]

"The long sad river" in "Cities" already points toward "the big rivers" of the later poem "Last Heard Of" published in *Vega* and initiates the slow descent into the painful memory of the lost anchorage that "The Anecdotes" put into the limelight:

> *Nostos* home: *algos* pain: nostalgia . . .
>
> The homing pain for such as are attached:
> . . .
> Home for most is what you can least bear.[119]

The world of "idleness" and "innocence" of "Cities," which is replaced by "pain" in "The Anecdotes," is strongly redolent of the dialectics of William Blake's *Songs of Innocence and Experience*. The subject's pain is reverberated by the broken syntax of the first line, where the series of colons and the italics further enhance the disjunction that rules the poet's world. Greek and English words echo one another, diffracting the pain through an etymological deconstruction that defeats language. On each side of the colons, "*Nostos* home" and "*algos* pain" are inevitably tied together, like inseparable refractions suggesting that one cannot go without the other, that every anchorage is intimately linked to its loss. Instead of following the rivers of time, the poet chooses those of language, yet this journey brings no deeper understanding as the word "nostalgia" finally closes upon itself at the end of the line, embracing both its Greek origins and its English essence, asserting an origin from which it is necessarily excluded. The line reverberates the foreign nature of a word, its uncanny belonging that mirrors the poet's ontological exile, and orients our gaze toward the oblique relationship to language established through poetry.

This paradoxical sense of belonging that only estranges one further has been deftly analyzed by Shmuel Trigano:

> One of the first discoveries made by the exilic subject is that of the power and depth of language which can bear the world as well as the consciousness and the experience of the world which has, however, disappeared. . . . The linguistic representation which is nurtured by exile leads to a radically new perception. Before departure, words referred to the extra-linguistic reality. During the time of exile, words carry and embrace what they refer to, language carries the outer reality, the abstract carries the concrete. Identity turns into a narrative, and reality into memory. . . . Dwelling becomes an effect of language.[120]

The poem "II In Cairo," just like the other fragments composing "The Anecdotes," reverberates this linguistic mode of dwelling. The two stanzas following the initial line that seems to float above the poem, like a tentative title, attempt to redefine "nostalgia." "The homing pain for such as are attached" ushers in a series of sensorial perceptions that break free from spatiotemporal references, as if the attempt to circumscribe nostalgia progressively erased any fixed bearing. The sailor reading the omens in Ursa Major at the end of the first stanza mirrors the poet's eternal exile, which forces him as well to steer "the hub of the green wheel." This wheel echoes "The Prayer Wheel" where the poet endeavored, a few pages earlier in the same collection, to solve within the cycle of its seven stanzas the dichotomy between the abstract and the concrete, between immanence and transcendence.[121] Yet just as the cycle of prayers spelled hopelessness and death—"What is known is never written / . . . / The Dumb petitions in the churchyard / Under the European sword / Spell out our tribal suicide"[122]—the sailor's astronomical observation unveils a world of endless suffering: "Ursa Major to the sailor could spell wounds, / More than the mauling of the northern bear." These sufferings are indissociable from the aftermath of the Second World War, which led Durrell's contemporary, the French poet Pierre Reverdy, to assert: "I do not believe that a man can write anything which is not just influenced by or fraught with but utterly saturated by what we have been through." At the abstract and intimate level such a writing discloses the inner sufferings of the subject who has realized that, as Shmuel Trigano said, his former "world has . . . disappeared" and who strives to found a new "home": "Home for most is what you can least bear." Home is thus redefined not as the origin of essence but as the essence of pain. In his attempt to discover the source of his suffering the poet stumbles upon the very suffering that acts as a screen, both reverberating and hiding the ungraspable object of desire.

In the wake of the path delineated in "Cities, Plains and People," "The Anecdotes" offers a symbolic and spiritual journey throughout which writing becomes the true home the poet can only reach by relinquishing nostalgia through a renunciation of what Pierre Reverdy calls "specific reality":

> The emotion is not conveyed by the object: it is shaped within the subject who is the one to express it once he has betrayed and transformed it so well that it has nothing left in common with the object that apparently prompted it; the subject becomes its true source.
> The object is the specific reality. In the passage from the object to the subject reality vanishes away. New bonds are born.[123]

The initiatory journey is thus more clearly sketched out: the mandala of writing and the wheel of time establish unsuspected kinships between distinct poems and collections, suggesting a quest for deeper knowledge that the poetic subject can only apprehend through writing. Such is indeed the journey that the Kalachakra mandala stands for:

> The mandala draws out an initiatory quest through a palace dedicated to emptiness. . . . But emptiness does not mean naught, the complete negation of existence. This emptiness, which is not 'empty' in the common sense of the word, means a greater awareness of the unsubstantial nature of phenomena.[124]

Therefore, the poet's quest leads him to break free from the world of matter, to engage into those "new bonds" that combine the contraries in order to shed a new light upon the world: "*Ego gigno lumen*, I beget light / But darkness is also of my nature." This quotation from Hermes Trismegistus[125] leads the reader away from the darker undertones of "Cities"—"Now darkness comes to Europe / [. . .] / Barbarians with secretaries move"[126]—and heralds a world where reality and sensations are artfully welded. Thus, the sixteen fragments composing "The Anecdotes"—not unlike the sixteen forms of emptiness taught by Tibetan Buddhism[127]—represent both the specific materiality of space and its symbolic abstraction through which new relations are born. The subject of the poem detaches himself from his childhood roots and earlier years of formation evoked in "Cities" in order to build up a depersonalized subject and become this "anonymous hand" that sketches a fragile, idyllic space-time:

> Anonymous hand, record one afternoon,
> In May, some time before the fig-leaf:
> Boats lying idle in the sky, a town

> Thrown as on a screen of watered silk,
> Lying on its side, reddish and soluble,
> A sheet of glass leading down into the sea . . . [128]

From the depths of writing, shimmering with the "merging, overlapping, liquefying" contours of Venice in *Bitter Lemons*[129] or the town of Rhodes ready to "dissolve again as you enter the little harbor,"[130] there emerges the impalpable reality of the poem's island town "reddish and soluble." It stands for the quintessence of the isle, which the recurring reference to Atlantis metaphorizes: it is an Arcadia that keeps appearing and disappearing, the very object of the writing's relentless quest, always about to be submerged by the tides of time. Just like any other island town in Durrell's texts, it vanishes in the perfect completion of its mirage, both visual and prosodic. The "twelve sad lines" make up three stanzas whose decrescendo pattern (stanza 1: 6 lines; stanzas 2 and 3: 3 lines each) underline the slow, pliant rhythm of a world that delicately moves toward emptiness:

> Shape of boats, body of a young girl, cicada,
> Conspire and join each other here,
> In twelve sad lines against the dark.

The perfect shape of the poem playing on binary and ternary patterns is mirrored by that of beings and things that progressively turn into abstract symbols of a reality that no longer belongs to the realm of phenomena and enacts the shift from immanence to transcendence announced in "The Prayer-Wheel." Such are the silent and intangible forms that enable the poet to ward off the dark.

The following poem, "IV At Rhodes," opens up a meditation on the essence of space and on the nature of reality, thus functioning as an abstract counterpoint to the previous fragment:

> If space curves how much the more thought,
> Returning after every conjugation
> To the young point of rest it started in?
>
> The fullness of being is not in refinement,
> By the delimitation of the object, but
> In roundness, the embosoming of the Real.[131]

The exploration of space brings one back to one's starting point and functions as a metaphor for the exploration of the subject and of its relationship with the outer world. The analytic approach—"We may expound, break into fields of thought, / But qualifying in this manner only spoil"[132]—is replaced by an all-inclusive one, defined in "The Prayer-Wheel" as "the human compromise,"[133] which is the natural logical and mythological consequence of the cosmic incoherence and of man's powerlessness and which the Yellow Emperor in "Cities" already heralded:

> Apparent opposition of the two
> Where unlocked numbers show their fabric,
> He laid his finger to the map,
> And where the signs confuse,
> Defined the Many and the None
> As base reflections of the One.[134]

The reader is thus allowed to trace down the slow maturing process of Durrell's metaphysics, which blends Eastern and Western thought. Attempting to go beyond the analytic perception he practiced at the Villa Seurat, he searches in Rhodes for a deeper understanding into man's mind that would enable him to bridge the gap between alien representations of the man and of the world, as his letter to Henry Miller evinces:

> I have been reading the second of Groddeck's books; just the world for it, this shining Greek light. . . . It is the rearrangement of the Freudian concepts into a philosophic system in which the individual sees all round himself. The IT concept is TAO. . . . In other words the mechanical view is replaced by the vitalist view. It is interesting in this book to read the long eulogy by Keyserling . . . in which he says that Groddeck of all men reminded him of Lao Tzu in his application of the Chinese idea of non-action. . . . Freud's part is the calculus. Groddeck's the attitude. Ah! If only we had known about him in Paris! This is all that we felt was missing from Howe and Rank and Jung![135]

This humanist vision, which replaces the "mechanical" one and embraces both body and mind, permeates both Durrell's creation and his philosophical reflection. Some thirty years later, he will dwell upon it again in his preface to the French edition of *The Book of the It*:

> Like any poet he is not any more systematic than dogmatic or didactic. . . . He is guided by selected "intuitions" and shows the skills of a born writer. . . . he refused to accept the division between mind and body into two categories; to him, they were different modalities of being. . . . His books have the magic confidence of poetry which is, after all, the ability to see . . .[136]

This "ability to see" the one in the many, to overcome the "signs [that] confuse," to solve divisions pervades Durrell's poetry. If one may say that "Cities" retraces the birth and the coming of age of the artist's conscience, then "The Anecdotes" could be considered as the outcome of this process, as if the poet had actually taken the place of Prospero who, at the opening of the third section of "Cities," holds in his hand the apple of a new world whose perfect circularity is folded within the curves of writing. The apple, the mandala, and the prayer-wheel thus operate as T. S. Eliot's objective correlatives for a particular space-time embodied by the dynamic paradox of the wheel, which remains fixed upon its axis while in motion. Likewise, the ongoing spiral of chanted prayers, or the expanding circle of poems echoing one another, symbolize the growing awareness achieved through a poetry whose various figures—Prospero, the Yellow Emperor in "Cities," Garcia, the sailor, Melissa, Clea in "The Anecdotes"—function as so many camera-eyes that step across temporal, spatial, and textual boundaries to announce a higher wisdom: "no saint or seer unlocks / The wells of truth unless he first / Conquer for the truth his thirst."[137]

Therefore the concluding lines of "IV At Rhodes" become programmatic:

> We used experience up. The rest precipitated.
> Soon we were still alive: but nothing else was left.

Intimate experience leads to a new form of knowledge whereby, as in an alchemical experiment, solid matter changes species. The same process is hinted at by Phaon in *Sappho*:

> . . . there is
> A factor, like some colourless precipitate,
> Unlike time, yet of it, that is the clue,
> The great clue to the world of unseen forms.[138]

Significantly the same process is at work in the writing of the poem itself. Thus, "VI At Alexandria" operates as the "colourless precipitate" of the unseen form of the *Alexandria Quartet*:

> At four thirty the smell of satin, leather:
> Rain falling in the mirror above the mad
> Jumbled pots of expensive scent and fard,
> And the sense of some great impending scandal.[139]

The reader immediately recognizes the poetic prose of *Justine* where Darley describes the train taking Melissa away:

> Five o'clock. Walking about in her room, studying inanimate objects with intense concentration. The empty powder-boxes. The depilatories from Sardis. The smell of satin and leather. The horrible feeling of some great impending scandal . . .[140]

Thus the poetic writing seeps into the later prose, breaking the barriers between self-contained genres and allowing the poem to reverberate in the prose as textual, spatial, and temporal boundaries collapse. Once again, the reader is reminded of the prophetic words of Diomedes in *Sappho*:

> Phaon
> In verse or prose, whichever pleases you.
> Diomedes
> It is the same to me. Whether it's prose or verse
> I can accommodate it, shape it, give it birth.[141]

Poetry may then be considered as the substrate of writing. It dwells in those marginal spaces, carving underground correspondences in which readers may fathom the latent echoes between the lines.

The same phenomenon is at work in "VII Alexandria," where the image of the egg reads as the poetic precipitate of the poetic end of *The Black Book*:

> Sometime we shall all come together
> And it will be time to put a stop
> To this little rubbing together of minimal words,
> To let the Word Prime repose in its mode
> As yolk in its fort of albumen reposes
> Contented by the circular propriety
> Of its hammock in the formal breathing egg.[142]

One easily recognizes here the concluding lines of *The Black Book*:

> From between your legs leaking, the breathing yolk, the durable, the forever, the enormous Now.
> This is how it ends.
> THE END[143]

This paradoxical ending, twice asserted, heralds a new world while folding back upon itself, through the polyptoton and the poetic echo to a text that promises a refunded space-time. The "Many" thus reverts to the "One" according to the Buddhist principle, which is reflected in the successive run-on lines giving the syntactic unit a smooth and flowing rhythm.

The central aim of "The Anecdotes" is then not to retrace the details of the poet's artistic progress but to build up a new mode of writing and of reading that is inseparable from a sharper awareness. The following stanzas unfold a series of metaphorical images of the poetic act: the "sculpture" that disengages itself from the thickness of matter, the "plumbline" used to fathom space, the "ideogram," sharp as "a knifeblade" that delineates a new reality until the final metaphor, which conflates the poem with the "metaphor / For perpetual and *useless* suffering exposed / By conscience in the very act of writing."

Not just a combination of metaphors, the poem is the essence of metaphor, it is a symbolic transfer, a displaced image, as Pierre Reverdy explains:

> A poem . . . is in fact a complex image which, once it has been created, becomes an autonomous object within reality. Yet, the image is, by definition, the means of incorporating reality in order to reduce it to such proportions that can easily be apprehended by man. It is the magical act of transmutation of the outer reality into an inner one.[144]

This "transmutation of the outer reality into an inner one," which is enacted through the poetic image, affects both the world and the subject. Thus, the exiled subject in "Cities" becomes in "The Anecdotes" the subject estranged from his own self who can watch at a distance "The exile I had already begun within myself" in "XIII In Paris" before he performs the final enunciative shift whereby time is reversed: "The heart must be very old to feel so young." This is the point when the poet, having truly "used experience up,"[145] reaches out to the life-giving force of the poetic world that endures when nothing else is left. The heart of the old poet reaching back into time is strongly reminiscent of Pierre Reverdy's description of the poet as

> this old man of thirteen years old waking up. . . . this child loaded with gifts that place him so much above his age level . . . has entered the world through a broken door. . . . However, this entrance might as well be a ruse and this world, the mere anteroom to another which he alone is somewhat miraculously empowered to create and, later on, from one surprise to the next, to lead us to explore.[146]

Therefore the real world would merely be a decoy out of which the poet attempts to guide us. One may easily recognize here the presence of Plato's cave as well as the Gnostic theories that gain such a prevailing influence in Durrell's later prose work. However, contrary to Akkad's tenets developed in *The Avignon Quintet* where man has been tricked by "the usurping god" into mistaking beauty for truth,[147] the Gnostic leap enacted through poetry seems to operate in a reverse fashion. Delving into the sensual matter of the world, instead of shutting oneself off from the world, becomes the very means the poet chooses to accomplish "the mystic leap."[148] And like a true initiator, he only brings his readers on the brink of that new world so that both "Cities" and "The Anecdotes" end on a threshold. "Cities" concludes on "the evergreen / Cell by the margin of the sea and land"[149] while the last fragment of "The Anecdotes" opens on a farewell: "And so at last goodbye."[150] Yet just as *The Black Book*, "The Anecdotes" present the reader with a paradoxical closure that simultaneously conjures up a new world:

> Yet the thing can be done, as you say, simply
> By sitting and waiting, the mystical leap
> Is only a figure for it, it involves not daring
> But patience, being gored, not to cry out.
> But perhaps even the desire itself is dying.
> I should like that: to make an end of it.[151]

This "mystical leap" accomplished through patience and renunciation foreshadows that of the Bodhidharma as well as the last words of the *The Avignon Quintet*. In both cases the mysterious cave opens on an endless silence whereby, as Corinne Alexandre-Garner has explained, "the author rejects the idea of finitude and offers an oriental definition of the passing of time."[152] The modals "can" and "should" that frame the stanza suggest the unaccomplished that lies at the heart of the poem, as if the end of desire were the poet's only true aim, an impossible, irrepresentable, immaterial end that eludes language. This "last goodbye" is strikingly different from the final parting suggested some forty years later in the "*disenfranchised last goodbye, / Goodbye*" that ends the poem "Le Cercle refermé" in *Caesar's Vast Ghost*. It is a farewell to the world of illusions, which enacts "the mystical leap" through the interplay of joining and dividing that characterizes the last three stanzas. The two penultimate ones are indeed both typographically separated by the blank and semantically linked by the translation of "to make an end of it" into "It is time we did away," which heralds further development in the previous stanza. Finally, the ultimate line "You kiss and make: while I withdraw and plead" both reads as a distinct clausula isolated from the body of the poem while acting as a perfect syntactic mirror to the last line of the antepenultimate stanza: "I should like that: to make an end of it." The "mystical leap" thus lies in the blanks that both separate and bind the various elements of this last fragment as well as the sixteen sections of the poem: it establishes a poetic community that remains permanently open and fluid through the staging of the enunciative shifters "I" and "you" that can refer, over time and space, to an infinity of speakers and addressees. This new, unassignable community heralds a new era that the poet and the reader are to explore jointly as the use of the first-person plural as well as the balanced symmetry of the modal structures—"As for me I must do as I was born / And so must you"[153]—evinces. Dissociation and unity, difference and conference are thus welded together in a form that abolishes dichotomies and summons what "Cities" defined as a "personal landscape built / Within the Chinese circle's calm embrace."[154] However, as "The Anecdotes" remind us, the completion of the circle can never be fully apprehended, only hinted at through imperfect patterns: "The egg, the cone, the rhombus,"[155] that act as so many moving and tentative clues, or the mandala, a simultaneously two-dimensional and three-dimensional representation interweaving the granular fluidity of color pigments and the shimmering volume of the wheel of time.

If one may concur with Corinne Alexandre-Garner that "the last 'goodbye' which ends the last book . . . only points to the space where time comes to be silent, to move from speech to silence, from presence to final absence,"[156] one may nevertheless remark that Durrell's earlier poetic work, and more specifically *Cities, Plains and People* and *On Seeming to Presume*, point toward "the infinite within the text."[157] The last hemistich "I withdraw and plead" suggests indeed "the signature of an open oeuvre,"[158] which is set against the final disappearance it purported to stage. Never is the poet so present and vocal as in the pregnant echoes of this infinite silence, calling back into mind the programmatic ending of *Justine*: "Does not everything depend upon our interpretation of the silence around us?"[159] In the same gesture, the poet obeys the code of classical closure within the scope of a single stanza comprising a single line that concludes the final fragment of the last poem in the collection, and simultaneously debunks it. The last word—"plead"—enacts the ultimate subversion by giving voice to the infinite echo that haunts the text. It materializes the quintessentially immaterial poetic voice born out of the very dematerialization, which is the prerequisite to its existence. This is how Durrell opens his reader to a new perception that is directly inherited from Zen Buddhism:

> It is only when you seek it that you lose it.
> You cannot take hold of it, nor can you get rid of it;
> While you can do neither, it goes on its way;
> You remain silent and it speaks; you speak and it is silent.[160]

A careful reading of Suzuki's *Manual of Zen Buddhism*, which Durrell thoroughly underlined and annotated, reveals his spiritual kinship with the Master of Zen. Thus, the final remark—"I will let him realize the great Tao"—is ended by Durrell's hand in the margin: "by shutting up!"[161] At the heart of this metaphysical silence the reader is led to explore the fundamental emptiness that rules the cosmos and the initiatory powers of poetry as a place of awakening, as the experience of an inner progress toward a truth that is yet to be discovered.

Through the disfiguration of space it stages, *On Seeming to Presume* marks a turning point in Durrell's poetic writing. Opening at an angle to the Greek world on the island of Revelation, the collection paves the way for a new relation to the world. Objects, places, and characters assemble in a moving picture that invites the reader to go beyond representation and question the bonds that make up our world and are, according to Yves Bonnefoy, the true essence of poetry, which is "not the production of poems but the deepening and therefore the reorganizing of the bonds between people or between them and the space where they live, what we call the world."[162]

Such an experience is indissociable from the personal, spiritual, and philosophical progress through which the poet, opening up words as so many doors onto the sensible, attempts to give meaning to his being in the world. Throughout the unending weaving of texts, he explores the substance where he belongs, which dwells in him, resists him, and endures. By contrasting the painful awareness of his own finitude against the timeless presence that breathes through his writing, he endeavors to inhabit a place that keeps eluding him and is perpetually reborn and whose critical importance Bonnefoy tirelessly asserted:

> Hence poetry. That is, within speech which has been turned into conceptual discourse, the act of recollection of a background which is entirely continuous, united, and which had unfolded from the dawn of sign. . . . in the verbal sign, since it continues to exist within language where it is born by the voice, its non-signifying facet (that is sound as such, a bare reality of the word) can recall to the speaker what he has lost in terms of presence to the world, and induce him towards a speech that will allow for rhythms born from the body to look over the wall of concept and into the garden of the dawn of day.[163]

Such a definition is in keeping with Durrell's reading of the sign:

> Poetically words are less important for their dictionary meanings than for the vibrations they set up in the middle ear—the pineal ear, so to speak. Poets are

simply handers on of the sound, like sea shells; and, yes, it is always the sound of the sea—*symbolon tees geneseoos*, in the words of Plato.[164]

Poetry is thus to be understood as an invitation to listen to the secret echoes that will enable us to decipher "the vocabulary of roses,"[165] which offers us a glimpse into Bonnefoy's "garden of the dawn of day"—a place where the multiple signs of loss are turned inside out to reveal the land the poet yearns for: the native soil of writing. Through this final "mystical leap" that pervades Durrell's entire oeuvre, exile and death are no longer synonymous with pain and suffering but disclose what Bonnefoy calls "a prospective return" whereby "a whole future of true life could be born from redeemed speech."[166] As any true redemption, that of poetry signals the end of solitude: the addressee who is inscribed within the text—"You kiss and make"[167]—is the poet's alter ego, his confidant, and the far-away neighbor entrusted with a new world.

Notes

1. T. S. Eliot's letter to Lawrence Durrell, January 27, 1948, quoted by Ian MacNiven, *Lawrence Durrell: A Biography*, London: Faber, 1998, p. 347.

2. ". . . I am on the last lap of the race finishing the labyrinth book," Letter to Henry Miller dated October 1945, *The Durrell-Miller Letters, 1935–80*, Ian S. MacNiven, ed., London: Faber, 1988, p. 186. *Cefalu* was first published in 1947 and reissued under the title *The Dark Labyrinth* in 1964.

3. *The Durrell-Miller Letters*, p. 187.

4. Letter to Henry Miller, January 1, 1946, *The Durrell-Miller Letters*, pp. 190–91.

5. "'Enter the dark crystal if you dare / And gaze on Greece,'" "Letter to Seferis the Greek," Lawrence Durrell, *A Private Country*, London: Faber, 1944 (first published in 1943), p. 69.

6. Letter to Henry Miller, September 25, 1946, *The Durrell-Miller Letters*, p. 198.

7. *The Durrell-Miller Letters*, p. 191.

8. Lawrence Durrell, *The Alexandria Quartet*, London: Faber, 1974 (first published in 1962), p. 668.

9. Lawrence Durrell, *The Alexandria Quartet*, p. 668.

10. Lawrence Durrell, *The Greek Islands*, London: Faber, 1978, pp. 164–65.

11. See the chapter entitled "Patmos" in Lawrence Durrell, *Reflections on a Marine Venus*, London: Faber, 1953, pp. 63–79, as well as the article "The Island of the Rose" published by Durrell in 1947 in the *Geographical Magazine*. For a critical translation and a detailed study of the latter, see Isabelle Keller-Privat, "L'île de la rose de Lawrence Durrell: aux confins du voyage, l'île palimpsest," *Les Artistes anglo-américains et la Méditerranée*, vol. 3, Paris: Michel Houdiard, 2010, chapter 6, pp. 106–30.

12. Lawrence Durrell, *On Seeming to Presume*, London: Faber, 1948, p. 9.

13. *The Durrell-Miller Letters*, p. 191.
14. *The Greek Islands*, p. 164.
15. Revelation 21: 1.
16. *Reflections on a Marine Venus*, pp. 66, 76.
17. *Reflections on a Marine Venus*, p. 94.
18. *The Alexandria Quartet*, p. 439.
19. Christian Doumet, *Faut-il comprendre la poésie?* Paris: Klincksieck, 2004, p. 81.
20. William Wordsworth, "Lines written a few miles above Tintern Abbey," *Lyrical Ballads 1798*, Oxford: Oxford University Press, 1993, p. 112.
21. "Lines written a few miles above Tintern Abbey," p. 113.
22. "In the Garden: Villa Cleobolus," *On Seeming to Presume*, p. 25.
23. "In the Garden: Villa Cleobolus," *On Seeming to Presume*, p. 25.
24. Letter from Rhodes dated January 20, 1946, *The Durrell-Miller Letters*, p. 201.
25. Pierre Reverdy, *Cette émotion appelée poésie. Écrits sur la poésie (1930-1960)*, Paris: Flammarion, 1974, p. 63.
26. *Reflections on a Marine Venus*, pp. 107–32.
27. *Reflections on a Marine Venus*, p. 122.
28. Lawrence Durrell, *Bitter Lemons of Cyprus*, London: Faber, 1957, pp. 15–16.
29. William Wordsworth and Samuel Taylor Coleridge, "The Rime of the Ancyent Marinere," *Lyrical Ballads 1798*, p. 17.
30. *Reflections on a Marine Venus*, p. 121.
31. "[. . .] we see the 'archaics' which the woman spoke of; a series of trenches and parapets cut in the red soil of the valley to form a square," *Reflections on a Marine Venus*, p. 110.
32. "Last Heard of," in Lawrence Durrell, *Vega and Other Poems*, London: Faber, 1973, p. 38.
33. *Faut-il comprendre la poésie?* p. 111.
34. *Reflections on a Marine Venus*, p. 128.
35. *On Seeming to Presume*, p. 11.
36. *Reflections on a Marine Venus*, p. 48.
37. Jean-Christophe Bailly, *L'élargissement du poème*, Paris: Bourgeois, 2015, p. 162.
38. *L'élargissement du poème*, p. 164.
39. *L'élargissement du poème*, p. 164.
40. Antonio Fregoso (1444–1512).
41. *On Seeming to Presume*, p. 18.
42. *Reflections on a Marine Venus*, pp. 110–11.
43. "In Europe," Lawrence Durrell, *Cities, Plains and People*, London: Faber, 1946, p. 30.
44. Lawrence Durrell, *The Avignon Quintet*, London: Faber, 1992, p. 1346.
45. "In Europe," *Cities, Plains and People*, pp. 29, 30.
46. "The Parthenon," *On Seeming to Presume*, p. 38.
47. *On Seeming to Presume*, p. 37.
48. *On Seeming to Presume*, p. 37.

49. *On Seeming to Presume*, p. 37.
50. *On Seeming to Presume*, p. 37.
51. Numbers 17: 8.
52. "Seferis," *Vega*, p. 54.
53. The copy of *Vega* held by the Bibliothèque Lawrence Durrell at the University Paris Ouest–Nanterre includes a blank page.
54. "We are the clay, and thou our potter; and we all are the work of thy hand," Isaiah 64: 8.
55. *On Seeming to Presume*, p. 11.
56. "Fangbrand," *A Private Country*, p. 7.
57. "To Argos," *A Private Country*, p. 15.
58. *A Private Country*, p. 22.
59. *A Private Country*, p. 71. In *Panic Spring* Marlowe, leaving England, heads for the same blue: "[. . .] life which could drag him off, sans destination, into the blue, southward," Lawrence Durrell, *Panic Spring: A Romance*, James Gifford, ed., Victoria, Canada: ELS editions, 2008 (first published in 1937), p. 10.
60. "Palme" was first published in 1919 before it was reissued in *Charmes* in 1922. Paul Valery, *Œuvres I*, Paris: Gallimard, 1957, "Bibliothèque de La Pléiade," 153–56. "Patience, patience, / Patience in the azure! / Every atom of silence / Holds the promise of a ripe fruit!"
61. *On Seeming to Presume*, p. 38.
62. "Στεριές και νησιά," "Steries kai Nissia," "Lands and Islands," from "O Ilios o Iliatoras," translated by Kimon Friar and published under the title *The Sovereign Sun: Selected Poems*, Temple University Press, 1974. I wish to thank Barbara Papastavrou for her help in identifying the quotation. Odysseas Elytis is among the circle of Greek friends mentioned by Durrell in *The Greek Islands* (p. 235).
63. *Reflections on a Marine Venus*, p. 15.
64. *On Seeming to Presume*, p. 18.
65. *On Seeming to Presume*, p. 17.
66. *On Seeming to Presume*, p. 22.
67. "Home for most is what you can least bear," in "The Anecdotes," "II In Cairo," *On Seeming to Presume*, p. 49.
68. T. S. Eliot, "The Love Song of J. Alfred Prufrock," *Collected Poems 1909-1962*, London: Faber, 2002, p. 5. Both poets are all the more intimately linked as the persona of "The Love Song of J. Alfred Prufrock" echoes Hamlet's: "No! I am not Prince Hamlet, nor was meant to be," p. 7.
69. *On Seeming to Presume*, pp. 39–40.
70. *On Seeming to Presume*, p. 39.
71. William Shakespeare, *Hamlet*, act 2, scene 2.
72. "Titania waked and straightaway loved an ass," William Shakespeare, *A Midsummer Night's Dream*, London: Routledge, 1994, act 3, scene 2.
73. Mark 10: 24.

74. Percy Bysshe Shelley, "A Defence of Poetry," *The Complete Works, Prose: Volumes V–VI–VII*, London: Ernest Benn, 1965, p. 115.

75. *The Alexandria Quartet*, p. 278.

76. Many characters are significantly made to cross the desert (Narouz, Nessim, Pursewarden, Mountolive), and the name "Nessim" means "the breeze" in Arabic.

77. See for instance *The Alexandria Quartet*, pp. 310, 381, 386.

78. *The Alexandria Quartet*, p. 121. In *Clea*, Darley is invited by Liza to retrieve Pursewarden's secret correspondence on a night when the khamseen is symbolically blowing (*The Alexandria Quartet*, p. 783).

79. "With that, I've said it all," interview with Michel Braudeau, June 1984, in Earl G. Ingersoll, ed., *Lawrence Durrell: Conversations*, Madison: Fairleigh Dickinson University Press, 1998, pp. 190–91.

80. Yves Bonnefoy, *La Beauté dès le premier jour*, Paris: William Blake & Co. Édit., 2009, p. 9.

81. "With that, I've said it all," interview with Michel Braudeau, June 1984, *Lawrence Durrell: Conversations*, pp. 190–91.

82. *On Seeming to Presume*, p. 40.

83. *On Seeming to Presume*, p. 40.

84. *La Beauté dès le premier jour*, p. 9.

85. W. B. Yeats, "To the Rose upon the Rood of Time," *The Rose* (1893), *W. B. Yeats: A Critical Edition of the Major Works*, Oxford: Oxford University Press, 1997, p. 12.

86. "The Rose of Battle," *The Rose* (1893), *W. B. Yeats: A Critical Edition of the Major Works*, p. 18.

87. "When I said. A rose is a rose is a rose is a rose. And then later made that into a ring I made poetry and what did I do I caressed completely caressed and addressed a noun," Gertrude Stein, "Poetry and Grammar," *Lectures in America*, Boston: Beacon Press, 1985, p. 231.

88. Notebook entitled "Endpapers and Inklings," dated 1988. Quoted in "Manufacturing Dreams or Lawrence Durrell's Fiction Revisited through the Prism of Chirico's Metaphysical Painting," Corinne Alexandre-Garner and Isabelle Keller-Privat, *Deus Loci: The Lawrence Durrell Journal* NS 13 (2012–2013), pp. 105–6.

89. *The Alexandria Quartet*, p. 879.

90. Paul Valéry, "Propos sur la poésie," *Œuvres I*, Paris: Gallimard, 1957, p. 1369.

91. "A Defence of Poetry," pp. 111–12.

92. *Cette émotion appelée poésie*, pp. 34–35.

93. Thierry Maulnier, *Introduction à la poésie française*, Paris: Gallimard, 1939, pp. 98–99.

94. "Mark of Patmos," *On Seeming to Presume*, p. 43.

95. Lawrence Durrell, *A Smile in the Mind's Eye*, London: Faber, 1982 (first published in 1980) pp. 50–51.

96. From Greek *anakhōrein*, ANA + *khōrein* withdraw, *The New Shorter Oxford Dictionary*.

97. "Basil the Hermit," *On Seeming to Presume*, p. 44.
98. *The Avignon Quintet*, p. 1229.
99. D. T. Suzuki, *Manual of Zen Buddhism*, London: Rider and Company, 1956, p. 87.
100. "Dmitri of Carpathos," *On Seeming to Presume*, p. 45.
101. The term *icon* is understood here as a sign defined by its resemblance to the "reality" of the external world, as opposed to the clue (characterized by its "natural contiguity") and the symbol (relying on mere social convention), based on the definitions elaborated by A. J. Greimas and J. Courtès, *Sémiotique: Dictionnaire raisonné de la théorie du langage*, Paris: Hachette Supérieur, 1993, p. 177.
102. "Three sailors stand like brooms. / The altar has opened like a honeycomb; / An erect and flashing deacon like a deposition," *Cities, Plains and People*, p. 55.
103. "If truth were needles surely eyes would see?" *On Seeming to Presume*, p. 40.
104. "Fangbrand," *A Private Country*, p. 10.
105. "Investigating a Nightingale," *Lawrence Durrell: Conversations*, p. 82.
106. *The Avignon Quintet*, p. 351.
107. "Panagiotis of Lindos," *On Seeming to Presume*, p. 46.
108. "A Rhodian Captain," *On Seeming to Presume*, p. 46.
109. *Cities, Plains and People*, p. 72.
110. *On Seeming to Presume*, p. 9.
111. Sylvie Crossman, "Le mandala de Kalachakra ou le vaisseau du grand voyage," *Tibet, les formes du vide*, Montpellier: Indigène éditions, 1996, pp. 25–26.
112. *Tibet, les formes du vide*, p. 27.
113. For a detailed study of the relationships between "Cities, Plains and People" and T. S. Eliot's *Four Quartets* see C. Alexandre-Garner, I. Keller-Privat, "When Elsewhere Is Home: Mapping Literature as Home in Lawrence Durrell's 'Cities, Plains and People,'" *Etudes Britanniques Contemporaines* no. 37 (2009), pp. 69–86.
114. Ian MacNiven, *Lawrence Durrell*, p. 280.
115. Letter from Rhodes dated January 20, 1946, *The Durrell-Miller Letters*, p. 201.
116. "I In Cairo," "The Anecdotes," *On Seeming to Presume*, p. 49.
117. *Cities, Plains and People*, p. 57.
118. *Cities, Plains and People*, p. 58.
119. "II In Cairo," "The Anecdotes," *On Seeming to Presume*, p. 49.
120. Shmuel Trigano, *Le Temps de l'exil*, Paris: Éditions Payot & Rivages, 2005, pp. 33–34.
121. For a textual and genetic study of this poem see Fiona Tomkinson, "Durrell's 'Poem in Space Time' at the Crossroads of the Arts and the Sciences," *Lawrence Durrell at the Crossroads of Arts and Sciences*, Presses Universitaires de Paris Ouest, 2010, pp. 117–29.
122. *On Seeming to Presume*, pp. 31–32.
123. "Le poète secret et le monde extérieur" (1938), *Cette émotion appelée poésie*, p. 129.
124. *Tibet, les formes du vide*, p. 27.

125. Both lines are a direct reference to "Ego gigno lumen, tenebræ autem naturæ meæ sunt," *Rosarium Philosophorum* (1550), *Artis auriferae II* (1593), quoted by Carl Jung, *Dreams*, London: Routledge, 2002, p. 186.
126. *Cities, Plains and People*, p. 68.
127. See *Tibet, les formes du vide*, pp. 33–34.
128. "III At Rhodes," *On Seeming to Presume*, p. 50.
129. *Bitter Lemons*, p. 15.
130. *Reflections on a Marine Venus*, p. 77.
131. "IV At Rhodes," *On Seeming to Presume*, p. 50.
132. *On Seeming to Presume*, p. 50.
133. *On Seeming to Presume*, p. 30.
134. *Cities, Plains and People*, p. 68.
135. Letter dated from February 28, 1946, *The Durrell-Miller Letters*, p. 195.
136. Lawrence Durrell, "Préface," Georg Groddeck, *Le Livre du Ça*, Paris: Gallimard, 1973, pp. 7–8.
137. *Cities, Plains and People*, p. 61.
138. Lawrence Durrell, *Sappho*, London: Faber, 1967 (first published in 1950), scene 1, p. 56.
139. "VI At Alexandria," *On Seeming to Presume*, p. 52.
140. *The Alexandria Quartet*, p. 87. For a stylistic study of this passage see Corinne Alexandre-Garner and Isabelle Keller-Privat, "Lawrence George Durrell (1912-1990)," *Guide de la littérature britannique des origines à nos jours*, Paris: Ellipses, 2008, pp. 321–22.
141. *Sappho*, scene 2, p. 63.
142. "VII At Alexandria," *On Seeming to Presume*, p. 52.
143. Lawrence Durrell, *The Black Book*, London: Faber, 1977 (first published in 1938), p. 244.
144. *Cette émotion appelée poésie*, p. 67.
145. "IV At Rhodes," *On Seeming to Presume*, p. 51.
146. "Preface to 'Souspente' d'Antoine Tudal" (1945), *Cette émotion appelée poésie*, pp. 200–201.
147. "Beauty is a trap," *The Avignon Quintet*, p. 116.
148. "XVI In Rio," *On Seeming to Presume*, p. 60.
149. *Cities, Plains and People*, p. 72.
150. "XVI In Rio," *On Seeming to Presume*, p. 59.
151. "XVI In Rio," *On Seeming to Presume*, p. 60.
152. Corinne Alexandre-Garner, "Durrell: la clôture impossible," *Études Britanniques Contemporaines* no. 10, 1996, p. 93.
153. "XVI In Rio," *On Seeming to Presume*, p. 60.
154. *Cities, Plains and People*, p. 69.
155. "IV At Rhodes," *On Seeming to Presume*, p. 50.
156. "Durrell: la clôture impossible?" pp. 94–95.
157. "Durrell: la clôture impossible?" p. 95.

158. "Durrell: la clôture impossible?" p. 93.
159. *The Alexandria Quartet*, p. 195.
160. *Manual of Zen Buddhism*, p. 98. This passage was underlined by Durrell in his personal copy.
161. *Manual of Zen Buddhism*, p. 111.
162. *La Beauté dès le premier jour*, p. 8.
163. *La Beauté dès le premier jour*, p. 10.
164. "The Kneller Tape" (1962), *Lawrence Durrell: Conversations*, p. 72.
165. *On Seeming to Presume*, p. 43.
166. *La Beauté dès le premier jour*, p. 10.
167. *On Seeming to Presume*, p. 60.

CHAPTER FOUR

"Dreams bursting at the seams to die"[1]
The Tree of Idleness, The Mauled Dream

The title of this fourth collection suggests the safe haven of a self-enclosed space, a place of anchorage and freedom placed under the auspices of the prefatory note[2] that functions as a prologue to Milarepa's introduction: "The notion of emptiness engenders compassion." The collection is thus introduced twice: once by its author, who traces its source back to "the name of the tree which stands outside Bellapaix Abbey in Cyprus, and which confers the gift of pure idleness on all who sit under it," and then by the Buddhist philosopher, who warns the reader to envisage the ontological emptiness of worldly forms.

Significantly, *The Tree of Idleness* sketches out a moving territory where the poet's persona keeps drifting and resurfacing, as if torn between distant writing anchoring points. The first poem, entitled "Lesbos," points both to the later song that will first be published in 1963[3] and to the earlier play, *Sappho* (1950), thus tearing apart the formal unity of the poem, which simultaneously partakes of the dramatic and musical genres. Unlike *On Seeming to Presume*, which was mostly centered on Rhodes, the following collection orients the reader's gaze toward the Greek space in poems such as "Niki," "Mneiae," or "Orpheus," the better to jostle the reader into the hostile universe of "River Water." The memory of Greece is thus dramatically pitted against the shores of Europe: Belgrade, where Durrell seeks a refuge from his exile in Venice ("A Water-Colour of Venice") and Ischia ("Deus Loci"). Greece thus functions as a central obsessing memory and as the fundamental gleam of light that sheds hope on darker places such as Alexandria ("A Bowl of Roses" and "A Portrait of Theodora") and Yugoslavia ("Sarajevo" and "Letters in Darkness"). Such a broken and jerky structure may be accounted for by the fact that this collection was not written in "the shade of the Greek sun"[4] but in various places of exile where Durrell was sent before reaching Cyprus:

> After five years of Serbia I had begun to doubt, whether in wanting to live in the Mediterranean at all, I was not guilty of some fearful aberration; indeed the whole of this adventure had begun to smell of improbability.[5]

This is why the reader finds himself constantly displaced, miles away from the reassuring shelter that the title seemed to promise and forced to share this "fearful aberration": finding peace and freedom through a journey punctuated by endless uprootings and in which each temporary harbor is proof to the unstable, improbable nature of human anchorage. This is how the collection sets to explore a deep anxiety rooted in belonging and loss, a paradox through which the subject strives to build up a dream that defeats the laws of causality and the rules of human time. Starting from the realities of a well-known universe, the poet unfolds a new order: "everything becomes strange, distorted. . . . Reality is severed from the rule of time and space" as well as from logic so as to "shock the reader. . . . The latter is no longer confident but thrown into a state of alarm."[6]

In the Bosom of Silence

We may remember Richard Pine's perspective on the structural unity of Durrell's poetry that was based on an analogical reading of his poetry and prose work:

> . . . we can examine the body of his poetry from 1931, when he was still in his teens, up to the poems written in his fortieth year (appearing as *The Tree of Idleness*, 1955) as a cohesive body of work, a self-contained metaphor in the long curve of his writing life parallel to regarding his first four novels as a preliminary quartet.[7]

According to such an interpretation, *The Tree of Idleness* should be considered as the conclusion to the cycle, solving past interrogations and bringing to an end Durrell's poetic opus that Pine sums up as follows:

> . . . poetry meant a celebration of the island as a haven and a way of analysing what the haven contained. Durrell re-entered the womb in order to leave it once more.[8]

And yet the pattern that evolves from the preceding collections we have just studied rather points toward the disfiguration of the island through a writing that veers away from its object in order to offer the reader not so much "a celebration of the island" as its transmutation into a poetic experience that opens up the subject's conscience to a never-ending questioning of himself and of the world at large. The poem entitled "The Tree of Idleness" looms out like the displaced shadow of the fifth chapter of *Bitter Lemons*,[9] thus pointing to the in-between space of creative freedom that shimmers in the woof of the text, in between poetry and prose, in between a visionary and a discursive writing. The island may therefore be considered not as the object but as the receptacle of a scriptural experience that roots itself in space in order to accomplish a metamorphosis through which poetry enacts what the German critic Hugo Friedrich calls "a mystery, a narrow conquest upon the ineffable, a miracle and a force."[10]

"The Tree of Idleness," placed at the heart of the collection, functions as another eponymous poem, in the tradition of "Cities, Plains and People" and "On Seeming to Presume." But the similarity between the three collections is not just a structural one. "The Tree of Idleness" strongly echoes "In the Garden: Villa Cleobolus," for they both open on a deceptive title: just as the villa vanished away in the previous collection to make way for the garden, the tree of idleness, which has been announced by the title of the collection, that of the poem, and by the preliminary note, disappears instantly to be replaced by "this old Turkish house"[11] that comes to symbolize the poet's future tomb. And yet the symbolism of the house in Durrell's oeuvre is a most pregnant one, as the writer has explicitly stated: "A house means property, succession, home and family order. It also, by association, stands for children."[12] The poem and the collection are marked by a twofold absence: that of the house that will never be the ideal home Durrell had dreamed of, and that he will be forced to abandon, and that of "the gift of pure idleness" fraught with peace, freedom, and wisdom the poet will longingly retrace in his writing, having experienced its cruel loss. We may recall that "In the Garden: Villa Cleobolus" sketched out the hope of eternity achieved in the embrace of the dancers motionlessly spinning through space and time; "The Tree of Idleness" attempts to capture another form of eternity that takes the shape of a peaceful, welcome death under the banana trees, a death that sounds like a comforting promise:

> I shall die one day I suppose
> In this old Turkish house I inhabit:
> A ragged banana-leaf outside and here
> On the sill in a jam-jar a rock-rose.

The mirrored run-on lines (lines 1–2 and lines 3–4) breaks up the stanza into two balanced halves as if to refract the perfect equation between this world and the next, between the house of the living and that of the dead. The "banana-leaf" and the "rock-rose" point to the lost life and to the upcoming one that is brought to the fore in the next stanza where the "pining mandolin" and the "cicadas" refer the reader to a twofold mourning: that of the island and of Greece conveyed in the poem and in the residence book and that of India haunting Durrell's Greece without ever being stated:

> . . . crowning every courtyard like a messenger from my Indian childhood spread the luxuriant green fan of banana-leaves, rattling like parchment in the wind. From behind the closed door of the tavern came the mournful whining of a mandolin.[13]

The residence book thus enlightens the subtext of the poem that hints both at the inner longing for a peaceful emptiness—the very same suggested by Milarepa and materialized by the tree of idleness—and at the ominous foreboding of an irrecoverable loss that pervades the poet's soul and "Scratches on silence like a pet locked in."[14]

The various temporal disjunctions between the present and the future as well as the enunciative duplication of a poetic voice torn between hypothesis, interrogation, and negation dramatize the "fearful / Gnawing"[15] that seeps through the poem and remind the reader of Durrell's unaccountable forebodings as he discovers the house he will inhabit with his young daughter:

> The wind moaned in the clump of banana trees, and at intervals I could still hear the whimper of the mandolin. . . . I, still obscured by premonitions of a familiarity which I could not articulate, walked to the end of the hall to watch the rain rattling among the pomegranates.[16]

This unreal familiarity is none other in the poem but that of death, which is why the poem revolves around a nonexisting temporal space that belongs to the imagination where it floats, unharmed by the violence of time and history. Death thus becomes the ultimate contraction of time and space, this personal peace the poet hankers after, as one would yearn for an out-of-bounds sanctuary that belongs to the unfigurable. The motionless time of present participles ("memory's dispersing / Springs," "a woman's wanting," "another sort of haunting," "nights of squinting rain," "landscapes of drumming cloud," "sleeping lips," "a poem imploring / Silence of lips") freezes the syntagm and fixes memory in the mode of the ever-present absence. Thus the village both recedes and insists "in memory's dispersing / Springs," just as the road that seems to flicker "in some cloud": the world of the past dwells in an oneiric present, borrowing from the dream the principles of association, compression, and rupture that are, according to Durrell, at the core of modernist poetry.[17] The poem can thus be likened to the dream process, as described by Valéry:

> . . . these well-known objects and beings somehow acquire a different value. They call out to one another, they merge in a radically new way. Thus they are . . . *musicalised*, for they have become commensurable, they echo through each other. Such a poetic world displays strong similarities with the world of dreams.[18]

Such is Durrell's poetic world where, as Valéry explains further, "we are given the familiar example of a *self-enclosed* world where all *real* things can be represented, but where everything appears and changes according only to the variations of our deeper sensibility."[19] In this world the material and the immaterial, the sensorial and the abstract, call out to one another, merge, and alter to summon a second genesis:

> By the moist clay of a woman's wanting,
> After the heart has stopped its fearful
> Gnawing, will I descry between
> This life and that another sort of haunting?

Life and death are no longer opposed but brought together in the last line that sheds a new light upon a life of past suffering and cleavage. The rime between "wanting" and "haunting" suggests the poet's slow detachment from desire and its corollary, memory. This renunciation, which heralds the realm of emptiness announced by Milarepa, is epitomized in the syntactic rift of the last line where the division between "this" and "that" no longer signals an opposition but an equation.

Anxiety is eventually annihilated in the second half of the poem, which unfolds that other life, a peaceful refraction of this one where the everyday is endowed with eternity in a landscape that lulls the senses and expands like a liquid, boundless watercolor bathing the poet's eye/I:

> No: the card-players in tabs of shade
> Will play on: the aerial springs
> Hiss: in bed lying quiet under kisses
> Without signature, with all my debts unpaid

> I shall recall nights of squinting rain,
> Like pig-iron on the hills: bruised
> Landscapes of drumming cloud and everywhere
> The lack of someone spreading like a stain.

The single sentence that makes up these two antepenultimate quatrains marks a definite structural and prosodic rift from the previous stanzas. The recurring colons operate as so many doors opening upon an unknown world whose strangely familiar music born from imperfect phonetic, morphological, and semantic echoes (linking "players" and "plays," "hiss" and "kisses," or "without" and "with") evoke not so much death itself as this oneiric world described by Valéry as "perfectly *irregular, unstable, involuntary, fragile.*"[20] The critic Clive Scott deftly analyzes the use Durrell makes of colons in this poem and reminds us that if we admit that colons momentarily suspend the logical articulation without suspending syntax, their function would then be to:

> . . . install a poetic transformation of the discursive into the intuitional. . . . The colon dynamizes perceptual relating and makes more pointed, more reciprocated, the exchanges between different phenomena, different observations.[21]

The run-on lines uniting the two quatrains coincide with the unfolding of the death dream that functions as a space of heightened perception: new relationships are born, former borderlines vanish, and the subject's acute "compassion" toward the universe announced by Milarepa reaches its climax in the enjambment of "bruised" that highlights the shared pain of the subject and place blending in the poet's holistic vision. The symbolic violence of the storm and the absence of the loved one blend the outer and the inner rift, the historical and the personal,[22] in order to conjure up a disfigured space where the future is already swallowed by the past.

From this cataclysmic wrenching a poem is born whose last stanza is paradoxically both linked to and cut off from the main body of the poem. It is indeed semantically linked to the first line of the previous stanza ("I shall recall nights of squinting rain") and yet opens upon an object that is syntactically and prosodically separated from its verb by the full stop that ends the previous stanza and the beginning of a new one:

> Or where brown fingers in the darkness move,
> Before the early shepherds have awoken,
> Tap out on sleeping lips with these same
> Worn typewriter keys a poem imploring
>
> Silence of lips and minds which have not spoken.

This ultimate vision of a man who dreams himself dead emerges like a broken fragment of memory endowed with the epiphanic power of brilliant shards that pierce through the haze of dreams, reflecting memories and sensations that have not yet reached consciousness. The reader recognizes here the author's own image as he reconstructs it for Henry Miller in one of his letters, opening a dialogue for silent "lips and minds":

> I am writing this at 4:50 a.m. A faint lilac dawn breaking accompanied by *bright moonlight*—weird. Nightingales singing intoxicated by the first rains. Everything damp. In a little while I take the car and sneak down the road towards a dawn coming up from Asia Minor like Paradise Lost.[23]

At the very moment when the writer watches himself, placing himself in the position of "'*Je est un Autre*,'" the writing operates like a mirror, this empty eye that sends him back the infinite act of repetition, as if every text, whether in prose or verse, reiterated the same quest for a peace that transcends pain and opens up a timeless space. Between night and dawn, in a surreal moonlit aurora, when the poet is the only one to be awake, a new poetic perception arises breaking free from the syntactic, discursive, and formal codes of letter writing. The letter paves the way for a radically new means of exchange, a paratactic and synaesthetic one rooted in vision and silence that enables the reader to feel, hear, and touch Cyprus before the writer's job has even started. Two years after Durrell's letter to Miller the poem echoes the same emptiness that lies within the folds of poetic images where a few initiates, sharing the same "Silence of lips and minds," can hear the poet's "imploring" voice. The last line, cut off from the last quatrain, seems to float free on the page, as if to materialize this leap into emptiness the poem yearns for. Poetry becomes the space where Durrell approaches and refracts Milarepa's emptiness, not as an absence but as a form of plenitude, as a springboard toward a new being in the world. Poetic language expels the word from its common semantic shell, just as the last verse is expelled here from the mold of the quatrain and brings forth a voice that is set free, a detached textual island/I-land. The infinite resonating power of the word has been strikingly expressed by contemporary French Haitian poet Frankétienne: "Words know more than we do; their knowledge is infinite and silently disseminates the subtle sap of the soul and the palpitating juice of boundless life."[24] The last stranded line highlights "the palpitating juice of boundless life" conveyed by each single word: the central place given to monosyllabic words ("lips" and "minds") framed by the disyllabic first and last words ("Silence" and "spoken"), whose antithetical meaning is counterbalanced by the alliterative pattern, transforms the line into an experimental symbolic, semantic, and musical exploration. Paradoxical though it may seem, although no sound is "spoken," silence is heard. Durrell joins here the modernist tradition developed by Mallarmé, who relentlessly delved into "the ineffable and the unspoken at the heart of the spoken word, the silence within the word."[25] A few decades later the critic Hugo Friedrich read this silence as:

> . . . the most acute form of tenderness, the most astonishing strangeness in word patterns, an evocative echo for the reader, a silence that conceals in its folds what is to come as well as a speech whose next step may be silence.[26]

The "Silence of lips and minds which have not spoken" suggests tender complicity of brotherly souls that gives birth to the poem, whether we think of real characters such as Durrell or Miller, or literary ones, such as Sappho and her daughter, whose dialogue inevitably acquires a metatextual resonance:

> Listen to the silence, child, do you hear it?
> It contains everything, drinks up everything,
> The ocean of our silence where such words
> As mothers and daughters use in meeting
> Can only make islands or peninsulas of meaning . . .[27]

The poetic gesture thus partakes of the same careful attention bestowed upon the unremarkable and that Sappho teaches to Kleis: it is an infinitesimal "peninsula of meaning" born from the silent expanse, returning to it and radiating light upon our world. Poetry is thus conceived as the antithesis to objective discourse; it is silent language that brings out hidden echoes and partakes of a form of eternity that Constance expresses much later in *The Avignon Quintet* when comparing herself to Affad: "I live in the contingent, he in the eternal—in prose rather than poetry."[28]

Durrell's writing crosses borders between Western and Eastern mysticism and points at silence as the absolute of poetic communication.

We may remember the poem "Conon in Alexandria" in *Cities, Plains and People*, which ended upon the aphorism "'*Music is only love, looking for words.*'"[29] The use of quotation marks and italics that seem to introduce an unknown voice combines with the odd comma dividing the verse into two hemistichs to disrupt the fluid musicality of the line and open it to an unexpected silence guiding the reader's ear toward the palpitating presence between the words.

The entire collection is placed under the auspices of this fruitful silence as early as the first poem, "Lesbos," that belongs to the cycle of musical poems, along with "Mneiae," "Style," or "Chanel," where the disruptive essence of poetic language is brought to the fore. In his collection of essays *Key to Modern Poetry* Durrell displayed his preoccupation with the specificities of poetic speech:

> I have thought to present poetry as one dialect of a greater language comprising the whole universe of ideas—a universe perpetually shifting, changing its relations and tenses as verbs do in speech, altering its outlines.[30]

"Lesbos," through its subtitle "*Song from a Play*," is reminiscent of the verse play *Sappho*, which is however never explicitly quoted, so that the poem acts once again as a disruptive force, breaking into the unmentioned world of the play to offer us throughout the four tercets in iambic pentameters an ode to the poet's island, a sort of exiled appendix to the play that partakes of what Frankétienne calls a "boundless life." The fascination for Lesbos that pervades the poem and the play is made explicit much later in *The Greek Islands*:

> Lesbos vibrates like a spiderweb with the names of high antiquity—the greatest of all being Sappho. . . . you receive your first impression of Lesbos as a place offering tranquility and beauty and a sort of repose which seems even to silence the *cicadas* at noon. Perhaps this impression is the result of finding such safe anchorages, where one can sleep on deck under the stars. . . .
> Lesbos has known nothing but the best of poetry, music, and philosophy—a very rich heritage for one small place!
> Its geographical strangeness also plays a part, for as you enter the narrow gullet of Iera or Kalloni the fissure closes behind you, sealed by the turning mountain. You lose sight of the narrow channel by which you have entered this anguish of silence and calm; a sense of unreality supervenes and you feel panicky.[31]

The formal perfection of the poem, the regular rhythm of the iambs underlined by the alliterative pattern, the fluidity of the verse often balanced by symmetrical hemistichs, the frequent correspondence between syntactic and metric units, the harmonious crescendo built up through the run-on line linking the last and the penultimate tercets, and finally the mirror effect of the ultimate line concur to the melodious flow of the poet's song and create at the onset of the collection a poetic island where language defies the laws of matter. The first stanza intertwines visual, tactile, and auditory images to convey what lies beyond representation—"The Pleiades" that embrace the land and the sky, the Greek goddesses and the Alexandrian and French poets, and usher in a cosmic vision of space:

> The Pleiades are sinking cool as paint,
> And earth's huge camber follows out,
> Turning in sleep, the oceanic curve:

The marine metaphor of the first line initiates an analogical conception of the world: the Pleiades sinking like a brushstroke into darkness mirror the shape of the earth that tilts like a ship so that the earth and the sky are at one and partake of the same peaceful slumber. The following stanza develops an anthropomorphic vision of space that combines long shots and close-ups to give human dimensions to the world. The comparison in the last line—"Like dancers to a music they deserve"—reasserts the fundamental correlation between cosmic and human harmony that was already at work in the previous collection: "The painted dancers motionless in play / Spin for eternity . . ."[32] The "balcony" that seems to hover under the stars, not unlike the star-spangled deck in *The Greek Islands*, draws the reader into the weightless density of the dream. Such is the dream of a perfect correspondence between the macrocosm and the microcosm that is conveyed by the run-on lines (l.9–10 and l.10–11), abolishing the rift between man and the universe. Once again, the poet crosses "the narrow gullet" and, turning his back to "the fissure clos[ing] behind,"[33] discovers true harmony:

> I slept. But the dispiriting autumn moon,
>
> In her slow expurgation of the sky
> Needs company: is brooding on the dead,
> And so am I now, so am I.

The sleep of death, relegated to the penultimate stanza, finally gives way to a second life. The symmetry of the hemistichs on each side of the colons announces the perfect mirroring pattern of the last line, where eye rhymes, assonances, and alliterations conjure up a harmonious and peaceful world that folds upon the subject like an embrace. Death is thus no longer conceived of as a loss but as the harbinger of a future fruitfulness and becomes the object of an ongoing meditation on hope at the source of writing, as the poem dedicated to Father Nicholas in *A Private Country* evinces:

> The dying and the becoming are one thing,
> So wherever you go the musical always is;
> . . .
> So sleep.
> All these warm when the flesh is cold.
> And the blue will keep.[34]

Durrell conjures up in these lines what he calls in his analysis of T. S. Eliot's *Four Quartets* "the 'stillness' of the dance,"[35] the paradoxical movement that reshapes the curves of space and time and weaves new bonds between man and the world through a poetic device that Durrell shares with Eliot: "recording ecstasy with intellectual control and detachment."[36] The meditation that concludes "Lesbos" sketches out a new poetic space: that of the atemporal marriage of contraries inherited from William Blake and revisited by modernism—"All time suspended in an instant of time, always renewing itself yet standing quite still. [. . .] It is a time which contains all opposites."[37] The echoes between Durrell's interpretation of *Burnt Norton* and his own poetry would justify further analysis of the intertextual links between Durrell and Eliot. However, in the wake of the often-unacknowledged Blakean subtext that underlies Durrell's verse, it might be wiser to focus at this stage upon the mysticism that pervades both Durrell's and Eliot's writings. Such is indeed, according to Durrell, one of the central definitions of "great poetry" that he considers as "initiatory and not didactic[38]":

> . . . great poetry reflects an unknown in the interpretation and understanding of which all knowledge is refunded into ignorance. It points towards a Something which itself subsists without distinction. . . . A poem is a congeries of symbols which transfers an enigmatic knowledge to the reader. . . . it reflects a metaphysical reality about ourselves and the world.[39]

Poetry and philosophy thus appear as the two sides of the same quest and entertain a complex relationship that Meschonnic describes as follows:

> . . . the poem *does* something. It does something to language, and to poetry. It does something to the subject—to the subject that composes it, and to the subject that reads it.
> But the poem is incapable of *thinking* what it does as a philosophical subject. And yet the subject of the poem *knows* it and accomplishes it. . . . Which is the equivalent of *showing* and doing with its own means what language cannot *say* in the ordinary transitive sense of the discontinuous units of the sign. . . .
> In that sense what the poem does has nothing to do with the *truth*, either in the logical, ethical or psychological sense. It is of a different essence—the invention of a relationship to oneself, to the others, and to the world.[40]

Therefore, according to Meschonnic, poetic illumination is an act (which is rooted in the etymology of the word poetry), but an act that is devoid of conscience since, as opposed to the philosophical subject defined as "conscious-unified-willful," the subject of the poem, which is not to be confounded with "the individual, the author," refers to what Meschonnic calls "the very act of subjectification of a discourse, of a practice."[41] The poem thus becomes the space of a third voice. It is neither explanatory, dialectic, nor descriptive. As Serge Ritman explains, the poem

> . . . cannot tolerate enclosure, assignation. From this point of view, the poem is a radical criticism of philosophies and religions as well as of explanatory methods. The poem ushers in a relation of relation, histories of voices.[42]

Poetry, the Art of Living

Poetry is thus to be considered not as the art of saying but as the art of living and becoming; it conveys an embodied, intimate knowledge rooted in sensation rather than in reason and triggers in the subject who composes and reads it the silent awakening of "the flesh heart."[43] The truth poetry attempts to unveil is indeed "of a different essence": as Durrell has explained in his lectures, "it is both mantic and semantic in its implications,"[44] both constructed and unpremeditated, "it is on the way. It is here, there, nowhere!"[45] as Pursewarden exclaims to Darley.

The poet's memory is the privileged medium of this sensual countergnosis deeply rooted in bodily perceptions and invested with a humanist purpose through which Durrell sketches out a new form of wisdom. The poem "Mneiae" highlights the prevailing role of memory through the explicit reference to Plutarch's nine Muses of remembrance, daughters to Zeus, and Mnemosyne, who "govern Thought under all its forms: eloquence, persuasion, wisdom, history, mathematics, astronomy."[46] The series of couplets in iambic tetrameters ends on the repetition of the last line that sounds like a mantra. As if to echo the Muses' song, the poem unfolds like an ode to "remembrance." Olfactory, tactile, and visual sensations bring to life a disjunctive vision whereby the subject is objectified into diffracted memories of the self. The poetic subject expands and multiplies simultaneously in the poet's and in the reader's memory. Indeed, the line "I, the watcher, smoking at a table" recalls the first stanza of "'*Je est un autre*'" in *A Private Country*:

> He is the man who makes notes,
> The observer in the tall black hat,
> Face hidden in the brim[47]

In between the lines of the two collections, Durrell points toward a new kind of awareness. Trying to overcome what he describes as Rimbaud's "deep-seated split in the psyche,"[48] he points to unity at the heart of the split:

> I, the watcher, smoking at a table,
> And I, my selves, observed by human choice,
>
> A disinherited portion of the whole:
> With you the sibling of my self-desire[49]

The opposition between the singular and the plural in the second line is reinforced by the symmetrical pattern of the first two lines ("I, the watcher" / "And I, my selves," "smoking" / "observed"). The disjunction of the subject in the following distich is further underlined by the deceptive punctuation as the colon introduces a prepositional clause instead of the expected main clause. The split self is thus mirrored by a split syntax playing on appositions and coordinations so that the linguistic matter, like memory, seems to dissolve, "Soft as puffs of smoke combining." This floating memory builds up a world where unity and multiplicity, past and present combine. The regular yet freely moving pattern of internal rhymes and alliterations culminating in the soft, fluid rhythm of the last two lines repeated like a burden gives the poem a mystic density: "Which time's the only ointment for, / Which time's the only ointment for." The voice of the poem that surges like a mantra is both the *telos* and the origin of writing. It rises out of that empty space materialized typographically by the blank separating the last line from the last distich, and returns to it, having reverberated in the poet's and in the reader's memory. As such it implicitly points to poetry as a spiritual tool intended to channel thought and free the subject's spirit so that he may catch a glimpse of this primordial unity Durrell refers to in *Key to Modern Poetry* when quoting Giordano Bruno: "the things that are becoming with those that are decaying are conjoined in one and the same composite being. . . ."[50]

Orpheus is naturally the hyperbolic emblem of the eternal paradox of the mnemonic process that both loses and grasps, mourns and celebrates, destroys and creates. Being the son to Calliope, the first Muse, he is the poet's secret alter ego in the poem "Orpheus":

> Do you contend in us, though now
> A memory only, the smashed lyre
> Washed up entangled in your hair,
> But sounding still as here,
> O monarch of all initiates and
> The dancer's only perfect peer?

The poet tactfully guides us back to the memory of the myth that narrates Orpheus's tearing apart by Thracian women and his slow journey down the river into the sea. The sea is said to have brought back his head and his lyre to the shores of Lesbos where the inhabitants built him a grave that sometimes resounded with the song of a lyre.[51] The poem thus brings us back to Lesbos, the land of lyric poetry and of the Pleiades. The "silent garden" of "Lesbos" is echoed by "the fecund silences" of "Orpheus." This descent into silence evokes the descent into the world of shades from which the poet returns, both maimed and victorious. The second stanza takes up the image of the "sea-bird's wings" in the first stanza to metamorphose Orpheus into "A great albatross" opening up the path to redemption, in the manner of Coleridge's and Baudelaire's poems[52]:

> . . . you steer like
> A great albatross, spread white
> On the earth-margins the sailing
> Snow-wings in the world's afterlight:
> Mentor of all these paper ships
> Cockled from fancy on a tide
> Made navigable only by your skill
> Which in some few approves
> A paper recreation of lost loves.

Placing himself under the protection of Orpheus, the poet enters the world of poetic mysteries. He becomes the sailor, the "self-appointed helmsman"[53] steering a "paper-ship" to bring back from Hades "A paper recreation of lost loves." Durrell sketches out in a few lines a recurrent characteristic of his poems and novels where the various personae and narrators keep recollecting the memory of their lost loves. The specificity of the poem lies in its capacity to intertwine those "lost loves" and "the fecund silences" they are born from, that is, to create what Durrell defines in *Key* as "a congeries of symbols."[54] "Orpheus" thus ushers in a secret descent into the mysteries of the poem, into the "dark congeries / Of intimations from the dead" that echoes the end of "Lesbos," "brooding on the dead."

In the wake of Orpheus singing Eurydice, Durrell sings the memory of his beloved in "The Dying Fall," whose title equally suggests Orsino's words at the beginning of *Twelfth Night*:

> If music be the food of love, play on,
> Give me excess of it, that, surfeiting,
> The appetite may sicken, and so die.
> That strain again! It had a dying fall.[55]

Yet unlike *Twelfth Night*, Durrell's poem stages a separation and harks back to Eliot's song: "I know the voices dying with a dying fall."[56] The first quatrain opens on a series of nominal sentences that function as so many minimalist stage directions:

> The islands rebuffed by water.
> Estuaries of putty and gold.
> A smokeless arc of Latin sky.
> One star, less than a week old.

This first stanza sketches out a self-enclosed landscape, akin to the weather-beaten islands, and devoid of any reality, as flat as a décor. Memory opens the doors of time and action in the second quatrain: it unveils a three-dimensional landscape when time and space combine to transform the landscape into a living monster: "When the sea wears bronze scales and / Hushes in the ambush of a calm." The descent into the world of memory, although "haltered," breathes life into a dead love, endlessly taken up and abandoned:

> The old dialogue always rebegins
> Between us: but now the spring
> Ripens, neither will be attending.

As opposed to the closed structure of the first stanza, the third one plays on successive run-on lines that paradoxically underline the subject's isolation. The increasing number of alternate, crossed, and enclosed rhymes combine with the run-on line, linking the last two quatrains to give the poem a prosodic and mnemonic depth that highlights the hopeless quest for a kiss as impalpable as the lovers' breath:

> For rosy as feet of pigeons pressed
>
> In clay, the kisses we possessed,
> Or thought we did: so borrowing, lending,
> Stacked fortunes in our love's society—
> Each in the perfect circle of a sigh was ending.

The "feet of pigeons pressed / In clay" echoes "the moist clay of a woman's wanting" in "The Tree of Idleness"; yet the material texture of the image seems to dissolve under the poet's hands, just like the syntax. The comparisons, appositions, and interpolated clauses protract the verb until the very end of the poem, as if to mimic the ungraspable nature of the object and recall once more the end of the dream conjured up by Eliot's song:

> We have lingered in the chambers of the sea
> By sea-girls wreathed with seaweed red and brown
> Till human voices wake us, and we drown.[57]

In Durrell's poem, just as in "The Love Song of J. Alfred Prufrock," the pattern of end rhymes and internal rhymes mirrors the slow dissolution of the object of desire that sinks into the deep waters of memory before disappearing "in the perfect circle of a sigh" that sends the reader back to the "arc of Latin sky." The breath of the poem encapsulates the circle of the absent kiss whose memory becomes the source of writing and the source of life.

It is then no wonder that the following poems should be constructed as an exploration of death, such as "At Strati's":

> Remember please, time has no joints,
> Pours over the great sills of thought,
> Not clogging nor resisting but
> Yawning to inherit the year's quarters;
> Weaving you up the unbroken series
> Of corn, ammonites and men,
> In a single unlaboured continuum,
> And not in slices called by day and night,
> And not in objects called by place and thing.

One instantly recognizes Hamlet's words—"The time is out of joint"[58]—that conjure up a devouring time that wrecks man's destiny, breaks up the world into splinters, dismantles time and space. Not unlike the spiral of the ammonite that suggests the ram horn of god Amon—"the Hidden," the irrepresentable—the time of writing revolves upon itself like a fossil, trapping in its folds fixed sensations, as Durrell explains in *Key*: "Memory, reflections, desire . . . inextricably tangled up."[59] The poem functions as a spontaneous linguistic spiral, characterized by alliterations, internal rhymes, syntactic and prosodic symmetry, that reminds the reader of the metatextual definition of the poem hinted at a few pages earlier in "Style": "Something like the sea, / Unlaboured momentum of water." The second stanza is precisely based on that very "momentum" played out in such a simple language that the reader immediately hears Durrell's analysis of Eliot's technique in *Key*: ". . . the full weight of the poetry lies behind the multiple impact of simple statement, almost conversationally introduced."[60] Following the informal statement of its first line, the second stanza progressively leads us backward, from the general to the particular. Syntactic and prosodic mirror effects foster an isolated poetic voice, severed from time and space: the absent clocks, the drinkers "embalmed in reverie," compose a still life—

> You say I do not write, but the taverns
> Have no clocks, and I conscripted
> By loneliness observe how other drinkers
> Sit at Strati's embalmed in reverie:
> Forms raise green cones of wine,
> And loaded heads recline on loaded arms,
> Under a sky pronounced by cypresses,
> Packed up, all of us, like loaves
> Human and plant, memory, wish.
>
> The very calendar props an empty inkwell.

The "empty inkwell" reminds the reader of "this dry inkwell" in "Blind Homer"[61] and leads him to take part in the mnemonic exploration that nurtures poetic meditation. The empty receptacle functions as another empty chamber where the poet, like Homer, "Conspires with introspection against loneliness"[62] and paves the way for a new temporality, a calendar of silent time. The known world is reified into fossilized dead matter and guides us into a still time that penetrates and petrifies forms and beings and progressively pervades one poem after the other. Hence, "On Mirrors":

> Time amputated so will bleed no more
> But flow like refuse now in clocks
> On clinic walls, in libraries and barracks,
> Not made to spend but kill and nothing more.

Starting with "the mirrors all reverted" in the house of the dead, the poem unveils the hidden face of time, the eternal end that resists man's measure and turns against him. Reverting mirrors, the poet also reverts our perspective and ushers in a new temporality:

> Yet mirrors abandoned drink like ponds:
> (Once they resumed the childhood of love)
> And overflowing, spreading, swallowing
> Like water light, show one averted face,
>
> As in the capsule of the human eye
> Seen at infinity, the outer end of time,
> A man and woman lying sun-bemused
> In a blue vineyard by the Latin sea,
>
> Steeped in each other's minds and breathing there
> Like wicks inhaling deep in golden oil.

The successive reversals rely on an infinite process of refraction: the ternary rhythm of "And overflowing, spreading, swallowing" mirrors that of "On clinic walls, in libraries and barracks." The successive run-on lines ease the shift from the mirror to the pond, and finally to the eye. Death becomes the door onto a series of metamorphoses up to the ultimate reversal through which the human eye leads into "the outer end of time," that is time freed from finitude, as described in *Key*: "All time suspended in an instant of time, always renewing itself, yet standing quite still."[63] This perspective into "infinity" is linked to the image of eternal union that belongs neither to time nor space but to a Fauvist vision ("In a blue vineyard") where art and color conspire to draw an outlandish setting. The lovers' absolute unity and freedom is materialized in a singular final distich by the verbal and alliterative chiasmus that ties up "Steeped in each other's minds" and "deep in golden oil," on the one hand, and "breathing" and "inhaling" on the other. The perfect mirror born from these last two lines that float free from the previous five quatrains suggests "the perfect circle of a sigh" concluding "The Dying Fall." The textual mirror thus expands between the lines, bridging the rift between the lives, between the loves, and bringing the reader once more to ponder upon the other face of death. The poet's gesture may then be read as an ultimate mirror to Pursewarden's advice:

> Try to tell yourself that its fundamental object was only to invoke the ultimate healing silence—and that the symbolism contained in form and pattern is only a frame reference through which, as in a mirror, one may glimpse the idea of a universe at rest, a universe in love with itself. . . . We must learn to read between the lines, between the lives.[64]

The various poetic, prosodic, syntactic, or generic mirror effects answer the same purpose: to open up a new vision that tears man away from time, that is, from finitude. In the silence of the pages that keep echoing one another, the mirror of the poem acts as a "frame" that paves the way for an unexpected liberation.

Rivers and Cities of the Orphic Journey

Through the prism of mirrors the poems "River Water" and "A Water-Colour of Venice" build up a textual space that substitutes itself to the topography as if the outer reality could only exist through the mediation of art.

In "River Water" the "Curve of the Danube's wrist" surfaces from the layers of the "oil-paint" that the poem decomposes in successive brushstrokes:

> The forest wears its coats
> of oil-paint as lightly can
> what only brush-strokes built,
> feather and leaf and spray,

After the apparent simplicity of the painting in the first stanza where the iambic trimeter reminds the reader of the rhythm of ancient Greek poetry, the Danube emerges as an allegory of a divided country that is set in sharp contrast against the landscape of "Lesbos." Although "The camber of earth and sky" echoes "earth's huge camber" in the first poem, the world conjured up in this textual painting stands poles apart from that of the Greek island: the "Curve of the Danube's wrist / [. . .] divides with a ruler of lead" and hints at Tito's military regime in Serbia. Yet just as the pictorial representation, the poetic form stages the displacement and disfiguration that metamorphoses military patrols into "an ant's patrol / fingers to fingers warm." The lover's soft touch echoes the painter's brushstroke as the poet's eye invites us to recompose the hidden body ("finger and wrist and arm") that mirrors the fragmented landscape of the first stanza ("feather and leaf and spray"). The poet already reveals what the later text "On Mirrors" calls "the capsule of the human eye / Seen at infinity," that is, the deep voyage into an inward gaze that embraces past and future in order to unveil what lies beyond death.

The mirrored perspectives pave the way for the exploration of absence: the absence of the loved one is a metonymy for the ontological absence that pervades the last three stanzas. The anadiplosis linking the fourth and fifth stanzas underlines the perfect mirror effect between the world of the living haunted by absence and that of the dead that haunts the time of the living. The loss of the beloved is emblematic of the ultimate dispossession and triggers in the last stanza a decomposition process that scars the flesh as much as the memory of the living:

> Dead kisses revisit the living
> in guises our bodies abet,
> for mouth or elbow or thigh:
> for the living must always remember
> what the dead can never forget.

The river waters never cease to discharge the flotsam and jetsam of life: "feather and leaf and spray," "finger and wrist and arm," "mouth or elbow or thigh" sketch out the fluctuating landscape of the memory of mourning. However, death is not equated with the void but as the only, paradoxical, form of permanence, as a stasis that opens up perception, what Durrell calls "time as the 'still centre,' the timeless moment when past and future are joined and compressed into one moment of vision."[65] The disfiguration of the landscape works though the incorporation of pictorial representation to free the signs and open up a dormant space-time.

Venice belongs to that dormant space, whether we think of the watercolor ushering in the narrative of *Bitter Lemons*,[66] or of the poem "A Water-Colour of Venice" that offers us a decomposed vision where the colors wash out and leave us with a ghost-like, lusterless, "Unreal city."[67] In a conversational tone the first stanza unfurls in a single sentence what Durrell analyzes as "a long, unstressed line which looks at first formless"[68] opening up the long-dead world of Corfu that saw the birth of Zarian and Durrell's friendship renewed once more in Cyprus in 1954.[69]

> Zarian was saying: Florence is youth,
> And after it Ravenna, age,
> Then Venice, second-childhood.

As early as the first lines Venice appears as the door to limbo, the ultimate place that welcomes the living after death before their actual disappearance in an apocalyptic décor that comes to symbolize the dying Europe that Durrell and Zarian ceaselessly deride[70]:

> The pools of burning stone where time
> And water, the old-siege masters,
> Have run their saps beneath
> A thousand saddle-bridges,
> Puffed up by marble griffins drinking,
>
> And set free to float on loops
> Of her canals like great intestines
> Now snapped off like a berg to float,
> Where now, like others, you have come alone

In the stone that liquefies like lava, in the water that runs out, like human time, in this drifting town ripped open the reader does not so much recognize the Venice that opens the doors to Cyprus as the first of the "Lost Cities" swollen and distorted beyond measure, as if the poet had walked back toward the putrefying "Venice blown up, and turning green."[71] Venice thus becomes the archetype of all Durrellian cities, outrageously disfigured—"Bloated among her ambiguities"[72]—which is later to take the shape of anthropomorphic Alexandria in *The Quartet*:

We turn a corner and the world becomes a pattern of arteries [. . .] two men in their own time and city, remote from the world, walking as if they were treading one of the lugubrious canals of the moon. [. . .]
'If you think of yourself as a sleeping city for example . . . what? [. . .]'[73]

A few decades later Venice and Alexandria will be reincarnated as Avignon through Bruce's walks that reveal a timeless city freed from the constraints of geography, a floating, uprooted city that stands as a metonymy for the crumbling memory building up a rhizomatic pattern of oneiric, multifaceted Durrellian cities:

Avignon! . . . it had stayed pegged here at the confluence of its two green rivers. The past embalmed it, the present could not alter it. . . . It had always waited for us, floating among its tenebrous monuments, the corpulence of its ragged bells, the putrescence of its squares. . . . It haunted one although it was rotten, fly-blown with expired dignities, almost deliquescent among its autumn river damps.[74]

Avignon is the scroll upon which time has inscribed its print and which resists it; it is a city preserved like a mummy and reborn through writing, insensitive to present time, a paradoxical city placed under the twofold auspices of eternity and death and that keeps resurfacing in the narrator's eye like a dead fish. Like Alexandria, Geneva, Paris, or Venice it both falls apart and endures: it is the city of Petrarch, of Laure de Noves and of the Marquis de Sade's Laure, the city of the Templars and of the Pope, and Saint Augustine's *City of God*. In *The Quintet* Avignon and Venice function as so many archaeological layers refracting the slow decomposition of memory as Rob Sutcliffe's description evinces—"Old Venice glittering and liquefying among her multiple reflections"[75]—and echoing the city of Alexandria subsiding under the narrator's feet: "He determined there and then that the whole city lay in ruins about him."[76]

The novelistic and poetic corpus does not so much represent a series of cities as it sketches out a unique, protean city of the soul that belongs to a network of literary routes offering the reader multiple ways into and out of the literary cities and textual spaces the better to suggest a form of spiritual journey. As Deleuze has explained:

The town is the correlate of the road. The town exists only as function of circulation, and of circuits; it is a remarkable point on the circuits that create it, and which it creates. It is defined by entries and exits. . . . It is . . . a network, because it is fundamentally in contact with other towns.[77]

Just as in the novels, the town of the poems, like an iceberg carried away by deeper currents, breaks free from any geographic anchorage to open the way to inner exploration and suggest the ultimate exit of death. When facing the city, whether watching it, walking through it, or recalling it, the subject is alone, just as he is alone in front of death. "A Water-Colour of Venice" ends on the fleeting essence of life ("Here sense dissolves"), and the gondolier is none other but Charon: "A boatman singing from his long black coffin. . . ." The final embrace of sleep in the last lines evokes a serene departure materialized by the isolation of the final line. Thus, the last two stanzas strikingly echo the end of "Lesbos":

Thick as a brushstroke sleep has laid
Its fleecy unconcern on every visage,

At the bottom of every soul a spoonful of sleep.

This last brushstroke is that of death completing the watercolor in the perfection of the smooth lexical and alliterative echoes characterizing the last three lines. The syntactic and musical unity is paradoxically broken by the prosodic structure mimicking the harmonious, painless, and fully accepted drifting away of the subject carried by death unto eternity.

The ode to the city is an ode to death and to the resilience of memory beating its rhythm in the deeper layers of conscience. This is the origin of a vanishing line that joins "Mneiae" ("remembrance of past lives"), "Orpheus" ("A paper recreation of lost loves"), "River Waters" ("Dead kisses revisit the living"), and "Asphodels: Chalcidice." "Asphodels" is based on a dialogic exchange that reiterates the opening of "A Water-Colour of Venice" while recalling the dramatic form of "In Europe" in *Cities, Plains and People*. However, the voices are anonymous and allow the reader to imagine the protagonists. The dialogic form that rules the entire poem is reminiscent of Durrell's critical hypothesis in his study of *The Waste Land*: "Suppose we arranged the poem for a number of voices—would that not give one some insight into the sort of poem it is?"[78] The harmony of the poem relies on balanced, mirrored responses that create unity out of a duality. The first, undecided and concise answer of the second speaker ending the first stanza—"'I wonder'"—is further developed at the beginning and in the end of the third stanza, summing the complex nature of memory and ushering in a meditation on death: "'Memory is all of these.' / 'Nor does death.'" The brief answers spur a retrospective reading that forces one to pay attention to the silent interpretation of the Other inscribed within the poem and wedging his way into the persona's reflection. Indeed the first answer calls into question not only the penultimate line but the entire stanza:

> 'No one will ever pick them, I think,
> The ugly off-white clusters: all the grace
> Lies in the name of death named.
> Are they a true certificate for death?'
> 'I wonder'

This last line sends the reader back to his own uncertainty, allowing the question to reverberate endlessly, as if the question did not so much aim for an answer as for its own perpetual echo, just as the polysemy of the answer itself—which can be understood as an expression of surprise or doubt. Thus the entire process of naming is called into question through a series of hesitations that begins in the mirrored halves of the title and develops in the following stanza where the asphodel comes to symbolize death:

> 'Death being identified, forgave it language:
> Called it "asphodel", as who should say
> The synonym for scentless, colourless,
>   Solitary,
>
> Rock-loving. . .' 'Memory is all of these.'

Therefore the question of the definition of death is tightly linked to that of memory: every trip down memory lane takes the poet further into the world of shades: just as Orpheus is but another name for the poet, the asphodel is but another name for death. Such an equation suggests a perfect symmetry between the world of the dead and that of the living if we are to agree with the concluding aphorism of "River Water": "for the living must always remember / what the dead can never forget." The persistence of death in the present, the endurance of the past and of human conscience that challenges the passing of time, is symbolized by the resilient flower rooted both in Chalcidice and in Hades, and is materialized by the dialogic reversal through which the second enunciator comes first in the last part of the poem:

> 'You mean our dying?' 'No, but when one is
> Alone, neither happy nor unhappy, in
> The deepest ache of reason where this love
> Becomes a malefactor, clinging so,
> You surely know—'

Unlike previous statements, this one asserts nothing since it relies on an ambiguous subject. "No, but" echoes "No one" in the first stanza and can be read both as an answer and as a refusal to answer: should it be interpreted as a definition of death or of memory, of the uncertainty of a heart caught in limbo, "suspended like a hair or a feather in the cloudy mixtures of memory,"[79] like Darley in *The Alexandria Quartet*? The dichotomy between "happy" and "unhappy," "reason," and "love," the unfinished sentence that ends on an aposiopesis and breaks up the syntactic unit while preserving the form of the stanza, conjure up an indefinite weightlessness, a paradoxical sensitive numbness that foreshadows the atmosphere of *The Quartet*.

From then on the two voices are perfectly balanced, reflecting the mirroring of memory and death, and the last stanza develops a dual assertion. The interrogative mode disappears, suggesting that the anxious questioning of the living has been replaced by the certainty of death: "Death's stock will stand no panic, / Be beautiful in jars . . . / Exonerate the flesh . . . / Or mock the enigma . . ." The allegory of death is both the subject and the object of discourse and cannot be circumscribed: ". . . an epitaph / It never earned.' / 'These precisely guard ironic truth, / . . . to fill your jars / With pretty writing-stuff . . .'" The ultimate ironical twist lies in its escape through and away from discourse, in this perpetual distance that culminates in the emblem: "'These comfortless, convincing, even, yes, / A little mocking, Grecian asphodels.'" The ternary rhythm of the adjectives sends the reader back to the initial description of the flowers in the second stanza ("scentless, colourless, / Solitary") and suggests that only the emblem, not the flower itself, can be described. The poem, a blason of death, opens and ends on its heraldic motif: neither a simile nor a metaphor for death, the asphodel conveys a form of presence that cannot be explained or summed up. It stands as a personal symbol for a higher, eternal reality that escapes discourse. One cannot then but remember Emmanuel Lévinas's meditation on death as an "irremediable divergence" that takes away both life and meaning:

> "Death is decomposition; it is the unanswerable. . . . Death, instead of being describable as an event as such, affects us as a non-sense. The mark it seems to leave upon our time (our relation to the infinite) is a pure question mark: it opens upon what can bring no possible answer. This question is already a modality of the relation with the hereafter of our being.[80]

Questioning "the hereafter of our being" implies establishing a dialogue with the other, sharing what Lévinas calls "an emotion, a concern for the *unknown*"[81] that is at the heart of the poetic gesture. Thus, "Sarajevo," with its regular iambic pentameters and its limpid architecture, unexpectedly ends on the indefinite, the "unanswerable," "the pure question mark": "A village like an instinct left to rust, / Composed around the echo of a pistol-shot." Only in the very last lines does the reader understand the silent, unmarked question of this apparently descriptive piece that starts as a letter: "Bosnia. November." One recalls the pattern of "Letters in Darkness" and recognizes the hand that wrote those dark, solitary letters to Henry Miller:

> Sarajevo is a strange place—a narrow gorge full of rushing waters; granite-red mountains and the town perched up on a cliff in a series of coloured bubbles of minaret and mosque; veiled women. Narrow streets full of mountaineers and mules. Wild crying of eagles in the air above it and all around a petrified ocean of rock with roads bulging round mountains, coiling and recoiling on themselves. I had a poem for the road which wouldn't get any further than
>
>> Ideal because their coils were apt
>> To these long sad self-communings
>> Among alien peoples . . .
>> So I threw it in a gorge and took the flat road over the plain to this dreary white city on its dirty rivers.[82]

Although the letter and the poem share the same lexical field, thus narrowing the gap between poetry and prose (which also resorts to elision and alliteration), the inverted perspective that marks the beginning of the poem initiates a striking rupture. Unlike the letter, the poem discovers Sarajevo from above, opting for a high-angle view over Serbia[83] and creating in the abysmal vision of a petrified city an uncanny vision that upsets our relationship to space and conveys the subject's anxious contemplation of the void:

> Balanced on scarps of trap, ramble or blunder
> Over traverses of cloud: and here they move,
> Mule-teams like insects harnessed by a bell
> Upon the leaf-edge of a winter sky,
>
> And down at last into this lap of stone
> Between four cataracts of rock: a town
> Peopled by sleepy eagles, whispering only
> Of the sunburnt herdsman's hopeless ploy:
> A sterile earth quickened by shards of rock
> Where nothing grows . . .

The blank separating the two stanzas, followed by the enjambment between lines 1 and 2 in the second stanza, materializes the fall into mineral matter. The city trapped in rock becomes the emblem of man's downfall into a barren world that is reminiscent of man's exile from the Garden of Eden.[84] Beyond the evocation of a historical era, the poem metaphorizes man's experience of finitude and the end of hope. The last lines of the penultimate stanza—"a peace / Harmless with nightingales. None are singing now."—sound as a perfect antithesis to the Greek world of Corinth where "Men, women, and the nightingales / Are forms of Spring"[85] or of "Education of a Cloud" ("Say spring, provinces of the nightingale"[86]) and foreshadow the ultimate reversal in the last stanza where the poem folds upon itself, trapping its object. The all-embracing cold and silence rule over the landscape and the poem, transforming the textual space into a deathly tomb where the intimations of life are smothered ("Dark beauty flowering under veils, / Trapped in the spectrum of dying style"), where the city shrinks like a lifeless body and becomes an empty shell echoing the sound of death, not of birds. Death, far from appearing as the natural outcome of life, becomes a shared crime that engages the other, as Lévinas explains:

> Everything takes place in death as if man were not a mere perishing being but offered us the event of finishing, of perishing itself—albeit as an ambiguous unknown. . . . One must think about the part of murder in death: every death is murder, is premature, and it engages the survivor's responsibility.[87]

One cannot ignore the political context of the poem and of the collection that endows the first line of the last stanza with a singular poignancy: "No history much? Perhaps." Operating as a hinge that shatters the smooth rhythm of the poem, this unsolved question marks history as an unknown and unknowable force ushering in the final perplexing ambiguity of "the echo of a pistol-shot." Indeed, the reader is simultaneously brought to hear both the echoes of Tito's political murders and those of the British repression in Cyprus. In both places Durrell was a powerless witness, and one may truly wonder whether and how he engaged his "survivor's responsibility." The hesitant answer to the interro-negative might point toward poetry as the tentative space where the poet breaks free from political and historical discourse the better to scrutinize the responsibility that is haunting him.

Opening the Doors of Conscience

This haunting comes to the fore in "A Bowl of Roses," where the poet addresses Melissa, the muse and alter ego who opened *Cities, Plains and Peo-*

ple,[88] thus summoning both one of his poetic masks—"nurse, augur, special self"[89]—and the character of *The Quartet* embodying one of the many lovers whose names have vanished memory: "I remember bodies, arms, faces, / But I have forgotten their names."[90] "This tattered old café" suggests both Melissa and Clea successively sitting at the same table in *Justine*[91] and in *Clea*,[92] and wearing the same dress. The "roses trapped in blue tin bowls" conjure up the lost loves haunting the poet. The rose operates as a metonym for the woman and symbolizes the poet's failure to keep love alive. Simultaneously, it connects the collection with the previous one, for the rose is also associated in the reader's memory with Manoli's in "Eternal Contemporaries": "The red rose Manoli picked himself / From the vocabulary of roses on the hill by Cefalû."[93] The rose is the flower of language brought alive, the red rose of the Greek land that turns black in the lover's hands:

> I think of you somewhere among them—
> Other roses—outworn by our literature,
> Made tenants of calf-love or else
> The poet's portion, a black black rose
> Coughed into the helpless lap of love,
> Or fallen from a lapel—a night-club rose.

The rose is the only one to survive and becomes the ideogram of love that will flower throughout Durrell's opus, from Darley's love for the "night-club rose" Melissa embodies to "the two roses [who] belong to the same family and grow on the same stalk—Sade and Laura, the point where extremes meet" in *The Avignon Quintet*.[94] Eventually it stands for the city itself, or more precisely for the love the city is unable to give, as Balthazar's prophetic words reveal: "'A rose from Alexandria' he said 'from the city which has everything but happiness to offer its lovers.'"[95] The repetition of the word "rose" that gives the poem its rhythm underlines the abstract essence of the flower that is progressively divested of its material connotations and becomes a pure symbol:

> No, you should have picked one from a poem
> Being written softly with a brush—
> The deathless ideogram for love we writers hunt.

This peculiar rose rising from the painter's brush—as if the poet hesitated between discourse and abstract painting in an unreal dialogue whose final question is left unanswered—is equally doomed to disappear:

Now alas the writing and the roses, Melissa,
Are nearly over: who will next remember
Their spring remission in kept promises,

Or even the true ground of their invention
In some dry heart or earthen inkwell?

The disappearance of the rose seals the silence of the lonely voice, the death of sensibility, and the end of writing. The "earthen inkwell" echoing the "dry heart" suggests a new form of awareness leading toward a subliminal discourse: behind the dichotomies, the ellipses, the silent addressee, the poem builds up what Friedrich calls "an indirect action upon the layers of being that do not yet have access to the rational world."[96] This is how the poem "Chanel" operates; its first line—"Scent like a river-pilot led me there"—encapsulates Durrell's poetic program:

> To speak of reality at all is to limit and debase it; in understanding poetry it is always the words which get in the way. It is a great pity that we cannot inhale poems like scents—for crude as their medium is, their message, their content is something which owes little to reason.[97]

The poem relies on a paradoxical enunciation that introduces a phantasmal dialogue detached from time and space and in which every word is specifically designed to carry us beyond the signified, toward the symbolic, rhythmic, and sensual vibrations that enfold us like scent. One may remember the perfume "*Jamais de la Vie*" used by Justine and Constance and that connotes their unreachable essence. Significantly, the scent in the poem is linked to absence, to the erasure of traces, and to the fading away of visual perception, the most rational of all five senses:

Bedroom darkness spread like a moss,
The polished wells of floors in blackness
Gave no reflections of the personage,
[. . .]
'Kisses leave no fingerprints.'

Out of darkness a new perception is born in the second half of the poem where the scent functions as an allegory for inner vision:

Yet as if rising from a still,
Perfume whispered at the sill,

> All those discarded husks of thought
> Hanging untenanted like gowns,
> Rinds of which the fruit had gone . . .

The phonetic loss from "still" to "sill," the shift toward parataxis that matches the sensorial shift from smell to hearing convey the progressive excavation of a writing leading to the final ellipsis. Just as the writing seems to run out, exhausting itself in the infinite quest for an ever-receding sensation, the subject is carried away by the surge of writing, like a shade ferried into darkness by the "river-pilot":

> Still the long chapter led me on.
> Still the clock beside the bed
> Heart-beat after heart-beat shed.

The exhausted subject of "Chanel" answers that of "Style" a few pages earlier:

> Turning away, to notice the thread
> Of blood from its unfelt stroke.

Should this be read as a forerunner of the pervading theme of blood in *The Red Limbo Lingo* or as the subtle displacement of the unacknowledged bloodstained reality the poet refuses to face and that nevertheless seeps through his writing? The poem might then stand for the tenuous red thread linking the artist to a silenced reality that resurfaces through the forms of various wounds and mutilations.

Indeed Melissa is not the only wounded female figure. So is Theodora, whose portrait is also highly evocative of the Alexandrian women: "cheap summer frock" and "cruel iron bed"[98] remind the reader of Melissa's and Clea's dress as well as of the hospital bed where Melissa dies and Clea recovers.[99] Theodora embodies the memory of lost loves: she is the ideal form taking the shapes and names of various female lovers in *The Quartet* and in *The Quintet*, the incarnation of an unceasingly displaced, ever remote object of desire. From one city to the next, Theodora functions as an oneiric projection that dwells in the poet's eye:

> I saw the street-lamp unpick Theodora
> Like an old sweater, unwrinkled eyes and mouth,
> Unbandaging her youth to let me see
> The wounds I had not seen before.

> How could I have ignored such wounds?
> The bloody sweepings of a loving smile
> Strewed like Osiris among the dunes?
> Now only my experience recognizes her
> Too late . . .

Theodora unrolling her bandages like Melissa in *The Quartet*[100] reveals another excavated portrait that is subsumed in its gaping wounds: the epanadiplosis "The wounds" / "such wounds" bridging the gap between the two stanzas materializes the gutted-out, unreal body that ushers in a silent exploration of deeper, invisible wounds that is the true purpose of the poem. The poet's blindness mirrors the unreal "strawberry-gold" eye that shines at the heart of the text:

> I recall her by a freckle of gold
> In the pupil of one eye, an odd
> Strawberry-gold . . .
>
> . . . I recalled no more
> For years. The eye was lying in wait.

The patient eye is both that of memory and of conscience, the eye that turns back inward and traps the poet between an irradiating visual memory—"I recall"—and a maimed vision—"I recalled no more." The sight of the loved one is intimately linked to the awareness of the loss of the other and of oneself and to a final, paradoxical recovery that unfolds the gaping wounds of time. Instead of the lover's face the poet discovers the wounding irradiation of love that sheds light upon his own blindness to the world and impairs his own vision. The dismembered figure of Osiris "strewed . . . among the dunes" maps out his erratic wandering into the sensible world.

Dwelling upon the wounds inflicted by love leads the poet to question his own end in the epistolary poem "Letters in Darkness," where the love relation veers to a death relation, thus exemplifying once more Lévinas's theory:

> . . . the death of another affects me more than my own. Love for another is the emotion triggered by the other's death. My hospitality towards the other, not the fear of the death that awaits me, is the true measure of death.
> We meet death in the other's face.[101]

These eight fictitious letters, dated from February 19, 1952, to January 12, 1953, and written from Belgrade, echo the writer's anguish in the deathly trap of the world that "River Water" conjured up at the beginning of the collection. Once again the reader faces the unstable nature of a world characterized by a jerky rhythm and the repeated colliding of disjointed space-times.

The first letter opens on an inverted Christian sacrifice where Dionysus, the poet's alter ego, ends up with a maimed divine body. The doctrine enshrined in "the grape-vine of ideas" is debased into a bodily sacrifice that annihilates desire and destroys the flesh: "A star entombed in flesh, desirelessness, / In some ghostly bedroom rented for a night." The following letter concludes this parody of Christian passion by debunking the prayer wheel that solved the conflict between immanence and transcendence, turning it into the wheel of crucifixion that spells out what "The Prayer-Wheel" called "our tribal suicide":[102]

> Hermits and patron-saints
> On the great star-wheel crucified
> Pinned out to lie burning, burning,
> And life is being delivered to the half-alive.

The destruction of love and the religion of death partake of the same cosmogony in which the reader can trace back Durrell's Gnostic as well as Taoist influences nurturing a paradoxical, inverted rewriting of history. Indeed, the explicit reference to antinomianism in the first letter conjures up the memory of those Gnostic heretics who interpreted freedom from law as freedom for license; simultaneously the crucifixion of "Hermits and patron-saints" is strongly reminiscent of Zhuang Zhou's counter eulogy of holiness: "Overthrow saints and free villains, the entire world will be in order. . . . Once the saints are dead, villains are no longer to be seen; peace instantly rules the world."[103]

> The fourth letter plays on the paradoxes of marriage:
> So marriage can, by ripeness bound,
> From over-ripeness qualify
> To sick detachment in the mind—

The regular iambic tetrameters and the repetition and combination of the word "ripeness" highlight the aphoristic nature of those lines, hinting at Greek Gnomic poetry of the sixth century BC and opening up a new space for meditation:

> Now logic founders, speech begins.
> Symbols sketch a swaying bridge
> Between the states at peace or war

The first line foreshadows the opening of "Deus Loci" ("All our religions founder, you / remain")[104] and ushers in the poetic momentum that underlies the poet's hope in a redeemed world. Once again Durrell's vision is strongly evocative of Reverdy's contemporary poetic inklings:

> So that poetry might be the only way to bridge the gap between existing things. Everything that is most useless, most gratuitous in this world rises from the failure of reality to satisfy the tremendous appetite of man and of his soul. Those bridges no one ever does or ever will cross, but for shadows—the innumerable hosts of fierce and taciturn shadows that enable him to hold silence at bay when he is alone.[105]

This swaying bridge thrown by poetry between peace and war, love and violence leads us all the way at the end of the letters to Pan, "The little hairy sexer, Pan, / The turning-point—pure laughter," who heralds "Deus Loci" ("Your panic fellowship is everywhere")[106] and ushers in a new form of love, free from what the first letter called "the lumber love can leave." Love then stands for an inner, secret, and sensual harmony conveyed by the symmetrical balance of the final lines of the third letter: "He lies in his love in shadowless content / As tongue in mouth, as poems in a skull." However, the following letter, bearing the symbolical date of the poet's birthday, destroys this harmonious relationship through a bestial representation of human passions: "the man-bull," "the squat consorts of the passion / Twisted like figs into the legs" evoke Darley's description of the prostitute's booth in *The Quartet* and his meditation upon this "clumsily engaged . . . incoherent experimental . . . means of communication."[107] Such a conflicting vision of love can easily be traced back to Durrell's reading of Rilke's *Letters to a Young Poet* where Rilke distinguishes between "Loving . . . becoming a world, for the love of another, a world unto oneself" and, on the other hand, the behavior of "young people who pour out as they are, unstable, disorderly, confused."[108] Likewise, the poem is torn between opposite poles and offers us, as Pan's counterpart, the image of the lover sinking into madness and mirroring the poet's own death:

> I watch the faultless measure of your dying
> Into an unknown misused animal
> Held by ropes and drugs; the puny
> Recipe society proposes when machines
> Break down. Love was our machine.

Both the subject and the act of loving are deprived of any humanity and turned into a faulty mechanism that fails to give birth to the "panic fellowship" extolled in "Deus Loci." At the point when "the infected face of loneliness / Smiles back wherever mirrors droop and bleed" the reader recognizes both the lovers' private fate[109] and the echo to the poet's ominous lines in "On Mirrors": "You gone, all the mirrors reverted, / . . . / Time amputated so will bleed no more / But flow like refuse now in clocks / On clinic walls...."[110] Facing one's "love for another" amounts then to a descent into madness that parallels the descent into death: "Our self-disdain being mirrored in / Each others' complicated ways of dying." The beloved woman's fate becomes the private place where the poet observes the slow progress of death surrounding him and pervading the silence—not the peaceful, contented silence that the previous line "As tongue in mouth, as poems in a skull" suggested but, on the contrary, the silence that betokens a ruined communication:

> The white screens they have set up
> Like the mind's censor under Babel
> Are trying to keep from the white coats
> All possible foreknowledge of the enigma.

The stanza attempts to circumscribe a twofold "enigma"—that of madness itself and that of the scientific language warding off madness. Poetry delves into the unspeakable as words turn to screens in the broken epanadiplosis "the white screens" / "the white coats." Language thus acts out its own dismantling, depriving the poet of what Alexis Nouss calls "any ontological support and any relation to reality" while endowing him with speech, "a vehicle of mutual understanding."[111]

Interestingly, Durrell never directly refers to the horrors of concentration camps in his poetry. And although the Second World War serves as a background to *Clea* it does not come to the fore as it does in *The Quintet*.[112] Madness operates as an ambivalent screen both shielding the reader from recent historical violence and projecting a personal and collective experience that cannot be dealt with through words. In so doing the poet reveals the Janus-like face of madness that encapsulates both the hopeless confinement of delirium and the irrational hope in a newly founded communication. The "possible foreknowledge of the enigma" that concludes the stanza conveys Durrell's relentless struggle against the world of Babel for "a vehicle of mutual understanding" that shines through the lines and pervades his poetry as much as his prose. Thus we may remember *The Quartet*:

> . . . the café where I waited for her: El Bab. The doorway by the shattered arch where in all innocence we talked; . . . we were possessed only by a desire to

communicate ideas and experiences which overstepped the range of thought normal to conversation among ordinary people.[113]

The complexity of Durrell's poetic world is here laid bare: it relies upon the intimations of the inventions of fragile exchanges that lie beyond the reach of ordinary communication and run the risk of a perpetual floundering, of turning the door—El Bab, in Arabic—into Babel, of toppling over into darkness, as "Letters in Darkness" evince:

> Some few have what I have:
> Silent gold pressure of eyes
> Belonging to one deeply hurt, deeply aware.
> . . .
> So, having dispossessed himself, and being
> Now for the first time prepared to die
> He feels at last trained for the second life.

The new vision from pain is conveyed through the dissociation of the subject. In this final letter "Je est un autre:" he is the writer looking at himself in the very act of writing—"He condenses, prunes and tries to order / The experiences which gorged upon his youth"—very much like the narrator in *The Quartet* who explains: ". . . only there, in the silences of the painter or the writer, can reality be reordered, reworked and made to show its significant side."[114] Therefore "the writer's / Middle years" herald the advent of a new time, "the second life" that foreshadows the redemption that takes place in "Deus Loci." However, this dissociation of the subject through which the "I" sees itself as the other appears to rest upon the disappearance of the other. Thus, "The lumber love can leave" is replaced in the last one by:

> . . . He matches now
> Old kisses to new, and in the bodies
> Of younger learners throws off his sperm
>
> Like lumber just to ease the weight
> Of sighing for their youth, his abandoned own;
> And in the coital slumber poaches
> From lips and tongues the pollen
> Of youth, to dust the licence of his art.

The relation to the other becomes synonymous with predation; love disappears and leaves in its wake what Darley calls "the whole portentous scrimmage of sex itself."[115] Eventually one may wonder whether it is not the death of the other that is celebrated in "these ripe and terrible / Years of the *agon*" as the poet faces with "Calm foreknowledge" the slow consummation of the lover, just as Darley, who distances himself from the fate of Melissa "dusted by the pollen of his kisses."[116] The thin line that separates love from estrangement points to the ultimate dispossession whereby the subject himself runs the risk of losing himself in the ruins of Babel.

"Letters in Darkness" thus echoes "Cities, Plains and People" and the "Anecdotes," reiterating the same descent into darkness, a descent into the abyss of time through which the poet attempts to free himself from what Reverdy calls "a conscience in discontent"[117]:

> ... poetry is the field where conscience is freed, where it ceases to know itself in the sole purpose of questioning itself without ever being able to justify or to explain itself. It is the state in which faculties are exercised with no other purpose but action itself; it is pure act, the supreme act of liberation, the only one whereby a man, as a poet, can grant himself the intense feeling of unfettered existence.[118]

In writing "Deus Loci" Durrell conjures up the dream of the absolute liberation of the poetic act that would be "the noblest outlet for man's conscience in discontent facing a reality hostile to his dream of divine fulfillment, of happiness and of freedom."[119] Exiled from his Serbian exile, the poet enters a space that connects him back to the Mediterranean and to the network of poetic friendships (Zarian, Norman Douglas, W. H. Auden[120]) that has never ceased to nurture him. This long poem masterfully stages the advent of "the second life" promised in the last lines of "Letters in Darkness," this new birth born from writing.

Throughout its ten stanzas "Deus Loci" embodies "poetry as a flamboyant form of life."[121] It opens as a prayer that turns into an incantation in a crescendo rhythm as the iambic tetrameters freely develop into pentameters, so that the poem is never caught in the web of a fixed pattern. It is built on an ascending impetus that starts from collapse ("All our religions founder, you / remain . . .") and roots itself in dust ("This dust, this royal dust, our mother") in order to anchor its dynamics in the enjambment signaled by the absence of capital letters at the beginning of the line so that the poetic breath expands until the epizeuxis "dust" leading to an antanaclasis whereby dust is metamorphosed into the source of life. The poem heralding the poet's rebirth uses an incantatory voice to give the "*deus loci*" the colors of the myth and replace darkness by a flood of light. The "spring-belonging rain" and the "body of damp clay" enable the poet to shape a second genesis:

1

All religions of the dust can tell—
this body of damp clay that cumbered so
Adam, and those before, was given him,
material for his lamps and spoon and body;

Out of the same "clay" surge the "putti" and "amorini" embodying the timeless forces of life that metamorphose dead man's dust into living matter ("curled up like watchsprings in a kiss").

The sixth stanza allows the reader to behold Pan's distorted body imprinted upon the landscape ("The saddle-nose, the hairy thighs / composed these vines, these humble vines"). The epizeuxis ushers in an allegory of the vine and accomplishes a symmetrical inversion: just as man reverts to clay in order to "curl up . . . in a kiss," the sanctified vine presented to God is offered back to man: "offering / in the black froth of grapes their increment / to pleasure or to sadness . . ." This inverted offering paves the way for the mirror effect through which wine reflects both human finitude and eternity:

7

Image of our own dust in wine!
drinkers of that royal dust pressed out
drop by cool drop in science and in love
into a model of the absconding god's
image—human like our own. Or else in other
mixtures, of breath in kisses dropped
under the fig's dark noonday lantern, yes,
lovers like tenants of a wishing-well
whose heartbeats labour though all time has
  stopped.

"This royal dust" in the second stanza becomes "that royal dust," thus completing between stanzas 2 and 7 the complete refraction between mother earth and the wine that give rise to a new being, to a new vision. Wine flows like blood ("drop by cool drop") in order to found a new faith in a human, manlike God that gathers and unites, unlike the God of Babel.[122] The stanza materializes this newly found harmony: the apposition, separated by the dash ("—human like our own") acts as a hinge linking, in the first half of the stanza, the man's refraction in the divinity and, in the second half, the lovers' refraction in the love act that partakes of the same eternity. "Dust in wine" and "breath in kisses" are part of the same creation welding the human and the divine, science and love, breath and flesh, and finally light and darkness in the powerful oxymoron "the fig's dark noonday lantern."

Just as the "*deus loci*" seeps into every nook and cranny of reality ("part animal, part insect, and part bird"), it lies at the heart of every rift in the world. This is how the symbols of loss and division enumerated in the following stanza ("the exile of objects lost / to context") paradoxically serve to reassert the supreme power of life ("Your panic fellowship is everywhere") that can be neither explained nor justified: "your provinces extend / throughout the domains of logic." Poetry thus becomes what Reverdy calls "the supreme act of liberation" that can metamorphose madness into a creative and healing principle, "the nurse and wife of fools" of the penultimate stanza.

The end of the poem, which corresponds with the end of the collection, offers the reader one last instance of a writing that mirrors its own end through the mirrored structure of the last stanza opening and ending upon "So today, after many years, we meet / [. . .] / And here met face to face," as if the world conjured up by the poem closed upon an Edenic independence. Simultaneously, the final words "Forio d'Ischia" recall those of "Letters in Darkness," ending on "Belgrade," as if the two poems reverberated the same unreal mindscape. These two self-contained worlds pointing to opposite directions—the Adriatic and the Mediterranean—suggest, through their perfect closure, the unbridgeable gap that sets them apart. *A Tree of Idleness*, which connects Greece and Egypt and forays briefly into Italy and Cyprus, thus concludes upon two estranged lands, as if to underline the vulnerable, precarious nature of the very space where poetry dwells. This "supreme act of liberation" thus translates into a great escape as the poet achieves freedom by breaking away from the place he writes from. This may account for the paradoxical presence of Cyprus that stands both as the root of writing and as the pervading absence shaping the entire collection. Significantly, Durrell will equally exclude Cyprus from his prose in *The Greek Islands*:

> One important question that will raise itself in the reader's mind is why there is no mention of Cyprus, that most Greek of Greek islands; an island where the local peasant speech contains the most ancient Doric forms and where, at Paphos, Aphrodite was born. There is good reason. The present tragic situation has given its contemporary history a provisional nature which at any moment may be resolved or altered by fruitful Greco-Turkish negotiations. In order not to prejudice any such negotiations, or to envenom issues which have done enough harm already to the relationship between these two great countries, it was deemed best to leave the island out.[123]

Twenty-three years earlier, the same question haunts the reader as he looks in vain for the island concealed behind "The Tree of Idleness," whose central function within the collection highlights a poignant absence. Durrell's ode to Cyprus seems to lie elsewhere, in the poem "Bitter Lemons" that was initially published in *Private Drafts*, a limited edition dated 1955 and comprising only 100 copies,[124] before it was reissued in 1957 as a conclusion to the residence book *Bitter Lemons of Cyprus*. Eventually, the poem will appear again on the disc *The Love Poems of Lawrence Durrell* published in 1962 and finally in *Collected Poems*, which includes the eight poems of *Private Drafts*.

"Bitter Lemons" thus belongs in the margins: it is estranged from the collection and exiled at the end of the residence book—just as the other poems published in *Private Drafts* ("Near Kyrenia," "The Meeting," and "Nicosia," bearing the title "Episode" in *Collected Poems*). It is an off-centered text whose absence belies the impossible confrontation with the Cypriot land that equally evades the writer throughout the residence book. Its original publication in a private collection aimed at a selected audience and printed by the author sets it apart: it is part of a tiny and delicate booklet that opens up the poet's private country to a narrow circle of initiates. Read as an intimate poetic confidence, the poem is fraught with the nostalgia of departures and irrevocable uprooting:

> And the dry grass underfoot
> Tortures memory and revises
> Habits half a lifetime dead

The same longing haunts "Near Kyrenia" ("A victim of memory") and "Nicosia" (whose first two stanzas start with "I should set about memorising this little room" and the last one by "This is probably the very moment to store it all"). In "The Meeting" the same wrenching pain floods the poet's memory: "Through meadows of tears unshed" echoes the last burden of the last two lines of "Bitter Lemons"—"Keep its calms like tears unshed."

This repeated last line detached from the final stanza, like an antiphon to the sea, echoes the end of "Mneiae" that ended upon the repetition of "Which time's the only ointment for." Just like "Mneiae," "Bitter Lemons" sets to explore "love, the grammar of that war"[125] on a musical pattern where the alternating iambic and trochaic tetrameters marry the enjambments from one stanza to the next so that the poem seems to flow endlessly, relentlessly, like this "unshed tear" that fills up the silence:

> Better leave the rest unsaid,
> Beauty, darkness, vehemence
> Let the old sea-nurses keep
>
> Their memorials of sleep
> And the Greek sea's curly head
> Keep its calms like tears unshed
>
> Keep its calms like tears unshed.

Significantly, the poet describes the island through an abstract language that stands at odds with the sensorial evocation of "The Tree of Idleness" as if he were not so much concerned with remembering the past as with setting it apart through the conceptual distance imposed by nouns. This detachment wrought by abstraction and silence pervades both the lexicon and the rhythm of the text where final rhymes are only used in the last three lines as if to mimic the backwash of the sea relentlessly lapping against memory.

The exclusion of the poem "Bitter Lemons" from the collection *The Tree of Idleness* might then be interpreted as a sign of repression, as if the poet refused to acknowledge in the end the loss of the beloved land, just as he has previously ignored the injured body of the loved woman in "A Portrait of Theodora": "How could I have ignored such wounds?"

Simultaneously, if the poem is considered within the context of the residence book *Bitter Lemons* it can be read as a poetic, insightful coda where the reader recognizes the garden of the Turkish house in Bellapaix, the scented trees and the shades of the sea that bore Aphrodite. The poem thus brings the reader back to the prose and is endowed with the symbolic value of the derelict Abbey described in the narrative:

> . . . as a testimony to the powers of contemplation which rule our inner lives. . . . a testimony to those who had tried, however imperfectly, to grasp and retain their grip on the inner substance of the imagination, which resides in thought, in contemplation, in the Peace . . . [126]

Poetry thus stands out as the space of displaced fulfillment and harmony denied by the narrative, a sanctuary where the soul may rest in peace, sheltered from the violence of the world, the idle *locus* for this idleness that Clive Scott aptly defines as "not a concept but a mode of creative being . . . a nonchalance at an angle to being, a gift of, and a response to a particular kind of being."[127] Feeling powerless to placate the winds of history, the writer withdraws into his private country where Babel can be transmuted into El Bab, opening the door to an inner awareness that defeats the death drift of history.

The residence book, like the collection of poems, points to the same emptiness conveyed by the ellipsis of "Bitter Lemons" that encapsulates the eclipse of a peace the narrative fails to recreate as well. There can be no final conclusion then, either to the collection or to the prose, as the writer admits his incapacity to heal the wounds of history.[128] ". . . no book is genuinely free from political bias. The opinion that art should have nothing to do with politics is itself a political attitude,"[129] George Orwell asserted in 1946. Yet Lawrence Durrell refused to "give the Greek press grounds for believing that [he] had resigned on policy grounds, which would have been unfair to my masters,"[130] and eventually leaves the island condemning "a state at war with itself."[131] Taking refuge in poetry as in a private cell where "the old illusion of timeless peace"[132] can be preserved, the poet chooses, like Darley, the atemporal kingdom of the imagination in a perplexing silence that dramatizes his ultimate alienation from the lost Eden.

The Tree of Idleness, initially placed under the auspices of Milarepa, ends on a silence that underlies the entire collection, placing emptiness at the heart of the poetic endeavor. One may easily recognize here the very principle of creation of the macrocosm that rests upon an original void[133] materialized through various images in Durrell's poems: the everlasting Greek sea permeating Durrell's world, the dissolution of the subject in the final lines, the receding presence of the material world, or the ungraspable nature of the truth that is brought to the fore in "Thasos":

> Only their poets differed in being free
> From the historic consciousness and its
> Defeats: . . .
> told
> The truth in oracles and never asked themselves
> In what or why they never could believe.[134]

The enunciative source vanishes away so that the reader fails to pinpoint the origin of discourse: are we listening to the obedient civil servant eluding reality or to the poet echoing the voice of the oracles? Eventually, the collection ends on an aporia that echoes one of Durrell's favorite Zen aphorisms: "'To talk is blaspheming, to remain silent is deception. Beyond silence and talking there is an upward passage, but my mouth is not wide enough to point it out to you.'"[135] Such might well be Durrell's ultimate message: a poetic art anchored in the distilled wisdom of aphorisms as so many splinters of truth that are allowed to flash upon our memory long after the poet's mouth has gone silent.

Notes

1. "Letters in Darkness," Lawrence Durrell, *The Tree of Idleness*, London: Faber, 1955, p. 39.
2. The same note reappears when the poem is published within Lawrence Durrell, *Collected Poems*, London: Faber, 1960, p. 237.
3. See *Autumn's Legacy Op.58*, music by Lennox Berkeley (London: J. & W. Chester, 1963), followed by *Songs about Greece* and *Contemporary Poets Set in Jazz*, music by T. Wallace Southam (London: Jupiter Recordings, 1964); *Lesbos*, music by T. Wallace Southam (Oxford University Press, 1967); and *In Arcadia*, music by T. Wallace Southam (London: Turret Books, 1968).
4. This expression is a reference to the yet untranslated literary biography written by Corinne Alexandre-Garner, *Lawrence Durrell: Dans l'ombre du soleil grec*, Paris: La Quinzaine Littéraire, Louis Vuitton, 2012.
5. Lawrence Durrell, *Bitter Lemons of Cyprus*, London: Faber, 1959 (first published in 1957), p. 16.
6. Hugo Friedrich, *Structure de la poésie moderne*, Paris: Librarie Générale Française, 1999 (first published in 1956), pp. 15, 17.
7. Richard Pine, *Lawrence Durrell: The Mindscape*, New York: St. Martin's Press, 1994, p. 130.
8. *Lawrence Durrell: The Mindscape*, p. 129.
9. "The Tree of Idleness," Lawrence Durrell, *Bitter Lemons*, London: Faber, 1955, pp. 75–91.
10. *Structure de la poésie moderne*, p. 230.
11. "The Tree of Idleness," *The Tree of Idleness*, p. 31.
12. Lawrence Durrell, *Key to Modern Poetry*, London: Peter Nevill, 1952, p. 12.
13. *Bitter Lemons of Cyprus*, pp. 56, 57.
14. *The Tree of Idleness*, p. 31.
15. *The Tree of Idleness*, p. 31.
16. *The Tree of Idleness*, p. 57.
17. See Durrell's analysis in *Key to Modern Poetry*, pp. 53–69.
18. Paul Valéry, "Propos sur la poésie" (1927), *Œuvres I*, Paris: Gallimard, 1957, p. 1363.
19. "Propos sur la poésie," pp. 1363–64.
20. "Propos sur la poésie," p. 1364.
21. Clive Scott, "Lawrence Durrell: The Poet as Idler," *Deus Loci: The Lawrence Durrell Journal* NS 13 (2012–2013): pp. 14–15.
22. We may remember that Eve Cohen was unable to follow Durrell to Cyprus and entrusted him with their baby daughter; see Ian MacNiven, *Lawrence Durrell*, London: Faber, 1998, p. 384.

23. Letter of November 1953, *The Durrell-Miller Letters 1935–80*, Ian S. MacNiven, ed., London: Faber 1989 (first published in 1988), p. 275.
24. Frankétienne, *Spirale, Premier mouvement des métamorphoses de l'oiseau schizophone, D'un pur silence inextinguible*, Vents d'ailleurs, La Roque d'Anthéron, 2004, p. 13.
25. Max Kommerell, *Gedanken über Gedichte* (1943), quoted by Hugo Friedrich, *Structure de la poésie moderne*, p. 225.
26. *Structure de la poésie moderne*, p. 225.
27. Lawrence Durrell, *Sappho*, London: Faber, 1967 (first published in 1950), scene 8, p. 185.
28. Lawrence Durrell, *The Avignon Quintet*, London: Faber, 1992, p. 861.
29. Lawrence Durrell, *Cities, Plains and People*, London: Faber, 1946, p. 51.
30. *Key to Modern Poetry*, p. xi.
31. Lawrence Durrell, *The Greek Islands*, London: Faber, 1978, pp. 184, 185–86.
32. "In the Garden: Villa Cleobolus," Lawrence Durrell, *On Seeming to Presume*, London: Faber, 1948, p. 25.
33. *The Greek Islands*, pp. 184, 185–86.
34. Lawrence Durrell, *A Private Country*, London: Faber, 1944 (first published in 1943), pp. 21–22.
35. *Key to Modern Poetry*, p. 159.
36. *Key to Modern Poetry*, p. 158.
37. *Key to Modern Poetry*, p. 156.
38. *Key to Modern Poetry*, p. 106.
39. *Key to Modern Poetry*, p. 90.
40. Henri Meschonnic, *Célébration de la poésie*, Paris: Verdier, 2001, pp. 36–37.
41. *Célébration de la poésie*, p. 36.
42. Serge Ritman, "Interview with Patrice Beray," *Mediapart*, June 15, 2013, http://www.mediapart.fr/article/offert/ff80a348bcb676ed322700d48a8ebdf6, last accessed June 15, 2013.
43. Such is the mystical image concluding Livia's yoga practice: "'. . . like an inverted lotus the valves of the flesh heart open by day and close by night during sleep,'" *The Avignon Quintet*, p. 411.
44. *Key to Modern Poetry*, p. 42.
45. Lawrence Durrell, *The Alexandria Quartet*, London: Faber, 1974 (first published in 1962), p. 761.
46. Pierre Grimal, *Dictionnaire de la mythologie grecque et romaine*, Paris: PUF, 1951, p. 304.
47. *A Private Country*, p. 50.
48. *Key to Modern Poetry*, p. 42.
49. *The Tree of Idleness*, p. 13.
50. *Key to Modern Poetry*, p. 43.
51. *Dictionnaire de la mythologie grecque et romaine*, pp. 332–33.
52. Durrell's albatross harks back to Coleridge's in "The Rime of the Ancyent Marinere" (*Lyrical Ballads 1798*, Oxford: Oxford University Press, 1993, pp. 7–32) and to Baudelaire's in "L'Albatros" (*Les Fleurs du Mal*, Paris: Gallimard, 1996, p. 38).

53. See Diana Menuhin's letter to Durrell previously quoted in our introduction: "like some self-appointed helmsman."
54. *Key to Modern Poetry*, p. 90.
55. William Shakespeare, *Twelfth Night*, Oxford: Oxford University Press, 1994, act 1, scene 1, l.1–4.
56. T. S. Eliot, "The Love Song of J. Alfred Prufrock," *Collected Poems 1909–1962*, London: Faber, 2002, p. 4.
57. "The Love Song of J. Alfred Prufrock," *Collected Poems 1909–1962*, p. 7.
58. William Shakespeare, *Hamlet*, act 1, scene 5, l.196.
59. *Key to Modern Poetry*, p. 9.
60. *Key to Modern Poetry*, p. 157.
61. "By this plate of olives, this dry inkwell," Lawrence Durrell, *On Seeming to Presume*, p. 10.
62. "Blind Homer," *On Seeming to Presume*, p. 10.
63. *Key to Modern Poetry*, p. 156.
64. *The Alexandria Quartet*, p. 763.
65. *Key to Modern Poetry*, p. 158.
66. *Bitter Lemons*, p. 15.
67. T. S. Eliot, *The Waste Land*, *Collected Poems*, p. 54.
68. *Key to Modern Poetry*, p. 157.
69. David Stephen Calonne, "The Discovery of Yourself: Lawrence Durrell and Gostan Zarian in Greece," *Lawrence Durrell and the Greek World*, London: Associated University Presses, 2004, p. 72.
70. See "the English Death" in *The Black Book* as well as *The Traveller and His Road* where Zarian exclaims: "Hideous disintegration." (New York: Ashod, 1981, p. 6).
71. "The Lost Cities," *On Seeming to Presume*, p. 28.
72. "The Lost Cities," *On Seeming to Presume*, p. 28.
73. *The Alexandria Quartet*, p. 116.
74. *The Avignon Quintet*, p. 13.
75. *The Avignon Quintet*, p. 185.
76. *The Avignon Quintet*, p. 202. Compare with *The Alexandria Quartet*, pp. 77, 177.
77. Gilles Deleuze and Felix Guattari, *A Thousand Plateaus: Capitalism and Schizophrenia*, London: Continuum, 2002, p. 432.
78. *Key to Modern Poetry*, pp. 148–51.
79. *The Alexandria Quartet*, p. 20.
80. Emmanuel Lévinas, *Dieu, la mort et le temps*, Paris: Grasset, 1993, pp. 20, 30.
81. *Dieu, la mort et le temps*, p. 25.
82. *The Durrell-Miller Letters*, letter dated October 12, 1949, pp. 240–41. We may remember here Blanford's gesture at the beginning of *Quinx*: "He had thrown away all his notes for the new book, shaking out his briefcase from the window of the train. [. . .] The sum of all their parts whirled in the death-drift of history—motes in a vast sunbeam," *The Avignon Quintet*, p. 1178.
83. See the espionage novel Durrell was simultaneously writing: *White Eagles over Serbia* (1957).

84. See Genesis 3: 17–19.
85. "At Corinth," *A Private Country*, p. 18.
86. *The Tree of Idleness*, p. 22.
87. *Dieu, la mort et le temps*, p. 84.
88. See "Eight Aspects of Melissa," *Cities, Plains and People*, p. 7.
89. "The Anecdotes, XIII In Paris," *On Seeming to Presume*, p. 55.
90. "Conon in Exile," *A Private Country*, p. 51.
91. *The Alexandria Quartet*, p. 54.
92. *The Alexandria Quartet*, p. 711.
93. *On Seeming to Presume*, p. 43.
94. *The Avignon Quintet*, p. 923.
95. *The Alexandria Quartet*, p. 215.
96. *Structure de la poésie moderne*, p. 15.
97. *Key to Modern Poetry*, p. 84.
98. "A Portrait of Theodora," *The Tree of Idleness*, p. 33.
99. *The Alexandria Quartet*, pp. 54, 843, 188, 854.
100. *The Alexandria Quartet*, p. 52.
101. *Dieu, la mort et le temps*, p. 121.
102. *On Seeming to Presume*, p. 32.
103. Zhuang Zhou, *Œuvre complète*, Paris: Gallimard, 1969, p. 88.
104. *The Tree of Idleness*, p. 44.
105. Paul Reverdy, "Préface à 'Souspente' d'Antoine Tudal" (1945), *Cette émotion appelée poésie (1930–1960)*, Paris: Flammarion, 1974, p. 198.
106. *The Tree of Idleness*, p. 47.
107. *The Alexandria Quartet*, p. 152.
108. Rainer Maria Rilke, *Lettres à un jeune poète*, Paris: Librairie Générale Française, 1989, pp. 70–71
109. One cannot ignore here the autobiographical echoes to Durrell's struggle against Eve Cohen's hallucinations and deep depression. See Corinne Alexandre-Garner, *Lawrence Durrell: Dans l'ombre du soleil grec*, p. 319.
110. *The Tree of Idleness*, p. 25.
111. Alexis Nouss, *Paul Celan. Les lieux d'un déplacement*, Paris: éditions Le Bord de L'eau, 2010, p. 27.
112. For insightful analyses of the representations of WWII in *The Quintet* see Corinne Alexandre-Garner, "La représentation de la deuxième guerre mondiale et du nazisme dans *Le Quinette d'Avignon*," *Parcours Judaïques III*, Presses Universitaires de Paris X, 1996, pp. 99–111, "Je est / hait l'Autre: la femme juive comme double et autre dans *The Avignon Quintet* de Lawrence Durrell," *Parcours Judaïques IV*, Presses Universitaires de Paris X, 1998, pp. 179–93, and Dianne Vipond, "The Politics of Lawrence Durrell's Major Fiction," *Deus Loci: The Lawrence Durrell Journal* NS 13 (2012–2013), pp. 47–63.
113. *The Alexandria Quartet*, p. 26.
114. *The Alexandria Quartet*, p. 20.

115. *The Alexandria Quartet*, p. 151.
116. *The Alexandria Quartet*, p. 19.
117. *Cette émotion appelée poésie*, p. 72.
118. *Cette émotion appelée poésie*, p. 73.
119. *Cette émotion appelée poésie*, p. 73.
120. For biographical details see Ian MacNiven, *Lawrence Durrell*, pp. 367–69.
121. *Cette émotion appelée poésie*, p. 219.
122. "Therefore is the name of it called Babel; because the Lord did there confound the language of all the earth: and from thence did the Lord scatter them abroad upon the face of all the earth," Genesis 11: 9.
123. *The Greek Islands*, p. 9.
124. The "Note" at the end of this thin volume explains: "Of these private drafts of poems in progress 100 copies have been printed as curiosities for personal friends at the Proodos Press." The Lawrence Durrell Library at the University Paris Ouest owns copy no. 18. Apart from "Bitter Lemons," this issue includes "Near Kyrenia," "Nicosia," "The Meeting," "John Donne," "Poem," "Ballad of Psychoanalysis," and "At the Long Bar."
125. *The Tree of Idleness*, p. 13
126. *Bitter Lemons of Cyprus*, pp. 78–79.
127. "Lawrence Durrell: The Poet as Idler," pp. 3, 5.
128. However, one must note that Durrell published in 1964 an article supporting Enosis in *London Magazine* (see Corinne Alexandre-Garner, *Lawrence Durrell: Dans l'ombre du soleil grec*, p. 322). Moreover, unsigned articles published in *The Economist* by Durrell as he was still on Cyprus testify to his attempt at dealing with what he called "The Cypriot's Dilemma."
129. "Why I write," *The Collected Essays, Journalism and Letters of George Orwell*, vol. I, Harmondsworth: Penguin Books, 1968, p. 26.
130. *Bitter Lemons of Cyprus*, p. 214.
131. *Bitter Lemons of Cyprus*, p. 217.
132. *Bitter Lemons of Cyprus*, p. 192.
133. One may remember Genesis as well as Durrell's philosophic sources, in particular Zhuang Zhou (see *Œuvre complète*, p. 104).
134. *The Tree of Idleness*, p. 35.
135. D. T. Suzuki, *Essays in Zen Buddhism*, London: Rider and Company, 1956, p. 55. This passage has been underlined by Durrell.

CHAPTER FIVE

The Ikons

Greece in the Mind's Eye

Eleven years have elapsed between the publication of *The Ikons* and that of the previous collection, *The Tree of Idleness* (1966). In the meantime, Durrell mainly published prose work[1] and drama,[2] contenting himself with publishing some scattered poems in reviews and issuing the first anthologies[3] that already foreshadow the final collection[4] and testify to the silent composition of an ambitious poetic opus. *The Ikons* bear the print of this ongoing poetic quest that pervades the fictional production and invites the reader to look for the hidden traces of a secret exploration.

This new collection marks a radical break in composition: as the prefatory note explains, it brings together poems that have already been published, either in literary reviews or in the first edition of *Collected Poems* (1964). The dust jacket introduces a medley of poems that veers away from the careful, self-enclosed composition of the previous collections and is rather conceived of as a "selection of his recent work."

For the first time, the collection is no longer defined by a specific spatio-temporal frame; rather, it follows in the wake of *The Tree of Idleness* where different times and places are pitted against each other. Thus, Greece, Italy, and Languedoc are superimposed in a borderless territory that opens up the dark recesses of the private creation underlying the better-known and widely acclaimed fiction. Moreover, this is the first collection that does not include any explicitly autobiographical text, as if the lyrical "I" were progressively wiped out. This shift was already under way in *On Seeming to Presume* where the lyrical "I" was less pervasive, although still present. Throughout the various collections the lyrical "I" does not in fact so much disappear as it is refunded into an exploration of the quintessential enunciative instability of the poetic subject. As Dominique Rabaté deftly points out in his study of "East Coker," the modernist lyrical "I" is best described as "a questioning subject, a disquieting, moving force:"[5]

> The "lyrical subject" is not the original core of a speech through which it is expressed but rather a tangential point, the desired horizon of possibly subjective utterances which he tries to link together. . . . The complex enunciative shifts are at the heart of lyricism; modern poetry has turned these fragmented voices into its own field of exploration.[6]

This broken-up enunciation, "ringing with disconnected voices echoing one another,"[7] is in keeping with a modernist space-time where hesitation and indecision prevail. This new collection thus appears to be less preoccupied with the sublimation of a personal experience than with experimenting with an abstract composition that further expands the disfiguration process initiated in the previous collections and echoes the aphorism concluding "Press Interview": "One cannot copy to unearth the new."[8]

This newness that the entire collection strives to bring forth (". . . I just fict / Unfashionable if you wish, or even unreal / So to evict the owner from his acts / In propria persona; spit out the bones")[9] seems at odds with the title *The Ikons*, whose eponymous poem is, for once, placed at the onset of the book and opts for a spelling that reminds the reader of the Greek etymon *eikōn*, and of the tradition of painted wooden panels celebrating orthodox saints and patriarchs. Paradoxically, this collection that breaks free from the representation of space, from the "copy," chooses a title that encapsulates a form of representation based on symbolic analogies with the real. This tension between two contradictory forms of relationship to the real is characteristic of Durrell's poetics, both in its prose and poetic achievements.

Thus, we may remember *The Alexandria Quartet* and the twofold process of representation and deconstruction that characterizes *Justine* and *Balthazar*, or the various forays into the painter's art embodied by Clea, who eventually opts for abstraction[10] after the accident that enables her to discover her artist's hand: "But the hand has proved itself almost more competent even than an ordinary flesh-and-blood member! [. . .] IT can *paint!* I have crossed the border and entered into the possession of my kingdom, thanks to the Hand."[11] The new artificial steel and rubber hand is freed from the laws of biology and verisimilitude. Hidden inside its green velvet glove, it leads a life of its own, not unlike the writer's hand leaving its green furrows in *The Black*

Book and paving the way for those improbable Mediterranean poetic icons that throw the reader into the world of the irrepresentable.

The Icon of the Irrepresentable

Devoid of any epigraph that may guide the reader, the collection opens upon "The Ikons," a programmatic text that holds the key to the entire set of poems. Yet, as is often the case in Durrell's work, the key is a mere illusion and the hidden meaning is revealed when least expected.

The first poem consists in a fragmented icon, a jarring triptych in three stanzas whose only coherence seems to lie in the multiple forms of disjunction. The first stanza introduces the end of Greek myths through the bastardized modern figures of excess formerly embodied by Dionysus:

> They have taken another road,
> Dionysus and all his cockledom,
> . . .
> A madman walks alone in the dark wood
> Swinging a lantern; nobodies march,
> Lute player, card-sharper, politician

The disappearance of the kingdom of Dionysus is matched, at the other end of the stanza, by the rise of Byzantium: ". . . the condign / Majestic stance of something else / Apparelled for death: Byzantium." Byzantium foreshadows another poem, "Byzance," that ushers in some fifteen pages later the vanishing of another world relegated, like Antiquity, to museums:

> Only objects of their past estate remain,
> Dispersing now like limbs in different museums.
> . . .
> Only the eye in an ikon here or there,
> Amends and ponders and reflects neglects
> Dead monarchs toughened to a stare.

Both similar and distinct, these two cultures share two equally rich civilizations, a cultural, artistic, and economic worldwide influence and an equally dramatic fall. Byzance disappears along with the Greek world and becomes Constantinople, and later on Istanbul, also called Polis, after the Greek word *city*; it is the setting chosen by Durrell for *The Revolt of Aphrodite* and whose descriptions in *Tunc* remind the reader of the "cerements of damp" and the "lichen covered" stones of the poem "Byzance"[12]:

> by now I had come to see what an immense graveyard Stamboul is, or seems to be. The tombs are sown broadcast, not gathered together in formalised squares and rectangles . . . here death seemed to be broadcast wholesale in quite arbitrary fashion. A heavy melancholy, a heavy depression seemed to hang over these beautiful monuments.[13]

In the novel, as in the collection, Byzance is the epitome of disjunction and abstraction in a twofold manner: it stands for a space where history and human bodies slowly disintegrate ("Her dust has pawned kings of gold"),[14] and it functions as the paradigm of impossible representation that is deliberately devoid of any kind of resemblance to reality. "Byzance" thus reverberates a defunct abstract world that traps the poet's eye in the coil of its dismembered bodies: "Only the eye in an ikon"[15] encapsulates in the poem the novelistic exploration of "the scar tissue of old wounds upon which the blood has dried black."[16] The act of representation is thus caught in the aporetic figuration of ruins that "Amends and ponders and reflects" and opens up, instead of the expected icon of the city, the irrepresentable intimate meditation of a single, disembodied eye contemplating death.

Like a ship "appareled for death,"[17] Byzantium in "The Ikons" and the poem "Byzance" pave the way for the secret motif at the heart of the icon—and faithfully echo the onomastics derived from the Greek verb *buzō*, "to tighten," which is at the root of the name Bosphorus, denoting a "narrow crossing" (*poros*)—while expanding, beyond the boundaries of a single poem, the disjunction process that precludes any linear reading of the opening poem as well as of the entire collection.

The second stanza of "The Ikons" relies on a temporal shift that throws the reader into the future ("The eyes won't change")[18] in order to lead him back toward a modernist form of death punctuated by a fragmented time ("Here the population of clocks multiplied / They bore the suffocating fruits of chime, hours") that echoes "Time amputated . . . / Not made to spend but kill and nothing more"[19] in the poem "On Mirrors" in the previous collection *On Seeming to Presume*.

Following the historical collapse of the past in the first stanza, and the future indomitable breaking down of society in the second one, the last stanza explores the present, personal embodiment of inner collapse:

> A café is the last Museum and best,
> To observe a great man in the middle
> Of a collapse; but parts work still,
> The crutches are incidental, adding variety.

This human specimen is anything but human: it is a dismembered manikin, broken up through the successive run-on lines and derisively equipped with the paraphernalia of infirmity, as if to foreshadow the disjointed dummy of Iolanthe in *The Revolt of Aphrodite* where the final crashing of the living doll epitomizes the fallen civilization observed by the "great man" in the poem:

> He sits before the tulip of old wine,
> In a red fez, by some sunken garden,
> Watching for shooting stars.

The triptych of "The Ikons" symbolically ends on the "sunken garden,"[20] the garden of the Fall thrown into darkness where "shooting stars"[21] bring an uncertain, fleeting light, borne from the cosmic explosion and dislocation of a further world. The only source of light thus originates in a far sweeping destruction, echoing the disappearance of the Greek god Dionysus and suggesting the unnamed iconoclastic figure of Lucifer, the fallen light-bearer.

The mask of death that slowly takes shape behind the icon of a lost civilization is further developed in the following poem: "Aphrodite." The reader initially thinks he can recognize the luminous figure that presides over the world of *Prospero's Cell* and *Reflections on a Marine Venus*, another Greek icon often associated to Dionysus in Durrell's texts. Thus, one may remember the sand statue carved by the narrator at the end of *Prospero's Cell* and that summons Botticelli's Venus Anadyomene: ". . . we build in gleaming sand the figure of a gigantic recumbent Aphrodite. . . . the sea creeps up and gnaws her long rigid fingers."[22]

When it resurfaces in *Reflections on a Marine Venus* it is endowed with a temporal dimension that turns it into an icon of eternity:

> through her we learned to see Greece with the inner eyes . . . as something ever-present and ever-renewed: the symbol married to the object prime—so that a cypress tree, a mask, an orange, a plough were extended beyond themselves into an eternality they enjoyed only with the furniture of all good poetry. In the blithe air of Rhodes she has provided us with a vicarious sense of continuity not only with the past—but also with the future. . . . Time is always aspiring to a dance-measure which will entangle the two in a dance, a dialogue, a duet: dissolve their opposition. The radiance of that worn stone figure carries the message to us so clearly . . .[23]

Yet Aphrodite in *The Ikons* stands miles apart from the goddess encountered in Durrell's travel narratives. It belongs to a fragmented time in which the past destroys any form of harmonious relationship between the human and the heavenly worlds:

> Not from some silent sea she rose
> In her great valve of nacre
> But from such a one—O sea,
> ...
> Time-scarred, bitter, simmering prophet.

In contrast with the Venus of Rhodes ("disregarded, sightless"),[24] this one is defined by her scopic drive ("Wide with panic the great eyes staring") and stands sharply against Pompeii's fresco showing Venus sailing freely and happily on her conch, as if sheltered in a shrine of beauty and grace. On the contrary, the apparition of the goddess is a violent, painful act underlined by the staccato rhythm at the beginning of each line in the second half of the first stanza where the hammering of past and present participles ("Scourged / Boiling / Carded / Time-scarred"), as well as the broken syntax of the last line framed by a double aposiopesis (marked by the ellipsis and the dash on either end), highlight the disappearance of the subject. Far from the incarnation of an antique ideal, the bulging-eyed Venus mirrors man's raging and fatal desire:

> Of man's own wish this speaking loveliness,
> On man's own wish this deathless petrifact.

The new Aphrodite stands out as an object of desire just about to break apart in the incomplete anaphora and the imperfect chiasmus of the last couplet. She presides over a dead world, revealing the worthlessness of man's quest, just as Iolanthe, the embodiment of Aphrodite in *Tunc*: "'I-O-lanthe!' Note that the stress falls upon the second syllable not the third, and that its value is that of the *omega*."[25] Just like Aphrodite in the poem, Iolanthe prophesizes the end of the world in the missed encounter with love, which is the true root of a fallen civilization:

> The sex act misses fire if there is no psychic click: a membrane has to be broken of which the hymen is only a parody, a mental hymen. Otherwise one can't understand, can't receive. So very few men can do this for a woman.[26]

Aphrodite and Iolanthe call to each other beyond textual boundaries and offer the reader the unexpected twofold icon of the goddess of love exposing man's incapacity to love. As such, they embody the platonic two-faced representation of Aphrodite as Aphrodite Urania, the seaborne goddess of heavenly love, and as Aphrodite Pandemos, the goddess of common love. This dichotomy pervades Durrell's entire opus.

A few pages later, Aphrodite reappears in the poem "Near Paphos," where its marine birth reminds the reader of the mesmerizing rhythm of the sea in *Bitter Lemons*:

> With the same obsessive rhythms it beat and beat again on that soft eroded point with its charred-looking sand: it had gone on from the beginning, never losing momentum, never hurrying, reaching out and subsiding with a sigh.[27]

This time, Aphrodite is not named, yet her mystic presence seeps through the regular beat of the tetrameters and the soft, musical lilt of the alliterative pattern through which the sea is transformed, as if by divine breath:

> Her sea limps up here twice a day
> And sigh by leaden sigh deposes
> Crude granite hefts and sponges
> Sucked smooth as foreheads or as noses;
> No footprints dove the labouring sand,
> For terrene clays bake smooth
> But coarse as a gipsy's hand.

Aphrodite reborn is both a marine and an earthly being that rises as the joint fruit of nature and man's work: it is simultaneously the object and the subject of creation. The chiasmus of the last two lines linking "terrene clays" to "gipsy's hand" and "smooth" to "coarse" suggests the fundamental harmony of which the goddess is the immanent form. The consecrated flower in the second stanza ("A rose in an abandoned well") opens up the primeval natural world ("The sexless babble of a spring") where the goddess's favorite birds disclose an undivided universe: boundaries dissolve and duality becomes a token of completeness.

This is a world that belongs to the present tense, as opposed to the divided one created by the temporal rift of the narrative in the past: "Before men sorted out their loves / By race and gender chose." The sea at Paphos is alien to any form of linear temporality and dwells in the eternal rhythm borne out of the incomplete anaphora that joins the first lines of the first and last stanzas, as if to avoid the pitfall of closure:

> This much the sea limps in to touch
> With old confiding foam-born hand
> While lovers seeking nothing much

> Or hunting the many through the one
> May taste in its reproachful roar
> The ancient relish of her sun.

The direct object of the verb "touch," "this much," is negated in the subsequent repetition, "nothing much," as if to suggest the dissolution of matter in the present eternity of the sea. The lovers' timeless embrace is bathed in the light of her heavenly body, just as the landscape of Paphos was bathed in the sweep of her sea. The possessive adjectives in "her sea" and "her sun" thus recreate the missing primordial harmony, reasserting Aphrodite's silent, anonymous, yet overpowering presence. She is the embodiment of the ongoing search for unity that brings the lovers together and that lies at the heart of the writer's quest whether in poetry or prose:

> She was a symbol . . . not of licence and sensuousness, but of the dual nature of man—the proposition which lay at the heart of the ancient religions from which she had been derived. . . . She belonged to a world of innocence outside the scope of the barren sensualities which are ascribed to her cult; she was an Indian.[28]

In the welding of the different generic forms the writer experiments with the creation of a redeemed vision that calls for a new, unassigned poetic voice inhabiting what Stéphane Baquey calls:

> . . . a space-time where the feeling of space and time is brought back, as opposed to the dispersal that characterizes common space and time. In that sense, the subject of the poem is devoid of both 'hic et nunc.'
> The utopia, or better, the uchronia of the poem lies in the invention of a voice that both shapes out a singular rhythm within language and the advent of a form of life . . . [29]

A few pages later, the poem "Io" conjures up Aphrodite as "the contemporary street-walker,"[30] the goddess of common love, and recalls once more the main character of *Tunc* who simultaneously embodies Aphrodite Pandemos and Io, the princess of Argos and priestess of the Goddess Hera who was changed into a heifer in order to escape the wrath of Zeus's wife. The poem plays on the same referential ambivalence:

> In the museums you can find her,
> Io, the contemporary street-walker all alive
> In bronze and leather, spear in hand,
> Her hair packed in some slender helm

> Like a tall golden hive—
> A fresco of a parody of arms.
> Or else on vases rushing . . .
> A hostage, someone's youngest daughter.
> All the repulsion and the joy in one.

The museum statue seems to copy the "street-walker," a living pagan icon, equipped like Diana Huntress and whose headdress suggests the numerous representations of Venus and Cupid. One may indeed remember Cranach the Elder's *Venus with Cupid*[31] where the latter, having been stung by a bee for stealing honey, complains to his mother Venus. He is shown holding the honeycomb, a symbol of immediate pleasure and its punishment. Io, with her mock attributes, is thus portrayed in the poem as the inverted blazon of Venus, just as the representation of sensual nakedness in Cranach's painting is subverted by the moral inscribed in its top right-hand corner.

The identification of the mythical figure keeps wavering throughout the poem, just as its representation mingling the sculptural and carnal images ("The slim statue asleep over there"), and calls forth once more the character of *Tunc* who stands out as the icon of Greece for the narrator: "Iolanthe now is an unidentified wave to sadness which reaches out for me whenever I see a slip of blue Greek sky, or a beautiful late evening breaking over the Plaka."[32] In the poem, just as in the novel, Io is an ode to a timeless melancholy that brings back the absent one:

> All that will keep, all that will keep.
> Soon we must be exiled to different corners
> Of the sky; but the inward whiteness harms not
> With dark keeping, harms not. . . .

One recognizes in the remanent figure of the vanished Io that of Father Nicholas, whose orison ended some twenty-three years earlier on the same words:

> . . . for the egg of beauty
> Blossoms in new migrations, the whale's grey acres,
> For men of the labyrinth of the dream of death.
> So sleep.
> All these warm when the flesh is cold.
> And the blue will keep.[33]

Father Nicholas and Io join in these "new migrations," belonging to the same "labyrinth of the dream of death" inhabited, in Durrell's cosmogony, by both real and mythical characters. Just as Durrell bade farewell in "Father Nicholas

His Death in the Ionian" to the man who partook of his intimate Greek landscape, he honors in "Io" what is left of Greece despite exile, "the inward whiteness" of the hunted heifer that sheds a fleeting, dazzling light upon the poet's eye and enables him to inhabit, if only briefly, the constellation that travels "to different corners / Of the sky."

The last stanza concludes upon a final farewell to the recumbent statue that stands on the threshold of death:

> . . . Yet perhaps
> I should sneak out and leave her here asleep?
> Draw tight those arms like silver toils
> The Parcae weave as their supreme award
> And between deep drawn breaths release
> The flying bolt of the unuttered word.

One remembers the reclining Aphrodite on the beach of Paleocastrizza in *Prospero's Cell* and whose first cry at birth ("her mouth open in an agonizing shriek, being born")[34] is transmuted in the poem into a last cry ushering in a new realm. Thus the poem revisits the classical myth of Aphrodite borne from the sea and offers the reader a goddess borne from and through death, unfolding her arms to welcome her fate and pointing in the slow dissolution of her stranded body to the further dissemination of a mysterious, initiatory word—"the unuttered word" of poetic inspiration that opens up consciousness and heralds veiled, undelivered beginnings.

The Icon of Awakening

This descent toward death heralding a new poetic awakening is characteristic not only of the representation of Aphrodite but also of the Greek space and, more specifically, of Cyprus. Thus, the poem "Salamis" offers an unexpected vision of the Greek and Roman ruins where scientists discovered in the 1950s, hidden under vast tumuli, the tombs of Cypriot Kings from IX to the VIII centuries BC containing the funerary chariots drawn by horses sacrificed on the spot and surrounded by magnificent Phoenician offerings. The poem is highly elliptical: apart from its title, it gives no clue as to the extralinguistic reality before the final lines ("a dead sea-king's / Face, a helm of gold, a mask"). Once more the icon seems to deny any form of representation but instead opens up a surprising perspective upon the irrepresentable:

> A treatise of the subtle Body,
> Dark van of winter-pledging stars,

> Spearheads of the advancing deep
> In seas whose commotions keep
> The tracery of ships' lace spars.
> Another island: another small eternity

The poem operates as a leap into the unknown and the invisible that can only be experienced by a conscience aware of the "subtle Body" that Yoga describes as the hidden face of the visible, common body and that is made of

> an infinity of channels that have naturally been compared to arteries, veins or nerves. The sacred texts refer to them as *nāḍī*, the Sanskrit word for 'river' that is used in the Vedas to refer to the Indus, the Ganges and their affluents. . . . These channels do not carry blood (like veins) or sensory-motor impulses (like nerves) but breath (*prāna*). . . . *prāna* and *apāna* refer to the air mass inhaled through the nose and exhaled through the mouth that, having invigorated the body, changes in nature. Simultaneously, and more essentially, *prāna* is the source of this invigoration. . . . Thus, the breath can legitimately be considered as a true cosmic element (*bhūta*) working its way within the body.[35]

Therefore the very place where mortal remains are excavated becomes, through poetry, the place where a new awareness of death and life is born, bringing the reader to consider a hidden force curled up at the heart of the microcosm, what the poem calls "Another island: another small eternity." The elliptical style thus leads to successive displacements hinting at the unknown. The funerary chariots are replaced by a voyage ("The tracery of ships' lace spars") that, in the context of the Upanishads, symbolizes the body drawn by the forces of the world of perception and action guided by thought. The soul is thus considered as undergoing a journey it neither controls nor desires and wishes to escape. Likewise, the lexical field of the sea journey sketches out the vicissitudes of former navigations and the various islands stand as so many isolated consciousnesses. The poem unfolds its erudite contemplation fostered by "yellowing books" in a space that belongs neither to geography nor to books but that functions as a standpoint where the poet questions the true purpose of art:

> Is the work of art really a work of nature,
> To mobilise the sense of wonder,
> Revise all time's nomenclature?

By interrogating the essence of the work of art, the poet lays bare the essentially metatextual nature of his quest, opening up the "*hic et nunc*" of the poem, sketching out an escape route toward a new space-time in which a spirit of wonder may be fostered by a singular and unadulterated perception.

The following stanzas develop the theme of the boundless journey, as if to "paraphrase" the departure of the dead, and nurture a meditation on the eternal nature of memory carving its empty mask in the mind's eye:

> A night of leavetakings and summaries,
> Inventory of the capes unwinding
> In their old smoke and cursing spray,
> In scarves of smoking suds—
> Never to leave, perhaps, never to go away,
> And yet past the heart's reminding
> See the soft underthrust of water sway

The still movement of impending departure is captured in the timelessness of present participles and infinitives, in the quiet pattern of alliterations, assonances, and interlocked rhymes welded into the present tense of the ripening vision. The "dead sea-king's / Face" although objectified as "a mask" reveals the persisting image of life crossing the vast expanse of death:

> Ringlets washed back from a dead sea-king's
> Face, a helm of gold, a mask
> In the autumnal water's writhing.
> To remain and realise were the hardest task.

This dramatic tension between memory and disappearance, persistence and destruction characterizes the entire collection, as the disjunctive title of the poem "North West" evinces.

> The dying business began hereabouts,
> A pewter plain, a shrubless frugality,
> An anarch sea, cliffs, nothing.
> It promised a local action merely
> But the death-rot somehow spread from
> Limb to limb and mind to mind,
> Became endemic. The body politic
> Was touched, began to suppurate once more.
> An empire began to have dizzy spells,
> One fever to cast out another
> One man to cast down another.

The entire poem focuses on man's perennial destructive impulse and on the entropy of history. Greek history functions as a metonym for universal history through the erasure of spatial landmarks. The anthropomorphic conception of the state echoes Shakespeare's tragedies and makes way for the poet's sharp criticism of contemporary politics as he witnesses the last convulsions of a dying Empire. The following question in the next stanza—"Who can apportion a historic fault?"—expresses the poet's sadness as he realizes his own powerlessness and the inevitable self-destruction of a world that devours its own children, after the manner of the Titan Kronos. Every beginning thus fosters its own end, from the initial stanza—"The dying business began hereabouts"—to the last one—"They spoke of starting again at the beginning"—which closes upon the image of the defeated gorgons covered "with self-renewing moss" that suggest the indomitable self-regeneration of destructive powers lurking in the depths of the earth. Like the Gorgon, whose petrifying powers endure on Athena's shield, death returns, giving birth to the cycle of renewed destructions that is materialized by the symmetrical pattern of the last two lines in the first stanza—"One fever to cast out another / One man to cast down another"—as well as by the implicit echo to T. S. Eliot's meditation on finitude in Part V of "East Coker" in *Four Quartets* where old age is not synonymous with wisdom but with defeat and alienation.[36]

Just as in "East Coker," the meditation on death developed in "North West" suggests the poet's limits and his inability to protect "the precious culture pilfered into dust"[37] and that is, in Durrell's own words, "the spiritual element that man adds to the material world. . . . The sum total of inventions, dreams, works of art, that he leaves behind for the rest of mankind, separate from himself and yet bearing his imprint."[38]

The poet's art would thus lie in his commitment to point at what lies beyond the horizon of the word, and carry on the struggle to convey the ineffable, the other life that keeps evading him, threatened as it is by the entropy of the world.

Seen in that perspective, the poet resembles the "lonely stroller" described by Stéphane Baquey: he is the man who has "retired from common time in quest of a form of life that lies in the folds of a language bent on the enigma of presence"[39] and only meets with death. This encounter is the cornerstone of the entire collection, which includes three central poems that can be read, like "The Ikons," as a triptych to Greece leaving:[40] "Olives," "The Initiation," and "In the Margin."

In the first one, the olives ("food and common tool") and the olive tree ("your tips in trimmings kindled quick") initially belie an anthropomorphic vision of nature ("Your mauled roots roared with confused ardours") before reverting to the eternal presence they spring from and that the poem addresses through them: "So the poets confused your attributes." Turned into a proper divinity the olive partakes of various natures: it is both sacred ("The Other"), and mundane ("the domestic useful"); it supports and surpasses man:[41] "Momentous, deathless, a freedom from the chain / . . .Who live or dead brought solace." It materializes man's sensual relation to a sacred space and the timeless union of the sacred and the profane.[42] It is an antidote to man's finitude. It penetrates memory and matter, and revises the contours of the known world:

> No need to add how turning downwind
> You pierce again today the glands of memory,
> Or how in summer calms you still stand still
> In etchings of a tree-defining place.

The olive thus plays a similar role to that of Gérard de Nerval's myosotis, which Yves Bonnefoy has magnificently analyzed:

> the myosotis translates as 'forget-me-not' in English, it is the flower that commands attention by inscribing its summons within the fabric of language, where it has become a figure of speech. Its 'forget-me-not' suggests the poet's task which is to remember the full reality of existing beings and things beneath the schematic representations fostered by a speech committed to conceptual understanding. And the minute the world thus built flounders, noticing the little flower in the surrounding non-being, seeing it not as the abstract entity described in dictionaries but as this very flower, in this place, in this most likely illusory existence that can nonetheless be experienced and pretends to be real, well, this is not something illusory, but new, drastically new; it inaugurates a new—or rather incipient—reality.[43]

It is this "incipient—reality" that Durrell attempts to capture, and the presence of the dash in Bonnefoy's sentence cannot be overstressed: it gives an almost palpable reality to the tension toward an ineffable presence that is made perceptible in Durrell's verse by the resisting texture of assonances ("you still stand still"). The ascetic vision of the poet reveals a new being to the world that metamorphoses living and inanimate matter into what Bonnefoy describes as "a place, a life-saving help . . . the only conceivable reality."[44]

The poem is therefore conceived of as an initiation. Symbolically, the poem "The Initiation" faces "Olives" in the collection. It introduces the reader to the death of material perception by transforming secular items ("Spoonful of wine, candle-stump and eyes") into "a life-saving help." This is why these desultory elements enumerated at the beginning of the poem reappear in the last stanza to compose the portrait of man's finitude: "What fruit the barbers shave / To the last dimple of the self-regard." In between these two poles the three decrescendo central stanzas sketch out the floating presence of the departed whose image still haunts the poet's inner eye. The last line of the first stanza, "A fever's point of no return," signals a hinge in the structure of the poem and paves the way for the surge of the child's voice calling for the one who no longer belongs to the world of images but whose dimly familiar presence echoes throughout the text: "The road leads softly down / On avenues of darkling recognition." The loss of the loved one challenges our perception of what lies beyond matter, which, according to Yves Bonnefoy, "can tear apart everything, yet consciousness and what it decides definitely evade its grasp."[45]

The nature of the icons announced in the first poem thus becomes clearer: these are abstract icons that do away with representation, paradoxical icons revealing what lies beyond the world of images, icons of an "incipient—reality" that breaks free from dead matter.

The last poem in this central triptych, "In the Margin," definitely wipes out the possibility of any form of representation in one long stanza of iambic trimeters that mimics the slow dissolution of the image. Opening on "One ikon still can move," the poem apparently still nurtures the hope of a pictorial image that is immediately debunked: "Grey eyes, whose graphic doubt / Smile to the last remove." This "graphic doubt" haunts the writing of the text, which plays on the polyptoton "move / remove" and displaces representation from the object to the paradoxical source of light that simultaneously drives away and foregrounds darkness:

> Light candles . . .
> Then softly frame your lips
> To blow the darkness out,
> In some forgotten room
> In some forgiven town
> Co-evals of wish
> Made half the darkness bloom.

The frame simultaneously widens and narrows through this shift in perspective that leads the reader's eyes from candles to lips before drowning them in the symbolic darkness of that little room in that little town that is to be read as a metonymy for a greater darkness ("Foreknowledge of the end"). The poem thus embraces the end of the day ("Calm as the night's serene / Erasure of the light") and the end of time ("So history bleeds on") so that the icon veers away from the representation of the loved one and focuses instead on the disappearance of the lovers haunted by doubt:

> Two pupils of the sense
> Knowing neither where nor whence
> So history bleeds on,
> And will not heed this wreath;
> Two spendthrifts of the death
> The dark bed held beneath.

The icon sketched out between the lines is a moving one in both senses of the phrase: it is an unstable, flickering image about to be swallowed in darkness that is meant to move the reader into the recognition of the universal fate embodied by the silent recumbent effigies. This symbolic death is the necessary threshold to a renewed perception, as the pun on the word "pupils" suggests, laying bare the metaphysical quest that rests on the deliberate renunciation of rational knowledge ("Knowing neither where nor whence"). Just as the lovers who choose to follow "sense" rather than reason, the poet holds no answer but allows for this ontological uncertainty to expand and reverberate in the reader's mind. This questioning is indeed at the heart of Eastern philosophy as Durrell's friend, the writer Mulk Raj Anand, explains:

> As Gandhi wrote, the truth about oneself should be the starting point of all writing. No use writing about others, when one has not written about one's own feelings, ideas, uncertainties, one's own agonies. "Agony, agony, dream and ferment" is the drama of every writer, and some small pleasures. A disciple once asked his master, the sage, in *Upanishad*: "What shall I do with my life?" The sage answered: "Ask yourself everyday who am I? Where have I come from? Where am I going?" . . .
> Unless one asks the questions "Who am I, where have I come from, where am I going," one cannot get over egoisms and achieve transcendence.[46]

Such is the abstract icon that stands in the margins of writing and of life and that teaches the gaze to see through the "spendthrifts of the death" and recognize the unrelenting quest that Durrell pursues through the various lovers who dwell in his poetry, his prose, and drama. Thus, Fabius in *Acte* aims at a similar transcendence:

> . . . We are the trash of history
> In a rotten Empire staggering to its doom.
> Ah, but with a knifestroke I could cut the girths
> And set the wild horse free.[47]

The freed horse in *Acte* is akin to Pegasus, the winged horse delivered by the beheaded Medusa: it embodies the desire for transcendence that is materialized in the poem by an ambivalent fleeting time that symbolizes both death ("running like a noose") and generosity ("spilling like a gland") as well as freedom and light when it flows unfettered from the writer's hands ("At leaf-pace gliding on / Or catching like a spark"). It brings forth an inner radiance that cannot be erased. Eventually the candles lit in darkness at the beginning of the poem lead toward the secret effulgence of poetry, not unlike the sacred oil lamps of Greece burning in invisible shrines.[48] Time is thus endowed with a new essence: it becomes a moment of light, of inner knowledge that, paradoxically, always arises out of darkness, as Bonnefoy explains:

> Yes, poetry is the unveiling of a truth; and as such, if it came fully into being, it would be its manifestation, its expression. But what about the poem? It is only a cluster of various harmonic patterns where the true poetic beam is often a very minor component. The poem expresses, in a thousand ways, both involuntary and unintentional . . .[49]

The poem ends on the image of "the dark bed," echoing the death bed behind the scenes in *Acte* where Petronius's last speech to his niece Flavia transforms death into an initiation, a displaced revelation of the irrepresentable, a mystic leap conveyed in verse:

> One day you will see that death is not merely
> To be 'died' but to be achieved. . . .
> . . . I simply pass the message on.
> Yes it *is* possible to become an adept of reality.[50]

What is referred to as "reality" is in fact the truth aimed at by the poet and that rises from the demise of representation and the invention of a new space-time.

It is thus no wonder that the following poems "Scaffoldings: Plaka" and "Acropolis" should focus on the collapse of matter, sending the reader back to the prophetic tone of "The Parthenon" in *On Seeming to Presume*. The reader remembers the latter poem, whose title introduced the Greek temple only to take the gaze further down into the city of Athens, an immaterial city, floating above the dismantled body of Western history and foreshadowing in the peaceful flight of "an eagle softly moving on the blue"[51] the hope of a recovered harmony in a space that belongs neither to common time or space. "Scaffoldings: Plaka," on the other hand, contrasts the city of whiteness of "The Parthenon" with a space that caves in prior to a descent into death that runs parallel to the vertical exploration of the demotic city. The lexical field of destruction and uprooting ("nibbled," "slipping," "melting," "disabused ruins," "pulled down," "uprooted," "wrinkle into dust") pervades the entire poem and contaminates language while history turns into a farce:

> For how long have we not nibbled
> At the immediate past in this fashion, words,
> Regretting our ignoble faculty of failing,
> Slipping between whose fingers?
> Melting between whose lips?
> The disabused ruins of history's many
> Many costumes we discarded.

Syntax, like reality, is torn apart in the postposition of "words" isolated between commas at the end of the sentence and of the line, in the anadiplosis of "many," in the accumulation of present participles ("regretting," "failing," "slipping," "melting") highlighting man's growing paralysis and helplessness. The anecdotal, anthropomorphic reference to "The little shop . . . pulled down / . . . / A sort of little face now uprooted . . ." triggers a descent into the excavated space of past history where the scaffold that gives its name to the poem no longer connotes architectural construction but instead uncovers the city's skeleton:

> We did not spot the scaffolding of bone
> Until the last winter, the immense despondency
> Once more gained full control, the immense despondency.

The belated perception of a wintry world climaxes in the epiphora that underlines the relentless progress of death and strikingly echoes the technique used by Eliot in "The Burial of the Dead":

> Unreal City,
> Under the brown fog of a winter dawn,
> A crowd flowed over London Bridge, so many,
> I had not thought death had undone so many.[52]

This world in decline is not only that of an ideal Greece, nor that of the poet's personal history, but more essentially, that of a culture that crosses frontiers, texts, and eras, reminding the reader of the early descriptions of Alexandria in *The Quartet*.[53] Eliot's "Unreal City" is echoed by equally unreal Durrell's "city loyal" that slowly metamorphoses into a death mask ("Old walls wrinkled into dust, windows / Poked out . . ."), hinting at the fate of exiled Greek heroes banished from ". . . squares and parks designed for someone's loving." The poem ends as an ode to the destroyed "heroic vision" that plunges the world into darkness:

> Say what you like it's gone.
>
> One blow can shatter the heroic vision.

The blank separating the last two lines materializes the fragmented perception and signals the fall of Athena's heroic city of the mind.

Facing "Scaffoldings: Plaka," the poem "Acropolis" focuses on the antique demotic city that lies, like Plaka, at the foot of the Parthenon and displays once more a lifeless city, composing a diptych with the previous poem where the fall of both the modern and the antique city is portrayed. The pictorial mimesis is underlined by the striking layout of the poem that relies on the elision of capital letters and on the asymmetrical combination of pentameters so that the syntactic and the prosodic patterns are systematically disrupted. The poem thus initially strikes the reader as a visual experiment, after the manner of Apollinaire's Calligrammes, thus rendering its semantic meaning secondary. Indeed, meaning is shattered as early as the first two lines—"the soft *quem quam* will be Scops the Owl / conjugation of nouns, a line of enquiry"—where the italicized onomatopoeia creates a myriad of polysemic echoes. The reader is thus simultaneously brought to hear the distorted song of Athena's favorite bird, the stuttering of the poet's voice, and the Latin declension of the indefinite pronoun *quisquam* in the accusative case. The poem's "line of enquiry" thus opens up a series of unanswered questions reverberating an ontological quest: "who walks here in the violet dust at night / by the tower of the winds and water-clocks?" The choice of the place adverbial throws the addressee into the city, at the north end of the Acropolis where the Tower of the Winds looms up. This octagonal marble monument, visible from the Parthenon and dated from the first century BC, is attributed to the Greek architect Andronikos of Cyrrhus. It displays an effigy of Triton as a weathervane, the symbolic representation of the main eight winds above its eight sundials, and a clepsydra. It stands as the perfect emblem of the passing of time and gives the poem a both historic and realistic anchorage that paradoxically opens up access to timelessness: while "the shattered pitchers" and "the fresh spring" refer to the mechanism of the water clock whose former circular tank and pipes can still be traced, they also connote the eternal fluidity of time. Yet the identification of this landmark of the antique Polis once again combines with a loss of meaning, for the reader is led astray from the opening question "who walks here . . . ?" which is left unanswered while the lonely late strollers may tentatively be identified as the community of poets and readers walking down the common grounds of memory. Thus the poet draws the reader into a joint quest by inviting him to hear, see, and feel a shattered landscape:

> the passive smells
> > bread urine cooking printing-ink
> will tell you what the sullen races think
> > and among the tombs gnawing of mandolines
> confounding sleep with carnage where
> > strangers still arrive like sleepy gods
> > dismount at nightfall at desolate inns.

The poem "Acropolis" thus sketches out an atemporal acropolis where the chords of mandolins, the smells of daily life, and the imprint of new faces cannot be circumscribed by time or space and where the poet experiments with the dislocation of language and time to offer the reader an infinite dance around the octagonal spiral of eight moving lines, like the eight faces of the Tower of the Winds.

Walking the Sacred Path

The Ikons thus unfurl as a multifaceted icon that relies on defamiliarization and conjures up a mystical Greece that is to be deciphered in the intertwining of cultural and literary allusions. As such, *The Ikons* partakes of the shift toward abstraction initiated in the earlier collections and explicitly invites the reader into an initiatory country in the poem "Eleusis" where the "echo of truth"[54] reverberates and expands the quest announced by "At Epidaurus" in *A Private Country*:

> Then smile, my dear, above the holy wands,
> Make the indefinite gesture of the hands,
> Unlocking this world which is not our world.[55]

This hieratic world finds its sensual achievement in "Eleusis" where the poet attempts to penetrate the secret of self-knowledge:

> How long will the full Unlearning take?
> How long the unacting and unthinking run?[56]

The poem shifts from a sensorial description of the sacred rites in the first three stanzas to an admonition between quotation marks, as if the poet were voicing a sacred call laying out man's eternal duties in the gnomic present:

> 'The issues change, alas the problems never.
> The capital question cuts to the very bone.
> Drink here your draught of the eternal fever,
> Sit down unthinking on the Unwishing stone.'[57]

"The eternal fever" belongs to a life cycle that encapsulates and transmutes death—and stands poles apart from the fever and frenzy of "North West." It places the poem within the antique tradition of the cult of Demeter in which the initiates hoped for life after death and were first introduced to the sacred rites through the worship of the dead:

> the mysteries of Eleusis . . . are both chtonian and epichtonian, if we may say so; this is why the bestower of bountiful harvests . . . is also the goddess of the dead.[58]

The poem ends on death, marrying, just as in the sacred rites, death and rebirth through a process of renunciation materialized by the recurring prefix –*un*, which highlights the material and spiritual dispossession imposed by the mysteries of Eleusis. "Eleusis" thus partakes of the ontological questioning of death that permeates Durrell's poetics and expands on the following page in "Apteros."

The underworld landscape of caving ruins in the former poem is contrasted by the rising temples in the latter, yet both convey a collapsing world. The bare stone of "Eleusis" is indeed replaced in "Apteros" by the antique friezes of the temple of Athena Nike where mineral matter reads like a book:

> Sky star-engraved, the Pleiads up,
> Autumn's old ikonography
> . . .
> Incised the crater of heaven burns
> . . .
> To die by the universal variable
> And scribble on a stone our scope
> . . .
> Kiss of white caryatids which lean
> With broken boxers' noses here
> On armatures of lead,
> . . .
> Shapes of the carnal void,

Cracked smiles of marble mouth,
Starred emblem of a stone embrace.

"Apteros" functions as the overhanging pediment that crowns the architecture of the entire collection: it is the final bastion above the ramp leading to the Propyleae and offers a panoramic view upon "Eleusis" and "Delphi," the following poem. "Apteros" thus stands at a crossroads between two mystic poles, but it also paves the way for the image of Athens that will be developed in "Scaffoldings: Plaka" and in "Acropolis" at the heart of the collection. Eventually Athens appears as a disparate, fragmented frieze that comprises the small temple to Athena Nike, the popular shops of the Plaka or the Tower of the Winds like so many remnants of an extinct world. "Apteros" is part of this frieze that reveals in its broken plaques the iconography of a lost era. It is stamped by the techniques of dismemberment and entanglement that characterizes Durrell's poetics. Thus, the fragments of friezes adorning the temple offer fleeting insights into the architectural iconography while shunning any form of pictorial representation. Instead, the frieze describes a circular pattern through the play of internal rhymes and repetitions: "In falling fruit and turning sea" heralds "Fruit, star and promiscuous wave," while the compound adjective "Sky star-engraved" recurs in "Starred emblem." And although the title of the poem explicitly refers to the temple of Athena Nike, the "Kiss of white caryatids" confuses the reader. Indeed the parapet of the temple includes sculptures of winged Victories flying above trophies and sacrificed animals in front of a seated Athena, Nike Apteros, wingless Athena, who, according to the legend, can no longer leave the city. Yet these are friezes, while the caryatids belong to the southern canopy of the Erechteion and its famous Porch of the Maidens.[59] The poem thus plays on the infinite "Shapes of the carnal void" by conjuring simultaneously the various vestiges of the Parthenon and destructuring a cultural common ground to the point that the reader fails to ascertain where to look for the "Cracked smiles of marble mouth." Should the last line—"Starred emblem of a stone embrace"—be understood as a reference to the circle of dislocated ruins overhanging Athens or to the star-spangled ceiling of the small temple? Once more the reader's gaze is torn between the finite and the infinite in an abstract icon that foregrounds man's essential frailty:

How much will time exempt in us
How much replace?

The eternal white figures that contain and challenge time question human finitude: "Year after summer year incline / To appear and reappear."

They are both devoured and preserved by time, and stand out as time's keeper as they epitomize a timeless inheritance—whether architectural, literary, or symbolic—that is akin to Paul Valéry's "soft columns" endowing man with an eternal aura:

> Nous marchons dans le temps
> Et nos corps éclatants
> Ont des pas ineffables
> Qui marquent dans les fables . . . [60]

Durrell's statues, temples, friezes, and caryatids lay bare the "armatures of lead" of a common anchorage that transcend, in the fabric of memory and art, the dissolution of time. Throughout the painstaking and slow excavation of matter that characterizes the entire collection, the rock wherefrom the poet contemplates the persistence of desire in the midst of despair shines through: "The phosphorescence of desire / To a season of wanhope." Thus, the "footsore stone"[61] in the poem "Eleusis," conjuring up the place where Demeter rested during her search for her daughter, recurs in the "stone"[62] of "Apteros" that heralds the "bitter rock"[63] of "Delphi," the following poem. They function as so many fragments of the "One Grey Greek Stone" that is the true eye of *The Ikons*.

This is the first time the title of a poem does not promise any identifiable landmark but instead sets the reader free to visualize either the poet's portrait in front of the omphalos in Delphi or the various stones scattered throughout the poems functioning as so many emblems of the little god Hermes, the messenger who joins the heavenly and the human worlds, the inheritor of the pre-Hellenic deity Herma, the pile of rocks or cairn. "One Grey Greek Stone" reads as the emblem of the crossing of temporal, spatial, and scriptural frontiers through which Durrell elaborates the abstract icon of his personal poetic quest.

> Capes hereabouts and promontories hold
> Boats grazing a cyclopean eyeball,
> No less astounding
> Snow-tusk or toffee-round hill
> In shaggy presences of rock abounding
> Charm the sick disputing will.

One may recognize in this first stanza the image of the insular Greece the poet explored and painted[64] as well as that of his many poems that stand out as so many capes and promontories offering the reader a textual Odyssey into a mythical space-time of "cyclopean" dimensions. The landscape of "One Grey Greek Stone" is the symbolic icon of the poetic space that appeals to our "sick disputing will" and magnifies the poet's healing voice in the perfect roundness of an unreal stone polished by the smooth rhythm of the rhymes. One may recall the shiny stone compositions of contemporary sculptor Henry Moore, his modest pebbles softened by the waves that testify to the presence of an overwhelming force, of an inner vitality, of a density and a perfection that surpass man's endeavor and that the artist tries to capture. Likewise, "One Grey Greek Stone," an "Old dusty gem" polished "to buff," fragile and luminous ("Trembles upon an eyelash into stars"), and endowed with chthonian powers ("Under such stones to sleep"), is transmuted: it is no longer a dilapidated vestige but points to a new way of writing and being in the world. In tune with the vital energy man shares with the landscape ("How strange our breathing does not stop") the poet's voice blends in with the rhythm of the earth that hints at a new, silent, and careful understanding:

> Tell me, the codes of open flowers,
> Lick up the glance to pocket a whole mind.
> Nothing precipitates, is left behind,
> The island is all eyes. Shout!
> The silence ponders, notes and codifies.
> We discover only what we set out to find.

Paradoxically, inanimate mineral matter becomes the source of a new awareness of life that springs from the primordial unity of the vegetal realm. The world becomes a book where flowers, islands, and words alike can be deciphered and silently answer man's questioning. One may recognize here the influence of Gérard de Nerval, who drew his reader's attention to "matter itself":

> 'Tout est sensible!' Et tout sur ton être est puissant.
> Crains dans le mur aveugle, un regard qui t'épie:
> A la matière même un verbe est attaché . . .
> . . .
> Un pur esprit s'accroît sous l'écorce des pierres![65]

Durrell shares Nerval's mysticism. The enunciative and syntactic ambiguity welded to the gnomic present creates a rift at the heart of the poetic voice, so that the reader may recognize another, differing voice that stands apart from the lyrical "I" of the following stanza:

> I am at a loss to explain how writing
> Turns this way this year, turns and tends—
> But the line breaks off as voices do, and ends.

The conflation of two distinct enunciative sources within a single utterance fosters a poetic vision that combines knowledge and ignorance, revelation and silence, resistance and fracture. The subject shedding his ego through the act of writing escapes the finite world of a single utterance and paves the way for an infinite silence conveyed by the aposiopesis, a silence transmuted into a paradoxical expressive gesture that "ponders, notes and codifies." The penultimate stanza performs the final metamorphosis of the subject that blends in the landscape and is no longer the subject of action but a passive, recording, patient, and sensitive presence opening our gaze:

> Image coiled in image, eye in eye,
> Copying each other like guesses where the water
> Only dares swallow up and magnify,
> So precise the quiet spools
> Gather, forgive, heap up and lie.

The twofold mirroring of the image and of the eye belongs to an elsewhere that is also an *elsewhen*: the perfect syntactic and prosodic symmetry enhances the all-encompassing gaze and ushers in a new mode of perception that links the object and the subject in a never-ending reciprocal relation. This abstract icon of poetic sensibility closes upon a tombstone that unveils the plenitude dreamed up by the poet:

> Under such stones to sleep would be
> The deepest luxury of the deliberate soul,
> By day's revivals or the plumblue fall
> Of darkness bending like a hoop the whole—
> Desires beyond the white capes of recall.

This last stanza metamorphoses the sleep of death into a serene bliss through the fluid alliterations, assonances, and enjambments; the smooth syntax; and the close phonetic kinship between interpolated rhymes. Thus may the soul awaken to another absolute form of life ("the whole") that finds its completion in the perfect circle[66] of days and nights, in the harmony of a refunded space-time that opens up a boundless perspective stretching beyond the shores of memory. This physical and poetic balance of forces and natural elements foreshadows the state of *nirvāṇa* the subject hankers after, this ultimate detachment from the world of sensations where desires and memory are inexorably bound together. This is consistent with D. T. Suzuki's analysis of *nirvāṇa*: relying upon sacred Pali writings, he interprets *nirvāṇa* as the psychological attitude that opens up the realm of endless possibilities and enables one to perceive unity amid the multitude of forms and stimuli. Such an expanded form of consciousness brings one into contact with "the silence of unity."[67]

"One Grey Greek Stone" adumbrates the realm of the absolute blossoming of abstraction, of totality and eternity, a boundless and timeless space mapping a new world that frees the subject from death.

This quest for the absolute is further developed in the poem "Poemandres" that summons once more Hermes Trismegistus, the Greek incarnation of the Egyptian god Thoth and the supposed author of the *Corpus Hermeticum*, a collection of seventeen dialogic treatises among which the first one, *Poimandres*, gave its title to the whole. Poimandres, the incarnation of "the Nous of the supreme,"[68] is believed to come either from the Coptic word *Peimente-rê* (knowledge of Rê) or from the Greek word ποιμήν ἀνδρῶν meaning "men's shepherd."

> A treatise on astrology, the *Corpus Hermeticum* blends scientific observations and pseudo-science; but, as a whole, these texts purporting to rely on a revelation, not on observation, presented themselves as an occult science.... The ideas they developed borrowed from Greek demotic thought and were arranged in an eclectic manner, mingling popular Platonic, Aristotelian, and Stoic philosophy. Here and there Judaic influences also seeped in, as well as traces of a religious literature that originally spread from Iran.[69]

Durrell's poem symbolically starts on an impossible deciphering:

> The hand is crabbed, the manuscript much defaced,
> Fly-spotted and faint even in good light.
> ...
> Yet beneath the enigma gnawed him like an acid . . .
> Men and women squirted into semblances,
> Their hair growing unpruned, foliage of eagles.

The poem unfurls as an exploration of the mysteries of the universe where species are no longer differentiated. Durrell's poetry mimics its own object through the use of a hermetic language that offers "revelations, not discoveries . . . implying and granting a sort of personal intimacy with the divine"[70] and adopting a dialogic form to stage a vision, a dream, a secret message or its communication. By borrowing the syntax and the lexicon of Gnostic texts the poem reads as a barely decipherable manuscript hinting at the presence of a secret subtext: "the angelic man," "the mystical spouse, his syzygy," "A vision of the soul," "the epoptic mystery," "The black backbone of death," "The gold back-bone of life," "spheres of self-delusion," "The black monitors of the Cabiri." As if to unveil the mysterious palimpsest of its own sources, the poem compiles allusions and images, taking the shape of a shimmering and confused vision that suggests the origins of the world while perplexing the erudite as much as the layman. The religious references, blending the Holy Chrism and the Cabiri—these mysterious divinities from Samothrace often associated with Jupiter,[71] Minerva, and Mercury and supposed to protect sailors—intensify in the second half of the poem where the sixth and eighth stanzas intertwine quotations that sound like the broken utterances of a lost Gnosis. The first one, in italics and in French, is made of fragments, suggesting that the very fabric of the text is "gnawed": "*Cri d'une âme qui fait éclater / Son enveloppe charnelle*" is taken from the critic Jean Richter,[72] who later developed, in the wake of André Breton, an esoteric interpretation of Nerval's poetry. The second part of the quotation is a rewriting of a letter dated July 15, 1854, sent by Gérard de Nerval from Frankfurt to Doctor Blanche:

> Le mal est plus grand que vous ne pensez. . . . Peut-être ce que j'ai éprouvé de bizarre n'existe-t-il que pour moi, dont le cerveau s'est abondamment nourri de visions et qui ai de la peine à séparer la vie réelle de celle du rêve.[73]

Like Nerval's text, Durrell's poem plays on the tenuous frontiers between reality and dream, between knowledge and the prescience of a hidden world, between its primary and secondary sources in a stanza where the enjambment is used to build up a factitious enunciative unit. The poem's persona seems to vanish amid the confusion of voices, as if to give way to the words of revelation quoted in the eighth stanza, where G. R. S. Mead's translation of *Poimandres* is poetically reworked:

> He in his turn beholding the form like to himself, existing in her, in her Water, loved it and willed to live in it; and with the will came act, and [so] he vivified the form devoid of reason.[74]

The union of man and earth, of the male and the female is part and parcel of the poet's questioning. Past and present inquiries blend in an unceasing dialogue that echoes those of hermetic texts and of Plato's philosophy, turning poetry into a hermetic and hermeneutic art.

The poem's final image sends the reader back to the Edenic myth of the first stanza where "Men and women squirted into semblances" and repeats the tragedy of the fall ad infinitum: "Yet she is still giving men apples printed / With the bite of her white teeth." From Aphrodite's to Eve's apple the mystery of the primordial division between "the angelic man" and "the mystical spouse," the Gnostic "syzygy,"[75] is an ever deeper one. The polysemy of the poetic image is an echo to that of the hermetic text itself, as G. R. S. Mead explains in the introduction to his translation:

> This is the most famous of the Hermetic documents, a revelation account describing a vision of the creation of the universe and the nature and fate of humanity. Authors from the Renaissance onward have been struck by the way in which its creation myth seems partly inspired by *Genesis*, partly reacting against it. The Fall has here become the descent of the Primal Man through the spheres of the planets to the world of Nature, a descent caused not by disobedience but by love, and done with the blessing of God.[76]

Just like *Poimandres*, the poem unfurls a kaleidoscope of overlapping references the better to baffle the reader in a maze of unassignable visions. Durrell's poetry thus revisits the tradition of occultism developed by Mallarmé, whose interest in Hermes Trismegistus has been analyzed by Hugo Friedrich:

> This is why [Mallarmé] used the word "hermeticism" and recommended its use in poetry. . . . In an article entitled Magic (*Variations on a theme. Major anecdotes*), he writes: "I contend that there exists between the old tricks and the eternal spell of poetry, a secret kinship." Poetry is the art of "conjuring in a deliberate shade, the unspoken object, through allusive, never explicit words" and the poet is "the wizard of words." The article goes on to explore the themes of the fairy, the magician, and the charm (in its Latin meaning of incantation, the very same meaning Valéry will refer to in the title of his poetry collection *Charms*).[77]

Durrell, a very knowledgeable reader of French poetry, especially of the symbolists, follows in Mallarmé's wake and uses occultism not only as a poetic theme but also as a prism magnifying the secret codes of poetic art. In his interview with Marc Alyn, Durrell defines his poetry through a dialogic exchange that testifies to the influence of hermeticism:

> M.A.—Behind this apparent simplicity and innocence your poetry is in fact a tight network of ideas and feelings.
>
> L.D.—Yes. I've always tried to create pills.

M.A.—Capsules of reality?

L.D.—And of sensuality and intellectual acuity. I don't know whether the mixture is always perfect (or the dose) but if I have written even one poem that is fully successful in that way, it is this 'mixing' that is responsible. That is what produces the surface, at the same time strong and fragile, hermetic and luminous. The shell knitted to the body.[78]

Inserting fragments from the *Corpus Hermeticum* Durrell seeks to achieve the alchemy through which the poet may engender a new world that no longer calls for understanding but for the timeless contemplation of the "luminous":

> 'And with the will came the Act and so at last
> In the due season of the fact
> He vivified naked Form devoid of Reason.'[79]

The tradition of the poet as an alchemist transmuting worldly matter naturally suggests Baudelaire's epilogue to the second edition of the *Fleurs du Mal*: ". . . j'ai fait mon devoir / Comme un parfait chimiste et comme une âme sainte. / Car j'ai de chaque chose extrait la quintessence, / Tu m'as donné ta boue et j'en ai fait de l'or."[80] Durrell's poem opens up a similar rift in his text by constantly undermining both literal and literary references to create a form of verse that denies immediate access, challenges semantics, and ushers in a poetic voice that heralds what Bonnefoy calls "the rise of the inexpressible over the expressible."[81] The poem thus becomes the place where "naked Form" is set free, where intense suffering ("the great harpoon buried in her," "the great wound," evocative of the sexual act) triggers a liberation that abolishes death and lays bare an invisible and inexpressible form of truth:

> A vision of the soul flashed across him
> With the great harpoon buried in her!
> And by the great wound set free the whole
> Wheat-ear and the epoptic mystery.[82]

The reader recognizes the wheat used in the sacred rituals of Eleusis, as well as the harpoon piercing Clea's hand at the end of *The Alexandria Quartet*. The multiple images of rebirth challenge death through a language that turns into a mystic experience.

The intertwined symbols and images pave the way for the following poem, "Paullus to Cornelia," where the poet, as a true "men's shepherd," takes his readers into the afterworld. The footnote, inviting the reader to "See the eleventh elegy of Propertius," reminds him that this poem also includes a subtext and highlights the erudite nature of the entire collection. This long poem reasserts the need not only to "read between the lines" but also to read backward and grasp the secret palimpsest that contains the key to the poetic mystery. The poem unfolds as an answer to Cornelia who, in the eleventh elegy of Propertius, addresses her husband from the world of shades and begs him to accept her death and departure, and cease to pray for her return. Durrell's poem takes the shape of a fictitious letter addressed by Paullus to Cornelia, as if words alone could cross the threshold of "the tomb where the grass grows."[83] The first stanza refers to Cornelia's description of the funerary pyre in Propertius and inverts the perspective of the Latin elegy by focusing on the husband's perspective. Symbolically, where Cornelia can only see ashes, Paullus contemplates the tokens of survival of human matter, the two rings that mock the flames:

> Cornelia, dry your cheek, poor shade,
> This last and most exact of visions,
> Old wedding-rings our fires won't eat
> Ash under grey cypresses,
> Old half-forgotten implausible decisions
> By going leaving you incomplete.

Durrell's first line is a perfect echo to Cornelia's prayer ("Desine, Paulle, meum lacrimis urgere sepulcrum") and ushers in a puzzling temporality that summons Propertius's poem, paying homage to its rhythm and tone while suggesting the anachronic image of Cohen's rings buried by the young Justine and Darley at the beginning of *The Alexandria Quartet*.[84] The foregrounding of inanimate objects that survive man's fate rings as a tenderly ironic answer to Cornelia's morose questioning: "What use was my marriage to Paullus, or the triumphal chariot of my ancestors, or those dear children, my glory?"[85] The poet's persona seems to inhabit two disjointed temporalities that are welded in the atemporal present participles of the last line ("going leaving"). This reassertion of the fundamental incompleteness born from the lovers' separation harks back to the two "syzygies" formed by "the angelic man" and "the mystical spouse" in "Poemandres." The text is thus torn by distant and closer ruptures—that of Cornelia's disappearance in the poem, that of Melissa in *The Quartet*, and that of the ontological rift that accounts, in the Gnostic creed, for man's fall. This rift is mirrored in the asymmetrical layout of the second and sixth stanzas. Both are set on the right-hand side of the page, as if pushed away into the margins, the better to follow Paullus's unspoken asides as he stops addressing Cornelia to ponder upon the void left by her death: "And now your message: yes, / Our house is very still," in the second stanza is echoed in the sixth by "From cellars full of dark air / An introspection costing life." This wavering between spoken and unspoken discourse paves the way for the intertwining of voices as the poem written in homage to Propertius also brings in references to Hermes Trismegistus:

> Water entering water forever keeps
> Her identical flavour: so one death into Death,
> The abstract portions of a simple whole,
> . . .
> With what precision we were given
> A form for all our looking-for in loving,
> The looking-glass, the spell

This encounter with water is not only a metaphor for Cornelia's journey down the Styx: the second half of the stanza metamorphoses the waters of death into those of life. Once again, the reader recognizes the echoes of "Poemandres," whose lines—"He beholding the form like to himself / Existing in her, in her Very Water, / Loved it and willed to live it"[86]—are directly related to the symbolism of water in the hermetic tradition and has been analyzed by G. R. S. Mead:

> The physical body, or body in the sense-world, is composed of the Moist Nature, which in a subsequent phase remains as Water-Earth, and in a still subsequent phase divides itself into the elements of physical earth, water, and air. The dissolution of the combination of these elements is effected by Death—that is, Darkness, the Drainer of the Water, the Typhonean Power. Water must thus here symbolize the Osirian Power of fructification and holding together.[87]

Far from being a mere dialogue with death, the poem also develops an ever-deepening meditation upon the essence of love, conceived as "The looking-glass, the spell," through which the subject mirrors himself in the other and escapes death. The marriage of opposites abolishes spatial, temporal, and linguistic distance and is subsumed in the elision—"eye to eye, mind mind, lip lip"—that brings together the living and the dead, the man and the woman, the present and the past: "And what you are and were become confounded."

In the second half of the poem Cornelia embodies the ideal twin the poet hankers after; she is the emblem of a timeless quest transcending death:

> You were that search for the Sovereign Form
> Which each of us owns, and each

> Must find and bury: all the disciplines
> We only summarise in simple dying.
> It is all there, we know it, within reach,
> Nor is there ever any hurry,
> For those who get beyond the maze of speech
> To where such vision waits, all knots untying.

This vision of the afterworld is not only the privilege of the one who has crossed the threshold of death, as in Propertius, and addresses the living. It is equally shared by the poet seer deciphering in his beloved's ashes the ultimate form, what "Poemandres" called the "naked form."[88] Death is thus conceived of as a learning "within reach," a passage toward the sought-for unity of the subject with himself and with the cosmos. This ultimate crossing "beyond the maze of speech / To where such vision waits, all knots untying" is materialized in the regular balance of the rhythm, the fluidity of alliterations and rimes that build up the musical lilt of the iambic pentameters where enjambments enact the recovered unity. This "Sovereign Form" the poet pursues on the other side of words, in the hermetic and literary images, in the exploration of ruins and of the antique palimpsest corresponds to what Bonnefoy calls the "poet's other language":

> When writing has turned into a voice, it is because the world is no longer conceived of as an aggregate of matter but as a reunion of presences and these are necessarily the essential realities that answer the fundamental needs of life and are therefore to be found beyond the specificities of idioms in a kingdom shared by all human beings—a land where no one walks as in a foreign country.[89]

"Paullus to Cornelia" adumbrates that "land where no one walks as in a foreign country," an ever-expanding in-between that simultaneously separates and unites Lawrence Durrell and the great master of Roman love poetry announcing Ovid's verse. This is how Durrell lays bare the fundamental archetypes of love and death and reasserts man's timeless anchorage in a universal kingdom:

> Yes, only there you know the search has ended,
> Cornelia, and she's rediscovered,
> Image of silence and all deaths befriended.

The crossing into the other world is thus fully accepted: the world of shades becomes a world of peace, contemplation, and creation that binds together the second and the third person, the past and the present, the one and the many, and orients the reader's gaze toward the complex philosophy of *The Avignon Quintet* where "the famous broken bridge"[90] points both to the remoteness and proximity of a further shore.

The End of Oracles?

The Ikons testify to the rise of Durrell's poetic voice that offers a new form of dwelling in the world that Bonnefoy describes as "the land of resurrection . . . coiled within us, if only like a peak that seems as much to recede in the distance as to draw closer."[91] Throughout the various poems, the collection explores the ambivalent figure of the seer poet resorting to silence and stasis to develop a mystic knowledge.

"Poemandres" introduces the voice of Hermes Trismegistus, "Paullus to Cornelia" brings back to life Propertius's elegy; similarly, "Stone Honey" conjures up Leonardo da Vinci and "Moonlight," Pliny the Elder's Natural History where the world is described both as an object and as a source of creation marrying opposites in a universal harmony:

> Not even are the forests and the spots in which the aspect of Nature is most rugged, destitute of their peculiar remedies; for so universally has that divine parent of all things distributed her succors for the benefit of man, as to implant for hint medicinal virtues in the trees of the desert even, while at every step she presents us with most wonderful illustrations of those antipathies and sympathies which exist in the vegetable world.[92]

Durrell sketches out the same cosmogony in his poem "Moonlight," where the tree is connected to various realms and the sap, following the lunar calendar, becomes "human sap" while the tree is affected with "bleeding." This cyclic process that brings together the human and the natural worlds contaminates the rhythm of the verse:

> It seems that in trees the sap
> Is moon-governed, rising and falling
> In absolute surrender, and if trees
> Then the menstrual pattern reconverts
> Some rhythms into human sap
> For the night's silver thermometer.

The regularity of internal rhymes, assonances, and alliterations ties in with the circular pattern of the sentence: from "moon-governed" to "night's silver thermometer" the first stanza is bathed in "Moonlight," which governs the entire poem until the last lines: "Waxing and waning in the ungovernable fury / Of something's phosphorescence." The interpenetration of vegetal, celestial, and human realms recalls the opening of Pliny's twelfth book where the natural philosopher asserts the divine essence of trees and their close bonds with man:

> The trees formed the first temples of the gods . . . indeed, we feel ourselves inspired to adoration, not less by the sacred groves and their very stillness, than by the statues of the gods, resplendent as they are with gold and ivory. Each kind of tree remains immutably consecrated to its own peculiar divinity, the beech to Jupiter, the laurel to Apollo, the olive to Minerva, the myrtle to Venus, and the poplar to Hercules. Moreover it is our belief that the Sylvans, the Fauns, and various kinds of goddess Nymphs, have the tutelage of the woods, and we consider those deities as especially appointed to preside over them by the will of heaven.[93]

The tree's central role in "Moonlight" is also perceptible in other numerous poems such as "Olives," "Blood-Count," and "Congenies" and evinces the strong influence of Roman literature upon Durrell's poetry, as the poet himself confessed to Marc Alyn:

> I have often found myself ringed by Roman ruins and I have to confess that while I appreciate the Roman attitude to landscape as well as their literature (Catullus, Propertius), I cannot take Roman landscape as a subject. I was steeped too young in the blue of Greece, which is both purer and more anarchic, subtleties that correspond more closely with my own sensitivity.[94]

Therefore, the subtle arrangements of Greek ruins, Roman literature, and Greek mythology that characterize Durrell's poetry collection compose the fragments that, in an Eliotic manner, he has shored against his ruins.[95] Such is the paradoxical, broken icon that proceeds from a prismatic vision allowing the poet to exclaim in "Moonlight": "I cannot tell, but so much is clear."

The same unspoken light pervades the entire collection, offering a vision that does not belong to sight but to insight. On the threshold of this new world, the prophet poet blends in with the mineral intensity of a magic space-time and relentlessly reaches out to the nameless other who gives meaning and impetus to his poetic endeavor:

> . . . at the same gate the same man
> Waiting, can be seen less as animal

> Than mineral, a besotted cistern
> For wine or blood, ebbing and flowing,
> Waxing and waning in the ungovernable fury
> Of something's phosphorescence. Yet he waits,
> He simply waits and smokes and goes on waiting,
> You know why, you know when, you know for whom.

The regular rhythm of symmetrical patterns, repetitions, and polyptotons allow for a peaceful, unchanging temporality where the poet is at one with the tree, "a besotted cistern, / For wine and blood." He is akin to Pliny's trees, whose wine invigorated man who, in turn, watered them with wine.[96] Belonging simultaneously to the vegetal and the mineral realm, the poet takes part in the celestial dance allowing the unidentified, uncircumscribed "phosphorescence" to shimmer. The solidly structured poem thus breaks apart into splinters of light that echo previous poetic flashes, such as those of "Apteros":

> To die by the universal variable
> And scribble on a stone our scope,
> The phosphorescence of desire
> To a season of wanhope.[97]

In the improbable light of the moon *The Ikons* give the reader a glimpse of the poet's secret desire: to enter the passive world conjured up in the last lines of the poem where the slow circumvolution of the last sentence opens the text to the mysterious presence of the other. The last line—"You know why, you know when, you know for whom"—reminds the reader of the earlier poem "Delphi" and of its mysterious oracle adumbrating a similarly immanent foreknowledge: "Tells you only what you know, / Know, but dare not realize."[98] Placed at either end of the collection, the poems echo each other and explore an intimate, sensible relation to knowledge.

This is how the seer poet pointing to the ineffable finds its counterpart in "Delphi" in the god Apollo who defeated the dragon Pytho, supposed to protect the oracle of Themis and slain by Apollo in order to put an end to the plundering of this monster engendered by Mother Earth, Gaia. Then, *The Hymn to Apollo* explains:

> darkness covered her eyes. And the holy strength of Helios made her rot away on the spot; wherefore the place is now called Pytho, and men call the lord Apollo by the name Pythian because this is the place where the power of piercing Helios made the monster rot away.[99]

In an article on Delphi published in 1965 and bearing the same title as his poem, Durrell delves into the myth of Pytho:

> But the oracle, the Pytho? Once again historians begin to stammer. Apollo killed the Dragon and left the corpse of this gigantic dead beast to rot. Out of this grew the oracular power of the Pytho. The word means 'to rot'. . . . The word 'to rot' for me is symbolical and suggests a spiritual truth into which the Delphic visitor was initiated. . . . The point at which the body begins to rot is the fertilizing point of death; this manner of trying to make death fertile may have had a symbolic value. . . . From 'ripe' to 'rot' is a short distance in English, as Shakespeare has told us in a famous passage.[100]

Through the myth itself to the rewriting of the myth, its reenactment and its interpretation, whether historical or poetic, the poet explores what Michel Butor calls the "rotting away of language"[101] that affects both the story of the monster and the various historical, scientific, and religious discourses eating away at each other. This rotting process fascinates Durrell, for it is the very essence of revelation, whether divine or poetic: "Truth, like the sword, has a double-edge. . . The oracle with all its theological sophistication knew this only too well," he explains. Such is indeed Butor's conclusion as he analyzes the rotting away of Pytho and the stuttering prophecies of Themis as the epitome of "Loxias, the oblique, the enigmatic, the embodiment of enigma itself."[102] In other words, truth naked. Thus Durrell's inquiry into the nature of truth seems to send us back to the initial chaos it stems from:

> But Greece . . . everything is confused, piled on top of itself, contorted, burnt dry, exploded. . . . It is as if nothing were provable any more, everything has become shadowy, provisional. The scholar begins to stammer.[103]

Announcing a quest into "the full Unlearning . . . / . . . the unacting and unthinking"[104] at the beginning of the collection, the poet deliberately plays on the reader's perplexity. The poem, combining irregular iambic tetrameters, finally opts for a trochaic pattern in the second stanza and progressively does away with the final rhyme, and ends on a baffling incantation addressed, oddly, not to the god but to the petitioner ("Beseech," "Try"). Language is thus turned upside down and offers the reader a final oracle bringing oracles to an end. Indeed the last stanza, shifting from the present to the past tense, creates a rift with the bygone days of Delphic oracles:

> Once upon the python spoke
> Now he lacks interpreters,

> Withering in his laurelled fires
> All the bitter rock inters,
> From within those jewelled eyes
> Tells only what you know,
> Know, but dare not realize.

The elision of "a time" in the first line strengthens the eye rhyme and the circular movement that draws the reader into the cave of "the bitter rock," the mouth of truth that voices the ultimate oracle: the end—in both senses of the word—of any prophecy, rendered pointless by self-knowledge. Poetic language functions as the red thread that enables the poet to fathom what Durrell calls in his article "the meaning of the oracle we so much need today" and that can only be conveyed "by a slender chain of gold links. . . Solomos, Palamas, Sekelianos, Cavafy, Seferis, Elytis"[105] . . . Durrell himself?

The slow dying away of those "voices from the dead" makes their absence even more portentous as the landscape tunes in to the ominous silence ("Hushed the marbles, choked the vase") and calls for an oblique approach. Such is the meaning of the following poem, "Keepsake," enumerating the laws of supreme renunciation. The first and second stanzas play on the balancing of imperatives and oxymorons ("increase / relax," "passionate indifference," "discipline of laziness") while the end of the poem reverses the familiar motto "So all that glitters may be gold," as if to mock received wisdom and further explore the disquieting philosophy announced in "Eleusis" and "Delphi." The imperative mode thus fosters a disruptive, anarchic moral that is characteristic of poetic truth, as Bonnefoy explains:

> . . . the "utterance" of the poem . . . the sort of teaching poetry conveys as to the relation the speaking subject should entertain with himself . . . the injunction to change one's life, to sharpen one's perception of what exists, of what is worthwhile. . . . The poem fosters thought, as if it willed itself into a thought in need of an utterance.[106]

Yet what is uttered is precisely the reversal of the expected utterance, whether in Delphi where "the bitter rock" remains sealed or in "Keepsake," whose title is ironically debunked by the utterance of the poem. The poetic utterance is thus to be understood as a shifty presence that deliberately refuses to be understood as "The Key to open all the locks / Of this insidious paradox."[107]

Following the principles enunciated in "Keepsake"—increasing yet not withholding, enjoying yet never exploiting, abandoning hope and desire—the poem "Persuasions" offers, in the last part of the collection, a teaching in the art of renunciation:

> We aliens are too greedy. They took their time,
> Being sure there was abundance of such
> Blueness, waters of mint in sheaves,
> Demotic and reasonable the sky through leaves.

The irregular iambic meter highlights the contrast between opposed poles—"We aliens / They took"—and each hemistich opens on a spondee mimicking the eternal rift between two worlds before the poem explores the recovered union between water and earth. "Blueness" subsumes the spirit of Greece and enacts the symbolic passage from water to sky ("waters of mint in sheaves"), which expands in the upward vision of "the sky through leaves" in the following line and, ultimately, in the nominalized adjective of the last stanza—"oar hankered for the blue"—thus completing the merging of the two realms. This shift from "blueness" to "the blue," which was already at work in *A Private Country*, transforms the color blue from a mere attribute into an essence and heralds further syntactic shifts such as that of the second stanza:

> Man sat a boat like a gull,
> Gull sat a rock like a star

The repetition of the same syntactic construction (erasing the preposition) creates a striking chiasmatic structure whereby "man" and "gull" are in symmetrical positions while the anadiplosis induces a tacit parallel between "man" and "star." The Greek space thus takes the shape of an "insidious paradox"[108] through which borders melt and liquefy under the weight of expanding water and sky. This "infinite extension"[109] is both temporal—"The future like the past was theirs"—and spatial—"oar," "Prow," "Anchor" are used as so many ploys to fathom boundless horizons and depths, whether physical or metaphysical:

> All fishermen's lecheries entangled were,
> Sharing the diversionary water-dream,
> The hunter's pious stare,
> Till finally the silence was supreme
> And neither any more was really there.

Therefore "the confidence of infinite extension," which corresponds to what Bonnefoy calls "the 'utterance' of the poem," is revealed in the central stanza, in that descent into the inner recesses of the dream where "water-dream" replaces the conventional daydream, where extremes meet—the lechers and the pious—in absolute silence. The final lines of the poem conjure up both silence and absence and lead to the mysterious closure of an unidentified quote—"'The perfect circle is incapable of further development'"—which mirrors the sacred circle of Eleusis and Delphi as well as that of writing itself, namely the opening line of "One Grey Greek Stone": "Image coiled in image, eye in eye."[110] "The perfect circle" mirrors the completion of the poetic image curling up in a visual and memorial refraction and summoning the earlier poems of *A Private Country* and its "blue circlets of stone, / On a sea blotted with fictions."[111] "Persuasions" asserts the poet's faith in the utterance of the poem detached from any recognizable enunciative source and in the intangible, interlinear unity that rises from the intense, sensible experience of an ever-expanding memory.

Poetry thus points at what cannot be reached in language but only through it: Byzance, Paphos, Eleusis, the Acropolis, the Plaka, Delphi, Salamis, Corfu, Troy, Athens, as well as Io, Aphrodite, Hermes, Apollo, Pliny, and Propertius map out a roaming memory that delineates, in the abstract icon of Greece, the presence of a receding Mediterranean, maimed by war, and which the poet in exile never ceases to revisit. Durrell's Mediterranean, like Bonnefoy's, is thus to be conceived of as "less a sea than shores,"[112] a crucible where cultures and languages have met and blended since the eves of time, where the first poets started "speaking next to the others' languages."[113] Durrell's poems enable us to listen to "the others' languages" in the fissures that open up the texts and the collections to a multiplicity of voices, exacerbating the tension between presence and memory, crafting a poetics between the shores.

The last poems in the collection celebrate Languedoc and highlight the predicament of the exiled poet in "Vidourle" through the image of the "Roman legionary" inhabiting "A stagnant home: a someone's home-from-home"[114] and a poem that incorporates the others' language: "He would repose the question with a sigh." The blending of English and French, the whiff of death approaching in "the lustrous nervous water" sketch out the icon of an evanescent world where the powerful Roman figure, "gone on furlough unregretted," echoes that of the "great man in the middle of a collapse"[115] in the very first poem of *The Ikons*. Both poems are equally "Apparelled for death"[116]—personal and universal death: the fall of Constantinople marking the end of the Roman Byzantine Empire appears as the mere repetition of the fall of the Western Roman Empire, leaving behind it the "stone gums"[117] of its bridge as testimony to the frailty of man's power.

"Vidourle" sketches out a watercolor—"Pour sky in water, softly mix and wait, / While birds whistle and sprain and curve. . ."—that conjures up, through a regular ternary rhythm and a balanced meter, the harmony of the Mediterranean. The suspension points that stand for the last foot of the second pentameter in the last stanza introduce a blank space where the desire for military power flounders and reveals instead the conqueror conquered:

> They must have faltered here at the very gate
> Of Gaul, seduced by such provender, such rich turf
> Bewitched, and made their sense of duty swerve.

The whistle of birds thus shatters the dreams of conquest and opens up the field of sensibility that takes hold of man's soul regardless of history: the fate of the "Roman legionary" meets, in the very last line of the poem, that of modern "civil servants loitering over aniseed."

Durrell's curving birds that reshape our dwelling in the world are evocative of Bonnefoy's description of Minerva's bird, which he sees as the essence of poetry:

> It is said—a beautiful Mediterranean image—that only at sundown does Minerva's bird begin flight but these words do not just mean that an event or a deed must have been fully completed, existed once, in order that they may be rationally or scientifically understood: they also have a meaning in poetry. Poetry is the memory of being. Walking through the shades of multiple conceptual forms of knowledge, poetry remembers realities that have come into being for us either because they can be immediately experienced . . . or because they help us perceive not the structure of things but what their full presence teaches us: the intensity of the moment, the importance of words that bore it, the depth within each of them, . . . in short, the poetic chances of being in the world. Poetry remembers those realities, however fleeting they may be in one life . . . . Like Minerva's bird that seeks to know, not to devour, it begins flight at sundown and soars up to these, patchy inklings of light.[118]

The poem "Congenies" pursues the same "patchy inklings of light" in its celebration of the soil and of the vine that seal the shared culture of winegrowers from Roman to modern times. Colors, textures, tastes, and smells blend ("In tones of dust or biscuit," "Loaves of the sunburnt soil," "Blood, rust, liver, tobacco")[119] while the "Dynasties" of vines corroborate the ageless ritual ("Dynasties of sturdy cruciform manikins," "Bonemeal grows necks of rock and teeth like dice") that makes man at one with the Mediterranean land. The references to crucifixion in the second stanza initiate a mystic union with the place through which the institutionalized religion is replaced by the power of the poetic word: "Their natural tutelary worship is the vine."

"The memory of being" described by Bonnefoy is thus freed from temporal constraints in the silent poetic space conjured by "this immensely quiet valley" while the violent historical strife ("In it you can read the bloody caucus of the past") is wiped away by the peaceful "clicking of the pruners' toil."

"Vidourle" and "Congenies" thus bring back to life realities that belong both to knowledge and experience, just as the Greek poems at the beginning of the collection commemorated the memory and the experience of myths, outlining what Bonnefoy calls "the poetic chances of being in the world" by expanding the spatiotemporal frame. This specific memory, that partakes both of science and of sensibility and transcends human time, adumbrates a new elusive and persisting reality that echoes Leonardo da Vinci's in the poem "Stone Honey":

Reading him is to refresh all nature,
Where, newly elaborated, reality attends.
. . .
So while renewing nature he relives for us
The simple things our inattention staled

Leonardo voices the poet's challenge: summoning an unexpected reality that calls for a new gaze, a gaze that "seeks to know, not to devour," that unlearns what we have so far apprehended conceptually and answers the question raised in the poem "Eleusis" at the beginning of the collection: "How long will the full Unlearning take?"[120]

The poetic quest thus joins the mystic one that strives for a knowledge whereby the subject of the gaze is thoroughly metamorphosed, as the poem "Kasyapa" evinces. The text refers to Mahā Kāśyapa, one of Buddha's disciples and the first Zen master who stands out as the archetypal figure of intuition, for he is said to have been the first one to understand Buddha's silent teaching. When Buddha took in his hand a flower that, according to tradition, only flowers once every three thousand years, and spun it in his fingers without a word, Mahā Kāśyapa was the only one to smile in return, thus manifesting his deeper understanding. The poem retraces this famous episode in the Buddha's life by recreating the silent arena of monks wherefrom the disciple's smile illuminates the world: "As ringed as a tree's old age / Or stone-splash circles in water / . . . To lap at the confines of our reason still."[121] The initially discrete smile in the first line ("When one smile grazed the surface") invades the entire space of the poem, outlining "'The perfect circle . . . incapable of further development'"[122] that Durrell's poetry extols. Just like the mystic experience, poetry is born from silence; it breaks free from the material "pattern of brush or pen,"[123] as much as from "The historian's dusty archives etc. / All the rhetoric of the unreal"[124]; it does not tell but conveys a smile that resists any narrative attempt just as it resists bodily confines and merges with the momentum of the universe at large:

> So the peculiar smile broke cover
> Sharp as the Pleiads of a new unknowing
> To lap at the confines of our reason still,
> The purposeless coming and going,
> The never quite never quite still.

"Kasyapa" adumbrates a new cosmogony where the dazzling, all-embracing smile enlightening the world like new Pleiades recalls the poem "Lesbos" at the beginning of *The Tree of Idleness*. In the perfect curve that crosses textual, spatial, and historical divides, the poet hints at a possible cosmic harmony welded in the folds of past and present writing. Yet, once again, the circle remains open to the "new unknowing" in the almost perfectly still breath of the last line that harks back to the refrain of "Nemea" in *A Private Country*—"Quite quiet, quiet there"[125]—ensuring that the reader's mind is "never quite still." Thus the poem truly keeps "Widening out to infinity the joke," perplexing the reader by simultaneously spurring and discouraging any form of recognition:

> Nor does it matter much, given the fact
> The date the season and the hour
> That I have forgotten not the smile
> Kasyapa, but the name of the flower.

The poem performs the very irony it conveys by enumerating the certainties shattered by the timeless, expanding smile ("the fact / The date the season and the hour") while conjuring a nameless, unidentified flower. "The flower," mirroring "the smile" at the end of the last two lines, is only determined within the narrow circle of the poem and is therefore devoid of any realistic anchorage although endowed with a universal presence. Such is the flower that arouses the reader's smile, the smile of a shared poetic intuition that exists both within and beyond the narrow confines of the poem.[126] The flower materializes the ineffable, the impossible unveiling and, concurrently, the impetus of an overpowering truth that defeats language. Like Nerval's myosotis, "it is the flower that commands attention by inscribing its summons within the fabric of language"[127] and that the poet attempts to decipher, as if to echo the prayer of "One Grey Greek Stone":

"Tell me, the codes of open flowers."[128] "Kasyapa" answers the mysterious code of flowers by a deeper mystery.

The Ikons signal a threshold in Durrell's poetic work: resolutely moving away from the representation of an inner reality, the poems open the field of the unrepresentable and the invisible. The collection veers away from the *hic and nunc* of figuration and unfolds a refunded temporality that is a prerequisite to a singular perception of the world. Thus, Durrell invites his reader to question the poet's art and role in these abstract icons where time, as much as reality, partakes of a new essence. Through the constant tension between absence and presence poetry tears apart the deathly linearity of human time and adumbrates a new mode of being in the world. The mythical and mystical Greece that underlies the structure of the collection nurtures an abstract icon in which the poet relentlessly explores the art of words. The lyrical "I" gives way to a broken enunciation that allows for the surge of multiple, disembodied voices that testify to the birth of a new, dispossessed poetic subject. One may then remember Paul Celan's prophetic words in his speech "Le Méridien," delivered a few years before the publication of *The Ikons*:

> The one who has art in sight and in mind, this one . . . forgets himself. Art places the 'I' at a distance. . . . Perhaps—this is just a question—perhaps poetry, like art, goes with an 'I' that has forgotten himself, towards this strange and foreign realm, and there—but where? in what place? with what? as what?—pulls away?[129]

Durrell's poetic awakening dwells in this "strange and foreign realm" where the subject disentangled from the self opens up to the variety of voices that haunt him, to their intense fluidity, and becomes this free, heedful conscience capturing and sharpening the other's gaze. Poetry is then no longer the recording of the self but a conscious leap into the unknown.

Notes

1. *White Eagles over Serbia*, *Bitter Lemons*, and *Esprit de Corps* were published in 1957; *Balthazar*, *Mountolive*, *Stiff Upper Lip* in 1958; and *Clea* in 1960.

2. *An Irish Faustus* was published in 1963 and *Acte* in 1964.

3. The first poetry collection, *Selected Poems*, was published in 1956; it was followed by *Collected Poems* in 1960 and by *Selected Poems 1935–1963* in 1964.

4. The complete anthology, *Collected Poems 1931–1974*, was first published in 1980.

5. Dominique Rabaté, "Enonciation poétique, énonciation lyrique," *Figures du sujet lyrique*, Dominique Rabaté, (ed.), Paris: PUF, 1996, p. 66.

6. "Enonciation poétique, énonciation lyrique," pp. 67, 75.
7. "Enonciation poétique, énonciation lyrique," p. 77.
8. Lawrence Durrell, *The Ikons*, London: Faber, 1966, p. 48.
9. "Press Interview," *The Ikons*, p. 48.
10. "You've gone abstract, Clea," Darley exclaims upon his return to Alexandria in *Clea* (Lawrence Durrell, *The Alexandria Quartet*, London: Faber, 1974 (first published in 1962), p. 726).
11. *The Alexandria Quartet*, p. 874.
12. "Byzance," *The Ikons*, p. 25.
13. Lawrence Durrell, *The Revolt of Aphrodite, Tunc*, London: Faber, 1990 (first published in 1974), p. 102.
14. "Byzance," *The Ikons*, p. 25.
15. "Byzance," *The Ikons*, p. 25.
16. *The Revolt of Aphrodite, Tunc*, p. 94.
17. The poem plays on the double meaning of the world "apparel": "something that covers or adorns" and "a vessel's gear and equipment" (*Collins English Dictionary*).
18. *The Ikons*, p. 11.
19. Lawrence Durrell, *On Seeming to Presume*, London: Faber, 1948, p. 25.
20. *The Ikons*, p. 11.
21. *The Ikons*, p. 11.
22. Lawrence Durrell, *Prospero's Cell: A Guide to the Landscape and Manners of the Island of Corfu*, London: Faber, 1962 (first published in 1945), p. 119.
23. Lawrence Durrell, *Reflections on a Marine Venus: A Companion to the Landscape of Rhodes*, London: Faber, 1953, p. 179.
24. *Reflections on a Marine Venus*, p. 179.
25. *The Revolt of Aphrodite, Tunc*, p. 29.
26. *The Revolt of Aphrodite, Tunc*, p. 230.
27. Lawrence Durrell, *Bitter Lemons of Cyprus*, London: Faber, 1959 (first published in 1957), p. 170.
28. *Bitter Lemons*, p. 171.
29. Stéphane Baquey, "Une voix sans appuis (À propos de Jean-Patrice Courtois)," *Singularités du sujet, huit études sur la poésie contemporaine*, Paris: Prétexte Éditeur, 2012, pp. 18, 21.
30. *The Ikons*, p. 22.
31. Lucas Cranach (1472–1533). *Venus with Cupid*, 1531 (176 x 80 cm). Royal Museums of Fine Arts of Belgium, Brussels. On the top right-hand corner one may read the following inscription: DV / PVER ALVEOLO FVRATVR MELLA CVPIDO. / FVRANTI DIGITV CVSPITE FIXIT APIS. / SIC ETIA NOBIS BREVIS ET PERITVRA VOLVPTAS / QVA PETIMVS TRISTI PIXTA DOLORE NOCET ("As Cupid the child was stealing honey from the beehive, a bee stung the thief's finger. Thus the brief and vain voluptuousness, inseparable from the pain it causes us when we seek it.")
32. *The Revolt of Aphrodite, Tunc*, p. 273.

33. Lawrence Durrell, *A Private Country*, London: Faber, 1944 (first published in 1943), p. 22.

34. *Prospero's Cell*, p 119.

35. Jean Varenne, *Upanishads du Yoga*, Paris: Gallimard, 1971, pp. 29–31.

36. T. S. Eliot, "East Coker," *Four Quartets, Collected Poems 1909–1962*, London: Faber, 2002, p. 190.

37. *The Ikons*, p. 21.

38. Lawrence Durrell, *The Big Supposer: A Dialogue with Marc Alyn*, New York: Grove Press, 1974 (first published in 1972), p. 33.

39. "Une voix sans appuis (À propos de Jean-Patrice Courtois)," p. 15.

40. One may recall here Durrell's translation of Cavafy's poem "The God Abandons Antony" and its concluding line: "And say farewell, farewell to Alexandria leaving," *The Alexandria Quartet*, p. 202. Likewise, it seems that Durrell's poetry never ceases to say farewell to Greece leaving.

41. See Jane Eblen Keller, "Durrell's Ode to the Olive," *Lawrence Durrell and the Greek World*, London: Associated University Presses, 2004, pp. 298–307, and James Gifford, "The Corfiot Landscape and Lawrence Durrell's Pilgrimage: The Colonial Palimpsest in 'Oil for the Saint; Return to Corfu,'" in *In-Between. Essays and Studies in Literary Criticism* 11, no. 2, 2002, pp. 181–96.

42. One may remember Durrell's return to the shrine of Saint Arsenius in Corfu where he brings olive oil he has carried with him from Provence and is suddenly struck by the eternal beauty of familiar faces lit by the oil lamp: "The wick flamed up . . . All of a sudden I saw the faces of my friends spring out of the gloom, touched by the yellow light . . . I thought of the Byzantine faces which stare out of the ikons in Salonika, Athens, Ravenna. . . . And behind this front rank, so to speak, the calm profiles of ancient Greek statues." "Oil for the Saint; Return to Corfu" (1966), *Spirit of Place: Mediterranean Writings*, London: Faber, 1988 (first published in 1969), p. 301.

43. Yves Bonnefoy, *L'Autre langue à portée de voix*, Paris: Seuil, 2013, pp. 14–15.

44. *L'Autre langue à portée de voix*, p. 15.

45. *L'Autre langue à portée de voix*, p. 15.

46. "Interview with Mulk Raj Anand about Lawrence Durrell," Ravindran Nambiar, *Indian Metaphysics in Lawrence Durrell's Novels*, Newcastle: Cambridge Scholars Publishing, 2014, p. 191.

47. Lawrence Durrell, *Acte*, New York: Dutton, 1966, III, i, pp. 66–67.

48. We may remember the oil lamps burning in Melissa or in Iolanthe's rooms, testifying to the unadulterated secret beauty of the prostitutes' inner being.

49. *L'Autre langue à portée de voix*, p. 9.

50. *Acte*, III, ii, p. 75.

51. *On Seeming to Presume*, p. 38.

52. T. S. Eliot, *The Waste Land, Collected Poems*, pp. 54–55.

53. See in particular the beginning of *Justine*: "Streets that run back from the docks with their tattered rotten supercargo of houses . . . Shuttered balconies swarming with rats . . . Peeling walls," *The Alexandria Quartet*, p. 26.

54. "Eleusis," *The Ikons*, p. 13.
55. *A Private Country*, p. 79.
56. *The Ikons*, p. 13.
57. *The Ikons*, p. 13.
58. Jean Humbert, Homère, *Hymnes*, Paris: Les Belles Lettres, 1951, p. 31.
59. Durrell was photographed there with his Greek friend Katsimbalis in 1949. Ian MacNiven, Coll. IMN, *Lawrence Durrell*, illustration #34.
60. "We walk in time / And our shimmering bodies / Take ineffable steps / That are imprinted in fables . . . ," Cantique des colonnes, Paul Valéry, *Charmes, Œuvres I*, Paris: Gallimard, 1957, p. 118.
61. *The Ikons*, p. 13.
62. "And scribble on a stone our scope," *The Ikons*, p. 14.
63. *The Ikons*, p. 15.
64. See Durrell's painting archives held by Southern Illinois University, Carbondale, Ill.
65. "'Everything is sensible!' And everything wields power over you. / Within the blind wall beware of a an eye spying on you: / At the heart of matter itself a word dwells . . . / . . . / A pure spirit grows beneath the rind of stones!" "Vers Dorés," Gérard de Nerval, *Les Chimères, Œuvres de Gérard de Nerval*, Tome I, Paris: Garnier, 1966, p. 709.
66. One may remember here the last line of the poem "The Dying Fall": "Each in the perfect circle of a sigh was ending," Lawrence Durrell, *The Tree of Idleness*, London: Faber, 1955, p. 18.
67. D. T. Suzuki, *Essays in Zen Buddhism*, New York: Grove Press, 1961, pp. 145–46.
68. *Corpus Hermeticum*, Tome I, Paris: Les Belles Lettres, 1945, p. 6.
69. Arthur Darby Nock, "Préface," *Corpus Hermeticum*, Tome I, Paris: Les Belles Lettres, 1945, pp. ii, v.
70. "Préface," *Corpus Hermeticum*, p. ii.
71. One may remember here Anaïs Nin's inscription on the copy of Otto Rank's *Art and Artist*, which she offered to Durrell upon his arrival in Paris: "To Lawrence Durrell—protégée of Jupiter and Neptune, born at the foot of the Himalayas . . ."
72. "Nerval et ses fantômes," Mercure de France, numéro spécial: *L'Univers de Nerval*, June 1, 1951. The exact quotation runs as follows: "Cri d'une âme qui fait éclater son masque charnel," quoted by Eduardo Aunos, *Gérard de Nerval et ses énigmes*, Paris: Aryana et Gérard Vidal éditeur, 1956.
73. "The disease is greater than you can imagine. . . . It may be that what I have experienced as bizarre only exists for me whose brain has nurtured abundant visions and is at pains to distinguish real life from that of dreams," Arlene Devine, *Le mythe de la femme dans l'œuvre de Gérard de Nerval*, Thèse, Faculty of Graduate Studies and Research, McGill University, 1969, p. 172.

74. *Thrice Great Hermes: Studies in Hellenistic Theosophy and Gnosis, Volume II*, London: Theosophical Publishing Society, 1906, p. 10. http://www.gnosis.org/library/grs-mead/TGH-v2/th202.html, last accessed August 4, 2013.

75. Valentinian syzygies are, in the Gnostic creed, complementary male and female forms. They are the successive and individual components of the divine essence, the "Pleroma," the state of wholeness, which is the higher reality.

76. *Thrice Great Hermes*, p. 1.

77. Hugo Friedrich, *Structure de la poésie moderne*, Paris: Librarie Générale Française, 1999 (first published in 1956), p. 188.

78. *The Big Supposer*, p. 126.

79. "Poemandres," *The Ikons*, p. 39.

80. ". . . I've done my duty / Like a perfect chemist and a holy soul. / For out of everything I have extracted the quintessence / You gave me your mud and I turned it into gold," Charles Baudelaire, *Les Fleurs du Mal*, Paris: Gallimard, 1972 (first published in 1855), p. 250.

81. *L'Autre langue à portée de voix*, p. 23.

82. "Poemandres," *The Ikons*, p. 39.

83. "Desine, Paulle, meum lacrimis urgere sepulcrum: / panditur ad nullas ianua nigra preces; / cum semel infernas intrarunt funera leges, / non exorato stant adamante uiae. / Te licet orantem fuscae deus audiat aulae, / nempe tuas lacrimas litora surda bibent. / Vota mouent superos: ubi portitor aera recepit, / obserat herbosos lurida porta rogos. Sic maestae cecinere tubae, cum subdita nostrum / detraheret lecto fax inimica caput." ("Paullus, no longer burden my grave with tears: the black gate opens to no one's prayer. Once the dead obey the law of infernal places, the gate remains like adamant, unmoved by pleas. Though the god of the dark courts may hear your request, surely the shores of deafness will drink your tears. Entreaty moves the living: when the ferryman has his coin, the ghastly doorway closes on a world of shadows. The mournful trumpets sang it, when the unkindly torch was placed below my bier, and raging flames dragged down my head," Properce, *Élégies*, Livre IV, "Elégie XI," Paris: Les Belles Lettres, 1995, p. 161.

84. *The Alexandria Quartet*, p. 21.

85. "Quid mihi coniugium Paulli, quid currus auorum / profuit aut famae pignora tanta meae?" *Elégies*, p. 161.

86. "Poemandres," *The Ikons*, p. 39.

87. "Commentary of Vision and Apocalypsis," *Thrice Great Hermes*, p. 39.

88. "Poemandres," *The Ikons*, p. 39.

89. *L'Autre langue à portée de voix*, p. 24.

90. "I even walked out gingerly upon the famous broken bridge, clutching the handrail as well as my hat, for here the wind whirled. A frail ghost-light lit the chapel, but there were no worshippers at that hour. A broken and renowned relic of man's belief, pointing its amputated fingers of masonry westward," Lawrence Durrell, *The Avignon Quintet*, London: Faber, 1992, p. 12.

91. *L'Autre langue à portée de voix*, p. 25.

92. "Ne siluae quidem horridiorque naturae fgacies medicinis carent, sacra illa parente rerum omnium nusquam non remedia disponente homini, ut medicina fieret etiam solitudo ipsa, sed ad singula illius discordia atque concordiae miraculis occursantibus," Pline l'Ancien, *Histoire naturelle, livre XXIV*, Chapitre 1, Paris: Les Belles Lettres, 1972, p. 24.

93. "Haec fuere numinum templa . . . Nec magis auro fulgentia atque ebore simulacra quam lucos et in iis silentia ipsa adoramus. Arborum genera numinibus suis dicata perpetuo seruantur, ut Ioui aesculus, Apollini laurus, Mineruae olea, Veneri myrtus, Herculi populus. Quin et Siluanos Faunosque et dearum genera siluis ac sua numina tamquam e caelo attributa credimus,"*Pline l'Ancien, Histoire naturelle, livre XII*, Chapitre 2, Paris: Les Belles Lettres, 1949, p. 20.

94. *The Big Supposer*, pp. 128–29.

95. "These fragments I have shored against my ruins," T. S. Eliot, *The Waste Land, Collected Poems 1909–1962*, p. 69.

96. "Ex his recreans membra olei liquor uiresque potus uini . . . Conpertum id maxime prodesse radicibus, docuimusque etiam arbores uina potare" (". . . it is from these that we now derive the oil of the olive that renders the limbs so supple, the draught of wine that so efficiently recruits the strength . . .Thus have we taught the very trees, even, to be wine-bibbers"), *Histoire naturelle, livre XII*, pp. 20–21.

97. "Apteros," *The Ikons*, p. 14.
98. "Delphi," *The Ikons*, p. 15.
99. Homère, *Hymnes*, Paris: Les Belles Lettres, 1951, v. 370–74, p. 94.
100. "Delphi," *Réalités*, Paris and New York, 1965, *Spirit of Place*, pp. 275–76.
101. Michel Butor, *Le génie du lieu*, Paris: Grasset, 1958, p. 76.
102. *Le génie du lieu*, p. 77.
103. *Spirit of Place*, p. 273.
104. "Eleusis," *The Ikons*, p. 13.
105. *Spirit of Place*, p. 277.
106. *L'Autre langue à portée de voix*, p. 8.
107. "Keepsake," *The Ikons*, p. 16.
108. "Keepsake," *The Ikons*, p. 16.
109. "Persuasions," *The Ikons*, p. 32.
110. "One Grey Greek Stone," *The Ikons*, p. 23.
111. "Fangbrand," *A Private Country*, p. 7.
112. "Moins une mer que des rives," *L'Autre à portée de voix*, pp. 297–305.
113. *L'Autre à portée de voix*, p. 302.
114. "Vidourle," *The Ikons*, p. 45.
115. "The Ikons," *The Ikons*, p. 11.
116. "The Ikons," *The Ikons*, p. 11.
117. "Vidourle," *The Ikons*, p. 45.
118. *L'Autre à portée de voix*, pp. 304–5.
119. "Congenies," *The Ikons*, p. 46.
120. "Eleusis," *The Ikons*, p. 13.

121. "Kasyapa," *The Ikons*, p. 37.
122. "Persuasions," *The Ikons*, p. 32.
123. "Kasyapa," *The Ikons*, p. 37.
124. "Kasyapa," *The Ikons*, p. 37.
125. "Nemea," *A Private Country*, p. 25.
126. Indeed, Sylvie, Bruce, and Piers compose the same mystic flower in *The Avignon Quintet*, thus corroborating the mysterious kinship between the writer's art and mysticism: "Our wet fingers touched and we formed a circle like the corolla of a flower, floating into the silence of the desert dawn with the ancient sun on our bodies," *The Avignon Quintet*, p. 125.
127. *L'Autre langue à portée de voix*, pp. 14–15.
128. "One Grey Greek Stone," *The Ikons*, p. 23.
129. Paul Celan, "Le Méridien," *Le Méridien & autres proses*, Paris: Seuil, 2002, p. 69.

CHAPTER SIX

The Red Limbo Lingo
"Thus words in music drown"[1]

The Red Limbo Lingo, published only five years after *The Ikons*, immediately baffles the reader. It is composed of prose fragments followed by twenty-one poems that will be taken up at the beginning of *Vega*. The first half corresponds to the "sort of poetic diary called the Vampire Notebook"[2] announced by Durrell in his letter to Henry Miller, seemingly suggesting that the poet intends to resort to the autobiographic inspiration that characterized his earlier work and to deny the distance from the self elaborated in *The Ikons*. Like *The Ikons*, *The Red Limbo Lingo* is contemporaneous with Durrell's fiction, as he explains to Miller in the same letter: "A ground map for a new book just sketching itself. Some good new poems."[3] *Nunquam*, the first volume of *The Revolt of Aphrodite*, has just been published (1970), while *Monsieur*, the first volume of *The Avignon Quintet*, is issued in 1974. Standing at a crossroads between two major narrative productions, *The Red Limbo Lingo* is also built as a crossroads between prosody and prose. The dust jacket introduces the opus not as a "poetic diary" but as a "notebook": "In this 'Notebook' Lawrence Durrell has recorded his strange thoughts, in prose or verse, in English or French, around the notion of blood . . ."[4] The inverted commas suggest that the author is as uncertain about the exact definition of his work as he was in his letter to Miller. Halfway between a diary and random notes, the text plays on its own indetermination, calling to mind the novelistic ploys simultaneously used by Durrell and aimed at bewildering and losing the reader. Should this collection be considered as the drop shadow of the author's life story, as an incomplete achievement, as an echo to the *The Revolt of Aphrodite*, as a forerunner to *The Avignon Quintet*—both of which are characterized by the predominant theme of blood, either as a diegetic or as a symbolic thread—or as the dismembered, unraveled form of a frayed poetic writing that *Vega* ultimately attempts to piece together? Throughout the various texts, the poet seems to be groping for shape and meaning, for a unified "I" that contemplates its impending fall in the rifts that yawn between formal, generic, and linguistics units. The reader is thus led to experience the increasing uncertainty of the poetic voice repeatedly striving to "reopen its original space; . . . to break up the song that bears it, to tear the text asunder."[5]

The private publication limited to 1,200 copies implies only a select readership, as opposed to that of *Vega*, which was qualified by the author as a "general edition."[6] Only a few are expected to enter the secret curves of Durrell's "constellation, star cluster of thoughts,"[7] which explicitly places the volume in the margins of the more well-known poetry collections, in a limbo—this intermediary and imaginary realm where everything that was once lost, forgotten, or repressed is hidden. The volume thus materializes the abyss that the poetic voice rises from and reverts to, the world of the dead and the unborn where unbaptized children are said to await Christ's return. Christian references are indeed predominant—"It's all about Jesus and vampires and the blood of the lamb etc."[8] as Durrell notes in his letter to Miller—but they also blend with alchemical, folkloric, and anthropological interpretations of the symbolic import of blood, as the jacket explains: "from its sacrificial aspect . . . to its association with vampires. . . . The ideas, he says, 'burgle anthropology, alchemy, etc. etc.'"[9] The surprising quotation incorporating the poet's words within his own text in the third person is resonant with the sense of enclosure and chaotic depth that generally stamps the representations of limbo. The reader is thus invited in the paratext to step down into "the red limbo lingo." The simultaneous disclosure and partial blurring of the poet's heterogeneous and potentially limitless sources ("etc. etc.") gives rise to a multilayered and self-reflexive writing, as if the constellation of poems was meant to branch off into ever-new poetic beams: "'. . . But a notebook of this sort is like a constellation, a star cluster of thoughts which may set off poems on quite other preoccupations.'"[10]

The descent into limbo is thus wrought within language itself, an obscure language that points at its own inadequacy, a "jargon" aimed at initiates only. The notebook ushers in a poetic excursion into an unexplored and disquieting territory, hovering between life and death, an in-between space where language deliberately runs the risk of incomprehension. *The Red Limbo Lingo* may then be read as the poetic counterpart to the cave in the fiction: it is an impenetrable and undecipherable space, the place where "meaning disseminates . . . instead of the expected final revelation,"[11] where writing precipitates, in the (al)chemical sense of the word.

The broken echoes between the prose fragments and the fiction simultaneously contribute to the coherence and to the dislocation of the whole, testifying to the inner rift of a writing that works toward its own depletion by building up a system of mirrors that reverberate and magnify the poet's angst and sends the reader backward to the "agon" that opened *The Black Book*. Through the unachieved dialogue with absent figures Durrell pursues his quest for a spiritual and visionary freedom in a collection that both extols an unfettered poetic momentum and forebodes its end.

Fathoming the Abyss

Some ten years before the publication of *The Red Limbo Lingo* Durrell declared in an interview that "poetry is form, and the wooing and seduction of form is the whole game. You can have all the apparatus in the world, but what you finally need is something like a—I don't know what—a lasso . . . a very delicate thing for catching wild deer."[12] And yet this collection strikingly disrupts poetic form through its structural, linguistic, and prosodic hesitations. Divided into two parts that both oppose and answer each other, it is both an autobiographic and an experimental poetic sketch in search of a lost unity. The first part, which could be entitled "the Vampire Notebook," is composed of thirty pieces written either in verse or in prose—a number that is decoded in the sixteenth fragment: "the 28 day menstrual cycle."[13] Thus, the reader follows the flux of writing—"black as the very blood of prose,"[14] the twenty-ninth fragment explains—within a structure that plays on French and English as well as on the irregular length of its fragments separated by asterisks the better to frustrate all expectations. The text flows out drop by drop, at an unpredictable rhythm, following the jerky pace of the poet's inner breath. The image of the "lasso . . . for catching a wild deer" thus begins to make sense: Durrell's poetic writing reflects the intense momentum toward a living organism that stands out of bounds and that the poet, like a hunter, tries to reach through a mimetic approach. The poem, like the lasso hanging in midair, is a suspended gesture that fails to ensnare its goal.

This is why the poet watches himself as an estranged third person in a metapoetic discourse that endeavors to circumscribe both its object and its shape:

> Thought-clusters, constellations of ideas linked by private associations, characterize poetic thinking as against the ratiocinative, noetical operations of

philosophers. In this dossier his speculations (which were devoted to wondering what our culture is all about) concerned the symbolic meaning of blood.
    The crucifixion as a prelude to a love-feast.[15]

By partly quoting the introductory words of the dust jacket, this eighth fragment creates an unusual *mise en abyme* through which the poet refers the reader to the paratext, to the limbo of the poem, as if its essence were irredeemably lost in an irrecoverable elsewhere, in a discourse upon discourse both belonging to and cut off from the poetic voice. Such a technique is reminiscent of the ploys used in *The Avignon Quintet* and forebodes the slow dissolution of the poetic "I" that can only be observed obliquely, like a monstrous phenomenon. This enunciative shift from first to third person creates an eerie poetic voice that foreshadows more disquieting shifts throughout the thirty fragments that seem to belong to an uncircumscribed elsewhere/elsewhen. The interplay of prose and poetry and the overlapping of different languages emphasize the alien and unreliable nature of the collection. Some of the poems lead to prose developments, as if the poem included its marginal notes. Thus, the last line in this last fragment is an analepsis referring the reader to the fifth fragment that intertwines both verse and prose:

> . . . the extraordinary blood-splattered figure of a man nailed to a wooden cross, like an expiring frog. . . .
> What he learned he did not like.
> What he learned he did not like.
>
> Who was this white crucified fish?[16]

The reader enters an unchartered territory where frontiers between genres melt away while the analepsis implies a regressive movement that contaminates the entire collection and is acknowledged at the end of the tenth fragment: "A poet may start at the end of his diary and work back towards the present."[17] The reader's uncomfortable position is not only explained by the choice of the theme or by the generic transgressions but also by a disruptive enunciation that simultaneously plays on poetic and narrative codes. *The Red Limbo Lingo* rejects any temporal or spatial anchorage, which makes analepses all the more confusing, as if Durrell's writing kept turning back upon the void.

The only anchorage would then be thematic. However, although some of the poems match the introductory definition—"strange thoughts . . . around the notion of blood"[18]—others appear only loosely related: the first one focuses on birth; the sixth and fourteenth on crucifixion; the ninth and thirtieth on alchemy; the sixth, fifteenth, sixteenth, twenty-first, and twenty-ninth on the cult of vampires; the thirteenth on the hidden kinship between magic rituals; the eighteenth, nineteenth, and thirtieth on symbolic echoes; and the twentieth on the medicinal virtues of blood drinking. They may alternately be read as a scholar's notes, or as clues to the works of fiction. One may thus remember *The Revolt of Aphrodite* and its impressive hunting scenes,[19] or Benedicta's violent self-mutilations as she flees Felix, running away like a hunted animal. The conclusion of *Tunc* thus acquires a cinematographic forcefulness in which the reader instantly recognizes most of the variations on blood developed in *The Red Limbo Lingo*:

> I hardly took in at first the bloody spoor which here and there marked the scarlet staircase-carpet . . . it was like following a wounded lion to its lair—I came upon a red pug-mark freshly impressed in the carpet. What could it mean? How on earth could I guess that Benedicta had been at that double toe of hers with a kitchen knife? . . . I vaguely surmised that her period had surprised her, that was all. But everything was quite different. She was standing on the bed naked, her arms raised in rapture, her face burning with gratitude and adoration; it was clear that the ceiling had burst open to reveal the heavens, clouded and starry, with its vast frieze of angels and demons—figures of some great Renaissance Annunciation. . . . the figures in the frieze held up their hands to bless, or to point to breasts, or crowns of thorns.[20]

The themes of menstruation, wounding, crucifixion, and hunting are all present and herald the hunting of the gypsy depicted by Sabine to Sutcliffe in *The Avignon Quintet*: "He heard her screams, and those of the little boy, and then everything was silent and the water of the estuary turned carnation-red as the hounds ate their fill."[21] Likewise, the thirteenth fragment describing Astarte "riding a white foal with the menstrual blood trickling down her thighs"[22] foreshadows Constance's description before she first makes love with Affad:

> In all that whiteness and steam he tiptoed to close the tap, and was turning away to leave when he noticed the blood flowing down from the couch, from the half-opened gown, the half-opened legs—a red pool into which he had inadvertently trodden with his bare foot and printed the tiles.[23]

From *The Revolt of Aphrodite* to *The Red Limbo Lingo* and *The Avignon Quintet* blood becomes the very fabric of writing upon which the artist imprints his characters' sufferings and their lifeless petrifaction—such as Benedicta leaving Felix and appearing "heavily veiled, like a statue of the Virgin Mary"[24]—

or the eternal haunting that preys upon their soul—such as Von Lupian's obsessive collection of paintings representing the same heartless carnage—as well as the urge that drives them away from a deathly world—such as Constance and Affad, who, shortly after the love scene, "lay exhausted in all that blood and steam like stricken martyrs to human bliss."[25] Blood is thus endowed with thaumaturgic powers, as in the twentieth fragment:

> The invitation to 'come down to the abattoir for a warm glass' was no joke in fin-de-siècle Paris as the prints attest. . . . A cow was hobbled and an incision was made to its side; a glass captured the hissing blood.[26]

Just like the scene of the hunted gypsy, this one keeps recurring within *The Avignon Quintet*, as if Durrell's writing was helplessly haunted by its own nightmarish projections. It is taken up for the first time in *Monsieur* where Pia reveals her homosexuality to Sutcliffe. The scene takes on a sadistic tone as the performance of human suffering bounds back upon the viewer, who becomes its first victim:

> Those scenes had marked his mind as if with a branding iron. . . . Huge sides of oxen were delivered to the house in the Via Caravi, whole beefs split down the middle. In these bloody cradles they would lie and make love while the men in blood-stained aprons stood around and jeered. He could see the pale Pia like Venus Anadyomene in a thoroughly contemporary version of Botticelli lying pale and exhausted in a crucible of red flesh. . . . Once there had been a little blood in her footprint on the wet bathroom floor, but this was her period, or so she said.[27]

Unlike the fertile blood running throughout the love scene between Constance and Affad, this one reveals the perversion of love turned into a sacrilege: the sex act has become an utterly sterile performance, a parody of Venus's adultery and of her subsequent imprisonment by Hephaestus in a magic net. The birth of Venus Anadyomene, "born from the sperm of God,"[28] is replaced by a degrading immersion in animal blood: the "bloody cradles" are an ironic rewriting of the magic nets where Venus lay exposed to the gods' gibes.

The scene recurs in *Livia*, where it is displaced from Venice to Geneva, but described in the same words: the old American lady, the beef carcasses, and the butchers with their blood-stained aprons are identical. The textual echo blurs the reader's temporal and spatial landmarks as both scenes seem interchangeable. Venice and Geneva, just as the old lady's house and the slaughterhouse overlap: diegetic space is no longer a definite and reliable anchorage but a sprawling and indeterminate entity that partly accounts for the monstrous, labyrinthine narrative. This blurring climaxes in the poems where genres, voices, and texts intertwine so that the scriptural space itself evades the reader's grasp and forces him to wander in an in-between, in a limbo where language comes apart at the seams. Thus, the collection borrows the form of an erratic, desultory notebook composed of chance remarks that echo the mnemonic flashes separated by asterisks at the beginning of *The Alexandria Quartet*. However, the reader well remembers that such apparently random snippets of thought were carefully organized, as the palindrome opening of the third fragment evinces: "Notes for landscape tones . . ."[29] Through imperfection and fragmentation, the writer was already looking for a perfect achievement, giving the reader the illusion of gaining access to a previous, intimate, and unformed writing material. Such a warning encourages the reader of *The Red Limbo Lingo* to grasp the underlying coherence beneath the obsessive theme of blood. For not only does the collection point toward past and future texts on a syntactic level, but it also points to the paradigmatic depths of a writing that explores the poet's metatextual angst, questioning his relationship with poetry by delving into a language that is necessarily wrought in limbo. This projected in-between space shared by poet and reader can only exist in a twilight zone, on the page where men's laws are temporarily abolished, where time and space are suspended. The space of this imaginary, and yet real, encounter is the very same conjured up by Eliot in *The Waste Land*—"You! hypocrite lecteur!—mon semblable,—mon frère"[30]—and stated as early as the second fragment:

> Drunk from the shameless garrick of lovelingo.
> Poem?

These two lines sound like a distich interrogating the essence of poetry. The second line is ambiguous: does the question bear upon the nature of the text itself or upon that of poetry at large? Is poetry a question of form and should this last line be read as what Agamben calls "a transgression towards prose"?[31] Or is poetry a question of language, as the first line suggests where the words "garrick" and "lovelingo" hamper our reading? One may feel tempted to read "garrick" as an allusion to David Garrick, the actor made famous by his interpretations of Shakespeare's plays and the director of the Drury Lane theater. "The shameless garrick of lovelingo" might then refer to the flamboyant swirl of couples in love in Shakespeare's comedies, which Durrell particularly favored. But one may also recognize a paronomasia on the French word "garrigue," this sunburned, calcareous land celebrated in the second half of the collection in the poems "One Place," "The Land," and "Mistral," and ultimately in "A Patch of Dust,"[32] published one year after *Vega*. The literary space thus takes over the geographic one: it is a space born from a new language that revels in neologisms whereby "lovelingo" both resumes and develops the language adumbrated in the first fragment: "A destiny predetermined by his / Limbotalk and limbothink / He learned how to lovejingle the limbs' lingo."[33] The involuted movement of a writing that feeds upon itself, divides and joins again, as if to mimic cell division, suggests that this first fragment stages the birth of writing. Poetry would then arise from the recreation of language, as in this singular distich that gives shape to the "constellations of ideas" announced in the introduction and recaptured in the eighth fragment where the poet redefines the aesthetic codes by which his work is to be judged. Durrell is here walking in the footsteps of William Wordsworth, whose voice is recalled in the epigraph to *Quinx* and commented on at length by Durrell in *Key to Modern Poetry*: "Every great and original writer . . . must himself create the taste by which he is to be judged."[34] Thus Durrell subtly manages to situate himself along the chain of Romantic poets while playing with repeated metatextual comments (namely in fragments 8, 9, 10, and 12) that foreshadow the second half of the collection and simultaneously deconstruct the poetic form.

This marginal, self-creative space, freed from the constraints of established codes, that both belongs to the written page and transcends it, is characterized by an organic temporality whereby time flows like an open vein. We are taken from the time of the poet's birth in the first fragment to the astral calendar of bloodletting in the last one: "The calendars of barbers carefully set out the times propitious to bleeding . . ."[35] However, chronological linearity is denied in favor of a cyclic time: the menstrual cycle is echoed by the astral one, birthing by sacrifice, so that the blood flow sketches out a paradoxically still and moving rhythm, a present that never dies. Within this disquieting space-time temporal markers become meaningless: "The day which we call today will tomorrow become yesterday; tomorrow will become today in twenty-four hours. Is Time then a superfluous concept?"[36] The annihilation of a temporal *telos* anchors the poem in a timelessness materialized here by the negation of shifters that create an unfamiliar temporal pattern momentarily trapping the reader in limbo. Likewise, the chain of cause and consequence is disrupted, the better to create what Judith Balso calls "poetic anachronism"[37] whereby "the present must no longer be conceived in relation to the past (which is powerless to explain what exists) but, on the contrary, by projecting oneself decisively into the unknown present."[38] This is a time of disengagement from the known world, but it is also the time of a return to the primordial and inaccessible sources of the psyche: "He asked himself who first thought of punctuating time. The memory of unpunctuated process still hangs on in the unconscious—the first time pieces were shaped like an egg."[39] The egg symbolizes both the genesis of the world, the force of creation, and its cyclic renewal, the principle of rebirth, as has been explained by Mircea Eliade:

> the ritual virtue of the egg . . . lies in the symbolism embodied in the egg which is not so much that of birth as that of a repeated *re-birth* based on the cosmological pattern. . . . The egg confirms and promotes resurrection which, once again, is not a birth, but a 'return,' a 'repetition.'. . . the egg never misses its essential purposes: ensuring the *repetition* of the creative act which gave birth to all living forms *in illo tempore*.[40]

As such, the egg in Durrell's poetics signals the persistent presence of an incorruptible, enduring life cycle celebrated in a poetry that is itself "the art of time. It has the taste of the fruit Tantalus would fain grasp in Hades, and which eludes the hand that reaches out to them; it has the taste of the everflowing water he can never drink."[41] Both a temptress and a prison, both a trap and a way out, Durrell's poetic space-time conjures up Henri Michaux's ideal: "render the uninhabitable habitable, the unbreathable, breathable. . . . Relinquishing the line, the verse, the internal rhyme, even rhythm, divesting itself further and further, it [the poem] searches for the poetic territory of the inner self."[42] The decomposition of language is intimately linked to the forays into bodily matter: the syntagmatic line of worldly dispossession thus crosses the paradigmatic line of a deeper, intrinsic renunciation, bringing about an in-between space where flux and stasis, the material and the immaterial, the unique and the same meet and part.

The reader is thus caught in the weft of a text that expands both horizontally (through textual analepses and prolepses) and vertically, blending genres and forms, performing its own "tapestry of carnal violence."[43] Just as when reading Durrell's prose, one is thus forced to abandon a linear approach and to consider the distinct sections of the collection as two parallel yet opposed doors into the text: that of the "notebook" and that of the poems, both dedicated to Miriam Cendrars, the daughter of the famous French novelist, traveler, and poet who was also a close friend of Henry Miller.[44]

Like Durrell, Freddy Sauser was fascinated by Rimbaud's phrase "Je est un autre" and chose the pseudonym Blaise Cendrars, thereby demanding, as Claude Leroy explains, "to be translated into embers and ashes. In so doing, he conjures up the legendary phoenix as the emblem of his writing wish: being reborn through his works and being eternally reborn."[45] Just like Durrell, Cendrars plays on the various literary genres and chooses free verse in his poetry. His writing plays on visionary insights and the reverberation of echoes to create a spiraling pattern materializing "the perpetual movement of writing that can alone keep the phoenix awake."[46] His early poems testify to a dysphoric vision of the human condition that strikingly echoes the first fragment of *The Red Limbo Lingo*:

> A Pity
> Man is alone—very much alone. As early as birth he fell into a tub. . . .
> I reach everywhere for Man's smashed heart, that dark, smashed heart crushed
> by sorrow's heavy feet, and crying.
> It sheds tears of blood.[47]

Cendrars's verse testifies to the modern poet's painful relation to his own material, such as Durrell asserting: "In the beginning was the Word, and the word was blood. . . ,"[48] or French contemporary poet Louise Dupré writing in "The blood of words": "Reaching the blood of words, such is the choice made by each poem. It strives to arouse the suffering in the world. . . . The blood of words is the blood that ties me to the immemorial memory of sorrow."[49] This ontological suffering, which takes its roots in man's personal and collective history, precedes it. It is an absolute pain that foregoes birth. The secret kinship between the two poets becomes obvious when one compares the first lines of *The Red Limbo Lingo*—"First of all, / He did not ask to be born. / He did not ask to find himself in the Red Limbo"[50]—and those of Cendrars's 1922 poem entitled "My Mother's Womb":

> I painfully allowed myself to be carried along
> And you flooded me in your blood
> . . .
> Had I been able to speak
> I would have said:
>
> Shit, I don't want to live![51]

Unlike Cendrars, Durrell opts for the third person throughout this first part in order to build up an ironic distance through which he endeavors to disengage himself from his own suffering and project himself into the other, "the man who makes notes / The observer in the tall black hat, / Face hidden in the brim."[52] Whereas the last stanza of the above poem from *A Private Country* still left room for the poetic "I," albeit as an objectified mask—"He watches me now, working late, / Bringing a poem to life"[53]—*The Red Limbo Lingo* starts from the dispossession of the "I": the poet is thus the abstract object of a satirical study, a protean, monstrous other, both ludicrous and scary, the unexpected outcome of an excruciating birth that was already adumbrated in the first lines of "Cities, Plains and People": "I give you here unending / In idleness an innocent beginning / Until your pain become a literature."[54] The reader is taken away from the bright world of childhood into the jargon of a limbo darkened by the blood of writing that reveals both the embodiment of the principle of life and the alchemical metamorphosis of poetic matter. "Nine months awash in the seablue sac / Of the amnion" suggests the boundless sea and the narrow amniotic pouch before the fetus is finally "washed ashore in the bulrushes," like Moses, deprived of any human identity, the debased fruit of "an ape's wish."[55] He is only born to be sacrificed: "When he reached civilisation the gallows was / Still warm."[56] His coming into the world is thus synonymous with his impending death: the tightened rhythm of the two iambic feet in the central line "Our daily noose"[57] not only parodies Our Lord's Prayer but also mimics the narrowing breath of the future dead. This feeling of entrapment and suffocation culminates in the paranomasia "womb / tomb" and the enclosed rhymes that characterize the very last poem concluding *Collected Poems* in 1974:

> Lonely product of a ninepenny womb,
> Full of a fierce psychic reticence
> One gladiator of the simple sense
> Carving out poetry for his tomb[58]

In the opening fragment of *The Red Limbo Lingo* the only rhymes are flat ones, almost identical, and placed at the beginning and at the end of the fragment ("sac," l.4 and "back," l.5; "axe," l.26 and "wax," l.27). The self-enclosure of the textual space is also reinforced by the various mirror effects of the first stanza where syntactic echoes, anaphoras, and polyptotons abound:

> l.2 He did not ask to be born
> l.3 He did not ask to find himself in the Red Limbo—
> l.4 Nine months awash in the seablue sac
> l.6 Washed ashore in the bulrushes of an ape's wish
> l.11 Nine months of the blood's imprinting finely
> l.12 In the womb . . .

Birth is conceived as a fall into biological matter and as a spiritual death. The only hope for freedom and life lies in a return to the sources of this spontaneous flow that carries in its folds the secret of an alchemical relation to the world:

> Nine months of the blood's imprinting finely
> In the womb had filled his charts with lines;
> Pumped and ladled rich spagyrick[59] blood
> Direct into the plexus where all the dark
> Foreknowledge will abide and henceforth be . . .

The poet resists the entropy of a death-driven civilization through these prelapsarian maps of a world drawn in the eternal ink of blood before the advent of rational knowledge. The aposiopesis concluding this first stanza opens up the verse to the infinite possibilities of being, to its alchemic rebirth, and recalls Lawrence's letter to Aunt Prudence before she sails in *Down the Styx*:

> But like all great journeys this also has an end; unlike most journeys however, this turns out to be a beginning. You are sailing down, dear Aunt, towards the great beginning of nothing, which is the ending of everything. . . . You are being swallowed. This is a placental nightmare . . . this is the chamber where the sight of the usually sightless is unsealed. This is the womb of the Minotaur, the abyss . . .[60]

The poet's language rises out of the abyss. The "nine months" are those of the gestation of language ("Limbotalk and limbothink") that signals the poet's rebirth. Delving into the origins of life, the poet explores the origins of poetic language leading, in the second stanza, through compound nouns and adjectives, to a linguistic limbo where grammatical categories can freely blend, where language is no longer fettered by semantics, syntax, or logic:

> He learned how to lovejingle the limb's lingo,
> Even he hit headlines some-once like
> A punpampered pimp in a sunburst of
> Aeroplane eyewash; . . .

The rhythmic and alliterative pattern of Durrell's lines is reminiscent of Edith Sitwell's playful compositions where auditory sensations are brought to the fore in order to arouse what the poet calls

> the growth of consciousness . . . like that of a person who has always been blind and who, suddenly endowed with sight, must learn to see; or it is the cry of that waiting, watching world, where everything we see is a symbol of something beyond, to the consciousness that is yet buried in this earth-sleep . . .[61]

Durrell's poem opens up the doors to another form of consciousness, that which precedes the birth of consciousness, that of indifferentiation: ". . . the whole unscripted and quite / Untabulated cryptic fauna."[62] The accumulation of negative prefixes partakes of a "jargon" that denies established forms and that relies on the marriage of contraries in order to develop unexpected associations molding new alliterative, syntactic, and prosodic patterns:

> Because he was free he was bound,
> By double sex and double axe,
> By sun's waning and moon's mighty wax.[63]

These lines sum up the paradox of poetic birth, which both belongs to and evades the world: it is a birth in bondage and a spiritual birth to freedom that spurs the poet to travel back in time so as to recover the "dark / Foreknowledge"[64] he has been separated from and initiate the leap into the unknown materialized by the concatenated enjambments at the end of the first stanza.

The reader follows a similar backward journey throughout the collection that keeps referring him to time immemorial. Just as this very first fragment that takes us into an irrepresentable before, the following ones are to be read as the remaining traces of a past text. Indeed the third fragment can only be understood as a diffuse echo to the first one: "In the open prison of the gut, / The visions of Tiresias shut"[65] sends the reader back to "the dark / Foreknowledge,"[66] so that "The primal scene, the primal scene / Often heard but seldom seen"[67] may be interpreted as referring both to the sex act and to the birth scene. The repetitive pattern of the first line and the perfect symmetry of the second one, just as the flat rhymes mimic this backward movement to a preceding time and text. This enclosed scene "taking place offstage / In something like the lion's cage"[68] is thus both the scene of supreme knowledge and prescience, and that of innocence:

> Boy goats girl, and girl gets goat,
> The royal yoga of the stoat

If the sex act is, in fiction, the harbinger of death and rebirth, it triggers in *The Red Limbo Lingo* the rebirth of language through neologisms, compound words, and puns that disclose an "offstage" where the poet casts a new jargon. Reality thus opens up to a new perception that is conveyed by a language in limbo playing on paradoxes and displacements. In the aforementioned lines, the noun "goat" becomes a verb that stands in for "get" and performs the metamorphosis of the boy into a lecherous animal moved by physical desire only, which highlights the unsatisfactory exchange between male and female and accounts for the emotional havoc Affad denounces some years later in *The Avignon Quintet*.[69] But the goat also conjures up Pan, the shepherds' god known for his strong sexual activity. He is the incarnation of the All (the popular etymological interpretation of the name Pan) of the Universe, and of the irrepressible surge of life breaking free from the constraints of social rules. Within the poem Pan heralds a singular form of yoga that seems diametrically opposed to the "royal yoga," also called Rāja Yoga, which focuses on a sharpened awareness and favors meditation in order to broaden the mind and reach spiritual liberation. The royal yoga considers the mind as the real master of the psychic and physical structures; the body must then be tamed through an ascetic discipline that prepares the mind for meditation. According to Jean Varenne, Rāja Yoga is "the Indian equivalent for the royal art (*rājan* means 'king') of Western alchemists. This comparison is all the more effective as yoga also implies an alchemical process since it offers to transform the individual in order to free him from the phenomenal world, to allow him to leave existential multiplicity so as to reach essential Unity and merge with it."[70] Therefore, "The royal yoga of the stoat" combines two incompatible noun syntagms that are joined by the pun in order to arouse the reader's curiosity. The alchemy is thus born from a language where the rhyme scheme, the paronomasia and assonances transmute the linguistic code to conjure up the unsaid and throw the reader in a semantic limbo where meaning can no longer be ascribed.

Duplicating without repeating the first beginning, the poems that follow the first section of fragmentary notes offer a second threshold that opens on "The Reckoning." Surprisingly this poem opts for the first personal plural, as if to include the reader in the meditation. Suggesting a final settlement of accounts, the poem links the poet's fate to that of all those who will undergo the last judgment, whether they chose "the crown of thorns" or "the bridal wreath of love,"[71] equally exposed as "warring fictions"[72] breeding painful rifts. The true poet would thus be the one who, having undergone the ordeals of division and dispersal, succeeds, through love and death, in bringing back coherence and construing a form of wisdom out of the multiplicity of proffered choices: "May live out one thrift in a world of options."[73] Thus may the contradictions of multiplicity be solved through unity: "In one thought focus and resume / The thousand contradictions."[74] This unique form of wisdom, conjured up a second time at the end of the first stanza ("one thought") can be compared to the mental images that are used as an aid for meditation and enable the subject to withdraw from his environment and nurture a meditation that expands consciously. This revelation is symbolically placed at the center of the first stanza and isolated by inverted commas: "'As below, darling, so above.'"[75] This quote has been attributed to Hermes Trismegistus in *The Emerald Table*, a famous alchemical codex that was in fact composed in the eleventh century by an anonymous author. It comprises a dozen obscure allegorical statements, among which are those asserting the correspondences between the microcosm and the macrocosm. This theory is in keeping with the Elizabethan worldview and harks back to "the shameless garrick of lovelingo" in the first part of the collection. Moreover, the line evinces a perfect symmetry in which the dactyls "As below / so above" are balanced by the central trochee ("darling"), the better to engage the reader and endow the line with a performative impetus since the mere presence of the rhetorical apostrophe ensures the perfect poise between the two poles: that of the lower and of the upper orders, that of the living and the dead, that of the finite and the infinite.

The second stanza shows the path through "The limbo of half-knowing,"[76] following the one sketched out in the first fragment of the first part—". . . where all the dark / Foreknowledge will abide and henceforth be . . ."[77] Simultaneously, time lines dissolve in the flux of language, which replaces the blood flux in the first section of the collection: "Timeless as water into language flowing."[78] The regular rhythm of the stanza, relying on smooth run-on lines and alternate rhymes, combines flux and stasis through the circular rhyming pattern linking up the last and the first lines. This balance relies on the interplay of contraries—"Molten as snow on new burns"[79]—and on the redemption of a torn conscience through renunciation and utter dispossession: "half-knowing" leads to "unknowing" and recalls the philosophy elaborated in "Eleusis"[80] and "Kasyapa"[81] in *The Ikons*. Renouncing rational knowledge enables the poet to grasp the true nature of man's quest; "It is not peace we seek but meaning"[82] is thus echoed by "It is not meaning that we need but sight"[83] in the last line. In between these two lines the reader may reckon the distance crossed by the subject into the territory of "unknowing" where boundaries begin to crumble:

> To convince at last that all is possible,
> That the feeble human finite must belong
> Within the starred circumference of wonder

The finite and the infinite are thus joined, echoing the quotation from Hermes Trismegistus, but this can only be achieved through a transmutation of the soul that renounces all forms of excess, i.e., hatred as much as love:

> For you become what you hate too much,
> As when you love too much you fraction
> By insolence the fine delight . . .

This stanza illustrates the mystic statement by reasserting the perfect correspondence between the subject and the object while the aposiopesis, which breaks both the syntactic and the prosodic rhythm, creates the necessary opening to the final revelation: that of a vision that upsets the existing order of the fleshly world as much as that of the textual one. Therefore, the "royal yoga" announced as a playful twist finds its unexpected completion in the second part of the poem where the poet shares with us his silent meditation upon human desire. Durrell thus bequeaths to his reader his spiritual and poetic quest for an inner freedom and sketches out a heraldic vision of the world that welds words as so many ideograms: "Ideograms, then, of heraldic sense in the alchemical mode . . ."[84] But these can only be read from limbo, this third space between two worlds where man's true heart may blossom: "in the Red Limbo Lingo hearts are flowers."[85]

Touching the Immaterial

The world of flowers stands in sharp contrast with that of "computers" and "machines,"[86] and with the civilization of the "fat commonplace, a senior *colon* . . . [who] wrote poetry on his computer or triteness machine."[87] On the contrary, the true poet resists the rule of the machine: "The poet unlike the computer answers an unasked question in his work. Imprints the soft flesh of language with his love bites."[88] Poetry breaks apart from a mechanical world: it is an organic, living relation to language that may be compared to that between the vampire and his victim. This fused bond is exemplified in the lexical intertwining of the twenty-first fragment: "a Red Limbo Lingo poet-vampire."[89] This time, language itself stands for the other and becomes this life-giving force on which the poet feeds. Language is thus far more than a mere vehicle: it is the very flesh of the poet's work, composing the "tapestry of carnal violence"[90] announced in the first fragment and that perfectly tallies with Gregory Death's conception of literary production as explained some forty years earlier in *The Black Book*:

> Books should be built of one's tissue or not at all. The struggle is not to record experience but to record oneself. The book, then, does not properly exist. There is only my tissue, my guilt, transmuted by God knows what alchemy, into a few pints of green ink and handmade paper.[91]

If the book does not exist, as Gregory says, then the reader must be holding in his hands the inner substance of the poet's self transmuted, through writing, into an intimate language the collection refers to as "lingo" and shared only by "the chosen race, the poets."[92] This is why Durrell explicitly addresses a select readership: "(Spoken words are hidden from persons not intended to hear them—so says the alchemist.)"[93] Introduced as an aside isolated from the rest of the text by the parentheses, the statement is a warning to the reader and invites him or her to listen to the silence between the lines: "We speak in puns and ellipses lest the computers, our children, overhear."[94] This is another of the many definitions of the poet's work that Durrell will develop in a 1970 interview, explaining: "A theory of mine now is that you have to speak almost entirely in poetry and puns to confuse the computers."[95] This preoccupation prevails throughout *The Revolt of Aphrodite* where the computer Abel records words and thoughts to predict the characters' fate, thus converting individuals into mere data ruled by the firm.

The Red Limbo Lingo also stands apart from previous collections by including the reader, who takes part in the alchemical transmutation and fulfills the poet's early predictions:

> Everyone is an artist . . . but most people go through life in a state of vegetable slumber and the artist pushes up like a sort of brussels sprout here and there, always saying the same thing, always giving the same little signal—saying that there is a knack about living which can be found if you try hard enough, and that there is a source of secret joy in identifying yourself with the rhythms of the amazing and curious world in which we find ourselves.[96]

Poetry becomes a healing process whereby man is torn from his slumber. Such a conviction partly accounts for the increasing complexity of Durrell's poetic opus that interweaves forms and genres to draw the reader between the lines. We may remember, for instance, that the fifth fragment opens on a prose piece, follows up with a poem, and finally ends on prose. Yet the initial prose section might as well be read as a poem hinging on the two questions answered by the three central lines:

> What was he to do—
> Indignantly finding himself
> Born into a race which,
> Despising the idol-worshipping savage,
> Offered him in exchange
> The extraordinary blood-spattered figure
> Of a man nailed to a wooden cross

> Like an expiring frog.
> He asked himself 'what could we learn
> About people who could select
> This kind of bloody squirming thing
> As an idol?'
>
> What he learned he did not like.
> What he learned he did not like.
>
> Who was this white crucified fish?[97]

Prose and poetry thus actually become interchangeable and compose a harmonious whole to be deciphered between the lines, in the elliptic form that breeds new ones. Syntactic and semantic logic lead the reader to consider the first two parts of this fragment as developing the same argument through which one follows the metamorphosis of the "blood-spattered figure / Of a man" into "an expiring frog," a "bloody squirming thing," and finally into a "white crucified fish," while "the idol-worshipping savage" is once more offered "an idol"; thus, the two peoples, the colonized and the colonizer, are brought together as victims of the same illusion.

The alchemy of the poet's jargon thus lays bare what may be called the subtle body of the text that unfolds in the reader's sensible imagination, and it echoes the "treatise of the subtle Body" in "Salamis," in *The Ikons*.[98] The text is thus perpetually reborn on the page and operates as a network of secret correspondences, an invisible locus where meaning may be excavated and reshaped—the ultimate limbo. The various symbolic values of blood act then as so many "little signal[s]" that point to "the rhythms of the amazing and curious world"[99] and expose both our inadequate representation of reality and our all-too-faint understanding of life. Whether blood is considered as a physical or a metaphysical element—the alchemists' blood, the blood of the crucified god, the blood ritual of Holy Communion revisited as "cult of the dead vampire,"[100] the blood shed by the guillotine, menstrual blood, the blood of the holy lamb, the scarlet ink of emperors, the blood-stained earth, the life-saving blood, the blood of gods, men, and poems—it is, by essence, uncircumscribed. It stands out as a volatile essence, akin to man, who can successively take the shape of a "savage," a "blood-spattered figure," an "expiring frog," a "bloody squirming thing," an "idol," and finally a "white crucified fish," deprived of any color as if an inhuman substance. Therefore, throughout the inquiry "around the notion of blood"[101] initially announced, the poet keeps investigating the decomposition of human matter and exposing, after Spengler, whose theories Durrell carefully probed throughout *The*

Revolt of Aphrodite, the spiritual decline of society. Indeed, even when rebelling against religious institutions, Durrell never ceases to plead for an unfettered spiritual impetus that can alone save man from death:

> Yes, of course I believe in God; but every kind of God. But I rather dread the word religion because I have a notion that the reality of it dissolves the minute it is uttered as a concept. I don't like the political idea inherent in religions claiming to be the only exclusive path; that is sad and silly. All religions say the same thing in different dialects.[102]

A few years later he added: "I think we are suffering from this appalling plague of a.) Christianity and b.) scholasticism which has ruined us as philosophers and as human beings. Think of the bloodstained record of our Christian civilization . . ."[103]

This alchemical writing establishes a privileged relationship with the reader and thus endeavors to found a new covenant with the world at large: this is what the poet calls "the cannibal sacrament which had established the pedigree of the chosen race, the poets," which Christ comes to symbolize.[104] In the wake of Christian symbolism, the text extols blood as the sign of an intense suffering and regeneration by rewriting the beginning of St. John's gospel: "In the beginning was the Word, and the word was blood . . ."[105] The word, like blood, is both a reality and a symbol: it is the very matter of life that comes under both forms. Thus we may account for the metatextual references in the first part of the collection: purporting to be first a "notebook," and then a "dossier," that suggests a set of unbound sheets, the collection further on refers to its poems as "ideograms": "Ideograms . . . of heraldic sense in the alchemical mode."[106] The poem is thus defined in the margins, within the prose fragments, as an image as much as a text, a graphic symbol for a set of concepts, escaping representation and developing its own individual structure and inner meaning. We are then no longer dealing with a text modeled upon the world but with a token of the irrepresentable, that echoes the heraldic blazons whose function was initially, as the Book of Numbers explains, to distinguish the main tribes of Israel by "the ensigns of their father's house."[107] As a sign, the poem performs the material presence of the immaterial, a symbolic, invisible lineage that brings to the reader a new awareness of the irrepresentable, as defined by Jean-Marc Houpert and Paule Petitier:

> it is a paradoxical concept that can grasp nothing, that cannot account for anything, but that enables one to understand precisely what lies beyond our reach through a reflexive movement that strives to understand the object by focusing on how it evades us.[108]

The poem would thus be a negative sign, the inverted facet of a presence that escapes us but whose symbol persists and heals our conscience, not unlike the warm glasses of "hissing blood"[109] with which Parisian ladies "toasted love"[110]—this ever-present absence. Poetic writing thus unveils simultaneously what does and does not exist, and testifies to the poet's eerie foreknowledge: "The poet . . . knows to what degree things can unhappen."[111] One dimly recognizes here Pursewarden's assertion: "Truth disappears with the telling of it. It can only be conveyed, not stated; irony alone is the weapon for such a task."[112]

Durrell's concept of truth comprises all the forms of expression of a knowledge in keeping with phenomenological experience and in tune with the subject's deeper nature, independent of any content. It is what is left unsaid and nevertheless seeps through poetry as much as fiction, challenges representation, and conjures up a language that, as Pierre Jourde has explained in his analysis of Nerval,

> is an experimental place where the poet does not merely experience with forms or language. . . . It is not about expressing a past experience . . . but about what, in speech, tallies with the impetus of a desire to convey, at the heart of things, their presence.[113]

In *The Red Limbo Lingo* even irony is to be read as a negative sign, as a trace of the ineffable, since it both debunks its own object and the authority of the enunciative source:

> sumptuous lions
> brief toads
> telephoning giraffes
>
> apt as various fleshes
> recent as horses
> lucrative as swans[114]

These surprising tercets illustrate what the first fragment calls "the whole unscripted and quite / Untabulated fauna posed against / Its tapestry of carnal violence."[115] The interplay of adjectives related to the human realm and of the animal lexicon suggests an unreal scene while emphasizing the powerful achievement of the poetic language that manages to convey the irrepresentable: the invisible bestial essence of human nature. One may remember the *Human Physiognomy* of Giambattista della Porta, who, like Greek auguries, deciphered human nature and foretold men's future actions by relying on physical analogies between the human face and animal figures.[116] This erroneous scientific deduction can only make the modern reader smile as he understands the covert irony of the question concluding the short prose piece and introducing this poem: "How would you set about thanking life?"[117] Indeed, the poem offers an unexpected celebration of life through elisions and displacements, mimicking the process of creation through a parodic recreation that suggests the grotesque antique wall paintings representing fantastic scenes adorned with improbable plants and animals. Once more, poetic language experiences the irrepresentable: it unfurls a reality that belongs neither to the text nor to the world. It is the sign of an unassignable truth. This explains why the question raised in the first part of the collection is answered negatively in the second one: "It is simply not possible to thank life. / The universe seems a huge hug without arms."[118] The entire opus is paradoxically built upon this impossibility, as a search for the ineffable that both drives the artistic urge and forebodes its end. The homage to a living and loving principle rules the internal structure of the collection that progressively veers away from the theme of blood in the first part to explore that of love in the second. Out of the twenty-one poems, eleven deal with love and only five with death, leading the reader to doubt the coherence between the two sections of the collection. However, titles such as "A Winter of Vampires," "Pistol Weather," and "Revenants" testify to the persistence of the theme of blood that leads the poet to question death and probe into the irrepresentable nature of human suffering.

"A Winter of Vampires" stages in its first stanza a woman who resembles the mysterious lover of Pursewarden's tale in *The Alexandria Quartet*.[119] The story of Carlo Negroponte's meetings with the vampire includes a supposedly Italian poem quoted in italics by Pursewarden:

> "Lips not on lips, but on each other's wounds
> Must suck the envenomed bodies of the loved
> And through the tideless blood draw nourishment
> To feed the love that feeds upon their deaths. . . ."[120]

The choriambus at the beginning of the first line, the regular caesuras and iambic pentameter, the syntactic and lexical symmetry, the fluid run-on lines, the polyptotons and repetitions operate as so many textual refractions duplicating the mirroring of the lover-poet into the love object. Facing his own image, the subject finds himself emptied out of his own substance, not unlike Narcissus, whose life was swallowed up by his own reflection. The lover-poet staged by Pursewarden's tale is a suffering body abandoning himself to a slow dissolution, turning into the shadow of his own self, suspended between life and death, and finally eaten up by a desire that ushers in his demise.

On the contrary, the poem "A Winter of Vampires" in *The Red Limbo Lingo* substitutes a symbolic projection for the deathly one:

> It is not at all how the story-books say
> But another kind of reversed success.
> A transaction where the words themselves
> Begin to bleed and everything else follows.[121]

We are led away from the folkloric tale developed in the first part of the collection and underlying Pursewarden's tale to enter another kind of upheaval that affects language itself and that was heralded by the nineteenth metatextual fragment:

> It is not generally known that words, if cut open, will also bleed; a poem of pith may at once accuse, persuade and assuage. The Red Limbo Lingo holds a bloody flag up to nature.[122]

Blood thus heralds a new reading pact, leading the reader to question the very act of writing. The woman vampire is thus no longer an object of discourse, nor the goal of a love quest, but a metaphor for the fruitful encounter with the other:

> The dissolution of the egg
> In the mind of the lady suggests new
> Paths to follow, less improbable victories,
> Just as illusory as the old, I fear.[123]

The reader is brought back to "the first time pieces . . . shaped like an egg"[124] and to the symbolism of rebirth and regeneration developed in the first part. The recurring image of the egg in the second part testifies to the persistence of a periodic renewal and allows for the welding of the material and the immaterial, of human love and awareness that open up "new / Paths" as so many future struggles the poet intends to wage through writing.

This fruitful encounter with the other, through which the subject negotiates his relation to his own self and to death, is contrasted by missed encounters, "when the embraces go astray," thus reasserting the coherence of the quest, which is first and foremost a quest for unity and harmony that will be further developed in *The Avignon Quintet*.[125]

Following "A Winter of Vampires," "Pistol Weather" expands the search for an ever-fleeting love that was already the topic of "Nobody" and "Rain, Rain, Go to Spain" ending a few pages earlier upon the absent figure of the loved one. Just as "A Winter of Vampires," "Pistol Weather" offers no remedy and, attempting to unravel love, eventually deconstructs it: "Delicacy, constancy and depth— / We examined every artificial prison."

Oddly, this tentative definition is interrupted by a linguistic digression interrogating the word itself through a surprising comparison: "Such as your character for 'death', / Which reads simply 'A stepping forever / Into a whiteness without remission.'" The choice of the noun "character" reminds the reader of the ideograms introduced in the first pages of the collection: "Ideograms . . . of heraldic sense in the alchemical mode."[126] Just like death, love would then be another graphic symbol of the irrepresentable that would entertain neither a denotative nor a connotative relation with reality. Like death, love mocks semantics and is all the more ungraspable as it can only be perceived in the mirror of other "characters" whom the poet keeps exploring: "With no separation-anxiety I presume?" This question suggests the poet's attempt to reach beyond any form of attachment for a concept whose reality language fails to ascertain. Love would then be another form of death, a death to the world of sterile attachments and morbid anxiety, and to the binding rules of cause and consequence, a new space where one can at last "coincide":

> Surely to love is to coincide a little?
> And after I contracted your own mightier
> Loneliness, I became really ill myself.
> But grateful for the thorny knowledge of you;
> And thank you for the choice of time and space.

"Pistol Weather" ushers in a singular space-time where love and death are conceived as equal counterparts: love is constantly measured against death. Passion is then to be understood in the etymological sense of the word: it is a deliberate act of suffering that echoes Christ's passion while transmuting the Christian dogma. Thus, "the thorny knowledge of you" both repeats and reverses "the crucifixion . . . the crown of thorns"[127] conjured up in the first section of the collection. Indeed the thorns no longer connote the feelings of guilt and pain suggested in the first part: they have turned into the thorns of knowledge that summon the tree of knowledge in the Garden of Eden and the subsequent degradation and transcendence of love through crucifixion. Moreover, the thorns also connote the alchemical rose and remind the reader of the rose motif in Renaissance poetry, from Pierre de Ronsard to Thomas Campion. The deathly fate of love is finally rendered through an ironic execution that superimposes the poet's head and John the Baptist's: "But all the time I kept seeing the severed head, / Lying there, eyes open, in your lap." It would then seem that this third space freed from the binding ties of suffering remains to be conquered.

Love is then another word for the investigation into death, including in seemingly comic pieces, such as "Revenants," whose first stanza brings back the theme of vampires through the mischievous and phantasmagoric projection of the optical illusions early photographers enjoyed capturing: "Particular ghosts might then trouble / With professional horrors like / Corpses in evening dress, / Photoglyphs from some ancient calendar / Pictographs of lost time." Yet this enumeration of impalpable and artificial ghosts harbors a deeper reality: "To see them always in memory / Descending a spiral staircase slowly / With that peculiar fond regard." The encounter between those ghosts and the poet becomes all the more "particular," and meaningful, as the projection becomes an inner one whereby the subject enters "that peculiar fond regard." The visual mirror effect is heightened by the linguistic one that allows the reader to hear the French etymology of the word "regard," thus adding to the spiral movement of the text that keeps dragging our gaze into the deeper recesses of language. This descent paves the way for the flowering Elysian fields in the following stanza where the binary structure of the hemistichs, the syntactic symmetry, the rimes and anaphoras enhance the prismatic effects of the camera:

> Or else out in silent gardens
> Under stone walls, a snapped fountain,
> Wild violets there uncaring
> Wild cyclamens uncurling
> In silence, in loaf leisure.

The "particular ghosts" finally metamorphose into "a last specialised picture / Flickering on the retina":—they have become the inner life of the poet's secret vision. One cannot then fail to remember Clea and Darley's encounter with the dead sailors in *The Alexandria Quartet* and the intimacy between the living and the dead, the visible and the invisible foreshadowed in the novel:

> Yes, but the dead are everywhere. They cannot be so simply evaded. One feels them pressing their sad blind fingers in deprivation upon the panels of our secret lives, asking to be remembered and re-enacted once more in the life of the flesh—encamping among our heartbeats, invading our embraces....
> And when the dead invade? For sometimes they emerge in person.[128]

The poet's eye thus becomes the camera obscura simultaneously projecting and decomposing the image of death the better to reinvent it. If we agree with Darley that "the dead are everywhere," then we understand how death may be read as the textual other that haunts both the poet's gaze and language. Thus, the use of the word "photoglyph" harks back both to the words "photograph" and "hieroglyph" and suggests once more the ideogram combining the familiar and the symbolic in order to break free from an emotional representation of death—since emotions are rightly disparaged by the poet as "pampered mirrors"—and usher in an impalpable, irrepresentable reality. Such a lexical and semantic shift gives birth to a truly poetic vision whose specificity, according to François Dagognet, is "to shatter reality as it is perceived and to renew our vision of the world." He goes on to define the creative image as "orienting us towards absence and delivering us from reality."[129] This palpitating image ("Flickering on the retina") that keeps evading and haunting the text spurs an unachievable quest as the concluding line to the poem evinces: "How to involve all nature in every breath?" Poetic insight is thus explicitly correlated to the visionary inspiration that underpins the artistic quest. The yawning gap between "picture" and "breath," respectively placed at the end of the first and last lines of the last stanza, epitomizes the tenuous borders of Durrellian space-time that surreptitiously opens up to past ghosts. One may recognize here the echoes of Pursewarden's motto—"the symbolism contained in form and pattern is only a frame of reference through which, as in a mirror, one may glimpse the idea of a universe at rest, a universe in love with itself"[130]—or Wordsworth's celebration of Tintern Abbey:

> Though absent long,
> These forms of beauty have not been to me,
> As is a landscape to the blind man's eye.[131]

This throbbing poetic image inspires the dissolution of temporal and spatial frontiers, bringing back into the limelight the words of past poets and challenging death. By renewing our conception of life and death, Durrell deliberately creates the rift that opens up our minds to the perception of shimmering forms of presence and transforms history into "a superfluous concept"[132] in order to substitute for it a deeper temporality that enlightens and broadens our sensitive awareness.

The Quest for Freedom

The entire collection is driven by the need for "sight" explicitly stated in "The Reckoning." The love poems testify to the dissolution of commonly perceived reality in favor of an intimate, fragile space-time.

Thus, the poems "Nobody" and "Rain, Rain, Go to Spain" that follow each other in *The Red Limbo Lingo* and face each other in *Collected Poems* both express the lover-poet's painful sense of alienation as he addresses his beloved. The first person and free verse, the irregular stanzas playing on alliterations, assonances, and symmetrical patterns and addressing the absent lady directly partake of the epistolary genre. The similar textual form and theme creates an illusory mirror effect between both texts.

"Nobody" ushers in a paradoxical space as early as the title that opens the text on a negation and a closure:

> Nobody
> You and who else?
> Who else? Why Nobody.[133]

The poem seems to fold back upon itself as early as the second line, addressing an invisible and anonymous "you" who embodies the very concept of absence in an elliptical question. The echoing second line confirms the vanity of the quest and foreshadows the poet's ontological loneliness from beginning to end. The poem unfurls the space-time of absence that engulfs the subject:

> I shall be weeks or months away now
> Where the diving roads divide,
> A solitude with little dignity,
> Where forests lie, where rivers pine,
> In a great hemisphere of loveless sky:
> And your letters will cross mine.

The lovers' estrangement belongs to an unspecified, intimate time scale. The anthropomorphic landscape sketches out a personal landscape that hints at a torn self. The apposition "A solitude with little dignity" gives the reader an insight into the poet's pain and humility: the syntactic and symbolic gap endows the stanza with an inner depth, mimicking the subject's slow descent into the abyss of loneliness at the heart of a world where letters become symbols of a failed exchange.

The city mapped by the lover's lonely steps metamorphoses into a monstrous, sprawling trap. "A cobweb of skyscrapers" reminds the reader of Alexandria:[134] once again, the city becomes the space of an inner wandering ensnaring the subject: "Between Fifth and Sixth musing I'll go, / Matching some footprints in young snow, / Within the loving ambush of some heart / So close and yet so very far apart . . ." Snow is both the space of an imaginary projection and the writing page of this unachieved love dream. The poet walks in the steps of a haunting love and is trapped in a love ambush that is a source of both suffering and hope. Durrell develops here the symbolism of the snow that underpinned *The Black Book* where "the snow slowly becomes the element that paves the way from the world of pain and absence to the inscription of that absence and pain."[135] The regular rhymes offer a musical and rhythmical structure that replaces the collapsing urban architecture while the persistence of the unreal vision is made perceptible in the aposiopesis that gives a textual reality to the fleeting afterglow of a lost union. The following stanza delves further into a phantasmagoric city where shapes and things dissolve ("the skyscrapers fade," "the falling sleet"), where beings turn into shades ("Phantom green") and belong to an undefined species ("Like great cats at their toilet"). Unlike the first assertive previous stanza, the second part of the poem introduces doubt: "I shall hesitate and falter, that much I know." The prosodic symmetry of this last line echoes the last line of the second stanza ("I don't know, I just don't know") and plays on the semantic redundancy of "hesitate" and "falter" that belie a stuttering language, a vanishing point hinting at the presence of an elsewhere that words fail to circumscribe.

This stuttering language is echoed in the last stanza by a wavering spacetime that superimposes India ("When you reach India at last"), Europe ("your empty chair in our shabby bistro"), and America ("the New York snow"). But these geographic bearings belong to an empty world where things and beings have lost their substance, where lovers meet without touching each other, where the ineffable intimacy held in "a sigh" has vanished, just like footprints in the snow, where the mind is "Confined in memory." The poem thus ends like a solitary letter telling the end of a still journey enclosed in the perfect echo of its first and last lines:

> I shall be weeks or months away now,
> Where the diving roads divide,
> A solitude with little dignity,
> . . .
> I'll be back alone again
> Confined in memory, but nothing to report,
> Watching the traffic pass and
> Dreaming of footprints in the New York snow.

The lover-poet's inner journey leads to confinement and silence. Past love has been transmuted into the dream of an indelible trace persisting on the snow-white page.

On the contrary, the following poem, "Rain, Rain, Go to Spain," although focusing on the lovers' separation, builds up a radically different space-time. The rain acts as a mediating element linking distant geographic spaces. The meteorological phenomenon functions as a musical score structuring the entire poem, giving it rhythm and coherence, enhancing the poet's isolation and seeping through the paradoxical communication of an imaginary correspondence.

The poem mimics the music of the rain through repetitions, assonances, eye rhymes, and a syncopated syntax that testify to an acute perception of reality whereby the poet breaks away from logic and temporal linearity:

> That noise will be the rain again,
> Hush-falling absolver of together—
> Companionable enough, though, here abroad:
> The log fire, some conclusive music, loneliness.
> . . .
> But this hissing rain won't improve anything.
> The roads will be washed out. Thinking falters.

The elliptical subject in the third line and the enumeration of nominal syntagms build up a minimalist scene, as if reality was superseded by sensory exploration, ushering in the realm of imagination: "I can visualise somebody at the door." The end of the stanza reasserts the presence of elemental forces through the shift from "that" to "this," making the noise of the rain even more powerful. Yet this time, the mind does not turn toward the world of dreams but toward that of the past: that of reading and separation in the second stanza, that of rereading in the third one. The network of multiple correspondences forces the reader to follow the same iterative pattern and to decipher the various echoes—alliterative ("in an amused way," "In an amazed way," st. 3), lexical ("glassed in by the rain," st. 2, "rain-polished darkness," st. 3), or thematic: "I finger the sex of many an uncut book" (st. 2) refers to the nineteenth fragment in the first part: "It is not generally thought that words, if cut open, will also bleed . . ."[136] Likewise, the quote from the postcard—"'It is raining here and / Greco is so sombre'"—refers both to the writing context of the poem and to a further poem in the collection, "Joss," where the poet defines himself as the fruit of an Indian childhood "born again in Greece."[137]

Once more spatiotemporal frontiers lose meaning and substance and are replaced by a universe that creates its own rhythm and landmarks, its secret music presiding over the lovers' reunion:

> You and memory both become
> Contemporary to this inner music.
> Time to sift out our silences, then:
> Time to repair the failing fire.[138]

This is no longer the rhythm of nostalgic retrospection but that of a re-creation, opening a new time scale through the smooth alliterative pattern whereby space is reordered. The initial "log fire" becomes this inner fire the poem rekindles while the anaphora of the last two lines gives the poem a prophetic undertone that echoes Ecclesiastes: "A time to rend, and a time to sow; a time to keep silence, and a time to speak."[139]

Therefore the progression from "Nobody" to "Rain, Rain, Go to Spain" becomes obvious. While the first poem ends on the imaginary projection of an impossible union, the second one delves into the intimate present, into the experience of intense sensations that enable the poet to tear himself apart from the time line and to opt for "the anchorage in the present time that is, *per se*, an anchorage in eternity"[140] and can alone, as the philosopher Michel Hulin has explained, free man from angst.

The inner freedom the collection aims for implies a new temporality that redefines the subject's gaze on the self and on the world. Such a gaze is rooted in a constant asceticism as the poem "Stoic," pursuing the quest of "Pistol Weather," testifies:

> I, a slave, chained to an oar of a poem,
> Inhabiting this faraway province where
> Nothing happens. I wouldn't want it to.
> I have expressly deprived myself of much:
> Conversations, sweets of friendship, love . . .[141]

The poet deliberately chooses solitude and isolation the better to explore the essence of death through a negative definition developed in the second stanza at the end of which he singles out one characteristic: "From all these factors I select one, the silence / Which is that jewel of divine futility."[142] This new realm is reminiscent of the death experience of the Indian sage Ramana Maharshi as told by Michel Hulin:

> Ramana Maharshi . . . feels that the angst for death may, on the contrary, constitute a favorable occasion, and open up a door to ultimate reality. He considers angst as the promise of revelation. . . . He does not fight against it but uses it as a means of getting closer to his own death. . . . Thus is the threshold crossed. This is a near death experience, not, of course, as an encounter with

an objective extreme danger, but as an extreme form of self denial. All personal projects have been abandoned, whether worldly or 'religious.' One enters a state of openness, readiness, and acceptance of whatever will come to be.[143]

Entering this remote and deserted territory as a slave, the poet detaches himself from all bonds in order to approach those who have crossed the threshold and radiate freedom and peace: "Refusal to bow, the unvarnished grain / Of the mind's impudence: you see it so well / On the faces of self-reliant dead." This insolence is the gift of the wise man confronting his own angst and going against his instincts to resist any form of self-defense against death as Michel Hulin further explains: "he allows himself, through a thorough conversion, to be freely invaded by terror . . . in order to see what will come out of it."[144]

Poetry thus appears as the space of intimate meditation cut off from ordinary time and in tune with the undying self. Pursewarden hankered after the same revelation when he asserted in *The Alexandria Quartet*: "Death is a metaphor; nobody dies to himself."[145] The poem is thus built as a rising temple to meditation that acquires depth and height throughout the volume. Thus, in "One Place" the poet conjures up a unique space where dualities are abolished and ultimate reality asserted:

> Commission silence for a line or two,
> These walls, these trees—time out of mind
> Are temples to perfection lightly spent,
> Sunbribed and apt in their shadowy stresses,
> Where the planes hang heads, lies
> Something the mind caresses;

The performative language of the poem builds up, through the sheer force of the imperatives, an immaterial temple where nature and architecture, the vegetal and the man-made are in tune, and that the multiple intrusions from the outside world ("Bells bowling, the sistrum bonged") fail to disturb. The first stanza develops as an ode that is "to be whispered only," suggesting an intimate relation with the text that merges with the reader's breath, not unlike mantras whose ritual repetition channels mental activity and helps meditation. On the contrary, the last stanza breaks apart from that world of inner, silent meditation and throws the reader back into the world of dualism and hopeless questioning:

> To go or stay is really not the question;
> Nor even to go forever, one can't allow here

> Death as a page its full relapse.
> In such a nook it would always be perhaps,
> Dying with no strings attached—who could to that?

Durrell materializes the palpable rift between Eastern and Western representations of death as well as the subject's painstaking efforts to achieve the much-desired conversion whereby he may free himself from angst. Poetry experiences here with its very limits: it is incapable of explaining; it can only convey and disseminate the hope of an inner achievement that lies beyond language. This accounts for the last line of the poem that sends the reader back to his own personal questioning, to his own secret challenge.

As if to answer "One Place," the poem "The Land" offers the exploration of a space-time where fearless and curious intruders can roam freely[146] ("The rapt moonwalkers or mere students / Of the world-envelope are piercing / Into the earth's crust . . .").[147] These explorers are perpetual nomads who also dwell in a cyclic world where they plant, grow, and protect life so that their very tools are conceived as "manual extensions" through which man communes with his surroundings. Freed from "finite time," they are also freed from abstract questionings and fear:

> Not puzzled any more, having forgotten
> How brief and how precarious life was,
> But finding it chiefly true yet various,
> With no uncritical submission to the Gods.

The slow disappearance of run-on lines and the perfect symmetry of syntactic and prosodic structures underline the faultless balance between man and the universe. Past and future are superseded by the unmarred stillness of the present tense that throws the reader into a harmonious, eternal rhythm "Inside the uniform flow of the equinoxes."[148]

"One Place" and "The Land" thus offer a metaphysical journey that climaxes in the following poem, "Joss." The title suggests a sacred place where the subject connects with an eternal space-time through the singing rhythm of the poem. One easily recognizes Durrell's Indian past ("An Indian childhood")[149] as well as his Greek youth in the "Easter ikons" of the second stanza. However, the poem unravels a curiously depersonalized space-time: the erasure of determiners and verbs abolishes any form of temporal anchorage. Simultaneously, the enumeration of nominal syntagms, which coincide with the prosodic structure in stanza 1, followed by the successive run-on lines in the second one, blur the narrative line so that the poem no longer develops the testimony of a single subject, as if the voice of the poem sought to disengage itself from any individual utterance. The first stanza plays on an ascending movement from "old bones" to "Indian bones," then "slender batons" and finally "brown saints." The gaze is thus drawn from the material to the immaterial, from the perishable to the eternal. The last line—"An Indian childhood. Joss"—suggests the original separation through the syntactic rift that materializes the gap between the told and the untold, and the emotional breach at the source of a writing that sublimates space. The sheer strength of the isolated noun "Joss" echoes the title and conjures up the absent territory, the founding place, the birth of the poetic breath. One is then tempted to read this single word in the light of Durrell's interpretation of the poetic power of words: "Poetically words are less important for their dictionary meanings than for the vibrations they set up in the middle ear—the pineal ear, so to speak. Poets are simply handers on of the sound, like sea shells."[150] Likewise, the reader is invited to allow the word "Joss" to reverberate and understand that no higher music may ever conjure up the lost and present land the poet will seek through Greece and into Languedoc. The second stanza contrasts "Joss" with "frankincense" and "whiff of brown saints" by "Easter ikons" and signals the fall into matter through a rigid syntax that takes over prosody until the third stanza, where the memory of the original birth is recaptured in the melodious celebration of "A second childhood." Images and sounds combine as sensorial perceptions become the only existing reality, the only possible form of life defined as "chiefly true yet various"[151] in the previous poem "The Land." "Joss" reasserts the diverse, fluid essence of life in this third stanza, where verbs are reinserted in the present tense and the iterative mode and trigger the repetition of the first ten lines:

> The images repeat repent repent (*da capo*)
> A second childhood, born again in Greece.
> O the benign power, the providing power
> Is here too with its reassurance honey.
> After the heartbreak of the long voyage,
> Same lexicon, stars over the water.

The intertwining of images and sensations brings back to mind the "Thought-clusters, constellations of ideas"[152] announced in the first part of the collection that paved the way for a visionary writing shedding the constraints of time and cause. In that perspective, "joss" and "frankincense" belong to the "Same lexicon" and abolish geographic as well as linguistic barriers, ushering in the final bilingual stanza. The female figure in the fourth stanza ties in with the leitmotif of vampires ("Demon of Sadness, / . . . The necklace of cannibals' teeth") before metamorphosing into a protective, benevolent presence who belongs to a world of hope and harmony: ". . . a woman walking alone / In the reign of her forgiveness / In the rain." The fluidity of alliterations and homonymy places her among the enlightening stars "smiling under rain,"[153] like another incarnation of the mischievous, unassignable *deus loci*.

The two lines in French at the beginning of the last stanza create an ironic diversion and underline the gap between the subject's dualistic vision and the reclaimed unity in the last two lines where the anaphora sends us back to the initial "single name" in a final *da capo*:

> A single word to transcend all others,
> A single name buried Excalibur in a stone.

"Joss" is then the silent coda enshrined in the poem, the jewel of life akin to the sacred sword that can only be wrent away from the stone by the hand of the initiate.

Poetry is thus the secret place where Durrell endeavors to approach death by confronting the angst of a closing lifetime, as the last poems of the collection evince. "Avignon," for instance, sounds like a funeral march—"Come, meet me in some dead café— / . . . / Come, random with me in the rain, / In ghastly harness like a dream, / In rainwashed streets of saddened dark"[154]—that conjures up the subject's slow descent into melancholia. Likewise, "Mistral," despite the jazzy undertone of the French ballad inserted in this bilingual poem, suggests the dark fate of cabaret girls (such as Melissa in *The Alexandria Quartet* or Iolanthe in *The Revolt of Aphrodite*) and opens on a deathly dawn:

> At four the dawn mistral usually
> A sleep-walking giant sways and crackles
> The house, a vessel big with sail
> . . .
> Far away in her carnal fealty sleeps
> La Môme in her tiny chambre de bonne.
> 'Le vent se lève . . . Il faut tenter de vivre.'[155]

Durrell is explicitly echoing here the last stanza of Valéry's "Cimetière marin":

> Le vent se lève ! . . . Il faut tenter de vivre!
> L'air immense ouvre et referme mon livre[156]

This is not the first intertextual reference to Valéry, although it is one of the most striking. Durrell greatly admired the French poet, whom he compared to Seferis—"Basically Valéry is very close to Seferis. It's the gnomic quality, the density"[157]—before establishing a parallel between Valéry's poetic writing and his own: "I was a terrific word-hunter, an avid collector of images before the Eternal. But I was like Valéry when it came to the first line, 'the gift of the gods.' I would often have to wait ages for it."[158] This similarity is further corroborated by the end of "Mistral," concluding on the image of Golgotha ("the hills of bones")[159] as if to echo again Valéry's verse ("Ce crâne vide et ce rire éternel").[160]

Both "Mistral" and the entire collection conclude on an apocalyptic end that becomes utterly parodic in the final "Envoi":

> Be silent, old frog.
> Let God compound the issue as he must,
> And dog eat dog
> Unto the final desecration of man's dust.
> The just will be devoured by the unjust.

The iconoclastic humor debunking the biblical message[161] and the puns (the palindrome God/dog) that undermine ordinary logic (such as the common saying "Every dog has its day") fail to conceal the poet's growing despair that can only be expressed through a disrespectful writing that pushes linguistic and poetic boundaries to the point of nonsense. Poetry thus operates as this tangential force that reshapes reality, as Durrell explains:

> Perhaps poetry is a tangent of writing. . . . That intuition [of the essential] confers a sort of tangential vision. . . . One feels vaguely the subtlety of life, the nature at once limpid and obscure of the movement of existence. . . . And at the same time there comes an awareness of the inadequacies of language to convey that intuition. So one has to fall back on detours in language as in life; one looks upon beings and things differently, and that leads to a particular kind of irreverence, impregnated with a sense of the sacred.[162]

This new "lingo" meant for the initiates therefore opens up a very singular space, a "red limbo" that stands out as a boundless territory where extremes cohabit—angst and irony, fear and disrespect, desire and detachment—and through which the poet progressively guides us from a dualistic world to the hope of a peaceful relation to the world and to the self. The poet's "I" metamorphoses by renouncing the ego through a constant *agon*. Poetry is then both synonymous with a painful rift and a hopeful fulfillment: out of the gaps of writing a new self is born that breaks free from the subject and transcends death. *The Red Limbo Lingo* paves the way for the ultimate achievement Durrell's entire opus hankers after: "It is not meaning that we need but sight."[163] This quest for absolute vision is at the roots of Durrell's artistic endeavor, as he himself recalled when reminiscing his Indian childhood and his desire to reach for the ungraspable:

> In India when I was a boy they had great green lizards there, and if you shouted or shot them their tails would fall off. There was only one boy in the school who could catch lizards intact. No one knew quite how he did it. He had a special soft way of going up to them and he'd bring them back with their tails on. That strikes me as the best analogy I can give you. To try and catch your poem without its tail falling off.[164]

Apprehending living time in its frail and fleeting essence, unraveling a world of patience, knowledge, and precision that conveys the beauty and delicacy of life, such is the hope that keeps the poet's voice vibrant in limbo. Out of the wrenching pain of exile and loss, at the heart of the spatial, temporal, and linguistic gap that is the poet's true abode, a new writing is born that shatters boundaries between prose and poetry, narrative line and free association, discursive and rhythmic logic. Breaking away from literary codes and practices Durrell experiences with blurred frontiers to allow us to listen, in the clefts of the text, to the silent voice of poetry. Thus Durrell joins the ongoing modernist exploration of disjointed forms invoking in the drowning of language "all nature in every breath."[165]

Notes

1. Lawrence Durrell, *The Red Limbo Lingo: A Poetry Notebook*, London: Faber, 1971, p. 35.

2. February 10, 1970, Letter to Henry Miller, *The Durrell-Miller Letters 1935–80*, Ian S. MacNiven, ed., London: Faber, 1989 (first published in 1988), pp. 437–38.

3. *The Durrell-Miller Letters 1935–80*, pp. 437–38.

4. *The Red Limbo Lingo*, [n.p.]. [Copy held by the Lawrence Durrell Research Library at the University Paris Ouest].

5. Dominique Rabaté, "Enonciation poétique, énonciation lyrique," *Figures du sujet lyrique*, Paris: PUF, 1996, p. 78.

6. Lawrence Durrell, *Vega and Other Poems*, London: Faber, 1973, p. 8.

7. "But a notebook of this sort is like a constellation, a star cluster of thoughts . . . ," *The Red Limbo Lingo*, [n.p.].

8. May 5, 1971, Letter to Henry Miller, *The Durrell-Miller Letters 1935–80*, p. 449.

9. *The Red Limbo Lingo*, [n.p.].
10. *The Red Limbo Lingo*, [n.p.].
11. Corinne Alexandre-Garner, "Durrell: la clôture impossible?" *Etudes Britanniques Contemporaines* no. 10 (1996), p. 93.
12. "Talking Jolly Glibly," interview with Julian Mitchell and Gene Andrewski (1959), *Lawrence Durrell: Conversations*, Earl G. Ingersoll, ed., Madison: Fairleigh Dickinson University Press, 1998, p. 29.
13. *The Red Limbo Lingo*, p. 15.
14. *The Red Limbo Lingo*, p. 21.
15. *The Red Limbo Lingo*, p. 12.
16. *The Red Limbo Lingo*, p. 11.
17. *The Red Limbo Lingo*, p. 12.
18. *The Red Limbo Lingo*, [n.p.].
19. Lawrence Durrell, *The Revolt of Aphrodite, Tunc*, London: Faber, 1990 (first published in 1974), pp. 139–42. The previous scene where Felix is shown how "to break . . . in" the falcon is also exceedingly violent (p. 116).
20. *The Revolt of Aphrodite, Tunc*, pp. 289–90.
21. Lawrence Durrell, *The Avignon Quintet*, London: Faber, 1992, p. 1248.
22. *The Red Limbo Lingo*, p. 14.
23. *The Avignon Quintet*, p. 835. See Ravi Nambiar, "Lawrence Durrell's Recreation of D. H. Lawrence's *Constance*: Restoring Woman's Cosmic Place," *Lawrence Durrell, Borderlands & Borderlines, Confluences* no. 26, Presses Universitaires de Paris 10, 2005, p. 147.
24. *The Revolt of Aphrodite, Tunc*, p. 293.
25. *The Revolt of Aphrodite, Tunc*, p. 836.
26. *The Red Limbo Lingo*, p. 18.
27. *The Avignon Quintet*, p. 180.
28. Pierre Grimal, *Dictionnaire de la mythologie grecque et romaine*, Paris: PUF, 1996, pp. 39–40.
29. Lawrence Durrell, *The Alexandria Quartet*, London: Faber, 1974 (first published in 1962), p. 18.
30. T. S. Eliot, *Collected Poems 1909–1962*, London: Faber, 2002, p. 55.
31. Giorgio Agamben, *La Fin du poème*, Paris: Circé, 2002, pp. 134–35.
32. Lawrence Durrell, *Collected Poems 1931–1974*, London: Faber, 1985 (first published in 1980), p. 338.
33. *The Red Limbo Lingo*, p. 9.
34. Lawrence Durrell, *Key to Modern Poetry*, London: Peter Nevill, 1952, p. 7. Some twenty years later Durrell takes up the same quote in his introduction to the anthology of Wordsworth's poems he prefaced and edited (*Wordsworth Selected by Lawrence Durrell*, Harmondsworth: Penguin Books, 1973, p. 13).
35. *The Red Limbo Lingo*, p. 22.
36. *The Red Limbo Lingo*, p. 15.
37. Judith Balso, *Affirmation de la poésie*, Caen: éditions Nous, 2011, p. 58.

38. *Affirmation de la poésie*, p. 60.
39. *The Red Limbo Lingo*, p. 19.
40. Mircea Eliade, *Traité d'histoire des religions*, Paris: Payot, 1974, pp. 347–49.
41. Julien Brocard, "Grâce à la poésie, une présentation," in *La Poésie pour quoi faire? Une enquête*, Jean-Michel Maupoix (ed.), Paris: Presses Universitaires de Paris Ouest, 2011, pp. 19–20.
42. Henri Michaux, "L'Avenir de la poésie" (1936), *Œuvres complètes I*, Paris: Gallimard, 1998, p. 969.
43. "Its tapestry of carnal violence," *The Red Limbo Lingo*, p. 9.
44. See *Blaise Cendrars–Henry Miller, Correspondance 1934–1979: 45 ans d'amitié* (edited by Miriam Cendrars, introduced by Frédéric-Jacques Temple), Paris: Denoël, 1995.
45. Blaise Cendrars, *Poésies complètes*, "Préface," Paris: Denoël, 2005, p. xiv.
46. *Poésies complètes*, "Préface," p. xiv.
47. *Poésies complètes*, p. 321.
48. *The Red Limbo Lingo*, p. 11.
49. "Le sang des mots," *La Poésie pour quoi faire?* pp. 120–21.
50. *The Red Limbo Lingo*, p. 9.
51. *Poésies complètes*, pp. 131–32.
52. "'Je est un autre,'" *A Private Country*, London: Faber, 1944 (first published in 1943), p. 50.
53. Lawrence Durrell, *A Private Country*, p. 50.
54. Lawrence Durrell, "Cities, Plains and People," *Cities, Plains and People*, London: Faber, 1946, p. 58.
55. *The Red Limbo Lingo*, p. 9.
56. *The Red Limbo Lingo*, p. 9.
57. *The Red Limbo Lingo*, p. 9.
58. "In Deep Grass" (1974; *Collected Poems 1931–1974*, p. 340) is the last poem Durrell ever included in a collection. In an interview with Corinne Alexandre-Garner, who asked him in 1984 "What about writing poems?" he answered: "It's funny. It's like when a singer who's a castrato loses his high register. I haven't got a poem in me anymore," "Waking up in Scott Fitzgerald's Bed," *Lawrence Durrell: Conversations*, p. 217.
59. Spagyric n. & a. [used and probably invented by Paracelsus] A n. 1. The science of alchemy. 2. An alchemist. B *adj*. Alchemical. (*The New Shorter Oxford Dictionary*).
60. "Down the Styx" (1961), Lawrence Durrell, *Spirit of Place: Mediterranean Writings*, London: Faber, 1988 (first published in 1969), pp. 420–22.
61. Edith Sitwell, "Some notes on my own poetry" (1949), *Collected Poems*, London: Duckworth Overlook, 2006, p. xxxi.
62. *The Red Limbo Lingo*, p. 9.
63. *The Red Limbo Lingo*, p. 9.
64. *The Red Limbo Lingo*, p. 9.

65. *The Red Limbo Lingo*, p. 10.
66. *The Red Limbo Lingo*, p. 9.
67. *The Red Limbo Lingo*, p. 10.
68. *The Red Limbo Lingo*, p. 10.
69. *The Avignon Quintet*, p. 838.
70. Jean Varenne, "YOGA," *Encyclopædia Universalis* [online], last accessed June 15, 2017, https://www-universalis—edu-com.nomade.univ-tlse2.fr/encyclopedie/yoga/. There are many more occurrences of alchemy in the *Upanishads*, such as in the conclusion to "The perfect meditation." See *Upanishads du Yoga*, translated from Sanskrit and annotated by Jean Varenne, Paris: Gallimard, 1971, p. 92.
71. *The Red Limbo Lingo*, p. 23.
72. *The Red Limbo Lingo*, p. 23.
73. *The Red Limbo Lingo*, p. 23.
74. *The Red Limbo Lingo*, p. 23.
75. *The Red Limbo Lingo*, p. 23.
76. *The Red Limbo Lingo*, p. 23.
77. *The Red Limbo Lingo*, p. 9.
78. *The Red Limbo Lingo*, p. 23.
79. *The Red Limbo Lingo*, p. 23.
80. *The Ikons*, London: Faber, 1966, p. 13.
81. *The Ikons*, p. 37.
82. *The Red Limbo Lingo*, p. 23.
83. *The Red Limbo Lingo*, p. 23.
84. *The Red Limbo Lingo*, p. 12.
85. *The Red Limbo Lingo*, p. 10. The same image already appeared in *The Revolt of Aphrodite, Nunquam*: "your visions withered slowly like ageing flowers," p. 13.
86. *The Red Limbo Lingo*, p. 10.
87. *The Red Limbo Lingo*, p. 13.
88. *The Red Limbo Lingo*, p. 13.
89. *The Red Limbo Lingo*, p. 18.
90. *The Red Limbo Lingo*, p. 9.
91. Lawrence Durrell, *The Black Book*, London: Faber, 1977 (first published in 1938), p. 121. This passage is highly reminiscent of Rilke's words in *The Notebooks of Male Laurids Brigge*: "For the memories are not what's essential. It's only when they become blood within us, become our nameless looks and signs that are no longer distinguishable from ourselves—not until then does it happen that, in a very rare moment, the first word of a verse rises in their midst and goes forth from among them," Rainer Maria Rilke, *The Notebooks of Male Laurids Brigge*, translated from the German by William Needham, https://archive.org/stream/TheNotebooksOfMalte LauridsBrigge/TheNotebooksOfMalteLauridsBrigge_djvu.txt, last accessed June 12, 2017.
92. *The Red Limbo Lingo*, p. 11.
93. *The Red Limbo Lingo*, p. 14.

94. *The Red Limbo Lingo*, p. 18.
95. "The First of the New Romantics," *Lawrence Durrell: Conversations*, pp. 116–17.
96. "Coming in Slightly at a Slant," 1960, *Lawrence Durrell: Conversations*, p. 55.
97. *The Red Limbo Lingo*, p. 11.
98. *The Ikons*, p. 17.
99. *Lawrence Durrell: Conversations*, p. 55.
100. "Even today in the great churches they are still drinking by blood group. . . . The cult of the dead vampire still holds the stage; it begins with the crucifixion, which was the common fate of the vampire in classical times," *The Red Limbo Lingo*, p. 11.
101. *The Red Limbo Lingo*, [n.p.]. [Copy held by the Lawrence Durrell Research Library at the University Paris Ouest].
102. "The Kneller Tape (Hamburg)," 1962, *Lawrence Durrell: Conversations*, p. 72.
103. "Investigating a Nightingale," 1965, *Lawrence Durrell: Conversations*, p. 83.
104. *The Red Limbo Lingo*, p. 11.
105. *The Red Limbo Lingo*, p. 11.
106. *The Red Limbo Lingo*, p. 12.
107. Numbers II: 2.
108. Jean-Marc Houpert and Paule Petitier, eds., *De l'irreprésentable en littérature*, Paris: l'Harmattan, 2001, p. 11.
109. *The Red Limbo Lingo*, p. 18.
110. *The Red Limbo Lingo*, p. 18.
111. *The Red Limbo Lingo*, p. 12.
112. *The Alexandria Quartet*, Clea, p. 764.
113. Pierre Jouard, "Nerval, la voix, l'irreprésentable," *De l'irreprésentable en littérature*, p. 155.
114. *The Red Limbo Lingo*, p. 13.
115. *The Red Limbo Lingo*, p. 9.
116. See G. B. della Porta, *De Humana Physiognomia libri III*, Naples, 1586, quoted by Jurgis Baltrušaitis, *Aberrations. Essai sur la légende des formes. Les perspectives dépravées—I*, Paris: Flammarion, 1995, pp. 22–23.
117. *The Red Limbo Lingo*, p. 12.
118. *The Red Limbo Lingo*, "Mistral," p. 46.
119. *The Alexandria Quartet*, pp. 348–50.
120. *The Alexandria Quartet*, p. 349.
121. *The Red Limbo Lingo*, p. 29.
122. *The Red Limbo Lingo*, p. 17.
123. *The Red Limbo Lingo*, p. 29.
124. *The Red Limbo Lingo*, p. 19.
125. "They must both act towards each other with the highest degree of conscious effort . . . the purer the child and the more harmonious the race," *The Avignon Quintet*, p. 838.

126. *The Red Limbo Lingo*, p. 11.
127. *The Red Limbo Lingo*, p. 11.
128. *The Alexandria Quartet*, p. 833.
129. François Dagognet, "L'image: reproduction et création," *Philopsis*, 2007, http://www.philopsis.fr, p. 4, last accessed June 15, 2017.
130. *The Alexandria Quartet*, p. 764.
131. "Lines written a few miles above Tintern Abbey," in William Wordsworth and Samuel Taylor Coleridge, *Lyrical Ballads 1978*, Oxford; Oxford University Press, 1993, p. 112. Durrell explicitly singled out this poem as among those that profoundly influenced him: "the famous lines written above Tintern Abbey could be considered one of the great love-poems in the language," *Wordsworth Selected by Lawrence Durrell*, p. 14.
132. *The Red Limbo Lingo*, p. 15.
133. *The Red Limbo Lingo*, p. 24.
134. See "We turn a corner and the world becomes a pattern of arteries, splashed with silver and deckle-edged with shadow," *The Alexandria Quartet*, p. 116.
135. Corinne Alexandre-Garner, "L'écriture de la neige dans les premiers textes de Lawrence Durrell: essai de généalogie d'une écriture," *Bulletin de la Société de Stylistique Anglaise*, 2005, no. 26, p. 179.
136. *The Red Limbo Lingo*, p. 17.
137. *The Red Limbo Lingo*, p. 40. This is a Durrellian leitmotif. During his interview with Peter Adam in 1975 Durrell described Greece thus: "It's my second birthplace. You know the old Indian notion that one is born twice, once physically and then once you sort of wake up to reality," "Everything comes right," *Lawrence Durrell: Conversations*, p. 166.
138. The original edition offers a slight variation: "Time to relay the failing fire" (*The Red Limbo Lingo*, p. 27). I have chosen to comment here on the final version of the poem.
139. Ecclesiastes 3: 7.
140. Michel Hulin, *La face cachée du temps, L'imaginaire de l'au-delà*, Paris: Fayard, 1985, p. 40.
141. *The Red Limbo Lingo*, p. 32.
142. *The Red Limbo Lingo*, p. 32.
143. *La face cachée du temps*, pp. 43–44.
144. *La face cachée du temps*, p. 44.
145. *The Alexandria Quartet*, p. 881.
146. One is reminded again of Pursewarden writing to Darley: "the poet finds himself growing gills and a tail, the better to swim against the currents of unenlightenment . . . by reversing process in this way, he unites the rushing, heedless stream of humanity to the still, tranquil, motionless, odourless, tasteless plenum from which its own motive essence is derived . . . the poetic jump I'm predicting lies the other side of it," *The Alexandria Quartet*, p. 772.
147. *The Red Limbo Lingo*, p. 39.

148. *The Red Limbo Lingo*, p. 39.
149. *The Red Limbo Lingo*, p. 40.
150. *Lawrence Durrell: Conversations*, p. 72.
151. *The Red Limbo Lingo*, p. 39.
152. "Thought-clusters, constellations of ideas linked by private associations, characterize poetic thinking . . . ," *The Red Limbo Lingo*, p. 12.
153. "Deus Loci," Lawrence Durrell, *The Tree of Idleness*, London: Faber, 1955, p. 48.
154. *The Red Limbo Lingo*, p. 41.
155. *The Red Limbo Lingo*, p. 46.
156. Paul Valéry, *Charmes*, *Œuvres I*, Paris: Gallimard, 1957, p. 151. The translation of "The Graveyard by the Sea" by Cecil Day-Lewis reads as follows: "The wind is rising! . . . We must try to live! / The huge air opens and shuts my book . . ." http://homepages.wmich.edu/~cooneys/poems/fr/valery.daylewis.html, last accessed June 19, 2017.
157. *Lawrence Durrell: Conversations*, p. 142.
158. *Lawrence Durrell: Conversations*, p. 147.
159. *The Red Limbo Lingo*, p. 47.
160. *Charmes*, p. 151. "That empty skull, that everlasting grin," translation by Cecil Day-Lewis, http://homepages.wmich.edu/~cooneys/poems/fr/valery.daylewis.html, last accessed June 19, 2017.
161. See "There shall no evil happen to the just: but the wicked shall be filled with mischief," Proverbs 12: 21.
162. *Lawrence Durrell: Conversations*, pp. 251–52.
163. *The Red Limbo Lingo*, p. 23.
164. *Lawrence Durrell: Conversations*, p. 29.
165. *The Red Limbo Lingo*, p. 38.

CHAPTER SEVEN

Vega

The Star of Poetry

Lawrence Durrell's last poetry collection[1] symbolically opens on a backward move by inserting the poems that initially belonged to the second part of *The Red Limbo Lingo*. This last poetic opus dated 1973 reasserts the "impossible closure"[2] of a work that plays on dissemination in an ever-centrifugal structure that blurs frontiers and develops a "constellation"[3] that is posited as the fundamental pattern of poetry. There would then be no beginning or end, as Mary Byrne rightfully contends when comparing Durrell's neo-baroque fiction and E. M. Forster's injunction in *Howards End*: "Only connect the prose and the passion, and both will be exalted, and human love will be seen at its height. Live in fragments no longer. Only connect . . ."[4] *Vega* paves the way for the final stage of *The Avignon Quintet*, whose last volume Durrell is simultaneously composing and that will end on the mysterious and fortuitous coincidence of the multiple diegetic layers as characters and plots are all brought together:

> Be ye members of one another, he thought. If each had a part in a play perhaps they could also be the various actors which, in their sum, made up one whole single personality? . . . He had thrown away all his notes for the new book, shaking out his briefcase from the window of the train and watching the leaves scatter and drift away down the valley of the Rhône. . . . just clouds of memoranda filling the air—human memoranda. The sum of all their parts whirled in the death-drift of history—motes in a vast sunbeam.[5]

In a final "comic paradox"[6] the fragments thrown away by Blanford will be collected and bound by the gypsies of Avignon, who will then sell them to

Toby, the historian invented by Blanford, before Blanford himself buys them again, arguing that "the mere fact that they had escaped destruction was a portent concerning their value for his forthcoming book whose presence had begun to loom up strangely over his future life."[7] Dispersion is then irremediably bound to collection, just as loss is bound to memory. Time lost and dead beings keep resurfacing sporadically, not unlike the starred sprays that compose the orphic constellation of Lyra at the top of which Vega stands out as the brightest star in the northern hemisphere in summer. The gaps between these searing flashes are the place where writing is born. Thus in *The Avignon Quintet* the writer's "notes" turn into "motes in a vast sunbeam"[8] and partake of natural creation again as spontaneous flinders refracting light and returning to life, just as the "shining canvases" of van Gogh are recaptured "in a patch of dust."[9] The unpremeditated nature of creation extolled in Durrell's work relies in fact on a carefully arranged pattern that transpires in the paronomasia "notes" / "motes" hinting at an absolute form of freedom the text constantly reaches for in an attempt to fuse into a united creation. This absolute harmony sketched out in the shimmering wax and wane of beings, worlds, and words that can only exist as repetitions of an unredeemable absence suggests Maurice Blanchot's analysis of the pattern of repetition:

> There cannot be a successful fragment, whether satisfactory or showing the way out, the end of mistakes, if only because every fragment, even a unique one, repeats itself and through repetition is undone.
>
> Let us remember. Repetition: not a religious repetition fraught with regret or nostalgia, an unwanted reiteration. Repetition: repetition in the extreme, general collapse, destruction of the present.[10]

The "general collapse" of the present is vital to the emergence of a world that aims for another reality, that of a vibrant, out-of-reach form of life that Durrell locates in poetry:

> Notes scattered to the winds of old Provence. Reality is what is completely contemporaneous to itself: we are not completely in it while we still breathe but we yearn to be—hence poetry![11]

Durrell's last collection is therefore to be read as the climax of this writing of the rift, of the repetition of cleavage and loss, of the process of dissemination sketching out the poet's irrational and raging hope, which has been aptly described by Mary Byrne as "a felt need to inject new life, a furious exploration of the darkness before the light. . . . It is a world of form with little reason, of games, of *mise en abîme* . . . a world seen as a book of books [. . .]."[12]

Interestingly *The Avignon Quintet*, the "book of books" by essence, is fraught with poetic fragments that unfold as so many journeys into that other, "contemporaneous" reality through which the novel is broken apart and explodes into textual fragments where meaning and form dissolve. Poetry seeps into fiction in order to bring in a new breath that regenerates writing through the destruction of diegetic time and logic and throws the reader into a radically alien system whose coordinates he can never pinpoint. The narrative is thus cleft into two enunciations both inaudible and unreadable that build up a challenging, constellated text:

make his bed	perhaps some passages in primal scene
take his wife	verse? Maybe Sutcliffe would share a
mark his pillow	Hearts-and-Flowers act with his alter
'absent wife'	ego?
darn his heel	
smoke his quid	Scene of the epilepsy, the pearl saliva,
doing all	The tongue bitten in half, almost
the other did	swallowed.
hunt the slipper	"Cybele! What's for dinner?"
hunt the soul	"Uterus!" she said.
Eros teach him	
breath control!	

Carry thy balls high, Coz, *les couilles bien haut! Recuser, accoler, accusez, raccolez!*[13]

Not only does the text seem deprived of any coherence, but the layout is even more perplexing. The split paragraph becomes incomprehensible to the point of absurdity: spatiotemporal landmarks vanish, and the narrator's voice gives rise to two distinct utterances that do not match and run parallel to each other. This is no dialogue but a baffling visual cacophony, a properly "aberrant prose style."[14] The writing breaks free from the novel and becomes experimental. It deliberately runs the risk of destroying form and meaning. In so doing it pursues the poet's aim defined by T. S. Eliot in *Four Quartets*—one of Durrell's major sources of inspiration—where poetry is envisaged as an ever-repeated failure to use words, a perpetual struggle whose reiteration is the poet's sole purpose.[15] Durrell rekindles Eliot's "trying" through a disjointed text that produces a new, diffuse meaning. The fiction thus generates a distorted and differed writing whereby the second column may be read as Blanford's comments upon Sutcliffe's verse in the left one. However, the commentary seems to collapse and veers into differing interpretations: "primal scene," "Hearts-and-Flowers act," or "scene of the epilepsy." Eventually what is supposed to help the reader make sense further disrupts textual coherence. The commentary symbolically ends on the cry "Uterus!" which the epileptic voiceless mouth already foreshadowed. The carnivalesque inversion of mouth and sex ushers in the last sentence of the fragment welding italicized and nonitalicized characters, English and French, as well as the exclamatory mode concluding both columns. The two distinct enunciations are thus brought together in a confusing utterance reminiscent of the techniques of displacement and substitution used by a painter such as Magritte in his famous oil on canvas entitled *Le viol* (*The rape*) and dated 1945. Likewise, Durrell plays on the monstrous and disquieting analogy between mouth and sex to suggest one of man's recurring fantasies of consummation and castration and relies on the simultaneous paradoxical feelings of desire and fear triggered by the scopic drive. The reader is therefore brought into the realm of the "unbridled fantastic" defined by Bakhtin:

> The unbridled fantastic is of paramount importance, which explains how it can build up verbal syntagms. . . . All its word combinations, even those that appear to be objectively utterly devoid of meaning, aim at destroying the hierarchy of established values, at belittling the great, at annihilating the customary image of the world in every detail.[16]

Durrell's writing appropriates language to perform its own annihilation and unveil through its collapsing forms and meaning the "twilight kingdom"[17] wherefrom a new meaning may emerge that is not given but remains to be elaborated and reinvented within a new order where the struggle of the poetic endeavor is the only thing that endures. Thus the "customary image of the [textual] world"[18] is jeopardized: the narrator who purports to make sense and to found a new order gives birth to a self-destructive text that brings him back to the beginning. This double impetus of destruction and creation is the object of Henry Miller's admiration when he first discovers Vega:

> Dear Larry—
> Am reading slowly and thoughtfully your poems in *Vega* and am overwhelmed by the use of language you permit yourself. It's almost frightening. . . .
> For me it's like jumping suddenly from ordinary arithmetics to integral calculus.
> . . .
>
> P.S. I like those French lines you inserted occasionally.
>
> P.P.S. I think the whole bloody book is a tour de force. Vive le poète![19]

Henry Miller embodies the ideal watchful and patient reader Durrell had been calling forth since *The Quartet* when he wrote: "In a book of poems: 'One to be taken from time to time as needed and allowed to dissolve in the mind.'"[20] He is the one who allows himself to be moved by the forces of language, by the primal idleness that is, according to critic Clive Scott, the touchstone of Durrell's poetics:

> a nonchalance at an angle to being, a gift of, and a response to a particular kind of being. . . . in these unmotivated and disengaged acts, we begin to feel that consciousness is on the *qui vive*, is stalking the off-chance, the hoped-for elicitation which will take us to the heart of things, to a perception of presence, of expanded being. . . . Idleness in its optimal manifestation is akin to the state expressed by the Arab word *kayf* (*Bitter Lemons* 39), "the contemplation which comes of silence and ease" (68). But idleness also has to do with the uncontrolled, the improvisations of reality, those things which move us in another direction unexpectedly . . .[21]

Miller is not just touched by the poet's idleness: he is also carried into a new perception of language and of the world, as the potent simile of the jump "from ordinary arithmetics to integral calculus" suggests. This floating attention to reality ushers in new horizons that lead the subject away from the elementary level of reckoning to another dimension: a panoramic vision that integrates the curved line of the universe. And as a true reader, Henry Miller enters this moving universe and plays in turn with the "improvisations of reality"[22] to offer Durrell a poetic response:

> I never knew, until I read
> you
>
> That a poem is a renunciation of
> language, at least as most of
> us understand the term.
> I never realized that words could
> exist separately and brutally
>
> That the way a flower, crushed or
> uncrushed, lies upon the paving,
> has meaning and beyond that,
> makes music, albeit for assassins,
> monsters, idiots.
>
> I did not understand that
> you could call your shots, dis-
> regard all rules, ethics, meta-

physics.
. . .
or—
Completely deny all reason, all intelligence, all kindness and consideration and babble like a lost baboon.[23]

Durrell's writing experiments with renunciation and disjunction and composes a secret music from chance encounters, blurred forms, and fragmentary meaning to elaborate his personal poetry of revolt. Henry Miller's verse is not a mere homage to the poet but also enlightens the reader on the complex strata of Durrell's poetics, allowing him to glance at the underlying unity of the artist's quest: "The poetic form expresses what is most intimate, most profound in man as he relates to the world. . . . Poetry is all a question of density. . . . poetry is a way of breathing."[24]

Vega testifies to this vital search for the breath of poetry.

Learning the Cryptic Breath

The French poet Henri Michaux defined poetry as "what enables those who are suffocating to breathe"[25]; some thirty years later Paul Celan asserted "Poetry: this may mean a turning point in breath."[26] *Vega* offers another "way of breathing"[27] starting with a deep inspiration—the first twenty-one poems ending *The Red Limbo Lingo*—that serves as a springboard to the last eighteen poems completing the collection. This prolonged inspiration that brings back and withholds the previous poems and finally gives the impetus for the second part of the collection delivering the new poems is reminiscent of the techniques of Pranayama, the Hindu art of breath control. It relies on the end of the preceding breath cycle and starts with a deep, long, and slow inspiration that gives its lively momentum to expiration. The composition of this last collection conjures up a peaceful cycle in which the end signals a perpetual renewal and opens up to the initiates: "But cryptic as a breath / One crystal changed its hue; / Thus words in music drown."[28] The poem revolves around itself like a dark crystal to unveil in a breath a mysterious world where words are carried away by music, as if summoned to be reborn in a new form. It is highly significant that *Vega* should and should not be at the same time Durrell's final poetic opus, as it is both the last public collection and the harbinger of a private publication, *Lifelines*, followed by the widely acclaimed *Collected Poems*. As such, *Vega* materializes the inner, peaceful breath that rules the flow of poetic energy and accounts for the poetic insights seeping into Durrell's later prose, such as *The Quintet* and *Caesar's Vast Ghost*. Simultaneously, *Vega* also reads like the poet's final farewell.

Starting with "The Reckoning" the collection brings us back to the unconscious limbo that precedes language. The porous time line ("Timeless as water into language flowing"),[29] the steady and soothing rhythm that mimics the perfect balance between the infinite and the finite ("'As below, darling, so above.'"),[30] the renunciation to rational understanding ("It is not meaning that we need but sight")[31] belong to a new breath that shapes out the harmonious flow of writing whereby the poetic subject frees himself from material contingencies to imagine a renewed relation to the world. Acting as a truly initiatory poem, "The Reckoning" reiterates the experience of *The Red Limbo Lingo* and offers the reader a deeper, more subtle breathing anchored in a repetitive pattern that puts to the fore an embodied memory. Indeed, the mere repetition of the last poems of *The Red Limbo Lingo* endows the beginning of *Vega* with a specific texture: they become the space of a poetic (re)enactment, of a mnemonic as well as of a bodily incorporation. When rereading "The Reckoning" in *Vega* the reader has already internalized the need for "sight" and the absence of "meaning" that *The Red Limbo Lingo* asserted. The repetition of the poem is then not so much the repetition of a text as the repetition of a singular practice that consists in reiterating the quest for a heraldic vision anchored in the deliberate renunciation to meaning, in the acceptance of "contradictions" and "warring fictions," in the awareness that there can be no "reckoning" because there can be no *telos* but only repeated cycles. But if there is no apocalypse, no final revelation, there can only be an ongoing, self-reflexive quest that defines the poem as being "made of what we are walking to, what we do not know, what we withdraw from, and whose knowledge is vital."[32]

As Durrell's reader resumes his task, he understands that the repetition serves one vital purpose: discovering the path that will lead him out of the infinite cycle of desires ("Desires in all their motions")[33] and further into a poetic quest that opens up awareness. He thus becomes part of that collective subject through which Durrell joins Michaux as well as the implied reader: "We were touching that dharmic presence of poetic thought, its cocoon so to speak. The very concept which shaped reality and which dictated psychic growth."[34]

Poetry is thus understood as a lifelong quest that attempts to grasp the passage from "psychic growth" to "reality," the underlying "presence" that dictates personal and cosmic harmony and that Pranayama also seeks. The first half of *Vega* thus offers a second chance, akin to a second life that recalls the many reincarnated characters in Durrell's novels. Looking back upon the past writing allows the reader to gaze at the images that have settled down, like so many mnemonic strata that are the true soil of poetic sensibility. Reading explicitly conflates with remembering as the text performs the perpetual resurgence of the undying poetic breath nurtured both by repetition and expansion, after the manner of the refrain described by Deleuze and Guattari:

> the refrain is a prism, a crystal of space-time. It acts upon that which surrounds it, sound or light, extracting from its various vibrations, or decompositions, projections, or transformations. The refrain also has a catalytic function: not only to increase the speed of the exchanges and reactions in that which surrounds it, but also to assure indirect interactions between elements devoid of so-called natural affinity . . . thus the little phrase from Vinteuil's sonata is associated with Swann's love, the character of Odette, and the landscape of the Bois de Boulogne for a long time, until it turns back on itself, opens onto itself, revealing until then unheard-of potentialities, entering into new connections, setting love adrift in the direction of other assemblages. Here Time is not an a priori form; rather, the refrain is the a priori form of time, which in each case fabricates different times.[35]

The poetic refrain enters all the more freely "into new connections" as it is disconnected from a narrative line. It echoes and expands through reading and rereading and imprints its own internal rhythm upon the eye and the ear since the reader necessarily entertains a dual relation to the poetic voice leading him, as Christian Doumet explains, to "envisage written matter as an object of listening—a listening mediated by the eye. 'Poetry is designed for a listening eye,' as Jacques Roubaud said . . ."[36] The poetic refrain embraces silence—the silence of a voice that patiently transcribes rhythmic and prosodic devices, continuous and discontinuous patterns, as well as the silence of the reader opening up to listen to that voice where he encounters his own self but that he cannot circumscribe. "The voice of the poem is neither here nor there," Christian Doumet adds, "it lies in the passage, the transfer, the metaphor from one to the other. Phonation is not its complete fulfillment: it is only an image."[37] The poetic refrain follows musical and mnemonic, symbolic, and silent associations that unfurl as so many "unheard-of potentialities," not unlike the solitary "footprints in the New York snow."[38] The refrain ushers in the song that breaks from the mold—as "Swimmers" suggests: "While poems in their cages sing"[39]—and that can scarcely be heard. This vibrant silence, which Christian Doumet describes as "the vocal persistence of the dead . . . at the heart of the living's rumination,"[40] evinces what fails to reach our senses: the hidden facet of the prism, this out-of-bounds space-time signifying the ontological openness of poetry.

Just as the "book-lined walls"[41] that unveil the networks of infinite contemplation ("I finger the sex of many an uncut book"),[42] the poem reasserts its impossible closure by placing the poet and the reader in front of multiple possible "assemblages." Thus, the poem "Lake Music," which finds its parodic reassemblage in the second half of the collection under the title "Apesong," is composed as a network of multiple combinations and junctions:

> Deep waters hereabouts.
> We could quit caring.
> Deep waters darling
> We could stop feeling.
> You could stop sharing
> . . .
> We could abandon supposing
> We could quit knowing
> Where we have come from
> Where we are going.[43]

The simple prosody alternating spondees and trochees on lines 1 and 3, relying on anaphoras and flat rhymes as well as on simple sentences, is redolent of the "childhood or bird refrain" that Deleuze and Guattari analyze as "a first type of refrain, a territorial or assemblage refrain [that music carries along] in order to transform it from within, to deterritorialize it, producing a refrain of the second type as the final end of music: the cosmic refrain of a sound machine."[44] The childhood refrain of "Lake Music" entails its own deterritorialization as the poem moves from death to rebirth. The "deep waters" of death turn into "This lustful anointing," and water becomes an intimate element through the shift from "Deep waters darling" on l.3 to "the deep water moving" on l.14. Abandoning himself to water, the subject abandons himself to a performative love that brings life back: "The beautiful grenades" metaphorizing the woman's breasts suggest Aphrodite's fecundity as well as the myth of Persephone seduced by Hades.[45] However, although the pomegranate seed operates in the Greek myth as an evil spell, it also connotes "the spark of chtonian fire Persephone steals for the greater good of mankind"[46] each time she comes back upon the earth to visit her mother. Therefore the pomegranate in the poem paves the way for the metamorphosis of the lover's body into a symbol of death and rebirth as her bodily materiality progressively falls apart in an upward surge ("Breasts up to lips and eyes") that finally leads to the welding of the material and the impalpable: "The vertebrae of believing." The lover's body no longer exists as such but as the sign of a recovered faith, of a hope beyond knowledge anchored in the initiatory powers of the word expounded by Durrell: ". . . the symbol is initiatory and not didactic . . ."[47] "This lustful anointing" transforms the death refrain into a refrain for life by reverting the linear, deathly drift of time, the beginning and the end: "Where we have come from / Where we are going." It conveys the sacred anointing of a harmonious connection that ushers in a new mode of being through the renunciation of the flesh and of the mind that defeats the *telos* of history. The childhood refrain branches off into a mystic one to be reterritorialized in *The Quintet* where Sylvie and Bruce, following their gnostic initiation in the desert, join hands in the waters of Lake Macabru:

> I walked towards the looking-glass of the lake, eager to see my own reflection in it as if in some curious way I expected to have changed, to have altered in my physical appearance. . . . I broke into a run along the margins of the lake, looking sideways to see my reflection racing through the massed spear-points of the reeds. . . . I swam out of my depth and turned over to let the sun fire a million silver drops of prismatic light on to my wet eyelashes. . . . Our wet fingers touched and we formed a circle like the corolla of a flower, floating into the silence of the desert dawn with the ancient sun on our bodies. It lasted a long time, this swim which seemed to have some of the qualities of an esoteric act of lustration. . . .
>
> It was like an extension of our loving—a sort of new tropical flora and fauna, a private country in which we wandered now, luxuriating in all its poetic beauty and variety.[48]

The initiatory journey ends on the early revelation refracted in a mirror of a lake that gives birth to the future poet: the character's hallucinatory undoubling conveys the birth of a new gaze in the fragmented prism of dawn. Foreshadowing the poet's renewed vision Blanford will embody later on in Constance,[49] the narrator's gaze upon his own reflection paves the way for the harmonic welding of shapes and sounds in the mystic flower composed by Bruce, Piers, and Sylvie, floating between desert and sky and sheltering in its silent corolla the eternity of sensible experience.

Spiritual and aesthetic revelations thus become intimately linked both in Durrell's novels and poems. Writing is an initiatory experience and a spiritual journey that allows us to glance, if only fleetingly, at a new world lying across the unmapped shore where causality and time have been vanquished. Because the poem is divested of logic and narrative bonds and blends in with the free association of shapes, echoes, rhythms, and images, marrying the concrete and the abstract ("pockets of mischance," "vertebrae of believing"), it is undoubtedly the most adequate means to convey a spontaneous insight into the patterns and cadences of life. It is a direct experience of linguistic, literary, aesthetic, and ontological forms and meanings that opens up the subject to a new relation to the world symbolized in Durrell's novels, poems, and essays by the recurring image of the rose that diffracts *ad infinitum* T. S. Eliot's "Multifoliate rose."[50] Thus, Durrell explains in *Key to Modern Poetry*:

> It is a great pity that we cannot inhale a poem like scents. . . . Let them be totals to experience first of all; then afterwards see if your brains and your reading cannot add to the first impression and support it.
> . . . in the last analysis great poetry reflects an unknown in the interpretation and understanding of which all knowledge is refunded into ignorance. It points towards a Something which itself subsists without distinction . . . At its lowest power you can find the faculty in the nickname or the nursery rhyme: at its highest it reflects a metaphysical reality about ourselves and the world.[51]

The lovers entering the waters of desire are thus bound to resurface and flower, sinking into the reader's memory only to be brought back between the lines and give rise to a unique, unchartered space-time that borrows its associative logic from the world of dreams, as Durrell himself suggests in his analysis of Woolf's *Jacob's Room*: "Poetry and prose alike began to borrow the colours of the dream, and the new ideas of time can be seen in the loosening causal connections of the action."[52] This literary interpretation highlights Durrell's own modernist experiment.

Thus, in *Vega*, the images of "the New York snow,"[53] that of Spain in the shadow of El Greco in "Rain, Rain, Go to Spain," of Aphrodite in "Aphros Meaning Spume," or of the solitary poet in "A Winter of Vampires," "Pistol Weather," "Stoic," "One Place," "Revenants," "Joss," "Avignon," "Incognito," "Swimmers," and "Blue" function as so many echoes of a past refrain. Poetry operates as the prism of an unnamed reality at the heart of which new connections can be dreamed that revive and reshape writing to produce what Deleuze calls "a crystal of space-time."[54] *Vega* explores the scattered fragments of a conscience that moves up and down the spiraling staircase of free associations, memories, and questions haunting the mind to deploy the new, unfettered temporality announced in "Incognito": "time is boundless."[55]

The superimposition of shimmering, fleeting shadows from one collection to the next, from one poem to the next, contributes to this uniform, boundless temporality that unfolds as in a dream and that "Incognito" brings about through the deliberate blurring of voices and figures. The first-person plural ("Outside us smoulder the great / World issues about which nothing /

Can be done, at least by us two;")[56] encompassing the poet and his beloved gives way to the first-person singular, detached from the lover, and observing through darkness the forlorn figure of the street girl ("Remind her that time is boundless, / And for call-girls like business-men, money")[57] whose walking shadow entices the reader's memory to drift back toward the many forsaken lovers haunting Durrell's prose and poetry:

> Redeem pleasure, then, with a proximate
> Love—. . .
>
> Her darkness, her eye are both typical
> Of a region long since plunged into
> Historic ruin; yet disinherited, she doesn't care
> Being perfect both as person and as thing.

Symbolically, the dark, night-clad figure enlightens the entire poem. This mysterious shade conjures up a crowd of past yet vibrant characters: Melissa, Justine, Iolanthe, whose silent presence brings back to life the ruins of a dead world: ". . . the ruins / Of man's estate, death of all goodness, / Lie entombed with me here in this / Oldfashioned but convincing death-bed."[58] This symbolic shroud is the birthplace of a new poetic breath: "All winter now I shall lie suffocating / Under the debris of this thought."[59] The poet thus pictures himself on the margins of time, belonging to and stepping out of historical time, what lies "Outside us," the better to enter a creative inner time, "Inside, the smaller area of a life." This accounts for the systematic confrontation throughout the poem of finite time and matter on the one hand ("business-men, money," "Historic ruin") and, on the other hand, of the infinite, the "boundless," woven together by the poet's "I." The poetic voice therefore embodies the "fracture" described by Giorgio Agamben:

> The poet, as our contemporary, is this fracture, the one who prevents time from merging, and, at the same time, he is the blood healing the scar. . . .
> The poet—the contemporary—must gaze at time. . . . the contemporary is the one who gazes at his own time in order to descry not its light but its darkness.[60]

At the heart of darkness the desired and lost woman, abandoned and found anew, simultaneously lover, goddess and vampire, woman child and street girl, keeps haunting the reader's eye, "Flickering on the retina"[61] like the star that presides over the entire collection. "Her darkness, her eye" materializes the gap, the dark pupil that snatches the poet's eye and filters an invisible light through which the regions of the past are brought back into the living present. The poet thus inhabits that in-between realm where stars do not lighten up the darkness but, paradoxically, make it deeper. As a victim of "Historic ruin" he is both "suffocating / Under the debris of this thought" and conjuring out of his helplessness the breath of a new hope.

Vega is thus akin to the luminous clouds of stardust described by Agamben:

> Within the expanding universe, far away galaxies move away from us at such great speed that their light cannot reach us. The darkness we behold in the sky is this light travelling at great speed towards us but nevertheless failing to reach us because it belongs to galaxies that move away at a velocity greater than the speed of light.
>
> Catching sight in the present darkness of that light aiming for us and failing, such is the meaning of being contemporaries. . . .
>
> Our time, the present, is in fact not only what is most distant from us: it can never reach us. Its backbone is broken and we stand exactly at the point of fracture.[62]

The entire collection, split between the former writing of *A Red Limbo Lingo* and the forthcoming one, embodies this fracture between the not more and the not yet and simultaneously stages the past and the advent of the poetic breath that may well fail to reach us but whose absent light nevertheless infringes upon darkness.

Hence the symptomatic presence of the poem entitled "?" in the first half of the collection. The very title of the poem places the poetic voice at "the point of fracture" between the present and the past, the question and the answer, the questioner and the addressee, the incomprehensible and the comprehensible. Henry Miller's lines on poetry are thus forcefully brought back to mind: "a poem is a renunciation / of language . . . / you could . . . / Completely deny all reason, all / intelligence, all kindness and con- / sideration and babble like a lost / baboon."[63]

Right from the start, "?" is indeed an emblematic case of the "renunciation / of language": it is the unpronounceable sign that testifies to the meaninglessness of the sign, the point when linguistics and semantics collapse. The poem thus invites the reader to explore the hidden side of language and allow himself to be seduced and transformed by a sign that paradoxically denies its own essence, as Meschonnic has argued:

> The poem does not belong to the world of signs.
>   The poem teaches us not to use language any more. . . .
>   But the poem transforms us into a specific subject-form. It carves within us a subject that could not exist without it. And this is done through language.[64]

The first two lines of "?" are particularly striking as they only deepen the mystery of the title:

> Waters rebribing a new moon are all
> Dissenting mirrors ending in themselves.
>
> Go away, leave me alone.[65]

This imperious tone pleading for solitude and silence violently disrupts the poetic flow, as if the poet's voice attempted to break apart from these entrapping refractions that can have no beginning nor end and preexist the poem itself. Beyond the neologism and the surprising use of the verb "bribe," "rebribing" spurs the reader to look for the initial occurrence of the action of "bribing," which is surprisingly to be discovered at the end, on l.19–20:

> And waters bribing a new moon are all
> The flesh's memories beyond recall.[66]

This image is as disquieting as the earlier one, and the nearly faultless repetition of the first line that seems designed to strengthen the structural, formal coherence of the text only makes it more incoherent from the point of view of semantics. Its overall structure expands the mirror effects, sending the reader from the beginning to the end and vice versa and jeopardizing any rational interpretation. The poem traps the reader in an ironic, unfathomable logic that deprives the reader of his own abilities, as Durrell has explained in *Key to Modern Poetry*: "in the last analysis great poetry reflects an unknown in the interpretation and understanding of which all knowledge is refunded into ignorance."[67] Thus Durrell invites his reader to experiment with the unknown and go against his time:

> People don't want the experience
> Any more: they want an explanation,
> How you go about it, when and why.

Such an assertion is in keeping with Agamben's reading of our modern era in his analysis of Walter Benjamin's 1933 exposure of "the poverty of experience":

> For just as the modern man has been deprived of his biography, he has also been dispossessed of his experience—and his incapacity to convey experiences may well be one of the rare certainties he can hold about his own condition . . .
> It is indeed our present incapacity to translate our daily life into experience that makes it unbearable. . . .

Experimentation—the scientific foundation of experience that ensures the rational transformation of sensitive impressions into exact quantitative reckonings and, hence, the anticipation of future impressions—meets this loss of certainty by displacing experience as much as possible outside man, into instruments and figures.[68]

Poetry thus goes against the times and uses as "instruments and figures" meter, rhythm, and syntax, images and tropes that paradoxically rely on mundane experience to usher in the unknown. Thus, the third stanza simultaneously relies upon and disrupts the iambic tetrameter by inserting choriambuses on l.4 and 7.[69] The iambic rhythm also falters in the second hemistich of l.6 as the colons open up onto the unknown: a "confession" that fails to explain or exonerate. Simultaneously, the rhyme scheme disrupts the unity of the stanza through the echoes linking l.1, 7, and 8[70] as well as l.19 and 20.[71] In the third stanza "explanation" on l.10 rhymes with "confession" on l.6. Syntactic logic also founders through the juxtaposition of conflicting space adverbials ("everywhere nearby" l.4) or the handling of appositions. Thus l.6 reads as an apposition to l.5: "So full of fervent need the mouth / The jewelry of smiling. . . ." The indefinite pronoun "Someone" at the beginning of the previous line is summed up in "the mouth" petrified into a jewel of a smile. This mouth betrays the hypocrisy of our times and the "confession" it delivers—"Tidemarks of old intentions' dying fall"—conveys no justification, but only the poet's twofold homage to Shakespeare and T. S. Eliot. The reader is thus simultaneously brought back to the first scene of act 1 in *Twelfth Night* ("That strain again; it had a dying fall")[72] and *The Love Song of J. Alfred Prufrock*:

> For I have known them all already, known them all—
> Have known the evenings, mornings, afternoons,
> I have measured out my life with coffee spoons;
> I have known the voices dying with a dying fall
> Beneath the music from a farther room.[73]

This metatextual fabric includes Durrell's poem "The Dying Fall," published twenty years before in *The Tree of Idleness*[74] and blurring even further the poetic space-time and persona.

The last line of the third stanza—"Surely that is all now, that is all?"[75]—suggests the unredeemable estrangement of the poet uttering a final plea for a possible reversal. The interrogative abolishes all certainty and introduces a questioning relation to the world. The syntactic mirror effect of the two hemistichs places the reader in front of a stuttering language that hinders progress and prompts him to distrust his own reading. Through the anonymous figure of "someone," both "everywhere" and "nearby," and whose gaping mouth explains nothing but summons instead the echoes of past voices, the reader feels displaced, thrown out of bounds into an experience of *déjà vu* that keeps dismantling the sign.

The poem both fathoms and explodes syntactic, prosodic, and literary knowledge so as to make way for a mnemonic and sensitive experience that materializes the frailty of language, the fluidity of form and meaning, the inconstancy of past textual echoes, the advent of possible connections. Far from answering the questions it raises, the poem heightens and extols the experience of uncertainty and offers itself as the ideal place for an ontological questioning. "Surely that is all now, that is all?"[76] foreshadows the final ironic question in the penultimate line: "Which witch? Which witch? Witch!"[77] Poetic writing would thus amount to a witch's trick, the charm of words and sounds combining homonyms and mirror effects to tear us from old, erroneous certainties and prepare us for the ultimate experience that may be perceived but cannot be named:

> But all you can say is: Look, it's manifest
> And nobody's to blame: it has no name.

This central distich operates as a hinge in the reflexive process that characterizes the entire poem. Echoing the first and last stanzas, this distich relies on the perfect mirror effect of the four hemistichs on each side of the colons. The first line relies on a surprising reversal: it opens on an iamb followed by a trochee and a dactyl. Yet the second line is a regular pentameter and includes an internal rhyme. The reader thus experiences the disquieting sensation of walking through the looking-glass to encounter death, which Agamben reading Montaigne analyzes as the ultimate experience:

> Traditional experience . . . faithfully upholds the distinction between science and experience, between human and divine knowledge. It is precisely the experience of the limits separating both spheres. This limit is death. This is why approaching death is, for Montaigne, the ultimate purpose of experience: man reaches maturity by anticipating death as the extreme limit of experience. Such a limit can only be approached, not experienced . . .[78]

The following stanza opens onto a beyond that can only be approached by trespassing upon the boundaries of the self and of known time:

> Spades touch a buried city,
> Calm bodies suffocated by ashes

> It happened so quickly there was no time,
> Their minds were overrun
> The sentry stiffened over a jammed gun[79]

Poetry pushes further the limits of human experience by calling the sign itself into question. The buried city conjures up Alexandria, the City of Memory,[80] as well as all the other Durrellian cities. It stands out both as the bygone city and as T. S. Eliot's "Unreal City"[81] breaking through the surface of writing. The poem thus rises from the point of fracture between the dead and the living, the real and the imagined, as a shared instrument to approach what cannot be uttered: the essence of the voice(s) haunting the text and setting it in motion, simultaneously revealing and concealing the poet's voice—not to be confused with the author's voice—welding prophecy and memory and projecting itself out of time and space:

> The voice may have come from a cloud
> But more likely the garden's wet planes
> A bird or a woman calling in the mist
> Asking if anything remains, and if so
>
> Which witch? Which witch? Witch!
> I am the only one who knows.[82]

This unidentified voice combines with a disjointed syntax as the elision of the preposition "from" on the second line paves the way for the breaking up of the sentence in the last stanza and introduces another "dissenting mirror" in the disjunctive distich where the reader searches in vain for an improbable answer. The final line subsumes the irony of such a quest in the implicit pun on the true identity of the first person. Indeed, the "I" should not be mistaken for the poet: it is a fluctuating, ungraspable voice that "may have come from a cloud / But more likely the garden's wet planes / A bird or a woman."[83] It is the embodiment of the irrepresentable, unassigned subject as defined by Agamben in his reading of Benveniste:

> Benveniste shows that it is in fact impossible to refer to "an immediate representation" and to an "individual concept" that each subject would have of him/herself. . . . the subject exists "through discourse," . . . it is nothing else but the projection onto man of the discursive system of shifters . . .[84]

Therefore, the speaking "I" may be considered as referring neither to the poet nor to the reader: it is not so much a subject as a pure voice belonging to the textual space-time that begins and ends with its utterance. Its fate is to grow away from the page, swallowed by the silence of the poem and swallowing, in turn, any hope of transcending knowledge—unless, the knowledge sought after by poet and reader alike lay precisely in the confined silence of a self-enclosed meditation symbolized by the circular eye rhyme in "o."

Likewise, the overall structure of *Vega* thus takes us from the known to the unknown and relies on the reader's inner resources. This is why the last poem from *The Red Limbo Lingo* takes on an altogether different meaning when placed at the hinge between the first and last parts of *Vega*. By inserting "Envoi" at the heart of *Vega*, the poem stresses the crucial role devoted to the end: it is both the end point and a new departure, the welcoming of a final silence and the birth of a new breath rising from silence—

> Be silent, old frog.
> Let God compound the issue as he must,
> And dog eat dog
> Unto the final desecration of man's dust.
> The just will be devoured by the unjust.[85]

The sequence of enclosed rhymes followed by a couplet and the combination of short and long lines enhancing the symmetrical iambic pentameters on lines 2 and 5 concur to the illusion of a perfect ending. The poem thus reads as a twofold ending within *The Red Limbo Lingo* where it concludes the collection and answers the final question raised in the penultimate poem, "Mistral": "Where will I next be when the mistral / Rises in sullen trumpets on the hills of bone?"[86] However, once displaced in *Vega*, "Envoi" no longer signifies the end but rather the reversal of the end into a new beginning and highlights the peculiar nature of the poetic ending that is, so to speak, expelled from the poem. Agamben invites us to pay attention to poetic devices such as the envoi

> that seem to be solely aimed at signifying, almost enunciating, the end of the poem, as if the latter needed it, as if the end entailed for the poem such a disastrous catastrophe and identity loss as to call for the use of very specific metric and semantic ploys.
> ... poets seem to be aware that there lies here a decisive crisis for the poem, a true *verse crisis* that jeopardizes its very substance.[87]

In *Vega*, as in Durrell's last cycle of novels, *The Quintet*, this crisis is conveyed through a specific closure that is both "twofold and illusory since it throws the reader into the outer margins of the text where, thanks to his interpretative work, he will carry on the work beyond what the author has written and will go back to the text to pursue and expand it without really putting an end to it."[88]

Thus, unsurprisingly, "Envoi" is echoed at the end of *Vega* by the concluding poem "Seferis." This homage to Durrell's Greek friend, who died in Athens two years before the publication of *Vega*, reads as a second ending. This eulogy celebrates the great poet who inspired Durrell and whose poetry he started translating as early as 1948. It extols both the ongoing surge of poetic life in "A new Greek fire ignited by your pen"[89] and the acceptance of death ("So tilting into darkness go we must")[90] through which a poetic brotherhood and lineage is born. The poet contemplating the dispersion of his work is reminiscent of Blanford in *The Quintet* and embraces in his meditative posture the entire structure of the collection that celebrates, through the representation of death and dissemination, the invincible onrush of life:

> Thus the fading writer signing off
> Sees in the vast perspectives of dispersal
> His words float off like tiny seeds,
> Wind-borne or bird-distributed notes,
> To the very end of loves without rehearsal,
> The stinging image riper than his deeds.[91]

Germinating words, lines turning to music, the lively sting of the poetic image replace the poet's fading figure and the poetic gesture that dissolves, borne away by wind or birds, entering an elsewhere that preexists creation and is simultaneously conveyed by creation. Such a pattern precludes any ending since writing keeps drifting away in order to point to what lies beyond, well after the poet's demise:

> How marvellous to have done it and then left
> It in the lost property office of the loving mind,
> The secret whisper those who listen find.[92]

"Seferis" invites the reader to listen to this "secret whisper" and to bring the poem back to life and simultaneously propels him "into the outer margins of the text"[93] by constantly reinventing itself. The final line ushers in an endless beginning and opens up what Clea called "the kingdom of [the] imagination"[94]: ". . . even to die is somehow to invent."[95] The unspeakable that eludes the linguistic sign and guides the reader's eye toward the blank page facing the last poem paves the way for an elsewhere that belongs to both the poet's and the reader's imagination and is their true symbolic dwelling, where the distant echoes of Durrell's as well as Seferis's past poems keep ringing. Thus, the reader is brought to remember the 1939 poem "Les Anges Sont Blancs" dedicated by Seferis to Henry Miller and extolling loss and dispersion as the very principle of the life-giving force of writing.[96] According to Seferis, the miracle of poetry is none other than its circulation through language(s)—since Seferis borrows his title from Balzac—and through the reader, who therefore becomes both the subject and the place of passage and enjoys a symbolic as well as a symbiotic relation to the poem. The poem thus appears as the ideal mode of expression of the exilic subject since it cannot be anchored in a specific time, place, or source of enunciation: it is everywhere.[97] Durrell's poem is an invitation to journey along with Seferis, toward the remote horizons of an unbounded writing that crosses secular and linguistic borders. Like Seferis's, Durrell's poetry unfurls as a "logbook" into an unchartered territory where our only guide is the intellectual nomad as defined by Kenneth White:

> . . . he is the bearer of at least the beginnings of new language and new space. He has broken his way out of the labyrinth and moves in what may at first seem a void, but which is perhaps the high-energy field in which could emerge a (new) world.
> What if we tried to enter it subtly, getting rid of ourselves (our heavy selves) as we gradually move across and into the territory?
> Poetic meditations.
> Cosmo-poetic meditations. . . . And a cosmic consciousness, where there is no separation between the self and the world, but an experience of continuity.[98]

The second half of *Vega* is subsumed in this farewell hymn that passes through us and constantly displaces us, calling through death for "an experience of continuity."

The Heraldic Smile

The poems "Last Heard of," "The Outer Limits," and "A Farewell" introduce, in the early part of the second section of *Vega*, the slow death march that develops throughout many other poems such as "Confederate" ("now you tell me / It is time for those last few words"),[99] "Want to Live Don't You?" (ending on the last word concluding Durrell's ultimate poem in his final work: "goodbye"),[100] "Cicada" ("Transparent sheath of the dead cicada"),[101] "The Muses" (closing upon "the bullet in the neck"),[102] and finally "Vega," the love poem that rings like an echo to "The Grey Penitents." Just as "The Grey Penitents," "Vega" intertwines the motifs of the lover's separation and of death: "Ah! The beautiful sail so unerringly on towards death / Once they experience the pith of this peerless calm."[103]

The entire collection seems to aim for this absolute experience, for a horizon that focuses the gaze on the unfathomable that lies beyond the vanishing line, as Michel Collot has explained:

> What draws the eye towards the horizon is not what it reveals but the fact that it opens up a boundless perspective upon the invisible. This boundless perspective coincides for the poet with a loss of the self, a descent into the inner depths that elude the eye of conscience. This abysmal experience belongs rather to the field of feeling or sensation than to perception. . . .
>
> The feeling of depth experienced by the poet implies a double bottom: that of the landscape seemingly deepening over there in infinite space, but also that of his own body that both anchors him here and projects him into the distance . . .[104]

"Vega" exemplifies this shift from outer to inner space. The first stanza conjures up the Italian lakes whose lines and colors sharply contrast with Languedoc. The landscape superimposes the cutting edges of solid colors. Green is the only explicit one (lines 1 and 8) and catalyzes the entire landscape in the first stanza by emphasizing the chromatic hues of the surrounding elements. Thus the "thirst for green" ushers in the implicit blue of "water," gray of "the stone garrigues," then again the blue of "this lake" until blue and green implicitly merge in the "slopes of water" (l.7). This briefly polychromatic composition dissolves in the all-embracing, pleonastic "green verdure" (l.8) that swallows all other colors before the night swoops upon earth and sky, temporarily abolishing distance and depth: "All on a dark floor, the sincere flavour of stars . . ." (l.9).

The ellipsis foreshadows the structural and thematic reversal whereby the poem sheds its pastoral tone and descriptive mode and opts for a dialogic form in stanzas 2 and 3. But this reversal is a mere illusion: line 10 introduces a deepening landscape—"This we called Vega, a sly map reference"—that sends the reader back to the first stanza before returning to the infinite abyss of the night in stanza 4. Therefore, despite the explicit anchorage in a realistic space and a dialogue that ushers in a narrative tone, the love encounter belongs neither to real space nor time:

> The fixed star of the ancients was another Vega,
> A candle burning high in the alps of heaven,
> Shielded by rosy fingers on some sill

> Above some darkly sifted lake. They also knew
> This silence trying to perfect itself in words.
>
> Ah! The beautiful sail so unerringly on towards death
> Once they experience the pith of this peerless calm.[105]

The apparition of Vega—the beloved woman and the star—takes us beyond the confines of our known world and signals a break from the horizontal to-and-fro movement of "The little train" in the first half of the poem. The earth and sky deepen and meet "in the alps of heaven," opening up the text to a cosmic dimension that cannot be bound in words but only exists in a contemplation that is mediated but never framed by language. It eludes perception but seeps through the deepening breath of the penultimate stanza shifting from the iambic pentameter to the hexameter. The journey into silence and death is thus endowed with a sensible reality that welds the eternal light of Lyra, the white star Vega, and the slow, peaceful rhythm of the last distich based on ternary feet. The anapests of the penultimate line mirror the dactyls of the last one while the isolated last foot combines with the soft plosives of the last line to further deepen the space of the poetic voice. Classical prosody is thus used by Durrell both as a means of giving the poem a rhythmic anchorage and as the latent memory of an ancient form that fleetingly resurfaces in his free verse to suggest a hidden presence, an invisible depth wherefrom the distant echoes of a perfect harmony still reach out to us. As Clive Scott has explained, this is another instance of the close intertextuality linking Durrell and T. S. Eliot's verse:

> This "principle," whereby the poet can withdraw from regularity or return to it at any point, may have come to Durrell through Eliot and his comment in "Reflections on *Vers Libre*" (1917) on "the ghost of some simple metre," which "should lurk behind the arras in even the 'freest' verse; to advance menacingly as we doze, and withdraw as we rouse . . ."[106]

The perfect harmony aimed at by Durrell thus welds the natural and the literary worlds by building up a chain of poets whose voices join across time and space to convey "the pith of this peerless calm."

Interestingly, the poem "Want to Live Don't You?" plays on a similar reversal of space as the realistic "public gardens" with their "benches," "children," "municipal orchestra," and "prams" finally give way to a dislocated landscape:

> Somewhere in all this grace and favour green
> . . .
> Under the braying foliage mimeographed

> Like the Lord's Prayer for a computer
> In this fate-forgiven corner of reflection
> The genetic twilight of a race evolves:
> Dreaming in codes, you only think you think.[107]

The poet is addressing all those living on borrowed time who believe themselves to be alive while they are only the pale shadows of a dead world where machines are designed to fake life. The various inversions and syntactic mirroring such as the question tag in the title or the repetition of the subject and predicate in the last line are mimetic of the mimeograph that duplicates flat copies of the world, not unlike Abel, the computer in Durrell's *The Revolt of Aphrodite*. At the heart of this artificial world the encounter of "a pair of fine eyes looking out" is the only source of hope. Yet it is a gaze "so full / Of an immense and complicated mistrust / Of human ways" that the poet can only establish a connection through repetition: "Very reasonable indeed / I should say: very reasonable indeed." The poet's soul mate materializes the inward tension of the poetic perspective estranged from a world devoid of sensibility—"Our glances lie unfermented among statues"[108]—and calling for what Michel Collot defines as "the acknowledgement of an essential and intractable invisibility dwelling at the very heart of vision."[109] The invisible and the material world should not be opposed: on the contrary, they partake of another:

> . . . the invisible is wrought within the very fabric of the visible; they are inseparable, like face and reverse. . . . one can only exist through the other while they cannot be brought to converge . . .[110]

This is why the poetic space—comprising the space of representation and the space of writing—finally metamorphoses in the last stanza to unveil not the invisible but its absent presence, what Merleau-Ponty calls "the lining of the invisible"[111]:

> This very spot where the writings of solitaries
> Limp off, take passage for foreign lands,
> Falter to an end, there being nothing left
> With which to compare them,
> Never looking back. Well then, goodbye.[112]

Figurative space thus functions as a symbolic threshold, and the poet's farewell ushers in a new form of life that cannot, however, be framed in words. These last five lines deliberately "limp" and "falter" toward an unreachable end materialized in the dismantled syntax: the verb of the main clause is suppressed, the relative clause expands, the subject is missing. Simultaneously the verse slips from hexameter to tetrameter and trimeter before falling back upon the tetrameter. The last line breaks up, emphasizing the assonance "look" / "good" so that the poem seems to fold back upon itself while the last word seems to promise another kind of "Somewhere," the reverse side of line 1.

"Want to Live Don't You?" therefore reads as an echo to the last fragment of On Seeming to Presume—"And so at last goodbye"[113]—and to Durrell's very last poem, "Le cercle refermé," published in Caesar's Vast Ghost a few days before his death. Pursuing the autobiographic trend of "Cities, Plains and People," "Le cercle refermé" nevertheless shatters the chronology and superimposes past and present time in the third stanza: "Mere time is winding down at last"[114] is thus followed by "When young and big with poems / . . . / . . . I was crafty in loving." Just as distinct eras mirror each other, so do sensory perceptions: "Boom of the sunset gun"[115] heralds the final assonance: ". . . goodbye / Goodbye."[116] Eventually the poem reads as another "passage for foreign lands,"[117] a crossing toward death that reverts into life:

Corpses floating skyward
. . .
So dying you begin to sleepwalk and regain your youth.

Mere time is winding down at last:[118]

The upward movement of bodies carried upon water reverses the classical image of the descent into Hades and reminds the reader of the poem "Last Heard Of" in Vega where the river metaphorizes the flow of life. The mirror effect that conveys the irrepresentable is a cornerstone in Durrell's poetics that relies on inversion and repetition to conjure up both the visible and the invisible. Durrell's writing unfurls like a moiré pattern alternating matte and glossy images, presence and absence, like the one-side and one-boundary surface of a Möbius strip:

The big rivers are through with me, I guess;
Can't walk by Thames any more
. . . Yes, the big rivers are through with me, I guess;
Nor the mind-propelling, youth-devouring ones
Like Nile or Seine, or black Brahmaputra
Where I was born and never went back again
The stars printed in shining tar.
Yes, the big rivers, except the one of sorrows[119]

The river image gives the poem its form and rhythm and conflates disjointed space-times: England and the poet's adolescence, the Nile and the war years, the Seine and Durrell's early writing years, Brahmaputra and his childhood are the metaphoric spaces of a time lost and found again in "Le cercle refermé." Their simple juxtaposition mirrors the ease with which the poet moves from one to the other, as if temporal and spatial boundaries had been abolished, just as verticality is annihilated in the internal slant rhyme "stars" / "tar." Inner space is conceived here as a one-side and one-boundary reality that can be traveled through ad infinitum, like the Möbius strip, so that the poet becomes the unreal landscape of his own writing:

> I have been washed up here or there,
> A somewhere soon becoming an empty everywhere.
> My memory of memories goes far astray,
> Was it today or was it yesterday?[120]

This unique rhyming quatrain inserted in the midst of free verse detaches itself not visually but rhythmically through its marked iambs as well as through the shift from tetrameter to hexameter and finally to pentameter in the last lines that rhyme like a heroic couplet. The clear-cut caesura between balanced hemistichs is emphasized by lexical mirror effects ("somewhere" / "everywhere"; "today" / "yesterday") and makes for a balanced, soothing lilt that suggests the peacefully flowing river. The poet's voice is thus at one with the inner momentum of space itself. The river of sorrows thus appears as the natural course of poetic sensibility toward unity and peace. Contrasting with the ominous lexical field, the flowing river conveys the impetus of life that saves the poet from the disintegration of matter. It acts truly as the "stinging image"[121] that simultaneously wounds and heals. Such is indeed the function of the poetic image as defined by Bachelard:

> The poetic image is the emergence of language; it always rises slightly above signifying language. . . . poetry is language in a state of emergence. Life is portrayed as ebullient. These linguistic impulses arising from the ordinary life of pragmatic language are miniatures of the vital impetus.[122]

"The emergence of language" characterizes all of Durrell's poems where the river image operates as a "miniature of the vital impetus." Thus, the very first line of "Last Heard Of" conjures up the echoes of "Rivers of seeds flowing" in "Themes Heraldic—II,"[123] as well as "The River's quietly flowing muscle" in "The Prayer-Wheel,"[124] or "Exhausted rivers ending in the sand" in "Letter to Seferis the Greek."[125] The river image is thus far more than a mere theme or a stylistic trope: it is the life principle at the heart of writing that transcends the sensible world, the source and the future of writing. As Durrell himself acknowledged: "The river image is absolutely fundamental in my work: the unfurling of metaphors in the sands of everyday life."[126] Although this comment is meant to explain Durrell's fictional work, it does shed light upon his poetry as well and reasserts the strong links between poetry and prose.[127] The river thus operates as the ontological principle of Durrell's writing, as the poem "The Rhône at Beaucaire" concluding the sixth chapter of *Caesar's Vast Ghost* evinces:

> The poet's great laboratory and creed
> The word which flows on staunchless as human need,
> Or the river, rhythms of memory traced in the blood
> So graphic yet so untranslatable to others:
> Your beauty, Françoise, the Rhône at Beaucaire.[128]

The flow of water seeps into the rhythm of language and vice versa, initiating a perfect symbiosis: "rivers" and "rhythm" are practically indistinguishable as river and words merge. The conflation of the natural and the human impetus leads the stanza to drift away: the syntactic and the semantic meaning dissolve. The series of appositions separated by the comma or the semicolon create a fluid, ungraspable object, akin to the woman's slowly ebbing yet eternal and formidable beauty, washed away by time and simultaneously imprinted forever in the blood of memory.

Facing "Last Heard Of," the poem "The Outer Limits" offers the river a fleeting insight into the other remote horizon where the poet projects himself, hoping for absolute freedom beyond language, space, and time limits:

> The pure form, then must be silence?
> I'd tear out a leaf of it and spread it,
> The second skin of music, yes[129]

The poem attempts to convey the thin membrane of silence that cradles speech and defeats any form of utterance. By fathoming his own limits the poet seizes, in this hesitant questioning, a latent presence that finally asserts itself at the end of the poem:

> So full of a gay informal logic,
> A real reality realising itself,
> No pressures but candid as a death,
> A full foreknowledge of the breathing game[130]

Such lines conjure up the memory of another French surrealist poet Durrell enjoyed reading, Gaston Puel, who wrote in the literary journal *Dire*:

> He who experiments with chance knows that there is no Golden Age, but a perpetual becoming between the possible and the inevitable, an impulse at the heart of a latent presence, a beginning within the weary folds of contradictions, a renewal.[131]

Durrell's verse attempts to approach this "impulse at the heart of a latent presence" and make us feel the incomprehensible: this "perpetual becoming" sketching out a vast expanse free from logos but that can, paradoxically, only be apprehended through language, an unfettered language that has shed the constraints of syntax and semantics and makes room for a new "gay informal logic." Limits, their existence and their trespassing, are then the very condition of poetic language, if we trust Michel Collot's analysis:

> The modern poet is less sensitive to the power of the gaze than to its 'limits.' . . . The acknowledgment of an essential and intractable invisibility dwelling at the very heart of vision forces phenomenology to offer a new definition of conscience. . . . It must lead to reevaluate our very 'Being.' 'Seeing,' 'is reaching out to a latent presence'[132] that only breaks through to melt away in the depths of the body or of the landscape.[133]

Therefore the object of the gaze is bound to disappear, just as Durrell's "full foreknowledge of the breathing game" that precisely belongs to "The outer limits." The world of the living in search for this "latent presence" thus appears as "Taut as a bent bow,"[134] aiming at an infinite horizon. Its arrow vanishes into thin air, leaving only the faint traces of a life breaking through the limits of speech and vision: "memory / Will combine for you voice, odour, smile."[135]

Endeavoring to approach the limits, the poem turns into a "proem"—the apt title of a very small volume to which Durrell contributed in 1938 and whose preliminary note stated: "CHAMBER's DICTIONARY: Proem: an introduction, a prelude, a preface."[136] Unsurprisingly, "The Outer Limits" is followed by the poem "A Farewell," as if the poet had already left this world for that of "The pure form,"[137] what Yves Bonnefoy calls "the absolute of sensibility that preexists our limited senses"[138]:

> Colours have no memory, friend,
> And can therefore prophesy,
> Turn whiter than tea-roses can

With whom to exchange addresses
In a far away city for a good-luck goodbye.[139]

The fading colors herald the advent of silence and the revelation of a sparkling light at the other end of the poem: "One thing about death—it isn't far to fall, / Its brightness disfigures every silence."[140] The approaching death, although frightening ("The dangerous years approach, friend"),[141] is also perceived as a liberation from the law of time; the celestial landscape dissolves, just as physical constraints do:

Time slips her moorings soon, and the
Surf-gathering boom of candles can retrace
To the whisper of canvas on the sky
A tiller's lug, jerked like some big dog,
The muscle-softening farewell embrace.

The perspective is subtly displaced, as if Durrell were looking at departing life in the mirror of the sky, watching down from the stars in search of a lost vision—"from the unknown to the known"—[142] that recalls the last stanza of "Air to Syria":

So we might be sailors
In a sinking ship on this field
Of mirrors: the air still
Humming in the corridors, the fans
Playing in the cabins
Moving on mystery like a lighted pond.[143]

Durrell conceives of poetry as a journey into an ever-receding eternity he fails to penetrate ("Out there on the flailing waters of everness")[144] that drains out language itself: "In thoughts now, no more in words."[145] Yet poetic language precisely springs from this aporia that turns absence into a source of light. Thus, in "A Farewell," death is described as enlightenment: "Its brightness disfigures every silence." "A Patch of Dust"[146] also presents death as a source of knowledge: "In these fatal shining canvasses I commend / A fatal diagnosis of light, more light / . . . / But you directly saw the splendour of the / Dying light redeemed."

Durrell's poetry may thus be subsumed in its emblematic cicada, Apollo's insect alternatively silent and singing, in tune with the rhythm of daylight and symbolizing the light and night dichotomy. Likewise Durrell's poetry follows the intermittent beat of presence and absence:

> Transparent sheath of the dead cicada
> . . .
> Simply snap off the scaly integument of mica.
> You could make a tiny violin of such a body,
> Lanterns for elves, varnish into brooches
> And wear by lamplight this transparent stare of the noon[147]

The cicada stands out as the heraldic emblem of the ideal poetic form: it is the transparent presence of a radiating absence bathing the world in the light of its indomitable gaze. The shift from "Transparent sheath" to "transparent stare" metamorphoses the dead membrane into a living and glowing one, opening up the text to a new perception and to a new essence whereby words partake of the "precious allegorical metal."[148]

The paradoxical nature of poetry explored by Durrell also accounts for the ironical tone of some of his texts, such as "On the Suchness of the Old Boy." This dialogic poem contrasts the disciple's and the sage's voices, reminding the reader of the textual structure of Zen teachings where the truth is often hinted at through an exchange between the master and his pupil.[149] The discourse of enlightenment, in italics, is fraught with puns, paradoxes, and nonsense and unfolds like a mischievous refrain where rhymes, polyptotons, assonances, and mirror effects induce a knowing smile, that of Chuang Tzu's Tao in A *Smile in the Mind's Eye*:

> It was a great little look, full of mischievous impudence, of irony and laughter. It was a look of sardonic complicity—it shared an amused and slanting consciousness of how precious the Unspoken was. . . . it is Taoism, and the minute you try to say something explicit about it you damage it, like clumsily trying to pick up a rare butterfly in your fingers. . . .
>
> Taoism is such a privileged brand of eastern philosophy that one would be right to regard it as an aesthetic view of the universe. . . . A Taoist was the joker in the pack, the poet on the hearth. . . . it was towards the poem (the ideogram of a perfected apprehension) that Taoism of this kind tended.[150]

A similar smile hovers upon the words of "the Sage," whose voice echoes a philosophy best approached through poetry. The puns based on neologisms— "Umptious," "Umptiousness," "Sumptiousness," "Yolklore"—echoing similar lexical constructions such as "uproariousness," "Scrumptiousness" and "Folklore," the witty aphorisms ("Damn the deep freeze, bugger the cold storage"), and the semantic aberrations that debunk the rigid syntax ("Be umptious asleep, awake, dressed or undressed," "Umption the ultimate fruit / Of holy Gumption") partake of this new unexplainable awareness that language fails to disprove and that, in turn, reshapes our relation to language. Reading thus becomes a metaphor, a transfer toward another apprehension of reality that cannot be grasped directly, just as a butterfly may not be approached with naked hands. The poem is thus akin to the butterfly net described by Blanford in *Livia*:

> The poetic reality of which I speak, and which Sutcliffe might have deployed in his unwritten books, is rather like the schoolchild's definition of a fishing-net as 'a lot of holes tied together with a string.' Just as impalpable, yet just as true of our work.[151]

"The poetic reality" Blanford seeks remains beyond the reaches of writing. Reversing the biblical metaphor of the fisher's net that "gathered the good into vessels, but cast the bad away,"[152] the text describes an open net that goes against the very concept of the net in its daily use. Such an image challenges our common representations and is reminiscent of the koan, a Zen parable aimed at the enlightenment of Buddhist monks and conveying a message that cannot be revealed, a truth that can only be achieved in the inner recesses of conscience.[153] Likewise, poetic writing is an attempt at grasping a reality made manifest by its absence, its "holes," its free zones of associations, interactions, and combinations that defy logic. Thus the aphorisms of wisdom enshrined in the poem float free like "a rare butterfly,"[154] detached from logos: "If so things are, why let them be," "Until all the extremes agree to meet," "Look not for reason anywhere; but keep / Revelation for those who least care," "Why do the many never reach the most?". This new approach of the world combines poetry and philosophy—a philosophy that is not so much a system as "an aesthetic view of the universe"[155] in which extremes meet, as the one meets the many in a fluid space-time ("If time flowed more it would melt into dancers"), sharply contrasting with our rigid present time: "The present burns in iron symmetry / With love built in like geometry."

"On the Suchness of the Old Boy" thus materializes the Taoist experience at the heart of the collection: "It was another way of saying / That he had discovered the heraldic way."[156] But this new truth cannot be expatiated: it is an inclusive movement that opens up the mind to relativity, humor, self-detachment, science and poetry, the known and the unknown—

> As happy on my hilltop I review
> The vistas of a world it never knew
> To which my Umption is the only clue.

Poetry is thus conceived as a mysterious key opening the doors of a new and ancient world and ushering in a playful science that propels us beyond the limits of rational knowledge in order to arouse the sensible world within. It is, as Roland Barthes said, "a fishing-net writing. . . fraught with holes and lights" that paves the way for a life experience:

> It is an attempt to localize an experience, which itself is too comprehensive to be included in the mere confines of language. . . . one can feel the language probing, like pair of giant calipers, attempting to circumscribe a realm, for the expression of which we have nothing between the madman's idiom and the A minor Quartet. . . . words themselves are used as a kind of sculpture, to symbolize what cannot be directly expressed: the heraldry of language is called into play to accentuate, to attest to, to pierce through the rind of the merely cognative impulse. . . .[157]

The marriage of poetry and philosophy is rooted in the poet's and the philosopher's shared and "indomitable need for the freedom dwelling in man."[158] If poetry can be said "to stem from the painful contact between external reality and human conscience," the same is true of philosophy. As Mallarmé has asserted, "Poetry expresses, through human language brought back to its essential rhythm, the mysterious meaning and shapes of existence: it grants authenticity to our stay and is our only spiritual task."[159] This quotation has been extensively analyzed by Meschonnic, who explains:

> This is where the poem can and must defeat the sign. By destroying acknowledged, professed, canonical representation. Because a poem is a time for listening. And the sign only addresses our sight. It is deaf and it makes us deaf. Only the poem can lead us to the voice, bring us from one voice to the other, turn us into listening beings. . . . And the content of this listening induces, imposes, a continuum between the subjects we are, the language we become, and the performative ethics this listening is. . . .[160]

This struggle against the sign is conveyed, in Durrell's poetry, by the ever-present irony that dismantles meaning, parodies prosodic, linguistic, and scriptural conventions, and leaves us only with "the blue regard of a fixed star"[161]—the stare of poetry that travels between his poems, and narratives, pushing ever further the shores of writing and corroborating once more Meschonnic's intuition: "The poem shows that the Odyssey lies in the voice. . . . Listening is its journey."[162] Durrell's poetry deliberately severs its moorings and crosses the lines between forms and genres, compelling us to read "between the lines, between the lives."

Notes

1. In 1974 Lawrence Durrell published his very last and private collection aimed at a restricted audience (115 copies only were issued). It was entitled *Lifelines, Four Poems by Lawrence Durrell* and was, like *Private Drafts*, a very small and intimate collection. It included the poems "Certain Landfalls," "Postmark," "Picture of Geishas," and "A Patch of Dust." Except for the penultimate poem, which was first published in 1965 and which reappeared in the 1980 edition of the *Collected Poems* under the title "Geishas," all the other poems were written one year after the publication of *Vega* and are placed at the end of the *Collected Poems* that concludes on the final poem "In Deep Grass," also dated 1974.

2. I borrow the expression from Corinne Alexandre-Garner's title, "Durrell: la clôture impossible?" *Etudes Britanniques Contemporaines* no. 10 (1996): 83–97.

3. "Thought-clusters, constellations of ideas linked by private associations, characterize poetic thinking . . . ," Lawrence Durrell, *The Red Limbo Lingo*, London: Faber, 1971, p. 12.

4. E. M. Forster, *Howards End*, Harmondsworth: Penguin Books, 1967, pp. 174–75.

5. Lawrence Durrell, *The Avignon Quintet*, London: Faber, 1992, pp. 1177–78.

6. "Comic Paradox of Fate," *The Avignon Quintet*, p. 1318.

7. *The Avignon Quintet*, p. 1318.

8. *The Avignon Quintet*, p. 1178.

9. "All this I saw in a patch of dust at St Rémy," "A Patch of Dust" (1974), Lawrence Durrell, *Collected Poems*, London: Faber, 1960, p. 338.

10. Maurice Blanchot, *L'écriture du désastre*, Paris: Gallimard, 1980, p. 72.

11. *The Avignon Quintet*, p. 1299.

12. Mary Byrne, "The Neo-Baroque in Durrell's Major Novels," *Deus Loci: The Lawrence Durrell Journal* NS 13 (2012–2013), p. 119.

13. *The Avignon Quintet*, pp. 1187–88.

14. "And pray, why not an aberrant prose style to echo the discordance at the heart of all nature?" *The Avignon Quintet*, p. 1188.

15. T. S. Eliot, "East Coker," *Collected Poems 1909–1962*, London: Faber, 2002, p. 190.

16. Mikhail Bakhtin, *Esthétique et théorie du roman*, Paris: Gallimard, 1978, p. 323.

17. T. S. Eliot, "The Hollow Men," *Collected Poems*, p. 81.

18. *Esthétique et théorie du roman*, p. 323.

19. Letter dated March 6, 1974, *The Durrell-Miller Letters 1935–80*, Ian S. MacNiven, ed., London: Faber, 1989 (first published in 1988), pp. 471–72.

20. Lawrence Durrell, "Consequential Data," *The Alexandria Quartet*, London: Faber, 1974 (first published in 1962), p. 386.

21. Clive Scott, "Lawrence Durrell: The Poet as Idler," *Deus Loci* NS 13, pp. 5–7.

22. "Lawrence Durrell: The Poet as Idler," pp. 5–7.

23. Letter dated March 6, 1974, *The Durrell-Miller Letters 1935–80*, pp. 472–73.

24. Lawrence Durrell, "Poetry: A Tragic Game," *The Big Supposer: A Dialogue with Marc Alyn*, New York: Grove Press, 1974 (first published in 1972), pp. 89–92.
25. Henri Michaux, *L'Avenir de la Poésie, Œuvres complètes I*, Paris: Gallimard, 1998, p. 969.
26. Paul Celan, *Le Méridien & autres proses*, Paris: Seuil, 2002 (first published in 1960), p. 73.
27. "Poetry: A Tragic Game," *The Big Supposer*, pp. 89–92.
28. "Sixties," Lawrence Durrell, *Vega and Other Poems*, London: Faber, 1973, p. 19.
29. "Sixties," *Vega*, p. 9.
30. "Sixties," *Vega*, p. 9.
31. "Sixties," *Vega*, p. 9.
32. Henri Meschonnic, *Célébration de la poésie*, Paris: Verdier, 2001, p. 252.
33. *Célébration de la poésie*, p. 252.
34. Lawrence Durrell, "Henri Michaux, The Poet of Supreme Solipsism," in *Henri Michaux*, Montpellier: Fata Morgana, 1990, p. 36.
35. *A Thousand Plateaus*, pp. 348–49.
36. Christian Doumet, *Faut-il comprendre la poésie?* Paris: Klincksieck, 2004, p. 40.
37. *Faut-il comprendre la poésie?* p. 40.
38. "Nobody," *Vega*, p. 10.
39. "Swimmers," *Vega*, p. 27.
40. *Faut-il comprendre la poésie?* p. 40.
41. "Rain, Rain, Go to Spain," *Vega*, p. 11.
42. "Rain, Rain, Go to Spain," *Vega*, p. 11.
43. "Lake Music," *Vega*, p. 16.
44. *A Thousand Plateaus*, p. 349.
45. "But he on his part secretly gave her sweet pomegranate seed to eat, taking care for himself that she might not remain continually with grave, dark-robed Demeter," "Hymn to Demeter," l.370, The Homeric Hymns, http://www.perseus.tufts.edu/hopper/text?doc=Perseus%3Atext%3A1999.01.0138%3Ahymn%3D2, last accessed June 23, 2017.
46. J. Chevalier and A. Gheerbrant, *Dictionnaire des symboles*, Paris: Éditions Robert Laffont, 1982, p. 485.
47. Lawrence Durrell, *Key to Modern Poetry*, London: Peter Nevill, 1952, p. 106. Durrell's conception of the symbol was heavily influenced by French symbolists to whom he frequently refers in *Key*.
48. *The Avignon Quintet*, pp. 124–26.
49. Compare the passage quoted above with, for instance, the poetic description of fishermen on the Nile: "The fisherman took up a mouthful of water and blew it out in a screen of spray against the sunlight, revelling in the prismatic hues of the water-drops" (*The Avignon Quintet*, p. 624).
50. T. S. Eliot, "The Hollow Men," *Collected Poems*, p. 81.
51. *Key to Modern Poetry*, pp. 84, 90.
52. *Key to Modern Poetry*, p. 68.

53. *Vega*, p. 10.
54. *A Thousand Plateaus*, p. 348.
55. "Incognito," *Vega*, p. 26.
56. *Vega*, p. 26.
57. *Vega*, p. 26.
58. *Vega*, p. 26.
59. *Vega*, p. 26.
60. Giorgio Agamben, *Qu'est-ce que le contemporain?* Paris: Éditions Payot & Rivages, 2008, pp. 15–19.
61. "Revenants," *Vega*, p. 22.
62. *Qu'est-ce que le contemporain?* pp. 24–25.
63. *The Durrell–Miller Letters*, pp. 472–73.
64. *Célébration de la poésie*, pp. 246–47.
65. "?" *Vega*, p. 18.
66. "?" *Vega*, p. 18.
67. *Key to Modern Poetry*, pp. 84, 90.
68. *Qu'est-ce que le contemporain?* pp. 23, 25, 32.
69. "Someone still everywhere nearby," 1.4; "Tidemarks of old intentions' dying fall," 1.7.
70. "all" v.1; "fall" v.7; "all" v.8.
71. "all" v.19; "recall" v.20.
72. William Shakespeare, *Twelfth Night*, act 1, scene 1.
73. T. S. Eliot, *Collected Poems 1909–1962*, p. 4.
74. See chapter 4.
75. "?" *Vega*, p. 18.
76. "?" *Vega*, p. 18.
77. "?" *Vega*, p. 18.
78. Giorgio Agamben, *Enfance et histoire*, Paris: Éditions Payot & Rivages, 2002 (first published in 1978), p. 35.
79. "?" *Vega*, p. 18.
80. See the title of Michael Haag's *Alexandria, City of Memory*, Cambridge: Yale University Press, 2004.
81. "Unreal City / . . . / I had not thought death had undone so many," T. S. Eliot, *Collected Poems 1909–1962*, p. 54.
82. "?" *Vega*, p. 18.
83. "?" *Vega*, p. 18.
84. *Enfance et histoire*, pp. 85–86.
85. "Envoi," *Vega*, p. 31.
86. "Mistral," *The Red Limbo Lingo*, p. 47.
87. Giorgio Agamben, *La Fin du poème*, Strasbourg: Circé, 2002, p. 135.
88. Corinne Alexandre-Garner, "Durrell: la clôture impossible?" p. 88.
89. "Seferis," *Vega*, p. 54.
90. "Seferis," *Vega*, p. 54.

91. "Seferis," *Vega*, p. 54.
92. "Seferis," *Vega*, p. 54.
93. Corinne Alexandre-Garner, "Durrell: la clôture impossible?" p. 88.
94. " . . . I have a feeling that you too perhaps have stepped across the threshold into the kingdom of your imagination . . . ," *The Alexandria Quartet*, p. 877.
95. "Seferis," *Vega*, p. 54.
96. George Seferis, "Les anges sont blancs," *Logbook I*, in *Complete Poems*, London: Anvil Press Poetry, 1995, p. 131.
97. "Memory II," *Logbook III*, *Complete Poems*, p. 188.
98. Kenneth White, *The Wanderer and His Charts: Essays on Cultural Renewal*, Edinburgh: Polygon Books, 2004, pp. 15, 63–64.
99. "Confederate," *Vega*, p. 42.
100. Compare "Want to Live Don't You?" *Vega*, p. 45, and "Le cercle refermé," in Lawrence Durrell, *Caesar's Vast Ghost: Aspects of Provence*. London: Faber, 1990, p. 174.
101. "Cicada," *Vega*, p. 51.
102. "The Muses," *Vega*, p. 52.
103. "Vega," *Vega*, p. 53.
104. Michel Collot, *La poésie moderne et la structure d'horizon*, Paris: PUF, 1989, pp. 27–28.
105. *Vega*, p. 53.
106. "Lawrence Durrell: The Poet as Idler," p. 18.
107. "Want to Live Don't You?" *Vega*, p. 45.
108. *Vega*, p. 45.
109. *La poésie moderne et la structure d'horizon*, p. 32.
110. *La poésie moderne et la structure d'horizon*, p. 34.
111. Maurice Merleau-Ponty, *L'Œil et l'esprit*, Paris: Gallimard, 1964, p. 85.
112. *Vega*, p. 45.
113. "The Anecdotes," "XVI In Rio," Lawrence Durrell, *On Seeming to Presume*, London: Faber, 1948, p. 59.
114. "Le cercle refermé," *Caesar's Vast Ghost*, p. 174.
115. "Le cercle refermé," *Caesar's Vast Ghost*, p. 174.
116. "Le cercle refermé," *Caesar's Vast Ghost*, p. 174.
117. *Vega*, p. 45.
118. *Vega*, p. 45.
119. "Last Heard Of," *Vega*, p. 38.
120. "Last Heard Of," *Vega*, p. 38.
121. "Seferis," *Vega*, p. 54.
122. Gaston Bachelard, *La poétique de l'espace*, Paris: PUF, 1957, p. 10.
123. This set of nine poems was written between 1937 and 1938. Only the seventh, "Summer in Corfu," was published in *A Private Country*. The entire set was first published as "Themes Heraldic (Selections From)" in the volume *Proems*, in 1938. Although there are slight mistakes in the numbering of the nine poems, the set is

complete. It is reissued in 1980 in *Collected Poems*. The poems are briefly commented upon by Ray Morrison in *A Smile in his Mind's Eye: A Study of the Early Works of Lawrence Durrell*, Toronto: University of Toronto Press, 2005, pp. 61–62.

124. *On Seeming to Presume*, p. 30.

125. Lawrence Durrell, *A Private Country*, London: Faber, 1944 (first published in 1943), p. 71.

126. *The Big Supposer*, p. 18.

127. See the descriptions of the Alyscamps in le *Monsieur* (*The Avignon Quintet*, pp. 35, 152, 223) and in *Caesar's Vast Ghost*, pp. 84–85, as well as "The River Rhône" and "Down the Styx" in *Spirit of Place: Mediterranean Writings*, London: Faber, 1988 (first published in 1969), pp. 323–35, 417–22.

128. *Caesar's Vast Ghost*, p. 87.

129. "The Outer Limits," *Vega*, p. 39.

130. "The Outer Limits," *Vega*, p. 39.

131. Gaston Puel, *Dire, Revue Européenne de Poésie*, automne–hiver 1966–1967; back cover [n.p.]; Lawrence Durrell's personal copy (The Lawrence Durrell Library, Paris Ouest).

132. Merleau-Ponty quoted by Michel Collot, *La poésie moderne et la structure d'horizon*, p. 32.

133. *La poésie moderne et la structure d'horizon*, pp. 30–32.

134. *Vega*, p. 39.

135. *Vega*, p. 39.

136. Lawrence Durrell, *Proems*, London: The Fortune Press, 1938, [n.p.].

137. "The Outer Limits," *Vega*, p. 39.

138. Yves Bonnefoy, "La poésie objective," *Two Cities, La Revue Bilingue de Paris* (May 1960), p. 11.

139. "A Farewell," *Vega*, p. 40.

140. "A Farewell," *Vega*, p. 41.

141. "A Farewell," *Vega*, p. 40.

142. "A Farewell," *Vega*, p. 40.

143. Lawrence Durrell, "Air to Syria," *Atlantic Anthology*, London: The Fortune Press, 1945, p. 87. This volume, edited by Nicholas Moore and Douglas Newton, included works by Stephen Coates, Saul Bellow, Lawrence Durrell, Henry Miller, Lucien Freud, Patrick Heron, W. S. Graham, Wallace Stevens, Elizabeth Bishop, G. S. Fraser, Richard Eberhart, Antonia White, etc.

144. *Vega*, p. 40.

145. *Vega*, p. 40.

146. Lawrence Durrell, *Collected Poems 1931–1974*, London: Faber, 1985 (first published in 1980), p. 338. This poem, addressed to Vincent van Gogh, concludes *Lifelines, Four Poems by Lawrence Durrell*.

147. "Cicada," *Vega*, p. 51.

148. "Cicada," *Vega*, p. 51.

149. See R. H. Blyth, *Zen and Zen Classics*, vol. 4, Tokyo: The Hokuseido Press, 1978.
150. *A Smile in the Mind's Eye*, pp. 18–20.
151. *The Avignon Quintet*, p. 351.
152. Saint Matthew 13: 47–48.
153. See Isabelle Keller-Privat, "'With only his eyeballs for probes': Looking into the Buddhist Intertext of *The Avignon Quintet* by Lawrence Durrell," *Lawrence Durrell, Borderlands & Borderlines, Confluences* no. 26, Paris: Presses Universitaires de Paris 10, 2005, pp. 138–39.
154. *A Smile in the Mind's Eye*, p. 18.
155. *A Smile in the Mind's Eye*, p. 18.
156. *Vega*, p. 32.
157. *A Smile in the Mind's Eye*, p. 88.
158. Pierre Reverdy, *Cette émotion appelée poésie. Écrits sur la poésie (1930–1960)*, Paris: Flammarion, 1974, p. 62.
159. Stéphane Mallarmé quoted in *Célébration de la poésie*, p. 248.
160. *Célébration de la poésie*, p. 249.
161. *A Smile in the Mind's Eye*, p. 69.
162. *Célébration de la poésie*, p. 251.

Conclusion

> He knew full well that the reality he sought lay beyond life,
> and that life was a very fragile and provisional matter.
> The poem is an act of affirmation . . .[1]

Following the flow of Durrell's verse leads the reader to sail with the poet "Down the Styx," where the "lava, boiling and sheeting"[2] penetrates the dark caves of a rhizomatic memory and lead us into *"a mineral world"*[3] of poems rising like cairns on the way. The varied forms of Durrell's poetic writing thus appear as so many instances of "the multiple utterances of poetry's unique speech . . . —the immanent Pentecost that enables the mind to overstep boundaries,"[4] whether linguistic, textual, temporal, or spatial. The thematic and symbolic threads of the first collections sketch out a deep poetic exploration that testifies, through its formal and conceptual issues, to a slow maturing process that both precedes and exceeds writing. Durrell follows in the wake of the great Romantics, and of Wordsworth, whom he praised as the true helmsman: "he steers his verse around the rocks and shoals which lay in wait for it . . . towards the open sea of English poetry."[5] Durrell's poetry thus unfolds as a quest for knowledge delving into the cycle of life and rebirth in order to investigate the new territories of the self and the world through what Pursewarden called: "a form . . . sincerely honoured by an awakened spirit."[6]

The autobiographical cycle of *A Private Country* heralds a conception of poetic writing as a passage and a transmission conveyed by the interplay of broken constructions and suspended rhymes that combine with a circular structure to suggest a latent, ethereal presence—the bedrock of poetry. The linear and geographic syntagmatic organization progressively peters out to be replaced by the paradigmatic meditation on the abyss awaiting the poet: exile, death, and loss operate as the vertical axes drawing the reader's gaze into the inner recesses of the poet's conscience. As early as his first collection, Lawrence Durrell interrogates the poetic gesture and the poet's role and sets the tone for the more introspective collections of later years, preparing the reader for the reflexive dynamics of *Cities, Plains and People* and *On Seeming to Presume*. This quest for the inner self is always deeply rooted in the Greek soil: the shining beacon of Durrell's poetry slowly turns into the space of a metaphysical wandering. The song of the poems transforms the landscape into a material, sensual reality, a musical mapping of the inner self. In the mirror of writing the visionary poet contemplates the shattered fragments of his past selves. The numerous enunciative and temporal shifts are characteristic of the poet's broken identity and of the idealization of a distant, abstract childhood. The image of childhood plays indeed a key role: it is a fundamental ideogram foregrounding the symbol as an essential yet shifty signifier that ensures both the polysemy and the coherence of the entire oeuvre. The poem thus functions as a mirror held up to the poet and to each one of us, refracting the endless process of dispossession and rebirth. Durrell's Greek world, just as the world of childhood, operates as a space of mourning where mourning may at last be overcome. Like the mirror of Zen, the poem offers the glimpse of a completeness that outwits language. Thus Durrell renews our conception of the poetic space: beyond a mere object of representation or nostalgic incantation, it is the place where new ties are woven between absence and presence, between forms, sounds, and meanings; it is "the hearth of an entire horizon."[7]

On Seeming to Presume furrows the founding wound dwelling in every single poem that rises both as a surge of desire and as the trace of a deep rift. Cities are no longer meant to be crossed or inhabited but rather operate as screens precluding any return and projecting, through their slow excavation, the images of loss and collapse haunting the poet. Durrell breaks away from the figuration of the Greek landscape to investigate the relations between time and space, and the Greek land becomes the soil of a meditation on man's finitude, foreshadowing the poetic and symbolic issues at stake in his prose. The poetic writing—of the poems and of the prose—inquires into an unspeakable reality materialized in the receding metatextual and intertextual embeddings that highlight the increasing tension of Durrell's style. The interpolation and overlapping of spatiotemporal strata concur to destroy what Reverdy calls "exact reality."[8] As a result, Durrell not only offers his reader an artistic and spiritual journey but also challenges literary reception by welding reading and writing and, in so doing, paves the way for a new conception of poetry.

The Tree of Idleness further experiments with this disfigured space where geographic consistency is denied and realistic bearings are repeatedly uprooted: the island of Cyprus operates as a hollow core, the mysterious *omphalos* from which the poet's voice stems. Poetry markedly distinguishes itself from objective speech: it is the fruit of silence, the space of the untold. The world of the dead acquires a prominent role as the poet becomes the ferryman freeing all those born in human bondage. Death and memory are thus closely intertwined, and poetry operates as a threshold wherefrom the poet can gauge his own responsibility as a survivor. The central absence of the island is metaphorized by the rose, the ideogram for lost love that unfolds in the figures of abandoned lovers, the fleeting wafts of perfume, the scattered letters sent from a dying Europe, and in this bitter lemon of a poem confined to the margins.

The structural silence of *The Tree of Idleness* alienating the poem "Bitter Lemons" in a limited edition first, and then later in the residence book, is echoed by the silence that precedes the following collection where spatiotemporal unity is once again shattered. Despite its title, *The Ikons* signals the climax of poetic disfiguration. The arrangement of poems into mirroring diptychs or triptychs builds up an abstract and disjointed icon that nurtures a meditation upon the irrepresentable. This is why Aphrodite is thrice conjured up and thrice shattered while the slow shift from antique ruins to bare mineral matter foregrounds the quintessential frailty of a poetic writing that relentlessly probes its own limits. In order to tear man away from the law of entropy the poet points, through textual matter, at what lies beyond speech. The poems become truly initiatory and function as so many icons of a reality that disengages itself from matter and projects itself into the margins, teaching the gaze a new method in the etymological sense of the word: a way beyond.[9] Durrellian Greece defamiliarizes our perspective and turns into a mystic icon aimed at the few who can track the cairns that the dragoman, like Hermes, leaves us as secret landmarks to prompt a new relation to the text and to the world: the poem ushers in a hermetic quest for the last passage. *The Ikons* thus open up the field of the irrepresentable and the invisible, tear apart the linearity of mundane reality, and awaken in each of us a nomadic conscience, a wanderer, not unlike those imagined by Jacques Lacarrière:

> ... the sons of an Explosion, of a celestial Dispersion ... the wandering particles—be they comets or humans—of an expanding universe.... The wanderer is a space apprentice experimenting with elsewhere.[10]

The Red Limbo Lingo develops the hermetic quest through a baffling structure that hints at a deliberate, controlled groping for poetic reality. Not unlike *The Quintet* that throws its reader into the dark cave of fiction, *The Red Limbo Lingo* throws us into a limbo where frontiers between prose and verse melt away, where words "break, under the burden"[11] and are recast. Syntax and logic break apart, nonsense rules, meaning is displaced. Poetry, the new kingdom of language, conjures up an organic, overflowing relation to the world. The deconstruction of the polysemic symbolism of blood gives rise to a new covenant with poetry and with the reader so that the entire collection functions as a mischievous and hermetic experiment. Each poem reads both as a text and as the image of a text in which the layout, the inner structure, and the lexicon constantly challenge our reading, like the dismantled body parts of the dead Orpheus, whose music never dies. By shattering form and meaning, the poetic language appears as the climax of the writing experience that welds Western and Eastern thought, marries the contraries, and wrings freedom out of annihilation.

Vega stands out as a paroxysmal instance of such an experiment exacerbating extreme tensions. Opening on the last poems from *The Red Limbo Lingo*, the collection brings together forces of dispersion and cohesion. The repetition of the same reads as a trace, a ruin saved from limbo, and as the threshold of a new vision that heralds the forthcoming poems. *Vega* therefore comes to symbolize both the end and the absence of ending in Durrell's poetic opus that continues to develop over the years since *Vega* will be followed by another, private and smaller collection while poetry will keep seeping through the later prose. This opus, catching its breath, as it were, enables the reader to feel the poetic breath that underlies Durrell's poetics, the alpha and omega of his lifelong literary achievement.

Reading Durrell's poetry thus amounts to attempting to circumscribe his poetics that Meschonnic identifies as "the intrinsic functioning"[12] of an author's literary production and, thereon, embarking upon "an extensive research into the workings of language"[13] leading to investigate the very essence of poetry that Durrell's entire work relentlessly probes. In so doing, the poet always dances on the razor's edge, risking eternal misunderstanding, as he points out in his ironical poem "The Critics," where he derides literary criticism: "'From images and scansion can be learned. . . .'"[14] The bitter tone of the poem is reminiscent of Pursewarden's "Conversations with Brother Ass" where he warns Darley against those "still painfully trying to extract from art some shadow of justification for their way of life."[15] However, Durrell's open distrust toward literary criticism is counterbalanced by his deep desire to engage the reader in a personal exchange, to bring him to discover the hidden side of language, as his many imaginary conversations with an absent reader evince. This is why Durrell's reader is the object of such paradoxical representations: he is both the one who can master learned references to practice a short-sighted and elitist reading ("Emended readings give the real reason")[16] and the sensitive soul the poet entrusts with the secret of poetic language: "The whole secret is here, in a word which grows above snowline."[17] Durrell's silent purpose is to tease the reader out of his daily slumber and awaken his deeper desire for the voice of poetry, allowing for the inner realization it will bring. Durrell's reader might then as well pay heed to Rilke's cautionary words against the "partisan opinions . . . petrified and meaningless"[18] of literary criticism. Indeed Rilke, not unlike Durrell, invites us to become the soil fecundated by writing:

> Always trust yourself, your own feelings, as opposed to argumentations, discussions or introductions . . . Everything is gestation and then birthing. To let each impression and each embryo of a feeling come to completion, entirely in itself, in the dark, in the unsayable, the unconscious, beyond the reach of one's own understanding, and with deep humility and patience to wait for the hour when a new clarity is born: this alone is what it means to live as an artist: in understanding as in creating.[19]

Poetic reading develops in the margins of meaning, away from the signifiers of secular utterances, which is why, as Bonnefoy explains, "poetry cannot be turned into discourse. One cannot unfold a rose bud without wrecking it."[20] The poem experiments with textual, semantic, and aesthetic limits and shapes out the poet who appears both as the subject and the object of a research project he shares with his reader.

Durrell's poetry maps an open space, a radically differing space that escapes the binding folds of the book and opens our eyes to a promised freedom, man's utmost frontier. Reading Durrell's poetry affects one's approach and perception of poetry and brings us close to the essence of its object. Poetry is indeed best defined as an experiment understood by Philippe Lacoue-Labarthe in the etymological sense of the word, "from Latin *ex-periri*, passing through danger"[21]:

> I call it an *experience* because what allows the poem to "surge"—a dazzling memory, that is also the sheer vertigo of memory—is precisely what has not taken place . . . what the poem hints at and shows, its aim, is its source. . . . Therefore the poem says, or strives to say, the "surge" of the poem as a possibility, that is, as an enigma.[22]

Every reading engages the reader in a renewed experience of poetry, in this quest for the unsayable that Henri Michaux described as the quest for "the secret of the poetic state, of poetic substance."[23] The poetic object thus folds back upon itself: initially considered as the refraction of a previous experience and as the tool whereby the poet awakens our understanding of the world, it becomes "the eye, the witness of that search."[24]

Striding books and shores, Durrell sketches out the meandering flow of a boundless search. The young poet's Greek journeys, his cosmopolitan literary friendships, the beloved and forsaken women haunting his texts function as so many sensual and abstract realities both present and absent, whose slow metamorphosis testifies to the alchemical essence of poetry. These rising and fading shadows resurfacing in poems and novels, residence books, and plays enlighten by their distant flicker the darkness that gave them birth and engulfs them anew. They are images akin to the firefly images described by George Didi-Huberman, spanning the still horizon like a traveling comet:

> The image: a unique, treasured apparition, even though it is such an unremarkable thing, a burning, a falling thing. It rarely ascends to the motionless upper regions of eternal ideas: it usually goes down, wanes, rushes down to earth, somewhere before or behind the horizon. Like a firefly, it eventually hides away from sight and goes to a place where it will perhaps be seen by someone else, where its survival will be noticed again.[25]

The firefly image that rises and drowns in memory, strikes the eye, and eludes our grasp operates as the secret ideogram embodied by Vega, the poem-woman-star that subsumes in its polysemic shapes Durrell's artistic quest. Both frail and dynamic, it is the light the poem seeks for, loses, and recognizes. It brings together the echoes of foreign lands and languages, unites the dead and the living poets, and crosses borders. Its reckless stare enlightens peninsulas of mercy in the silent dark.

Durrell's poetic voice joins the throbbing constellation of all those for whom poetry was not so much an art form as a way of being-in-the-world. Thus Durrell, speaking of Wordsworth, indirectly sheds light on his own quest: "the mysterious sense of election to poetry as a whole way of life. . . . He felt he was hunting for what was most itself in nature, the poised and limpid truth of reality. Poetry was his lariat."[26] On the lookout for the firefly image whose survival, he senses, was meant for him, Durrell listens to past voices in his own, and acts as the silent reader of his own poems. Simultaneously reading and writing his texts where he pays heed to distant and foreign curves, he guides the reader toward the other. Wordsworth, T. S.

Eliot, Valéry, Cendrars, Cavafy, Seferis, Sikelianos, and Elytis are among the "unique, treasured apparition[s]" enlightening Durrell's horizon and contributing to the same poetic quest. These are some of the "Pleiades . . . sinking cool as paint"[27] composing the poetic cosmos celebrated in "Lesbos" and inviting the reader to penetrate the world of poetry "Like dancers to a music they deserve."[28] The poetic opus is a shared space where reading and writing mirror one another *ad infinitum.*

In an ultimate, paradoxical, poetic twist, Durrell subverts the rules of literary criticism by turning it into a poetic performance where one may recognize both the creative powers of reading and the faint, albeit real, hope of approaching a language that brings us closer to the poetic experience. Such are indeed the lines Durrell devoted to Henri Michaux and where he veers from discursive to poetic speech:

> The poet seems to have realized that it is true what the sages tell us, that you can actually find yourself bending reality and mastering it, provided your vision contains not a single shred of self-seeking. By not wanting, you get it free so to speak, you rumble into the whole essential cosmic abundance—the whole of nature is at your beck and call like a superb fruit. . . . Wholeness arrives! But as Michaux insisted: 'The smile must always be involuntary!'[29]

Criticism is superseded by poetic images before giving way to Michaux's voice that seems to come out of a passage from *A Smile in the Mind's Eye* and sounds like a comment upon "the enigmatic smile of Kasyapa."[30] These words also introduce a second text, Durrell's "Poem in Honour of Henri Michaux," which consists in a prose poem breaking free from both the constraints of verse and of discourse and following the rules of poetry as defined in *A Smile*, ". . . not thinking so loud, letting the heartbeats break the codes embedded in the vowels"[31]:

> . . . somewhere inside him there is always a timid child playing with his experimental colour box!
> One cannot help feeling that he has embarked on a prolonged research into the order of things which preceded human logic, into the order which preceded logic and language. . . . Clusters of points dancing a farandole from tribes of words.[32]

A Private Country, Cities, Plains and People, On Seeming to Presume, The Tree of Idleness, The Ikons, The Red Limbo Lingo, and *Vega* are one of the many "clusters of points dancing a farandole from tribes of words" in which the careful reader hears the heartbeat of a long chain of poets, follows the lines of a nascent music breaking the codes, and discovers the colors of an experimental language.

As a quest for an irrecoverable before, a vanished Eden, a wrecked childhood, poetry—as a writing and as a reading experiment—is both an Orphic descent aware of the sacrifice inherent to creation, and the enraptured welcoming of the never-ending momentum of lights and words, sounds and shapes haunting our silent dreams.

So the search must go on, poem by poem . . .[33]

Notes

1. Lawrence Durrell, "Introduction," *Wordsworth Selected by Lawrence Durrell*, Harmondsworth: Penguin Books, 1973, p. 21.
2. Lawrence Durrell, "Down the Styx," *Spirit of Place*, London: Faber, p. 418.
3. "Down the Styx," p. 419.
4. Yves Bonnefoy, *L'Autre langue à portée de voix*, Paris: Seuil, 2013, p. 110.
5. "Introduction," *Wordsworth Selected by Lawrence Durrell*, p. 21.
6. Lawrence Durrell, *The Alexandria Quartet*, London: Faber, 1974 (first published in 1962), p. 751.
7. Michel Collot, *La poésie moderne et la structure d'horizon*, Paris: PUF, 1989, p. 19.
8. Pierre Reverdy, *Cette émotion appelée poésie. Écrits sur la poésie (1930–1960)*, Paris: Flammarion, 1974, p. 129.
9. Method: L *methodus* f. Gk *methodos* pursuit of knowledge, mode of investigation, f. *meta* beyond, after + *hodos* way. *The New Shorter Oxford English Dictionary*.
10. Jacques Lacarrière, *Errances, mémoire des paysages, paysages de la mémoire*, Paris: Christian Pirot, 1983, pp. 9–10.
11. T. S. Eliot, *Four Quartets, Collected Poems*, London: Faber, 2002, p. 182.
12. Henri Meschonnic, *Célébration de la poésie*, Paris: Verdier, 2001, p. 46.
13. *Célébration de la poésie*, p. 47.
14. Lawrence Durrell, *On Seeming to Presume*, London: Faber, 1948, p. 39.
15. *The Alexandria Quartet*, p. 756.
16. *On Seeming to Presume*, p. 39.
17. *The Alexandria Quartet*, p. 750.
18. Rainer Maria Rilke, *Letters to a Young Poet*, translated by Stephen Mitchell, Malden, MA: Burning Man Books, 2001, p. 11.
19. *Letters to a Young Poet*, p. 11.
20. *L'Autre langue à portée de voix*, p. 164.
21. Philippe Lacoue-Labarthe, *La poésie comme expérience*, Paris: Christian Bourgeois éditeur, 1986, p. 30.
22. *La poésie comme expérience*, pp. 30–31.

23. Pierre Reverdy, "L'Avenir de la poésie," *Œuvres complètes I*, Paris: Gallimard, 1998, p. 969.

24. "L'Avenir de la poésie," p. 978.

25. Georges Didi-Huberman, *Survivance des lucioles*, Paris: Les Éditions de Minuit, 2009, pp. 101–2.

26. "Introduction," *Wordsworth Selected by Lawrence Durrell*, p. 10.

27. "Lesbos," Lawrence Durrell, *The Tree of Idleness*, London: Faber, 1955, p. 11.

28. "Lesbos," *The Tree of Idleness*, p. 11.

29. Lawrence Durrell, "Henri Michaux, The Poet of Supreme Solipsism," *Henri Michaux*, Montpellier: Fata Morgana, 1990, pp. 36–37.

30. Lawrence Durrell, *A Smile in the Mind's Eye*, London: Faber, 1982 (first published in 1980), p. 92.

31. *A Smile in the Mind's Eye*, p. 92.

32. "Poem in honour of Henri Michaux," *Henri Michaux*, p. 42.

33. *A Smile in the Mind's Eye*, p. 92.

Bibliography

Durrell Manuscripts

Lawrence Durrell Research Library Paris—Ouest University, France. Referred as [Bibliothèque Lawrence Durrell, Paris Ouest].

Carbondale, Southern University of Illinois, USA. Collection 42 / 9 / 2. Referred as [SIU].

The British Library, Archives and manuscripts, The Lawrence Durrell collections: M. J. T. Tambimuttu (1943–45), Alan G. Thomas (1992), Ghislaine de Boysson (2006), Bernard Stone (2008).

Bibliography

Agamben, Giorgio. *Enfance et histoire*. Paris: Éditions Payot & Rivages, 2002 (1978).

———. *La Fin du poème*. Paris: Circé, 2002 (1996).

———. *Qu'est-ce que le contemporain?* Paris: Éditions Payot & Rivages, 2008.

Alexandre-Garner, Corinne. "Durrell: la clôture impossible?" *Etudes Britanniques Contemporaines* no. 10 (1996): 83–97.

———. "L'écriture de la neige dans les premiers textes de Lawrence Durrell: essai de généalogie d'une écriture." *Bulletin de la Société de Stylistique Anglaise* no. 26 (2005): 173–91.

———. "Je est / hait l'Autre: la femme juive comme double et autre dans *The Avignon Quintet* de Lawrence Durrell." *Parcours Judaïques* IV (1998): 179–93.

———. *Lawrence Durrell: Dans l'ombre du soleil grec*. Paris: La Quinzaine Littéraire, Louis Vuitton, 2012.

---. *Le Quatuor d'Alexandrie de Lawrence Durrell, fragmentation et écriture: étude sur l'amour, la femme et l'écriture dans le roman de Lawrence Durrell.* Berne: Peter Lang, 1985.

---. "Regard d'exil—Naître de l'Inde: Lawrence Durrell." *Cahiers du SAHIB* no. 4 (1996): 11–25.

---. "La représentation de la deuxième guerre et du nazisme dans *Le Quintette d'Avignon*." *Parcours Judaïques III* (1996): 99–111.

Alexandre-Garner, Corinne, and Isabelle Keller-Privat. "Lawrence George Durrell (1912–1990)." In *Guide de la littérature britannique des origines à nos jours*. Paris: Ellipses, 2008, 319–22.

---. "'Manufacturing Dreams' or Lawrence Durrell's Fiction Revisited through the Prism of De Chirico's Metaphysical Painting." *Deus Loci: The Lawrence Durrell Journal* NS 13 (2012–2013): 85–109.

---. "When Elsewhere Is Home: Mapping Literature as Home in Lawrence Durrell's 'Cities, Plains and People.'" *Études Britanniques Contemporaines* no. 37 (2009): 69–86.

Aunos, Eduardo. *Gérard de Nerval et ses énigmes*. Paris: Aryana et Gérard Vidal éditeur, 1956.

Bachelard, Gaston. *L'Intuition de l'instant*. Paris: Stock, 1931.

---. *La poétique de l'espace*. Paris: PUF, 1957.

Bacry, Patrick. *Les figures de style et autres procédés stylistiques*. Paris: Belin, 1992.

Bakhtin, Mikhail. *Esthétique et théorie du roman*. Paris: Gallimard, 1978.

Balso, Judith. *Affirmation de la poésie*. Caen: éditions Nous, 2011.

Baltrušaitis, Jurgis. *Aberrations. Essai sur la légende des formes. Les perspectives dépravées – I*. Paris: Flammarion, 1995.

Baquey, Stéphane. "Une voix sans appuis (À propos de Jean-Patrice Courtois)." In *Singularités du sujet, huit études sur la poésie contemporaine*, vol. 1, edited by Lionel Destremau and Emmanuel Laugier, 13–24. Paris: Prétexte Éditeur, 2012.

Barthes. Roland. *Le degré zéro de l'écriture*. Paris: Seuil, 1953.

Bataille, Georges. *La littérature et le mal*. Paris: Gallimard, 1957.

Bauchau, Henry. *Poésie complète*. Arles: Actes Sud, 2009.

Baudelaire, Charles. *Les Fleurs du Mal*. Paris: Gallimard, 1972 (1855).

---. *Petits Poèmes en prose*. Paris: Garnier, 1962 (1869).

Beebe, Maurice. "Criticism of Lawrence Durrell: A Selected Checklist." *Modern Fiction Studies* 13, no. 3 (1967): 417–21.

Bible de Jérusalem. Paris: Les éditions du Cerf, 2001.

The Holy Bible. *Authorized King James Version*. London: Eyre & Spottiswoode Publishers.

Blanchot, Maurice. *L'écriture du désastre*. Paris: Gallimard, 1980.

Blyth, R. H. *Zen and Zen Classics*, vol. 4. Tokyo: The Hokuseido Press, 1978. [Bibliothèque Lawrence Durrell, Paris Ouest].

Bolton, Jonathan. "*Personal Landscape* and the Poetry of the 1940s." *Deus Loci: The Lawrence Durrell Journal* NS 4 (1995–96): 62–72.

———. *Personal Landscapes: British Poets in Egypt during the Second World War*. London: Macmillan Press, 1997.
Bonnefoy, Yves. "La Poésie objective." *Two Cities*, Paris (May 1960): 8. [Bibliothèque Lawrence Durrell, Paris Ouest].
———. *La Beauté dès le premier jour*. Paris: William Blake & Co. Édit., 2009.
———. *L'Autre langue à portée de voix*. Paris: Seuil, 2013.
Bousiou, Pola. *The Nomads of Mykonos: Performing Liminalities in a 'Queer' Space*. New York, Oxford: Berghahn Books, 2008.
Bowen, Roger. "'The Artist at His Papers': Durrell, Egypt and the Poetry of Exile." *Twentieth Century Literature* 33, no. 4 (Winter 1987): 465–84.
———. *Many Histories Deep: The Personal Landscape Poets in Egypt, 1940–45*. Madison: Fairleigh Dickinson University Press, 1995.
Brigham, James A., and Alan Gradon Thomas. *Lawrence Durrell: An Illustrated Checklist*. Carbondale: Southern Illinois University Press, 1983.
Brigham, James A., and J. A. Douglas. "City Full of Dreams: Durrell's Alexandria and the Ghost of Baudelaire." *Deus Loci: The Lawrence Durrell Journal* NS 6 (1998): 93–103.
Butor, Michel. *Le génie du lieu*. Paris: Grasset, 1958.
Byrne, Mary J. *Lawrence Durrell's Alexandria Quartet: A Work in the Baroque Spirit*. M.A. Diss. University College Dublin, 1985.
———. "The Neo-Baroque in Durrell's Major Novels." *Deus Loci: The Lawrence Durrell Journal* NS 13 (2012–2013): 111–33.
Calonne, David Stephen. "The Discovery of Yourself: Lawrence Durrell and Gostan Zarian in Greece." In *Lawrence Durrell and the Greek World*, edited by Anna Lillios, 62–75. London: Associated University Presses.
Calotychos, Vangelis. "Lawrence Durrell, the Bitterest Lemon? Cyps and Brits Loving Each Other to Death in Cyprus, 1953–57." In *Lawrence Durrell and the Greek World*, edited by Anna Lillios, 169–87. London: Associated University Presses, 2004.
Caplan-Philippe, Murielle. *La couleur dans l'œuvre de Lawrence Durrell*. Diss. Paris III—Sorbonne Nouvelle University, 2002.
Cavafy, Constantin P. *A Bilingual Collection of Poems by C. P. Cavafy 1863–1933*. London: Loizou Publications, 1995. [SIU].
———. *Poèmes*. Translated by Dominique Grandmont. Paris: Gallimard, 1999.
Celan, Paul. *Le Méridien & autres proses*. Paris: Seuil, 2002 (1960).
Cendrars, Blaise. *Poésies completes*. Paris: Denoël, 2005.
———. *Blaise Cendrars-Henry Miller, Correspondance 1934–1979: 45 ans d'amitié*. Paris: Denoël, 1995.
Chevalier, Jean, and Alain Gheerbrant. *Dictionnaire des symboles*. Paris: Éditions Robert Laffont, 1982.
Coleridge, Samuel Taylor. *Lecture on Poetry*, December 12, 1811. In *Lectures 1808–1819 On Literature II*, 5. Edited by R. A. Foakes. London: Routledge & Kegan Paul, 1987.

Collot, Michel. *La poésie moderne et la structure d'horizon*. Paris: PUF, 1989.
Corpus Hermeticum, Tome I. Paris: Les Belles Lettres, 1945.
Crossman, Sylvie. "Le mandala de Kalachakra ou le vaisseau du grand voyage." In *Tibet, les formes du vide*. Montpellier: Indigène éditions, 1996, 25–29.
Dagognet, François. "L'image: reproduction et creation," *Philopsis* (2007): 1–7, http://www.philopsis.fr/IMG/pdf_pdf_image_dagognet.pdf, accessed January 12, 2017.
Deguy, Michel. *L'énergie du désespoir ou d'une poétique continuée par tous les moyens*. Paris: PUF, 1998.
Delcourt, Marie. *L'Oracle de Delphes*. Paris: Payot, 1981 (1955).
Deleuze, Gilles. *Critique et clinique*. Paris: Les Éditions de Minuit, 1993.
Deleuze, Gilles, and Felix Guattari. *A Thousand Plateaus: Capitalism and Schizophrenia*. London: Continuum, 2002.
Devine, Arlene. *Le mythe de la femme dans l'œuvre de Gérard de Nerval*. MA. Diss. McGill University, 1969.
Didi-Huberman, Georges. *L'Homme qui marchait dans la couleur*. Paris: Les Éditions de Minuit, 2001.
———. *Survivance des lucioles*. Paris: Les Éditions de Minuit, 2009.
Doumet, Christian. *Faut-il comprendre la poésie?* Paris: Klincksieck, 2004.
Durrell, Lawrence. Acte. New York: E. P. Dutton, 1966 (1965).
———. *The Alexandria Quartet*. London: Faber, 1974 (1962).
———. *In Arcadia*. Set to music by T. Wallace Southam. London: Turret Books, 1698.
———. *Atlantic Anthology*. London: The Fortune Press, 1945. [Bibliothèque Lawrence Durrell, Paris Ouest].
———. *Autumn's Legacy*. Op.58, for voice, piano. Set to music by Lennox Berkeley and W. Chester. Commissioned by the Cheltenham Festival committee. Includes "Lesbos." London: Turret Books, 1963.
———. *The Avignon Quintet*. London: Faber, 1992.
———. *The Big Supposer: A Dialogue with Marc Alyn*. New York: Grove Press, 1974 (1972).
———. *Bitter Lemons of Cyprus*. London: Faber, 1959 (1957).
———. *The Black Book*. London: Faber, 1977 (1938).
———. *Blue Thirst*. Santa Barbara: Capra Press, 1975.
———. *Caesar's Vast Ghost: Aspects of Provence*. London: Faber, 1990.
———. *Cities, Plains and People*. London: Faber, 1946.
———. *Collected Poems*. London: Faber, 1960.
———. *Collected Poems 1931–1974*. London: Faber, 1985 (1980).
———. *Contemporary Poets Set in Jazz*. Set to music by T. Wallace Southam, sung by Belle Gonzalez. Includes "Lesbos." Jupiter Recording, JUR OA11, 1966.
———. *The Dark Labyrinth* (*Cefalû*). London: Faber, 1976 (1947).
———. *The Greek Islands*. London: Faber, 1978.
———. "Henri Michaux, The Poet of Supreme Solipsism." In *Henri Michaux*. Montpellier: Fata Morgana, 1990.

———. *The Ikons*. London: Faber, 1966.
———. "Introduction." In *Wordsworth: Selected by Lawrence Durrell*. Harmondsworth: Penguin Books, 1973, 9–21.
———. "Introduction by Lawrence Durrell" In *Return to Oasis, War Poems and Recollections from the Middle-East 1940–1946*. London: Editions Poetry London, 1980. [Bibliothèque Lawrence Durrell, Paris Ouest].
———. "Introduction and Commentary by Lawrence Durrell." In Paul Hogarth, *The Mediterranean Shore: Travels in Lawrence Durrell's Country*. London: Pavillion Books, 1988.
———. *An Irish Faustus: A Morality in Nine Scenes*. London: Faber, 1963.
———. *Key to Modern Poetry*. London: Peter Nevill, 1952.
———. *Lawrence Durrell: Conversations*. Earl G. Ingersoll, ed. Madison: Fairleigh Dickinson University Press, 1998.
———. *Lesbos*. Set to music by T. Wallace Southam. Oxford: Oxford University Press, 1967.
———. *Lifelines, Four Poems by Lawrence Durrell*. Edinburgh: The Tragara Press, 1974. [Bibliothèque Lawrence Durrell, Paris Ouest].
———. *Middle East Anthology of Prose and Verse*. London: Lindsay Drumond, 1946. [Bibliothèque Lawrence Durrell, Paris Ouest].
———. *Nemea*. Set to music by T. Wallace Southam. London: Augener, 1950.
———. *Nothing Is Lost, Sweet Self*. Set to music by T. Wallace Southam. London: Turret Books, 1967, 1969.
———. *Panic Spring: A Romance*. James Gifford, ed. Victoria, Canada: ELS editions, 2008 (1937).
———. *Pied Piper of Lovers*. James Gifford, ed. Victoria, Canada: ELS editions, 2008 (1935).
———. "Préface de Lawrence Durrell." In Georg Groddeck, *Le Livre du Ça*. Paris: Gallimard, 1973. [Bibliothèque Lawrence Durrell, Paris Ouest].
———. "A Preface by Lawrence Durrell." In David Gascoyne, *Paris Journal 1937–1939*. London: Enitharmon Press, 1978.
———. *A Private Country*. London: Faber, 1944 (1943).
———. *Private Drafts*. Nicosia, 1955. [Copy no. 18, Bibliothèque Lawrence Durrell, Paris Ouest].
———. *Proems*. London: The Fortune Press, 1938. [Bibliothèque Lawrence Durrell, Paris Ouest].
———. *Prospero's Cell: A Guide to the Landscape and Manners of the Island of Corfu*. London: Faber, 1962 (1945).
———. *The Red Limbo Lingo*. London: Faber, 1971.
———. *Reflections on a Marine Venus: A Companion to the Landscape of Rhodes*. London: Faber, 1953.
———. *The Revolt of Aphrodite*. London: Faber, 1990 (1974).
———. *Sappho*. London: Faber, 1967 (1950).

———. *Sappho. Opera in Three Acts. Libretto by Lawrence Durrell.* Set to music by Peggy Glanville-Hicks. Commissioned by The San Francisco Opera House for Maria Callas as mezzo soprano. London: Toccata Classics, 2012 (1963).

———. *On Seeming to Presume.* London: Faber, 1948.

———. *Selected Poems.* New York: Grove Press, 1956.

———. *Selected Poems.* Alan Ross, ed. London: Faber, 1977, p. 11.

———. *Selected Poems 1935–1963.* London: Faber, 1964.

———. *Six Poems from the Greek of Sikelianós and Seferis and The King of Asine and Other Poems.* Translated from the Greek by Bernard Spencer, Nanos Valaoritis, Lawrence Durrell, with an introduction by Rex Warner. London, 1948. [Bibliothèque Lawrence Durrell, Paris Ouest].

———. *A Smile in the Mind's Eye.* London: Faber, 1982 (1980).

———. *Songs about Greece.* Includes "Lesbos" set to music by Lennox Berkeley and "In Arcadia" set to music by T. Wallace Southam. Jupiter Recording, Jeo 0C36, 1964.

———. *Songs of a Sunday Composer.* Set to music by T. Wallace Southam. Includes "Nothing Is Lost, Sweet Self," "Nemea," "In Arcadia," and "Lesbos" sung by John Barrow and Belle Gonzalez. London: Turret Books, 1969.

———. *Sound of Eleven.* The Peter Compton Big Band. Musical themes inspired from *Clea, Balthazar* and *Mountolive.* London: 77 Records-Dobells, 77 LEU 12/14, 2007.

———. *Spirit of Place: Mediterranean Writings.* London: Faber, 1988 (1969).

———. *The Spoken Word: Lawrence Durrell.* Includes jazz themes played by Lawrence Durrell, poetry readings and interviews. London: The British Library, 2012.

———. *The Tree of Idleness.* London: Faber, 1955.

———. *Ulysses Come Back.* London: Turret Books, 1971.

———. *Vega and Other Poems.* London: Faber, 1973.

———. *White Eagles over Serbia.* London: Faber, 1993 (1957).

Durrell, Lawrence, and Alfred Perles, eds. *The Booster. September 1937–Easter 1939,* U.S.A: Johnson Reprint Corporation, 1968. [Bibliothèque Lawrence Durrell, Paris Ouest].

Durrell, Lawrence, and Henry Miller. *The Durrell-Miller Letters 1935–80.* Edited by Ian S. MacNiven. London: Faber, 1989 (1988).

Durrell, Lawrence, and Robin Fedden, eds. *Personal Landscape: An Anthology of Exile.* London: Editions Poetry: no. 1 Jan 1942, no. 2 March 1942, no. 3 June 1942, vol. 1 part 4, 1942, vol. 2 part 1, 1943, vol. 2 parts 2–3, 1944, vol. 2 part 4, 1945. [Bibliothèque Lawrence Durrell, Paris Ouest].

Eliot, T. S. *Selected Poems.* Harmondsworth: Penguin, 1948.

———. *Collected Poems 1909–1962.* London: Faber, 2002.

Forster, E. M. *Howards End.* Harmondsworth: Penguin Books, 1967 (1910).

Fraenkel, Michael. *Death Is Not Enough: Essays in Active Negation.* London: Carrefour Publications, 1962 (1939). [SIU].

Fraenkel, Michael, and Henry Miller. *The Michael Fraenkel-Henry Miller Correspondence called Hamlet,* vol. 1 and 2. London: Carrefour Publications, 1939. [SIU].

Frankétienne. *Spirale, Premier mouvement des métamorphoses de l'oiseau schizophone, D'un pur silence inextinguible*. La Roque d'Anthéron: Vents d'ailleurs, 2004.
Fraser, George Sutherland. *Lawrence Durrell, A Study, with a Bibliography by Alan G. Thomas*. London: Faber, 1968.
Frénaud, André. *La Sainte Face*. Paris: Gallimard, 1968.
Friedrich, Hugo. *Structure de la poésie moderne*. Paris: Librarie Générale Française, 1999 (1956).
Gascoyne, David. *Collected Poems*, Oxford: OUP, 1984 (1965).
———. *Collected Journals 1936–1942*. London: Skoobs Books Publishing Ltd., 1991.
Gifford, James. "The Corfiot Landscape and Lawrence Durrell's Pilgrimage: The Colonial Palimpsest in 'Oil for the Saint; Return to Corfu.'" *In-Between: Essays and Studies in Literary Criticism* 11, no. 2 (2002): 181–96.
———. *Critical Materials on Lawrence Durrell: A Bibliographic Checklist*. International Lawrence Durrell Society, 2007, http://www.lawrencedurrell.org/bibliog/, accessed June 12, 2017.
Greimas, Algirdas Julien, and Joseph Courtès. *Sémiotique: dictionnaire raisonné de la théorie du langage*. Paris: Hachette Supérieur, 1993.
Grimal, Pierre. *Dictionnaire de la mythologie grecque et romaine*. Paris: PUF, 1996.
Groupe μ. *Traité du signe visuel. Pour une rhétorique de l'image*. Paris: Seuil, 1992.
Haag, Michael. *Alexandria, City of Memory*. Cambridge: Yale University Press, 2004.
Herbrechter, Stefan. *Lawrence Durrell, Postmodernism and the Ethics of Alterity*. Amsterdam: Rodopi, 1999.
Homère. *Hymnes*. Paris: Les Belles Lettres, 1951.
Hubner-Bayle, Corinne. *Gérard de Nerval: la marche à l'étoile*. Seyssel: Editions Champ Vallon, 2001.
Hugo, Victor. *Morceaux choisis de Victor Hugo*. Paris: Librairie Delagrave, 1934.
Hulin, Michel. *La face cachée du temps. L'imaginaire de l'au-delà*. Paris: Fayard, 1985.
Humbert, Jean. "Introduction générale et notices." In Homère, *Hymnes*. Paris: Les Belles Lettres, 1951.
Jourde, Pierre. "Nerval, la voix, l'irreprésentable." In *De l'irreprésentable en littérature*, edited by Jean-Marc Houpert and Paule Petitier: Paris: L'Harmattan, 2001.
Jung, Carl. *Dreams*. London: Routledge, 2002.
Keats, John. *The Works of John Keats*. Hertfordshire: Wordsworth Editions, 1994.
Keller, Isabelle. *L'Anamorphose dans l'œuvre romanesque de Lawrence Durrell*, Diss. Toulouse II—Jean Jaurès University, 2002.
Keller, Jane Eblen. "Durrell's Ode to the Olive." In *Lawrence Durrell and the Greek World*, edited by Anna Lillios, 298–307. London: Associated University Presses, 2004.
Keller-Privat, Isabelle. "La chasse aquatique dans *Le Quatuor d'Alexandrie* de Lawrence Durrell: un motif obsessionnel aux sources de la création," http://imager.upec.fr/servlet/com.univ.collaboratif.utils.LectureFichiergw?ID_FICHIER=1259766104138 accessed January 12, 2017.

———. "De l'autre côté des frontières: l'écriture poétique chez Lawrence Durrell." In *Migrations/Translations*, edited by Maroussia Ahmed, Corinne Alexandre Garner, Isabelle Keller-Privat, Nicholas Serruys, and Iulian Toma, 397–416. Paris: Presses Universitaires de Paris Ouest, 2015.

———. "L'écriture musicale chez Lawrence Durrell." *Anglophonia, Musique et Littératures: Intertextualités*. Toulouse: Presses Universitaires du Mirail (2002): 295–304.

———. "Empreintes de l'euphémisme dans *Quaint Fragments* & *A Private Country* de Lawrence Durrell: la musique du silence." In *Empreintes de l'Euphémisme. Tours et détours*, edited by Denis Jamet and Manuel Jobert, 365–79. Paris: L'Harmattan 2010.

———. "Finding One's Way through 'the List of Viable Selves' or Lawrence Durrell's Lesson in Detachment from 'the Most Fragile of Illusions.'" In *Impersonality and Emotion in Twentieth-Century British Literature*, edited by Christine Reynier and Jean-Michel Ganteau, 155–65. Publications de Montpellier III, 2005.

———. "L'île de la Rose" followed by "'L'île de la Rose' de Lawrence Durrell: aux confins du voyage, l'île palimpseste." Translation and commentary of "The Island of the Rose" by Lawrence Durrell, in *The Geographical Magazine*, 1947. In *Les Artistes anglo-américains et la Méditerranée*, vol. III, edited by Christine Reynier, 106–30. Paris: Michel Houdiard, 2010.

———. "Poetry and the Myth of Creation." In *An Introduction to Poetry in English*, edited by Eric Doumerc and Wendy Harding, 63–73. Toulouse: PUM, 2007.

———. "'With only his eyeballs for probes': Looking into the Buddhist Intertext of *The Avignon Quintet* by Lawrence Durrell." In *Lawrence Durrell: Borderlands & Borderlines, Confluences*, no. 26. Paris: Presses Universitaires de Paris 10, 2005, 129–43.

Kháyyám, Omar. *Les Quatrains*. Paris: éditions Ivréa, 1992.

Kirby-Smith Carruthers, Virginia. "Memory's Seditious Brew: Mythic Resonances in Durrell's Greek Poetry." *Durrell in Alexandria, On Miracle Ground 9, Conference Proceedings Alexandria, Egypt, June 1996*. Baltimore: The International Lawrence Durrell Society (2005): 268–73.

Lacarrière, Jacques. *Errances, mémoire des paysages, paysages de la mémoire*. Paris: Christian Pirot, 1983. [Bibliothèque Lawrence Durrell, Paris Ouest].

———. *Les Gnostiques* (préface de Lawrence Durrell). Paris: Albin Michel, 1994. [Bibliothèque Lawrence Durrell, Paris Ouest].

Lacoue-Labarthe, Philippe. *La poésie comme expérience*. Paris: Christian Bourgeois éditeur, 1986.

Lamartine, Alphonse de. *Œuvres Poétiques Complètes*. Paris: Gallimard, 1965.

Lapaire, Jean-Rémi, and Wilfrid Rotgé. *Grammaire et Linguistique de l'anglais*. Toulouse: PUM, 1991.

Levinas, Emmanuel. *Dieu, la mort et le temps*. Paris: Grasset, 1993.

Louvel, Liliane. *L'œil du texte: texte et image dans la littérature de langue anglaise*. Toulouse: Presses Universitaires du Mirail, 1998.

MacNiven, Ian. *Lawrence Durrell: A Biography*. London: Faber, 1998.

Mallarmé, Stéphane. *Œuvres*. Paris: Garnier, 1985. [SIU].

———. *Avant-dire au* Traité du verbe *de René Ghil*. In *Œuvres complètes*. Paris: Gallimard, 1945 (1886).
Maulnier, Thierry. *Introduction à la poésie française*. Paris: Gallimard, 1939.
Maupoix, Jean-Michel (ed.). *La Poésie pour quoi faire ? Une enquête*. Paris: Presses Universitaires de Paris Ouest, 2011.
Mead, George Robert Stow. *Thrice Great Hermes: Studies in Hellenistic Theosophy and Gnosis, Volume II*. London: Theosophical Publishing Society, 1906. http://www.gnosis.org/library/grs-mead/TGH-v2/index.html; accessed January 12, 2017.
Merleau-Ponty, Maurice. *L'Œil et l'esprit*. Paris: Gallimard, 1964.
Meschonnic, Henri. *Célébration de la poésie*. Paris: Verdier, 2001.
———. *Nous le passage*. Paris: Verdier, 1990.
Michaux, Henri. *Œuvres complètes I*. Paris: Gallimard, 1998.
Montaigne, Michel de. *Essais*. In *Œuvres complètes*. Paris: Gallimard, 1962.
Morin, Edgar. *Amour, Poésie, Sagesse*. Paris: Seuil, 1997.
Morrison, Ray. *A Smile in His Mind's Eye: A Study of the Early Works of Lawrence Durrell*. Toronto: University of Toronto Press, 2005.
Nambiar, C. Ravindran. "Lawrence Durrell's Recreation of D. H. Lawrence's Constance: Restoring Woman's Cosmic Place." In *Lawrence Durrell: Borderlands & Borderlines, Confluences*, no. 26. Paris: Presses Universitaires de Paris 10, 2005, 145–52.
———. *Indian Metaphysics in Lawrence Durrell's Novels*. Newcastle: Cambridge Scholars Publishing, 2014.
Nancy, Jean-Luc. *Résistance de la poésie*. Bordeaux: William Blake & Co., 2004.
Nerval, Gérard de. *Voyage en Orient*. Paris: Gallimard, 1961 (1851). [SIU].
———. *Sylvie*. Paris: Bordas, 1967 (1853). [SIU].
———. *Œuvres de Gérard de Nerval*, Tome I. Paris: Garnier, 1966.
Nock, Arthur Darby. "Préface." In *Corpus Hermeticum*, Tome I. Paris: Les Belles Lettres, 1945.
Nouss, Alexis. *Paul Celan. Les lieux d'un déplacement*. Paris: éditions Le Bord de L'Eau, 2010.
Orwell, George. *The Collected Essays, Journalism and Letters of George Orwell*, vol. I. Harmondsworth: Penguin Books, 1968.
Papastavrou-Koroniotakis, Barbara. "The Classified File of Lawrence Durrell." In *Lawrence Durrell: Borderlands & Borderlines, Confluences*, no. 26. Paris: Presses Universitaires de Paris 10, 2005, 21–47.
Platon. *Timée*. In *Œuvres Complètes*, Tome X. Paris: Les Belles Lettres, 1956.
Perles, Alfred. *My Friend Lawrence Durrell*. London: Village Press, 1973 (1961).
Pfister, Gérard (ed.). *"La poésie, c'est autre chose," 1001 définitions de la poésie*. Paris: Orbey, Arfuyen, 2008.
Pine, Richard. *Lawrence Durrell: The Mindscape*. New York: St. Martin's Press Inc., 1994.
Pharand, Michael W. "'Personal Neurasthenia': Eros and Thanatos in the Poetry of Lawrence Durrell." *Deus Loci: The Lawrence Durrell Jouranl* NS 3 (1994): 98–112.

Pline l'Ancien. *Histoire naturelle, livre XII*. Paris: Les Belles Lettres, 1949.
———. *Histoire naturelle, livre XXIV*. Paris: Les Belles Lettres, 1972.
Properce. *Élégies*. Paris: Les Belles Lettres, 1995.
Puel, Gaston. *Dire, Revue Européenne de Poésie*, automne–hiver 1966–1967 [Bibliothèque Lawrence Durrell, Paris Ouest].
Rabaté, Dominique. "Enonciation poétique, énonciation lyrique." In *Figures du sujet lyrique*, edited by Dominique Rabaté, 65–79. Paris: PUF, 1996.
Rafroidi, Patrick. *Précis de stylistique anglaise*. Paris: Ophrys, 1978.
Raizis, Marios Byron. "Lawrence Durrell and the Greek Poets: A Contribution to Cultural History." In *Lawrence Durrell and the Greek World*, edited by Anna Lillios, 241–54. London: Associated University Presses, 2004.
Rank, Otto. *Art and Artist*. New York: Norton, 1989 (1932). [Bibliothèque Lawrence Durrell, Paris Ouest].
Reverdy, Pierre. *Cette émotion appelée poésie. Écrits sur la poésie (1930–1960)*. Paris: Flammarion, 1974.
Richer, Jean. *Nerval et ses fantômes*. Paris: Mercure de France, 1951.
Rilke, Rainer Maria. *Lettres à un jeune poète*. Paris: Librairie Générale Française, 1989 (1929).
Ritman, Serge. "Entretien avec Patrice Beray." *Mediapart*, June 15, 2013.
Rivaux, Albert. "Notice." In Platon, *Œuvres Complètes*, Tome X. Paris: Les Belles Lettres, 1956.
Robinson, Jeremy. *Love, Culture and Poetry: A Study of Lawrence Durrell*. Kidderminster: Crescent Moon, 1990.
Salbayre, Sébastien, and Nathalie Vincent-Arnaud. *L'Analyse stylistique. Textes littéraires de langue anglaise*. Toulouse: PUM, 2006.
Scott, Clive. "Lawrence Durrell: The Poet as Idler." *Deus Loci: The Lawrence Durrell Journal* NS 13 (2012–2013): 3–24.
Seferis, George. *Complete Poems*. London: Anvil Press Poetry, 1995.
———. *A Poet's Journal. Days of 1945–1951*. Cambridge, MA: Harvard University Press, 1974.
Shakespeare, William. *Hamlet*. Oxford: Oxford University Press, 1994.
———. *Twelfth Night*. Oxford: Oxford University Press, 1994.
———. *A Midsummer Night's Dream*. London: Routledge, 1994.
Shelley, Percy Bysshe. "A Defence of Poetry 1840." In *The Complete Works, Prose: Volumes V–VI–VII*. London: Ernest Benn, 1965.
Sitwell, Edith. *Collected Poems*. London: Duckworth Overlook, 2006.
Sitwell, Sacheverell. *Agamemnon's Tomb*. Edinburgh: The Tragara Press, 1972 (1933). [Bibliothèque Lawrence Durrell, Paris Ouest].
Stein, Gertrude. *Lectures in America*. Boston: Beacon Press, 1985 (1935).
Stewart, Jack F. "Painterly Writing: Durrell's Island Landscapes." *Deus Loci: The Lawrence Durrell Journal* NS 6 (1998): 40–63.
Suhamy, Henri. *Versification anglaise*. Paris: C. D. U. – SEDES, 1970.
———. *Stylistique anglaise*. Paris: PUF, 1994.

Suzuki, D. T. *Manual of Zen Buddhism*. London: Rider and Company, 1956. [Bibliothèque Lawrence Durrell, Paris Ouest].

———. *Essais sur le Bouddhisme Zen*. Paris: Albin Michel, 2003. [Bibliothèque Lawrence Durrell].

———. *Essays in Zen Buddhism*. London: Rider and Company, 1953. [Bibliothèque Lawrence Durrell, Paris Ouest].

Thomas, Gordon K. "Durrell and Wordsworth: Seekers of the Shrinking Shore," *On Miracle Ground II, Second International Lawrence Durrell Conference Proceedings, Deus Loci: The Lawrence Durrell Quarterly*, special issue 7, no. 5 (1984): 183–95.

Todd, Daniel Ray. *An Annotated, Enumerative Bibliography of the Criticism of Lawrence Durrell's* Alexandria Quartet *and His Travel Works*. Diss. Tulane University, 1985.

Tomkinson, Fiona. "Durrell's 'Poem in Space and Time.'" In *Lawrence Durrell at the Crossroads of Arts and Sciences*, edited by Corinne Alexandre-Garner, Isabelle Keller-Privat, and Murielle Philippe, 117–32. Presses universitaires de Paris Ouest, 2010.

Trigano, Shmuel. *Le Temps de l'exil*. Paris: Éditions Payot & Rivages, 2005.

Tshering, Lama Seunam. "Les seize formes du vide." In *Tibet, les formes du vide*, 33–34. Montpellier: Indigène éditions, 1996.

Tzu Chuang. *The Complete Works of Chuang Tzu*. New York: Columbia University Press, 1968. [Bibliothèque Lawrence Durrell, Paris Ouest].

———. *Œuvre complète*. Paris: Gallimard, 1969.

Valéry, Paul. *Œuvres I*. Paris: Gallimard, 1957.

Varenne, Jean. *Upanishads du Yoga*. Paris: Gallimard, 1971.

Vincent-Arnaud, Nathalie. "'This music settling like white-hot steel': Music and Transmutation in Lawrence Durrell's *The Black Book*." In *Lawrence Durrell at the Crossroads of Arts and Sciences*, edited by Corinne Alexandre-Garner, Isabelle Keller-Privat, and Murielle Philippe, 159–72. Presses universitaires de Paris Ouest, 2010.

Vipond, Dianne. "The Politics of Lawrence Durrell's Major Fiction." *Deus Loci* NS 13 (2012–2013): 47–63.

White, Kenneth. *The Wanderer and his Charts. Essays on Cultural Renewal*. Edinburgh: Polygon Books, 2004.

Wordsworth, William. *Poems*, vol. 1. London: Penguin Books, 1990.

Wordsworth, William, and Samuel Taylor Coleridge. *Lyrical Ballads 1798*. Oxford: Oxford University Press, 1993.

Zarian, Kostan. *The Traveller and His Road*. New York: Ashod, 1981.

Index

Agamben, Giorgio, 37, 231, 278–79, 280–81, 282–84
Alexandre-Garner, Corinne, 18, 55, 59, 119–20, 261n58
Anand, Mulk Raj, 190
Ancet, Jacques, 2, 50–51

Bachelard, Gaston, 69, 291
Bailly, Jean-Christophe, 90
Baquey, Stéphane, 182, 187
Bakhtin, Mikhail, 270
Baudelaire, Charles, 203
Blake, William, 111, 139
Blanchot, Maurice, 268
blood, 5, 225–32, 234–36, 241–44
blue (color), 95–96, 212
Bonnefoy, Yves, 46, 101, 102, 121–22, 188–89, 191, 203, 206–7, 211, 212–15, 293, 309
Bowen, Roger, 26, 63
Buddhism, 43, 61, 105, 113–14, 117, 120, 129
Butor, Michel, 210

Celan, Paul, 217, 272
Cendrars, Blaise, 233–34
childhood, 51, 54–57, 306
Chuang Tzu, 61, 295
Coleridge, Samuel Taylor, 1, 86, 170n52, 264n131
Collot, Michel, 287, 289, 293

death, 27–28, 30–34, 53–55, 58, 67–68, 91–92, 94, 97–98, 131–34, 146–54, 158–61, 177–92, 195, 203–10, 213, 235–38, 245–49, 253–55, 285, 294–95
Deguy, Michel, 52
Deleuze, Gilles et Felix Guattari, 149, 274–75, 277
Didi-Huberman, George, 66, 310
disfiguration, 87–88, 90, 92, 97, 101, 121, 131, 134, 147–48, 307
Doumet, Christian, 27, 67, 82–83, 88, 274
Durrell, Lawrence—drama: *Acte*, 190–91; *Sappho*, 7, 7n4, 28, 54–55, 60, 116–17, 136

Durrell, Lawrence—poems: "Acropolis," 193–94; "The Anecdotes," 48–49, 108–20, 124n67; "Apteros," 195–97; "In Arcadia," 18, 62; "To Argos," 19; "Asphodels: Chalcidice," 150–52; "Bitter Lemons," 166–68; "A Bowl of Roses," 154–56; "Byzance," 177–78; "Carol on Corfu," 16–17; "Le cercle refermé," 119, 290–92; "Chanel," 156–57; "Cicada," 294–95; "Cities, Plains and People," 48, 58–59, 109–11; "Congenies," 214–15; "Conon in Alexandria," 63–66; "Conon the Critic, on the Six Landscape Painters of Greece," 61; "Conon in Exile," 28–29; "At Corinth," 20–23; "The Critics," 99; "In Deep Grass," 235, 261n58; "Delphi," 209–11; "Deus Loci," 163–65; "The Dying Fall," 142–44; "Egyptian Poem," 27–28; "Eight Aspects of Melissa," 43–46; "Eleusis," 194–96; "Envoi," 258, 284–85; "At Epidaurus," 36–38; "Eternal Contemporaries: Six Portraits," 102–8; "In Europe," 55–58, 91–92; "Exile in Athens," 25; "Fangbrand," 9, 11–15; "A Farewell," 293–94; "Father Nicholas His Death in the Ionian," 138; "Freedom," 60–61; "In the Garden: Villa Cleobolus," 81–84; "The Ikons," 177–82; "Incognito," 277–79; "Inconstancy," 49; "The Initiation," 188–89; "Io," 182–84; "Ithaca," 24; "'Je est un autre,'" 140, 162; "Joss," 255–57; "Journal in Paris," 35–36; "Kasyapa," 215–17; "Lake Music," 275–77; "The Land," 255; "Last Heard Of," 88; "Lesbos," 137; "Letters in Darkness," 158–63; "The Lost Cities," 85–88; "In the Margin," 189–91; "Matapan," 26; "On Mirrors," 145–46; "Mistral," 257–58; "Mneiae," 140; "Moonlight," 207–9; "Nemea," 68; "Nobody," 250–51; "North West," 186–87; "For a Nursery Mirror," 47, 51, 53; "Olives," 187–88; "One Grey Greek Stone," 197–200; "One Place," 254–55; "Orpheus," 141–42; "The Outer Limits," 292–93; "The Parthenon," 92–97; "Patmos," 79–81; "Paullus to Cornelia," 203–7; "Pearls," 48, 59–60; "Penelope," 97–98; "Persuasions," 212–13; "To Ping Kû Asleep," 51–52; "Pistol Weather," 247–48; "Poemandres," 200–203, 206, 207; "Two Poems in Basic English," 12, 69–70; "A Portrait of Theodora," 157–58, 167; "Rain, Rain, Go to Spain," 252–53; "The Reckoning," 238–40, 273; "Revenants," 248–49; "The Rhône at Beaucaire," 292; "River Water," 146–48; "Rodini," 89–92; "Salamis," 184–86; "Sarajevo," 152–54; "Scaffoldings: Plaka," 191–93; "On Seeming to Presume," 98–99; "Seferis," 285–86; "Sonnet Astray," 49–50; "The Sonnet of Hamlet," 29–31; "Stoic," 253–54; "Stone Honey," 215; "At Strati's," 144–45; "Summer in Corfu," 16–17; "Thasos," 168; "The Tree of Idleness," 131–36; "Vega," 286–88; "Vidourle," 213–14; "Want to Live Don't You?," 288–90; "A Water Colour of Venice," 148–50; "Water Music," 67; "A Winter of Vampires," 245–46; "?," 279–84

Durrell, Lawrence—prose: *The Alexandria Quartet*, 100–101, 103, 116–17, 120, 140, 146, 148–49, 152, 155, 157–58, 161–62, 176–77, 244–45, 248–49; *The Avignon*

Quintet, 92, 105, 107, 119–20, 136, 149, 155, 229–30, 267–70, 276, 296; *Bitter Lemons of Cyprus*, 86, 114, 130–32, 166–68, 181–82; *The Black Book*, 32–34, 117, 240–41; *The Durrell—Miller Letters 1935–1980*, 15, 31, 40n37, 78, 85, 115, 135, 153, 225; *Down the Styx*, 236; *The Greek Islands*, 79, 137, 165; *Key to Modern Poetry*, 137, 139–42, 144, 146, 150, 156, 232, 277, 280; *Panic Spring*, 52, 124n59; *Pied Piper of Lovers*, 20, 53; *Prospero's Cell*, 62, 179; *Reflections on a Marine Venus*, 68, 81, 85–88, 90–91, 96, 179; *The Revolt of Aphrodite*, 178, 180, 183, 229; *A Smile in the Mind's Eye*, 104, 295, 297

Eliade, Mircea, 233
Eliot, Thomas Stearns, 58, 64, 116, 139, 143–44, 187, 192, 231, 269, 281
Elytis, Odysseas, 96

Fedden, Robin and Bernard Spencer: *Personal Landscape*, 9; 23, 37, 43, 47, 49, 60
Forster, Edward Morgan, 267
Fraenkel, Michael, 34
Frankétienne, 135, 137
Friedrich, Hugo, 2, 131, 136, 156, 202
frontiers, 82–83

Groddeck, Georg, 115

heraldic universe, 13, 38, 49, 243–44
home, 20, 22–23, 98, 111–12
Hulin, Michel, 253–54

India, 132
irrepresentable, 243–45, 249, 307

Jourde, Pierre, 46, 244

Kalachakra mandala, 109, 113, 120
Keats, John, 84
Keller-Privat, Isabelle, 59
Ko-an, 61

Lacarrière, Jacques, 307
Lacoue-Labarthe, Philippe, 309
Lévinas, Emmanuel, 152, 154, 158

Magritte, René, 270
Mallarmé, Stéphane, 136, 202, 297
Maulnier, Thierry, 103
Merleau-Ponty, Maurice, 289
Meschonnic, Henri, 139–40, 273, 279, 297
Michaux, Henri, 233, 272, 310–11
Miller, Henry, 270–72, 279; *The Michael Fraenkel–Henry Miller Correspondence Called Hamlet*, 34. See also Durrell, Lawrence—prose
Montaigne de, Michel, 60
Morin, Edgar, 45
music, 67–68, 137

Nancy, Jean-Luc, 63, 67
Nerval de, Gérard, 188, 198, 201
nirvāṇa, 200
nostalgia, 111–13
Nouss, Alexis, 161

Pine, Richard, 130
Pliny the Elder, 207–9
Propertius, 203–4
Puel, Gaston, 293

Rabaté, Dominique, 176
Rank, Otto, 32, 36, 38, 51, 59
Reverdy, Pierre, 85, 103, 112–13, 118, 160, 163
Rilke, Rainer Maria, 160, 309
Rimbaud, Arthur, 25, 46, 140
Ritman, Serge, 140

rivers, 87–88, 111, 146, 290–92
rose (flower), 102–3, 155–56, 247–48

Scott, Clive, 134, 167, 271, 288
Seferis, George, 45–46, 286
Shakespeare, William, 24, 31–32, 35, 40n36, 47, 98–99, 142, 144, 281
Shelley, Percy Bysshe, 100, 103
Sitwell, Edith, 236
Sitwell, Sacheverell, 68
space-time, 58, 87–88 109, 117, 176, 182, 200, 232, 250–51, 296
Stein, Gertrude, 102
subtle body, 185, 242
Suzuki, Daisetz Teitaro, 61, 66, 105, 121, 168

Tao, 22, 110, 115
Tomkinson, Fiona, 126n21
Trigano, Shmuel, 112

Valéry, Paul, 67, 75n120, 95–96, 103, 133–34, 197, 257–58

White, Kenneth, 286
Wordsworth, William, 232, 249, 305, 310

Yeats, William Butler, 102
yoga, 185, 238

Zarian, Kostan, 61–62, 148
Zen, 61, 66, 105, 120–21, 168, 215, 295–96

About the Author

Isabelle Keller-Privat is a senior lecturer, president of the International Lawrence Durrell Society, and codirector of the research team "Lieux Communs / Common Places" for the CAS Research Centre at the University Toulouse Jean Jaurès, where she teaches British literature, poetry, and translation. She was awarded the International Lawrence Durrell Prize for New Scholarship in 2000 and has since contributed to many conferences and publications on Lawrence Durrell, V. S. Naipaul, Jon McGregor, and David Gascoyne. She has published the first monograph on Lawrence Durrell's poetry collections at the University Presses of Paris-Ouest, *Between the Lines: L'écriture du déchirement dans la poésie de Lawrence Durrell* (2015), which she has translated for Fairleigh Dickinson University Press. She has published over 30 papers and book chapters in national and international peer-reviewed journals and has coedited four collections of papers on Durrellian studies, interdisciplinary studies on exile and migration, and Mediterranean criticism. She is presently coediting two forthcoming books on travel letters in modern and contemporary fiction and on the arts and literature of the suburbs.